transitional settlement
displaced populations

These guidelines were developed as part of the University of Cambridge **shelterproject**. The associated online and CD-Rom resources were developed by the NGO Shelter Centre.

University of Cambridge shelterproject

shelterproject is an informal group of physical planners, shelter specialists, and researchers committed to improving the transitional settlement sector by supporting the development of policy, best practice, and shelter non-food items. **shelterproject** is associated with the Martin Centre of the University of Cambridge for some funded research projects.

www.shelterproject.org

Shelter Centre

Shelter Centre is a humanitarian non-government organisation concerned with the transitional settlement and shelter of populations affected by conflict and natural disasters, supporting human rights, dignity, protection, health, environment, and livelihoods. Shelter Centre maintains the Shelter Library, an on-line resource of material from a wide range of humanitarian organisations. It also runs Shelter Training, an educational resource for the transitional shelter sector.

www.sheltercentre.org

Oxfam GB

Oxfam GB, a member of Oxfam International, is a development, humanitarian, and campaigning agency dedicated to finding lasting solutions to poverty and suffering around the world. Oxfam believes that every human being is entitled to a life of dignity and opportunity, and it works with others worldwide to make this become a reality.

www.oxfam.org.uk

Oxfam GB publishes and distributes a wide range of books and other resource materials for development and relief workers, researchers and campaigners, schools and colleges, and the general public, as part of its programme of advocacy, education, and communications.

www.oxfam.org.uk/publications

transitional settlement
displaced populations

executive editors and lead authors
Tom Corsellis and Antonella Vitale

University of Cambridge
shelterproject

Oxfam

First published by Oxfam GB in association with University of Cambridge shelterproject in 2005

© University of Cambridge 2005

ISBN 0 85598 534 8

A trial edition of this material was published in 2004

shelterproject, Martin Centre for Architectural and Urban Studies, Department of Architecture, University of Cambridge, 6 Chaucer Road, Cambridge, CB2 2EB, UK www.shelterproject.org

The right of Tom Corsellis and Antonella Vitale to be identified as the authors of this work has been asserted in accordance with the Copyright, Designs and Patents Act 1988.

A catalogue record for this publication is available from the British Library.

Available through Oxfam GB from:
Bournemouth English Book Centre, PO Box 1496, Parkstone, Dorset, BH12 3YD, UK
tel: +44 (0)1202 712933; fax: +44 (0)1202 712930; email: oxfam@bebc.co.uk

USA: Stylus Publishing LLC, PO Box 605, Herndon, VA 20172-0605, USA
tel: +1 (0)703 661 1581; fax: +1 (0)703 661 1547; email: styluspub@aol.com

For details of local agents and representatives in other countries, consult our website: www.oxfam.org.uk/publications

or contact Oxfam Publishing, 274 Banbury Road, Oxford OX2 7DZ, UK
tel: +44 (0)1865 311 311; fax: +44 (0)1865 312 600; email: publish@oxfam.org.uk

The Oxfam GB website contains a fully searchable database of all Oxfam publications, and facilities for secure on-line ordering.

Published by Oxfam GB, 274 Banbury Road, Oxford OX2 7DZ, UK.

Printed by Information Press, Eynsham

Oxfam GB is a registered charity, no. 202 918, and is a member of Oxfam International.

contents

list of figures

list of tables

acknowledgements

This book results from a project funded by the Conflict and Humanitarian Affairs Department (CHAD) of the UK Department for International Development (DFID) for the benefit of the humanitarian sector. The views expressed are not necessarily those of CHAD or of DFID.

The executive editors and lead authors are Dr Tom Corsellis and Antonella Vitale. Contributions to the text of this edition, and to the production of the trial edition, were made by the following:

John Arnold, Joseph Ashmore, Dr Samira Barakat, Richard Bauer, Neil Brighton, Gordon Browne, Dr Emily Corsellis, John Corsellis, Jon Fowler, Seki Hirano, Steven Hunt, Stephen Jones, Dr Ilan Kelman, Sheenaanne Law, Peter Manfield, Mark Richardson, Matthew Slater, Andrew Smith, Goran Vodicka, Hugo Zaragoza.

shelterproject has been supported by a great number of individuals and organisations who have kindly volunteered their time and services. There is not room to mention all of them here, but **shelterproject** particularly wishes to thank the following people for their support for its work since 1997:

Lizzie Babister, Dr Nick Baker, Rachel Battilana, Kate Crawford, Claire Grisaffi, Alison Killing, Maria Mascarucci, Allan McRobie, Nancy Peskett, Allen Rand, Olivia Stanton, Robert Youlton.

Professor Robin Spence acted as Principal Investigator for the project, on behalf of the University of Cambridge.

Professor Ian Davis of the Cranfield Disaster Management Centre acted as consultant during the first phase.

shelterproject gratefully acknowledges the support of the organisations listed on the inside front cover, which have participated in the peer-review process that refined these guidelines.

The authors are indebted to the publishers of the following works for permission to reproduce material in respect of which they hold the copyright:

Sphere Project, *Humanitarian Charter and Minimum Standards in Disaster Response*, The Sphere Project, Geneva, 2004

UNHCR, *Handbook for Emergencies*, UNHCR, Geneva, 2000

UNDP / IAPSO, *Emergency Relief Items – Compendium of Generic Specifications*, Volumes 1 and 2, UNDP, New York, 2000

The online and CD-ROM resources associated with this book were developed by the NGO Shelter Centre, which managed teams of volunteers sourced and trained by Engineers Without Borders (EWB) and Architectes Sans Frontières (ASF). These services were constructed for Shelter Centre by the following:

John Arnold, Neil Brighton, Dr Tom Corsellis, Valentina Evangelisti, Francis Li, Catarina Pereira, Alice Piggott, Daniel Reader, Towera Ridley, Matthew Slater, Stephanie Smithers, Henry Travers, Antonella Vitale, Goran Vodicka.

Shelter Centre acknowledges with gratitude the support of the Martin Centre for Architectural and Urban Studies and the Department of Architecture of the University of Cambridge.

introduction

This book is published for co-ordinators and specialists working in humanitarian relief who are concerned with the transitional settlement needs of displaced people and their hosts. The guidelines in it offer a common planning tool for developing and implementing settlement and shelter strategies for people affected by conflict or natural disaster. They are intended primarily to help specialists to communicate with each other and understand one another. Other readers may also find them useful, because many aspects of transitional settlement work are relevant to policy making for displaced populations in general.

The guidelines are divided into two sections:

part a gives a broad overview of the issues relating to transitional settlement, and the six settlement options that are open to displaced populations

part b offers technical information as reference for the implementation of transitional settlement options

Users are advised to start by reading part a. In this way they will become familiar with the relevant methods and issues before referring to any particular chapter in part b. The CD at the back of the book contains further resources and information for reference purposes.

part a: process

1 **overview:** a survey of transitional settlement and its impacts

2 **strategy:** an introduction to planning levels and tools

3 **options:** the six transitional settlement options, described in detail

part b: implementation

4   **assessment:** a description of current assessment tools

5   **labour:** guidance on how to employ various kinds of labour

6   **construction:** advice on siting and building techniques

7   **logistics:** guidelines for distributing non-food items

8   **camps:** detailed information about the physical planning of camps

9   **resources:** suggestions for further reference

The transitional settlement choices open to displaced people have been categorised into **six programme options:**

 1   dispersed settlement: with host families

 2   dispersed settlement: rural self-settlement

 3   dispersed settlement: urban self-settlement

 4   grouped settlement: collective centres

 5   grouped settlement: self-settled camps

 6   grouped settlement: planned camps

Our approach to the transitional settlement of displaced populations is based on a holistic interpretation of the need for 'shelter'. It goes beyond the traditional provision of tents and camps and aims to support all of the settlement and shelter options that are open to displaced people.

The guidelines are not intended to be exhaustive, and they should not be used in isolation. It is assumed that agencies and organisations have their own internal guidelines, and also that readers will consult some of the many publications that are available on specific subjects, including water and sanitation, and gender-related aspects of humanitarian relief (such as Adams 1999 and Anderson 1994 – see chapter 9 for details).

While many aspects of these guidelines may be useful to agencies working in other types of transitional settlement scenario, please note that they are not relevant to non-displaced populations in situations such as the following:

- **reconstruction following conflict**, including the return of displaced populations to permanent settlement

- **natural disasters** (although environmental risk assessment for displaced populations is covered briefly in chapter 6)

- **resettlement** on new permanent and sustainable sites.

It is important to note, therefore, that these guidelines are intended to be used only in support of populations who have been displaced. It is hoped that separate guidelines for work in contexts of reconstruction, natural disasters, and resettlement will be developed in the near future.

part a process

chapter 1 overview

1 overview

Chapter 1 gives a general survey of the transitional settlement sector, which provides for the needs of populations who have been displaced by conflict or natural disaster. It aims to put the guidelines into context, introducing the reader to relevant terminology and concepts.

This book offers guidelines which are intended as a common planning tool for co-ordinators and specialists in humanitarian aid who work to provide for the transitional settlement needs of displaced people and their hosts. The guidelines combine general planning considerations (**part a: process**) with technical information (**part b: implementation**). They are intended to help specialists to communicate with each other and understand one another.

This chapter provides the context for the guidelines, introducing some of the issues relevant to transitional settlement.

1.1 **introduction** explains the importance of transitional settlement and introduces the six transitional settlement options open to displaced people.

1.2 **terms** lists and defines relevant terms.

1.3 **stakeholders** describes the particular interests of the various stakeholders in transitional settlement.

1.4 **standards** introduces international standards and the key texts relating to them.

1.5 **legal context** reviews definitions relating to transitional settlement in international law.

1.6 **livelihoods** identifies the potential impact of transitional settlement on the livelihoods of displaced people and their hosts.

1.1 introduction

In the year 2004, the United Nations High Commissioner for Refugees (UNHCR) estimated that there were 20 million refugees living worldwide. In addition, 25 million people were displaced within the borders of their own countries and were thus classified as Internally Displaced Persons (IDPs). The provision of well-planned settlement solutions for people who have been displaced by conflict or natural disasters is crucially important. Bad planning of settlements can have a number of negative effects, in the worst case destabilising whole countries or even entire regions, as has happened in West Africa, for example. In contrast, well-planned settlements can have a positive impact which extends beyond the provision of basic shelter. They can help displaced populations in many ways: by strengthening their physical protection and supporting their livelihoods; by minimising natural hazards and the spread of disease; and by managing natural resources in a sustainable way. These guidelines aim to assist the strategic planning and implementation processes for the transitional settlement of displaced populations.

The term 'transitional settlement' (TS) has been defined by a peer-review process initiated by shelterproject and continued by Shelter Centre. It means *settlement and shelter resulting from conflict and natural disasters, ranging from emergency response to durable solutions.* The word originates from an approach which extends beyond the traditional response, with its limited focus on the provision of planned camps. The new approach considers the wider impacts of settlement and the options for settlement, emphasising the need for a transition to durable settlement solutions and local development.

These guidelines deal with the particular TS needs of displaced populations. Future publications will consider the needs of populations who find themselves without shelter but have not been displaced.

1.1.1 options for transitional settlement

The approach of these guidelines to the transitional settlement of displaced populations is based on a holistic interpretation of the need for 'shelter'. It goes beyond the traditional provision of tents and camps, aiming instead to support all the settlement and shelter options that are open to displaced people. The TS choices open to displaced people have been categorised into six 'transitional settlement programme options', shown in figure 1(a).

figure 1(a): six transitional settlement options

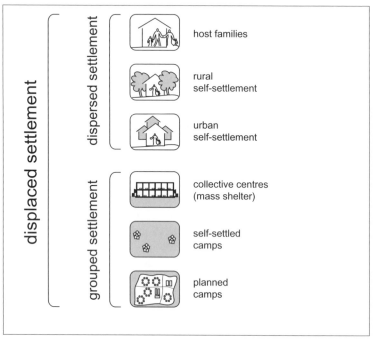

The options are discussed in detail in chapter 3, while the meaning of terms is defined in section 1.2 and in chapter 9.

1.1.2 impacts of transitional settlement

The influx of large numbers of displaced people into an area, and any TS response to their needs, will have consequences beyond the displaced population itself. Both the local and displaced populations can expect transitional settlement to have an impact on their lives in many ways:

- protection and security
- survival and health
- social needs, such as privacy and dignity
- livelihoods
- natural-resource management
- communal service infrastructure.

It is essential for organisations responsible for implementing TS programmes to be aware of these consequences, in order to reduce the negative effects and increase the positive effects of their work. For instance, TS responses which match the cultural expectations of the displaced population are less likely to fracture social structures, or to disrupt existing communities within the displaced population. Friction between or within families, or conflicts between clans or ethnic groups, may be reduced through appropriate TS responses. Adapting generic guidelines for the transitional settlement of displaced populations to local and cultural circumstances must be based on sound assessment, monitoring, and evaluation – matters which are discussed in chapter 4.

Each of the impacts of transitional settlement has potential consequences outside the sector. Support for communal service infrastructure, for example, can encourage the host population to accept the affected population, and it can influence all the activities of the aid community. The quality and appropriateness of shelter within transitional settlement have a major impact on health: for example, smoke produced by cooking on stoves or open fires is the fourth greatest risk to health and disease worldwide (Warwick and Doig 2004). Consequently, the provision of adequate cooking facilities for displaced populations should be viewed as vital for public health.

1.2 terms

Existing terminology does not adequately describe the range of needs and activities of stakeholders in the settlement and shelter of those affected by conflict and natural disasters. In 2002, organisations participating in the peer review of an early draft of this book asked for a new range of terms to be developed to describe all settlement and shelter activities, ranging from relief to development. This request resulted in the 'transitional settlement' approach. The glossary in chapter 9 lists new terms agreed upon by the peer review, together with other relevant terms. The new vocabulary builds on and is consistent with existing terminologies developed by organisations such as UNHCR.

1.2.1 'transitional settlement'

'Transitional settlement' is a new term, defined through the shelterproject peer-review process to mean *'settlement and shelter resulting from conflict and natural disasters, ranging from emergency response to durable solutions'*. These guidelines consider the transitional settlement of displaced populations only.

The term 'shelter sector' has been applied to the practice of responding to the settlement and shelter needs of refugees only, as covered by the mandate of UNHCR. The *'transitional settlement sector'* therefore encompasses the 'shelter sector' as well as the response to similar needs of non-refugees, such as internally displaced persons (IDPs).

There are a number of reasons why the term 'transitional settlement' is more appropriate than the term 'shelter sector' to describe operational activities. They include the following.

- There is a need to broaden the focus of shelter responses, to take account of their collective impacts as settlement responses: for example, their impact on local security.
- In the past, shelter response concentrated on family needs, at the expense of the collective needs of community and stakeholder groups, such as female-headed households (FHHs).
- The word 'transitional' emphasises the position of emergency shelter and settlement response within the wider continuum of relief, reconstruction/rehabilitation, and development.
- Donors, co-ordinators, implementers, and governments need a consistent terminology to describe similar circumstances, from emergencies to durable solutions and development.
- A common, consistent, and comprehensive terminology is crucial in order to assess, monitor, evaluate, design, manage, and hand over TS responses.

1.2.2 key terms

In table 1(a), key terms relating to transitional settlement are defined. Further terms and their definitions are presented in the glossary in chapter 9.

table 1(a): key terms in transitional settlement

term	description
transitional settlement	settlement and shelter resulting from conflict and natural disasters, from emergency response to durable solutions
transitional settlement sector	the field of providing settlement and shelter in the context of conflict and natural disasters, from emergency response to durable solutions. Aim: communities, families, and individuals affected by conflict and natural disasters should be afforded, together with any hosting populations, TS support to ensure their security, good health, privacy, and dignity, appropriate to their needs.
transitional shelter	shelter which provides a habitable covered living space and a secure, healthy living environment, with privacy and dignity, to those within it, during the period between a conflict or natural disaster and the achievement of a durable shelter solution
settlement	a community of covered living spaces providing a healthy, secure living environment with privacy and dignity to those groups, families, and individuals residing within them
shelter sector	abbreviation of the term 'site selection, planning and shelter sector', describing that part of the 'transitional settlement sector' which responds to the transitional settlement and shelter needs of refugees, within the mandate of UNHCR
shelter	a habitable covered living space, providing a secure, healthy living environment with privacy and dignity to those within it
shelter system	the combination of structural shelter items and 'shelter NFIs' (non-food items) which create shelter, such as tents with locally procured blankets and mattresses, and possibly stoves, appropriate to a cold climate

1.3 stakeholders

It is useful to consider the similarities and differences in the interests of stakeholder groups affected by transitional settlement. This might help to develop common operational guidelines which could improve co-ordination and co-operation between different organisations in the field.

table 1(b): stakeholders in transitional settlement

stakeholder groups	stake in transitional settlement includes:
local	
displaced and local populations	security; survival and health; social needs, including privacy and dignity; livelihoods, including economic stability; natural-resource management; communal service infrastructure, including transport
community-based organisations (CBOs)	capacity and skills; relations with local population, local and national government, national and international aid community, and donors
national	
host governments	internal and external security and stability; political and economic stability; national service infrastructure; national construction industry
police and military	internal and external security and stability; population mobility
local non-government organisations (LNGOs)	capacity and skills; relations with populations, CBOs, local and national government, international aid community, and donors
national and international	
co-ordinators	strategic effectiveness; local, national, and international relations

table 1(b): stakeholders in transitional settlement (cont.)

stakeholder groups	stake in transitional settlement includes:
specialists	sectoral effectiveness; strategic, government, and donor relations
other sectors of response	sectoral effectiveness, dependent on settlement options
development workers	operational continuity and assessment, monitoring, and evaluations
suppliers / contractors	economic stability; capacity; government and international relations
media	economic stability; local, national and international relations
international donors	strategic effectiveness; local, national, and international relations
United Nations bodies	strategic effectiveness; local, national, and international relations
international non-government organisations (INGOs)	local, national and strategic effectiveness; impact through sectoral range; local, national, and international relations with populations, governments, donors, and the media
peace-keeping forces	internal and external security and stability; population mobility

1.4 standards

Two basic texts provide the foundation for the response of the international community and aid organisations in humanitarian emergencies:

* *Handbook for Emergencies* (UNHCR 2000)

* *Humanitarian Charter and Minimum Standards in Disaster Response* (Sphere Project 2004)

Both texts are crucial to the transitional settlement sector. These guidelines are based on the guidance and information that are presented in them.

1.4.1 UNHCR *Handbook for Emergencies*

> Shelter must, at a minimum, provide protection from the elements, space to live and store belongings, privacy and emotional security. Shelter is likely to be one of the most important determinants of general living conditions and is often one of the largest items of non-recurring expenditure. While the basic need for shelter is similar in most emergencies, such considerations as the kind of housing needed, what materials and design are used, who constructs the housing and how long it must last will differ significantly in each situation.
> UNHCR (2000), p.144

The *Handbook for Emergencies* of the United Nations High Commissioner for Refugees (UNHCR) provides guidelines for the provision of protection to those covered by the mandate of UNHCR. It also aims to ensure that the necessary assistance reaches them in good time. Chapter 12, entitled 'Site Selection, Planning and Shelter', deals explicitly with best practice to meet the shelter-related and settlement-related needs of persons who are of concern to UNHCR. However, most of the guidance provided is directly applicable to the needs of all displaced persons, whether or not they are covered by the mandate. These guidelines, which address the needs of displaced people in general, are consistent with the UNHCR Handbook.

1.4.2 Sphere *Humanitarian Charter and Minimum Standards in Disaster Response*

> Beyond survival, shelter is necessary to provide security and personal safety, protection from the climate and enhanced resistance to ill health and disease. It is also important for human dignity and to sustain family and community life as far as possible in difficult circumstances.
> Sphere Project (2004), p.208

Humanitarian Charter and Minimum Standards in Disaster Response is intended to guide and inform decisions at all levels of response in a humanitarian emergency. The Minimum Standards were produced by consensus and are maintained by the Sphere Project. They aim to improve the quality of assistance that is provided to people affected by disasters, and to enhance the accountability of the organisations that provide it. One particularly important chapter describes quantifiable benchmarks and existing best practice used by a number of donor agencies, implementing agencies, and co-ordinating agencies when they fund, plan, and deliver assistance. Named 'Shelter and Site Planning' in earlier editions, in the 2004 revised edition it was renamed 'Minimum Standards in Shelter, Settlement and Non-Food Items'. These guidelines are consistent with the Sphere Project's Minimum Standards.

1.4.3 appropriate use

Standards and guidelines provide essential benchmarks by which humanitarian response can be monitored and evaluated. The inappropriate use of standards and guidelines may result in the under-provision or over-provision of support, which may, in turn, lead to some or all of the following results:

• resentment among groups within local or affected populations;

• the displacement of even more people, if over-provision acts as a 'honey pot', attracting displaced populations from other TS options, and even attracting elements of the host population when provision leads to a higher standard of living than they can achieve independently;

• the destabilisation of local economies, by affecting the availability of labour or materials and thereby undermining markets;

• the development of a culture of dependency among the displaced population, impeding the development of skills that are essential to self-sufficiency.

It is therefore important to implement international standards appropriately. Where necessary, the stakeholders in an operational context should debate and agree specific adjustments to general best practice and standards. However, any departure from international norms requires justification.

1.5 legal context

This section offers a brief introduction to the relevance of law and human rights to transitional settlement. While a consideration of specific legal tools and rights tools is beyond the scope of these guidelines, this section presents the legal context for the implementation of TS responses. It also highlights some of the legal considerations that should be taken into account when planning settlement strategies, programmes, and projects – matters which are discussed in chapter 2. It should be noted that there is a need to develop laws further, on both national and international levels, to deal with many aspects of the TS sector.

1.5.1 reasons for considering the law and human rights

The legal context is important for the following reasons:

- Human-rights law can be used as an advocacy tool, for example in presenting proposals to donors or negotiating with national and local governments.
- An awareness of local and national laws is essential in order to understand the socio-political context of a settlement: local and national laws will affect the use of land for settlements.
- An understanding of rights strengthens the ability of affected groups to make claims for resources and demand accountability from governments and other organisations that are mandated to provide assistance.

1.5.2 legal definitions relevant to transitional settlement

Many legal documents relating to the TS sector currently use the terms 'shelter' and 'housing' interchangeably.

shelter The United Nations has defined 'shelter' in the UN-HABITAT Agenda and the Istanbul Declaration on Human Settlements in a statement quoted in the box on the next page.

This definition is not legally binding. However, a UN Declaration can become binding if it achieves the status of customary law. While comprehensive in all other respects, this definition makes no specific mention of the rights of an individual to live within a family unit within a community.

Adequate shelter means more than a roof over one's head. It also means adequate privacy; adequate space; physical accessibility; adequate security; security of tenure; structural stability and durability; adequate lighting, heating and ventilation; adequate basic infrastructure, such as water-supply, sanitation and waste-management facilities; suitable environmental quality and health-related factors; and adequate and accessible location with regard to work and basic facilities: all of which should be available at an affordable cost. Adequacy should be determined together with the people concerned, bearing in mind the prospect for gradual development [...] [and] depends on specific cultural, social, environmental and economicfactors.
United Nations Centre for Human Settlements (UN-HABITAT) (1996), section IV B

---

housing The Office of the United Nations High Commissioner for Human Rights (UNHCR 1991) lists the characteristics of 'adequate housing' as follows:

- legal security of tenure
- availability of services, materials, facilities, and infrastructure
- affordability
- habitability
- accessibility
- location
- cultural adequacy.

In 1992 the UN developed 'Agenda 21', which notes: 'Access to safe and healthy shelter is essential to a person's physical, psychological, social and economic well-being and should be a fundamental part of national and international action' (UN 1992).

The 'Right to Adequate Housing' of UNHCHR states: 'Having a secure place to live is one of the fundamental elements for human dignity, physical and mental health and overall quality of life, which enables one's development' (UNHCHR 2005).

In addition, there are some links between housing law and TS provision for refugees and IDPs. The Committee on Economic, Social and Cultural Rights (CESCR) comments on laws regarding forced evictions:

Although the practice of forced evictions might appear to occur primarily in heavily populated urban areas, it also takes place in connection with forced population transfers, internal displacement, forced relocations in the context of armed conflict, mass exoduses and refugee movements. In all of these contexts, the right to adequate housing and not to be subjected to forced eviction may be violated through a wide range of acts or omissions attributable to States parties.
CESCR (1997)

1.5.3 levels of law and rights regimes

Law and rights can operate at a number of different levels, known as 'rights regimes'. While human rights are universally applicable in theory, other rights and laws tend to be specific to particular countries or communities.

Table 1(c), adapted from Conway (2002), describes the different levels of rights regimes, explains their relevance to transitional settlement, and suggests how these rights might be implemented.

table 1(c): rights regimes

rights regime	form of rights and domain	relevance for transitional settlement and refugees / IDPs	level of operation, institutional framework, and authority structures
international human-rights law	human rights with universal application	e.g. article 25, Universal Declaration of Human Rights; article 11 (1), ICESCR;* principles 1 and 18, Guiding Principles on Internal Displacement	international/global, implemented and monitored through UN
regional law	human rights which apply to regional populations	e.g. African Charter on Human and People's Rights, Article 14 ('right to property')	international/regional, increasingly with statutory power of endorsement

table 1(c): rights regimes (cont.)

constitutional law	national constitutional rights (mainly civil and political, starting to include economic and social, e.g. South Africa)	approximately 40 per cent of the world's countries have enshrined the right to adequate housing in their respective constitutions	national level, enforced through constitutional courts and other national legal mechanisms
statutory law	statutory rights deriving from criminal, commercial, and other law	e.g. may have to be taken into consideration when tendering	national or, under devolved government, local; formal legal system
religious law	religious rights and norms (domestic sphere, in some cases extended)	e.g. while few organisations may specifically provide mass shelter for religious purposes, community centres may fulfil similar roles	can operate at multiple levels (global through local): forms of authority depend on relations with the state
customary law	customary rights (kinship and resource rights), specific to localities and social/ethnic groups	e.g. customary land-use rights which have to be taken into account in planning	local level, enforced through customary authorities (e.g. chiefs)
living law	informal rights and norms (mostly re: kinship and resource rights), applying to localities through varying cultures	e.g. considerations for camp layouts, with regard to habitation norms	micro level; not formally incorporated into national legal system, but local elites may be able to co-opt elements of the state to help to enforce living law

(* ICESCR: International Covenant on Economic, Social, and Cultural Rights)

international human-rights law

International human-rights law provides an overarching framework in which to implement durable solutions for transitional settlement. However, the practical application and enforcement of human rights in the field in emergency situations is often difficult, if not impossible.

Some of the most important international laws with regard to the TS sector are those relating to housing rights. UN-HABITAT and the Office of the United Nations High Commissioner for Human Rights (OHCHR) assert the legal importance of 'adequate housing':

> Since the adoption of the Universal Declaration of Human Rights in 1948, the right to adequate housing has been reaffirmed and explicitly recognised in a wide range of international instruments as a component of the right to an adequate standard of living, and joined the body of universally accepted and applicable international human rights law.
> UN-HABITAT / OHCHR (2002)

The strongest reference to housing rights in the international legal context is the right to adequate housing as enshrined in Article 25 of the Universal Declaration of Human Rights and article 11 (1) of the International Covenant on Economic, Social, and Cultural Rights (ICESCR).

The 1967 Protocol Relating to the Status of Refugees (UNHCR 1951/1967), in Article 21 on Housing, states:

> The Contracting States...shall accord to refugees lawfully staying in their territory treatment as favourable as possible and, in any event, not less favourable than that accorded to aliens generally in the same circumstances.
> (Geneva Convention Article 20, 1951)

This means that countries which do not provide shelter rights to 'aliens' would not be obliged to provide shelter to refugees.

Some human-rights documents emphasise the right to property rather than the right to shelter or housing. For example, Article 14 of the African Charter on Human and People's Rights states that the 'right to property shall be guaranteed', but it does not comment on the right to shelter (OAU 1981). In contrast, the Charter of Fundamental Rights of the European Union guarantees the 'right to property' in Article 17, while Article 34 notes: 'the Union recognises and respects the right to social and housing assistance' (EU 2000).

The bibliography in chapter 9 of this book lists some of the most important documents relating to transitional settlement and the rights of refugees and IDPs. Some documents are universal in their intended application, while others are specific to refugees or IDPs.

1.5.4 rights to land

Access to land is often one of the most important issues to consider when planning transitional settlement responses. A number of different groups may have concurrent rights to land that is required for the siting of a transitional settlement. This is a source of potential conflict, for instance when local communities have traditional or customary rights to land that a national government has made available for transitional settlement. Site selection cannot therefore be determined simply by choosing the land that is most suitable for displaced persons. Access to that land must also be obtained, and it may have to be negotiated at a number of levels.

Local populations and governments are frequently reluctant to give up land required for the transitional settlement of displaced persons, especially if the settlement appears likely to become long-term or even permanent. There are numerous concerns, including the following:

- the current value of the land, and fear that it might depreciate;
- fear that displaced persons will refuse to leave their new location;
- resentment if displaced persons appear to receive better support than the local population;
- competition for local resources, and unsustainable resource use;
- political implications, if the ethnic balance within the host community or country is altered by the arrival of displaced persons;
- repercussions from the country of origin, threatening the security of the host population;
- possible destabilising effects, political or environmental, either locally or nationally.

The UNHCR *Handbook for Emergencies* describes in detail the process for dealing with land-use issues:

28. In most countries land for the establishment of refugee sites is scarce. Often, sites are provided on public land by the government. Any use of private land must be based on formal legal arrangements in accordance with the laws of the country. Headquarters should be consulted at once if this is a problem.

29. Once a possible site has been identified, the process of site assessment should always include clarification of land-ownership and land rights. Almost invariably, land rights or ownership are known, even though these may not be well documented in public record, or may not be obvious. Nomadic use of rangeland, for instance, requires huge areas and may not look used.

30. The refugees should have the exclusive use of the site, through agreement with national and local (including traditional) authorities. Traditional or customary land use rights are very sensitive issues, and even if there may be an agreement with the national government to use a site, local groups may disagree with the site being used even temporarily. Clarification of access rights and land use restrictions is also necessary to define the rights of the refugees to:

i. Collect fuel-wood, and timber for shelter construction as well as fodder for animals;

ii. Graze their animals;

iii. Engage in agriculture or other subsistence activities.

UNHCR (2000), p. 138

The *Sphere Minimum Standards* also acknowledge the importance of customary land rights:

Land ownership and usage: Appropriate consultation should be undertaken to establish not only who has ownership of the site but also who may have formal or customary use rights and would also be affected by the use of the site as a temporary settlement.
Sphere Project 2004, Chapter 4, p. 214

It is current UNHCR policy not to buy or rent land, because the country of asylum is obligated under international law to provide it without a formal charge. However, other mitigating measures and compensation may be offered. Site development for a camp, for example, might involve the construction of new road access; or support for host families may result in projects to improve communal service infrastructure. As the primary negotiator of land use, UNHCR should, when present, always be consulted on issues relating to land rights and access for displaced populations. Failure to consult with UNHCR can lead to unrealistic expectations, both on the part of aid agencies regarding access to land and on the part of land owners regarding compensation for loss of land.

1.6 livelihoods

'Livelihoods' are the ways in which people manage their lives in order to obtain the resources that they need, individually and communally: resources such as food, water, clothing, and shelter. Livelihoods are not simply forms of waged employment; they are both formal and informal activities undertaken in order to obtain resources. These guidelines adopt the 'livelihoods approach' in seeking to understand the effects of transitional settlement on displaced and local populations. Beyond questions of survival, security, and health, TS significantly influences the ways in which individuals and families make decisions and provide for their own needs. Support through TS can stimulate the recovery of their livelihoods, particularly because shelter and the land connected to it are major capital assets. However, governments and the aid community must recognise the non-permanent nature of their influence: their interventions constitute only one phase in the lives of the displaced populations and local hosts, who shape their own lives through an on-going process of decision making.

The livelihoods approach tries to understand the contexts of any transitional settlement from the perspectives of the displaced and local populations. This should result in TS responses which match the cultural expectations of both communities. Such responses are less likely than traditional ones to fracture social structures or to disrupt existing communities within the displaced population.

1.6.1 the livelihoods approach

The livelihoods approach defines 'poverty' not simply as a lack of financial means. It emphasises the integral links between poverty and the livelihoods of poor people, including the following factors:

- the context of their vulnerability
- the strategies that they adopt to support themselves
- capital assets that they possess to maintain those livelihoods
- their preferred outcomes in terms of their long-term settlement.

The livelihoods approach offers an analytical framework in which poor people are treated as active participants in the process of recovery, rather than as passive recipients of aid. It was developed for use in development contexts, yet in recent years it has increasingly been applied in emergencies too. Initially it focused on food security, but the approach is now used by many aid agencies, in many different forms.

1.6.2 livelihoods and transitional settlement

In emergency situations, displaced people have lost most, if not all, of their means to secure their livelihoods. While it is essential to provide emergency shelter to satisfy their immediate needs, the re-establishment of livelihoods should form an integral part of the aid effort. Programme planning should try to maximise the opportunities for displaced persons to begin to regain their livelihoods in some form. It should aim to promote dignity and self-respect, and to discourage the emergence of a culture of dependency.

The assessment of livelihoods is discussed in chapters 2 and 4. It is based upon the following categories of 'capital' available to displaced and local populations: social and political; human; natural; physical; and financial.

In times of hardship, people's coping strategies often involve maintaining their productive assets rather than meeting their immediate needs, such as food. Settlement and shelter are extremely important productive assets. Shelter, for example, provides a space in which to work and rest, and to care for children and elderly people. It makes available a place to care for animals, and to store tools, water, or goods produced. Supporting appropriate transitional settlement and shelter, therefore, develops a key productive asset, and hence allows displaced persons to concentrate on other immediate livelihoods-related needs.

chapter 2 strategy

2 strategy

This chapter presents a process for planning a response to a need for transitional settlement. It describes planning on the strategic, programme, and project levels. It gives guidance on how to develop profiles and plans, and then describes the phases of operation for planning.

Any transitional settlement (TS) response should be planned on the strategic, programme, and project levels. The overall process is the same on all three levels. It consists of developing the profile of a situation, followed by a detailed plan of action to reach the set objectives. The process described here does not constitute a prescriptive system. Instead it is intended as a checklist of factors which should be taken into account when planning transitional settlement. The chapter is structured in the following way.

2.1 **planning** presents the generic planning process for the strategic, programme, and project levels.

2.2 **developing profiles** explains how to undertake assessments, develop scenarios, and identify indicators.

2.3 **developing plans** suggests how to define objectives, describe activities, and create a schedule of operations.

2. 4 **phases of operation** presents the sequence of events in which planning and operations occur.

2. 5 **general planning considerations** identifies issues which planners should be aware of, such as concerns related to gender and to the physical environment.

2.1 planning

From the emergency phase onwards, the choice of TS options influences the protection and security of displaced populations, and the effectiveness of the work of the aid community. Often, humanitarian agencies have to expend a considerable proportion of their resources on efforts to reduce the damage done by inappropriate settlement options, such as the bad siting or planning of camps. It is therefore essential that any TS response is well planned and co-ordinated before implementation, from the regional to the local levels. In addition, TS plans should be integrated with other support for displaced populations and their hosts.

Co-ordinated planning is the key to engaging all stakeholders in the implementation of successful transitional settlement.

2.1.1 levels of planning

Any TS response should be planned on the strategic, programme, and project levels, which are illustrated in figure 2(a). The overall process is the same on all three levels. Good practice in planning is briefly described in section 2.1.2.

figure 2(a): three levels of planning

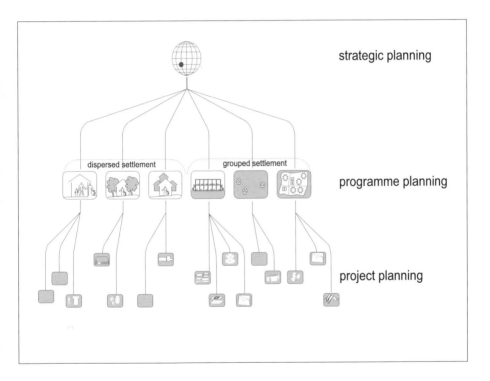

Planning should be well co-ordinated between levels, to ensure that any project activity in the field fits into the regional strategic plan.

strategic planning

Strategic planning manages transitional settlement on a national or regional level. It deals with the TS and shelter needs of the entire population displaced by a conflict, natural disaster, or complex emergency. Several or even all of the six TS programme options described in chapter 3 are combined to form a coherent strategy.

programme planning

Programme planning deals with the needs of a specific group of displaced people. For instance, all projects within a particular camp are combined to form a project plan to provide for the TS needs of the camp's inhabitants.

project planning

Project planning develops and manages the activities required to undertake each project within a programme. For example, the programme plan for a camp might require the expansion of a clinic. This would involve the production of tendering documents and schedules of work – activities which are co-ordinated within the project plan.

2.1.2 planning process

This section introduces the two steps in the process of developing a plan for the levels of strategy, programme, and project. First, a profile of a situation should be developed (2.2); based upon that profile, a plan of action (2.3) is worked out. Separate profiles and plans should be developed for each of the planning levels. It is crucial that the strategic, programme, and project plans are cross-referenced and co-ordinated with each other. Each profile and plan will offer different degrees of detail, and will be revised at different intervals. Crucially, planning must take into account the phases of operation (2.4) in an emergency.

profiles Understanding the social and physical contexts of a conflict, natural disaster, or complex emergency is essential to developing plans of action to implement responses. This understanding must be developed into a 'profile', or an analysis of current circumstances. Three steps are involved in the development of a profile:

- Assessments of the situation should be made, in order to understand livelihoods, capacities, and resources.

---

transitional settlement: displaced populations

- Scenarios of possible courses of events in the future should be developed.
- Indicators should be identified which can monitor the appropriateness of scenarios and warn of changing circumstances: for example, one indicator may be the refugees' rate of influx, which might enable planners to determine the scale of the emergency situation, which is often an important part of the various scenarios developed by them.

plans A plan is a report which presents a detailed course of action in response to a profile. It should identify which organisation is to undertake which particular activity, and over what period. Plans must be constantly revised, both through monitoring processes and through integration with other plans at different planning levels. A plan should include the following elements:

- the objectives agreed by all stakeholders, listing the intended achievements of each TS strategy, programme, and project;
- the activities required to achieve the objectives, identifying who will undertake them, and possible effects of the activities on the profiles;
- a schedule of operations, to ensure that activities are undertaken at an appropriate time and are co-ordinated to achieve the objectives.

Some of the steps in the planning process may be undertaken by individuals, teams, or formal committees, such as a strategic assessment committee. Whatever the formal structure, it is essential to the success of the aid operation that the relevant stakeholders are involved in the profiling and planning process (2.2.1). While it may be impractical to involve representatives from all stakeholder groups in all levels of planning, their guidance should be sought, and informal committees may be maintained for relevant discussion. The structure and accountability of committees need to be made clear, and they could become the foundation for the future management of relations between all stakeholder groups. For example, a 'camp committee' involving representatives of the displaced people and the local community should be able to resolve local disagreements and develop common strategies for managing natural resources.

The appropriateness, acceptability, and success of planning decisions usually depend as much on the quality of participation in the decision-making process as they do on the quality of the decisions themselves.

2.2 developing profiles

Maintaining profiles is essential for developing strategic, programme, and project plans (2.3). If appropriate, strategic profiles might include profiles of countries or regions that border the areas from where the displaced population are coming, and the areas where they are going. Programme profiles should be co-ordinated with profiles for other programmes, in order to cross-check information and add detail to the strategic profile. Project profiles should involve detailed studies of local conditions and population groups, to verify and add detail to the strategic and programme profiles.

The development of strategic, programme, and project profiles follows the same three-step process: undertaking assessments (2.2.1), creating scenarios (2.2.2), and identifying indicators (2.2.3).

Profiling, whether done by a committee or by an individual, must involve either participation or guidance by the relevant stakeholders. The involvement of all stakeholder groups will improve the quality and success of profiling and planning.

2.2.1 assessments

The assessment process for the development of profiles should seek the involvement of stakeholders; make reference to other plans and profiles; take into account people's livelihoods; and identify the capacities and resources available. A variety of tools and criteria for assessment are discussed in chapter 4. The livelihoods approach was introduced in section 1.6.

involvement Involve representatives from all stakeholder groups at all levels of planning, whether on formal or informal committees, or as sources of advice. The stakeholders in a TS context are as follows:

- national and local host governments
- the displaced population

- the local population
- local and national community-based and non-government organisations (CBOs and NGOs)
- the aid community, including sectoral technical personnel employed by UN bodies, international organisations (IOs), and international NGOs.

Stakeholder participation is valuable because it ensures that planning is appropriate to the context, and it increases the chances that decisions will be acted upon. It also offers a degree of continuity – which is especially important, given the high turnover of staff in many emergency situations.

reference Refer to relief and development plans and profiles prepared at local or national levels, and sectoral or strategic levels, by all of the stakeholder groups listed above ('involvement'). But bear in mind the assumptions made by previous planning processes, and the context in which they were implemented, when considering the degree to which they should inform new planning.

livelihoods Find out how displaced and local populations and individuals live and work in normal circumstances, and how they have been living and working since the emergency. Assess the livelihoods and the resources and opportunities available to the displaced people and the local population. The criteria listed in chapter 4 may be helpful in this process.

capacities Assess the opportunities and constraints presented by the resources, experience, and personnel of the organisations, groups, and individuals involved.

resources Assess in regional terms the nature, scale, and management structures of the physical environment, such as sites, infrastructure, housing stock, water supply, fuel wood, and construction materials. This will add to your understanding of the resources that are available locally to support the livelihoods of the displaced and local populations.

2.2.2 scenarios

Develop a series of scenarios into which a situation might develop, considering different likely patterns of future events. If such scenarios have already been identified as a result of other planning processes by national governments and the aid community, you should consult them.

The number of scenarios required, and their scope, depends upon the circumstances of each situation. However, common scenarios typically range between the following extremes:

- **best case:** where conflicts or risks from natural disasters diminish and co-ordination is possible, resulting in the early achievement of durable solutions to the settlement needs of the entire displaced population;

- **worst case:** where conflicts or risks from natural disasters escalate, and co-ordination is difficult, resulting in further displacement of the population.

Scenario development should conclude by selecting the most likely scenario, explaining the reasons for the selection, and the assumptions made. Scenario development and selection should make use of profile indicators. You might find that you need additional indicators as you refine a scenario.

2.2.3 indicators

Profile indicators enable the planners and implementers of aid operations to decide which scenario they should adopt as the basis for their decision making. They also help them to understand when one scenario is becoming more likely than another. For example, different scenarios for the future of an emergency situation may depend on different total numbers of refugees arriving. In this example, the rate of influx of displaced persons might serve to indicate which is the likely future scenario to be assumed for planning purposes.

2.3 developing plans

Plans should be developed on the basis of current strategic, programme, and project profiles (2.2). Strategic plans should integrate TS objectives with wider plans and objectives for relief and development. **Programme plans** should consider how each programme would influence profile considerations, such as security and resource management, locally and nationally. **Project plans** should offer detailed information on questions such as the form of labour that will be used, and on matters of management, sustainability, and handover.

The development of strategic, programme, and project plans follows the same three-step process: defining objectives (2.3.1), describing activities (2.3.2), and scheduling operations (2.3.3). The development of response plans must take into account phases of operation (2.4), including financial and technical implications, as well as general planning considerations (2.5), such as gender and age-related factors.

Planning might be done by a committee or an individual, but it is essential to seek participation or guidance from the relevant stakeholders. The involvement of all stakeholder groups will increase the quality and success of profiling and planning.

2.3.1 objectives

It is essential to identify consistent objectives for TS strategies, programmes, and projects. At each planning level, such objectives offer a point of reference throughout the phases of operation (2.4) against which to develop appropriate activities (2.3.2) and schedule their implementation (2.3.3).

When defining objectives, one should draw on the profile (2.2) of a situation; seek the involvement of stakeholders; make reference to other plans; and take into account generic and situation-specific objectives and 'centres of gravity' (see below). Objectives should also be quantified by means of planning indicators.

involvement Involve stakeholders in setting objectives, both to increase the chances of the objectives being reached, and to improve co-ordination. Stakeholder involvement is described in section 2.2.1. The involvement of sectoral specialists is particularly important, because planning for transitional settlement will have an impact on the operations of other sectors, such as water and sanitation and primary health care.

reference Refer to relief and development plans prepared at local or national and sectoral or strategic levels by all the stakeholder groups listed in section 2.2.1. TS objectives must be consistent with the objectives of other relief and development objectives and sectors of response.

For example, supporting dispersed settlement may seem appropriate from the perspective of transitional settlement, but it may be wholly unacceptable from the perspectives of local security, health-care infrastructure, the distribution of food, or the use of water resources.

generic and situation-specific objectives

Common generic objectives include the provision of the following:

- TS support for the transit process (2.4.3)
- access to a choice of appropriate TS options
- protection from threats external to the displaced population
- security from threats internal to the displaced population
- safety from natural hazards, including endemic diseases
- TS support for durable solutions.

In addition, a series of objectives that are specific to a particular situation should be set, such as the sustainable management of the harvesting of construction timber. These objectives may be modified and quantified with planning indicators (2.2.3) in response to the specific situation.

centres of gravity

Military planners often identify a 'centre of gravity': a single factor which will determine the outcome of a particular situation. For example, in a situation where displacement is likely, the security of a particular road may determine the rate of influx, the size of the influx, or whether the displacement will occur at all.

quantifying objectives with planning indicators

Planning indicators (2.2.3) should be attached to the objectives agreed for a specific situation, including a number of methods for with planning verification which can be cross-referenced. For example, success in maintaining secure access along a road might be indicated by the absence of security incidents, which might be verified by interviewing people who use the road, or even by patrolling the road. It is not good practice to use unquantifiable objectives, such as 'appropriate access', which are too general to make the objective meaningful in a specific situation.

When developing objectives, be aware of the assumptions that are made during the assessment stage (2.2.1) and when developing scenarios (2.2.2). Assumptions should be described next to any objectives offered in a plan.

2.3.2 activities

To meet strategic, programme, and project objectives (2.3.1), a range of activities must be carried out. These activities need to be identified and planned to suit the specifics of the given situation. This section describes typical activities on the strategic, programme, and project levels.

strategic activities

Strategic activities include the following:

- combining some or all of the six TS programme options (3.1.1) into a coherent plan of response to the needs for TS and shelter of the entire population displaced by a conflict, natural disaster, or complex emergency;
- co-ordinating TS programmes with other operations, such as the national or local provision of security and primary health care.

The planning and implementation of activities to support transitional settlement influences relations between the displaced and local populations, the local and national governments, and the aid community. The possible impacts of strategic activities on local, national, and regional security and development should be taken into account during strategic scenario development (2.2.2).

When considering which options to support, the aid community and local government should first consider the preferred settlement option of the displaced population. It may be the case, however, that the preferred option is inappropriate for the local population, or the local government, or the aid community, or even for the displaced population itself. The preferred settlement option can be implemented only if it is appropriate to the circumstances. Likewise, financial and political limitations must be recognised, and productive compromises must be reached.

programme activities

A TS programme will involve many projects. For example, a programme for one or more planned camps might include activities such as the following:

- supporting local services and facilities, and building new facilities through construction projects, such as road works (6.1)

- distribution projects for shelter materials and shelter non-food items (NFIs), involving assessment, procurement, and logistics (7.1)

project activities

Typical project activities might include:

- developing a project brief, based upon project objectives, including the assessment of project requirements and the resources available
- deciding upon arrangements for contracting materials and labour, such as undertaking a tendering process (5.4) or engaging direct labour (5.3)
- for construction projects: developing brief documentation for tenderers, and a bill of quantities (6.2.2)
- for distribution projects: defining the shelter NFI package and distribution system to meet project objectives (7.1).

A project brief is a clear description of the project's phased requirements – functional, social, physical, and developmental – in addition to performance specifications. For example, the project brief for a clinic might include the following elements:

- a description of who will use and staff the clinic, and how it will be used, based on assessments and interviews;
- a list of functions that the clinic should perform, such as medical screening, with a description of each function and its space requirements and functional requirements;
- a diagram explaining the relationship between those functions and common requirements, such as constant access to water and sanitation;
- any construction work required, such as the expansion or building of wards for in-patients;
- the use of and requirements for the clinic or the site of the clinic, once its role in the TS programme is finished;
- the materials and labour necessary to undertake the work, taking into account the capacities within aid agencies and local contracting organisations; skills; tools; and the availability of heavy plant, such as bulldozers.

2.3.3 scheduling

A schedule of operations needs to be agreed, specifying the range of activities (2.3.2) to be undertaken within a strategy, programme, or project plan. This is to ensure that the activities can be carried out within the required timeframe, given the resources available. For example, a schedule of works for a construction project is needed to enable the project manager, contractors, labour leaders, and suppliers to co-ordinate their work. The schedule of operations should be based upon the typical phases of operation understood throughout the aid community (2.4), but the impact of operations beyond the exit strategy should also be considered.

deadlines It is essential that all stakeholders should agree which specific activities should be completed in order to reach certain objectives (2.3.1). Deadlines can be identified by using the scenario planning (2.2.2) that was undertaken while developing profiles (2.2). Strategic, programme, and project deadlines should be integrated into a single timeline or schedule of operations. It is important that the schedule should balance the need to complete activities quickly with the need to maintain good relations between the displaced and local populations and labour forces.

The schedule will need to be updated regularly, and should be used as a management communication tool. For example, if displaced persons start to arrive at an increased rate, a deadline to build a new reception centre may need to be brought forward. This should be communicated to the responsible programme and project managers, in order to ensure that resources can be made available from other activities. Finally, the new deadlines have to be reintegrated into the schedule of operations.

In a highly changeable situation, unpredicted events will affect any schedule of operation, which must be sufficiently flexible to be adapted to the change. This is easier if the potential impact of alternative scenarios was considered when the schedule was drawn up.

critical path analysis

When developing a schedule of operations, there are likely to be factors upon which a number of activities depend: for example, there may be a lack of skilled craftspeople or a shortage of certain materials, without which a construction project cannot be completed. The process of identifying the factors that could determine the outcome of a situation is called 'critical path analysis'. These factors may affect a situation in either a positive or a negative way, constituting opportunities or risks. They need to be monitored constantly and used as planning indicators (2.3.1), to ensure that any changes can be identified immediately, and pre-planned responses can be implemented.

monitoring Schedules of operation are effective only if planning indicators are monitored. The aim of monitoring is (on the one hand) to maintain up-to-date information about a changing situation, and (on the other hand) to understand why a situation is changing. For example, it is essential to gain an understanding of why displaced population groups select certain TS options, and why they move between them.

schedule of operations diagram

Using the schedule of operations as a tool for planning and management communication can be made easier by visualising it in the form of a diagram, such as the fictitious example presented in figure 2(b).The diagram illustrates how populations move between different TS options; it thus allows the deadlines of different programmes to be compared. It also illustrates the importance of monitoring.

figure 2(b): illustrating a schedule of operations

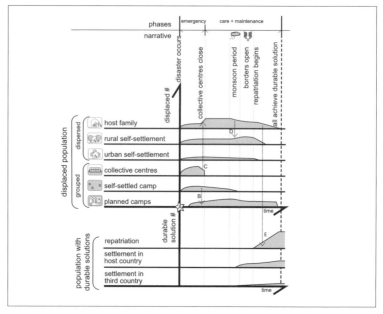

The diagram illustrates how displaced populations choose different TS options in response to the occurrence of certain events:

Event A: the disaster occurs, and a population movement follows. The displaced population chooses a number of TS options.

Event B: planned camps are opened after the initial period, and the population in the self-settled camps is transferred to the planned camps.

Event C: the closure of the collective centres is accompanied by population movement to host families.

Event D: during the care and maintenance phase, a monsoon occurs and some families move to rural self-settlement to begin farming.

Event E: the majority of the displaced population is repatriated. For others, durable solutions are reached by settling them in the host country or a third country.

scheduling checklist

Scheduling should consider the following questions, in addition to the criteria developed for any specific situation.

- Are the appropriate planning objectives and indicators in place (2.3.1)?
- What deadlines are appropriate, and how should they be combined into a schedule of operations?
- How should the schedule of operations be used as a management communication tool between strategic, programme, and project planning?
- Which factors or centres of gravity constitute the critical path for the schedule of operations?
- In which phase of the operation (2.4) is assistance being given, and how might this influence planning?
- What resources required for later phases need to be allocated within the first funding round (2.5.6)?
- What phasing of operations is appropriate for planning purposes, within each of the TS programme options under consideration? How do these phases influence each other?
- What factors are likely to influence the decision of displaced families to move between TS programme options?

- What upgrading of shelter facilities might be undertaken by the displaced population over time? How might this be integrated and supported?
- How might support within different phases or seasons increase the options for displaced populations to achieve levels of economic self-sufficiency?
- Which parts of the TS strategy need to involve specialists from outside the operational staff, and during which phases?

2.4 phases of operation

Developing a plan (2.3) must take full account of the wider phases of operation. Operations and planning occur in a sequence of events which is often described as consisting of seven phases.

figure 2(c): the seven phases of operation

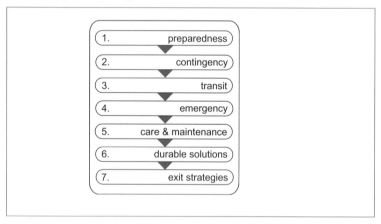

1. preparedness
2. contingency
3. transit
4. emergency
5. care & maintenance
6. durable solutions
7. exit strategies

2.4.1 preparedness phase

The preparedness phase can be described, for the purposes of TS programming, as the period before an emergency that is not necessarily imminent.

In the preparedness phase, planning for transitional settlement should focus on identifying, establishing, developing, and maintaining local and national capacities. Such activities might include the following:

- consolidating international law, such as refugee law, within national and regional statutes;
- building capacity within national institutions, line ministries, and external agencies: for example, by undertaking joint strategic planning (2.1);
- establishing early-warning mechanisms and capacities;
- establishing stockpiles of key shelter materials and equipment for the response in the emergency phase;
- public information campaigns, to raise awareness of the impacts of population displacement from another region or country.

Preparedness planning is particularly important in areas that are prone to natural disasters. Here, preparedness can in addition take the form of remedial work to restore infrastructure, housing, and land resources, to reduce the likelihood of damage to property and livelihoods, and any subsequent displacement.

early-warning mechanisms

Early-warning mechanisms and capacities are essential in respect of both conflicts and natural disasters. Triggers or indicators of pre-defined levels of emergency should be identified, along with the responses required. For example, a trigger might be the arrival of entire families of asylum seekers in a country from across a border where previously only individuals had arrived looking for work. This trigger might indicate that a response is required by local authorities, together with a scoping mission by a Protection Officer from UNHCR.

2.4.2 contingency phase

The contingency phase can be described, for the purposes of TS programming, as the period before an emergency which is yet to occur but is likely to happen.

Contingency planning should be undertaken to identify likely opportunities and constraints in responding to the expected situation, as well as to introduce the various stakeholders and engage them in planning processes. Activities in contingency planning may include the following:

- multi-stakeholder implementation plans, involving host governments, line ministries, humanitarian organisations, commercial contractors, the local population, and possibly members of the potentially displaced populations;

- social assessments of skills and capacities, as well as attitudes and historic relations between stakeholders;
- physical assessments of infrastructure and housing stock;
- site selection and planning for temporary and durable grouped settlements, possibly including reception, transit, planned and self-settled camps, collective centres, identification of host families, and options for integration within the host population;
- public awareness campaigns with the local community, in preparation for the likely consequences of an influx of displaced persons.

Contingency planning is usually based on scenario planning, with assumptions made about political, military, and other developments in later phases. As such, the accuracy of the contingency plan generally declines as time passes and the situation progresses, when new scenarios should be developed.

2.4.3 transit phase

The transit phase can be described, for the purposes of TS programming, as the period during which populations are being displaced and are moving away from their places of origin into TS options.

As part of any plan for TS response when displacement is on-going, support should be considered for the transit of displaced populations from a border or front line to a safer location. Transit should be supported with the following aims in mind:

- To increase the chances of survival of the displaced population.
- To form a better understanding of the nature and the scale of the influx of displaced people. (Information about their places of origin and points of entry, gender composition, and vulnerabilities will aid influx management and the preparation of further response.)
- To gain some control over the type and location of TS options chosen by displaced populations, in order to maximise protection and security and prevent relocation.

Support is often organised through a well-tried network of temporary facilities placed along the route of displacement. Way-stations positioned at a border or along the route lead to reception centres, either in the locality of the TS programmes, or within camps. Further guidance on transit and typical plans of facilities are presented in section 8.2. Controlling, directing, and limiting transit have frequently been manipulated for political reasons, and in order to disrupt humanitarian response, so aid organisations should be aware of this risk.

The transit process should allow the aid community to employ influx-management techniques to maintain a daily or even hourly understanding of the scale, speed, location, and direction of influx (8.2). This is the key to the planning and implementation of the transit programme. Based on the nature of the influx, decisions can be made to deploy and support teams for way-stations, and transit and reception centres can be prepared, allowing the aid community to stay one step ahead of the crisis.

blockage The state of transit may continue for some time, as families and communities re-group or delay making decisions about which TS option to choose. There is also a tendency for capacity in reception facilities to be taken up by vulnerable people and individuals wishing to make use of services or to await other family members who are still in transit. Such a use of settlement capacity by displaced groups may slow or block the transit network. It is important to ensure that the reasons for any blockage are understood, and that vulnerable people and others have appropriate alternatives to remaining in the transit facility.

There have been cases where transit facilities are occupied for months, whether for external or internal reasons. Negative impacts on social conditions and on health may be expected if people are accommodated in high-density accommodation for any period. Great care must be taken by the aid community to ensure that displaced persons are assisted on the basis of their vulnerability and are then moved on to a TS option as quickly as possible, ideally within days or weeks.

2.4.4 emergency phase

The emergency phase can be described, for the purposes of TS programming, as the period during which significant numbers of people are being displaced, with the result that a country or region is receiving a significant influx of displaced people.

Emergencies can be 'fast onset', where there is a large influx of displaced people over a short period of time, or 'slow onset', where influx rates appear low but remain constant over a longer period. The appropriate response might be different in the two cases, and the emergency phase needs to be described and understood for both. This section presents considerations which are common to both types of emergency.

influx management

Influx management during the transit phase (8.2) is the key to planning and implementation in the emergency phase. Preparations need to be made to meet the immediate needs of displaced persons, in terms of both infrastructure and services, such as health care. Influxes need to be predicted, to ensure that there is sufficient time to make these preparations.

When large unpredicted emergencies take place, the aid community is often unable to manage the influx. The following are common indicators that this is the case.

• Displaced families have no choice about TS arrangements, because the aid community has not made alternatives available to them.

• The aid community accepts TS programme options which it knows to be temporary, with the result that the displaced populations will have to be moved to a different site or option at a later point in time.

• Agencies accept lower standards than is internationally recommended, for example by Sphere (2004) and UNHCR (2000). (Note, however, that it is wholly acceptable to make emergency provisions for which upgrading is planned, such as designating defecation fields for immediate use in a camp, while leaving space for latrines to be constructed later.)

• Urgent requests are sent to headquarters for increases in resources and staff, outside a planned emergency response.

2.4.5 care and maintenance phase

The care and maintenance phase can be described, for the purposes of TS programming, as the period between the major influx of displaced people and the point when every member of the displaced population has either moved to another TS option, or has reached a durable solution and is no longer displaced. Therefore each TS option can be considered to have its own care and maintenance phase.

The core of any TS programme in the care and maintenance phase should be a deliberate and sustainable movement from the provision of services solely by external organisations to self-management and self-help. This involves enabling and empowering displaced communities to analyse and meet their own needs.

During the care and maintenance phase, different organisations often take responsibility for different sectors, such as food distribution, water and sanitation, and health care. It is important, therefore, to have a co-ordination body such as UNHCR to support the aid community and other stakeholders in identifying and meeting its common objectives. In some cases, especially with planned camps, different organisations take on this management and co-ordination role in different phases of operations. Similarly, TS needs will change with time. For example, the displaced population might begin to cultivate land, or the demographics might change through natural population growth, leading to a rapid large-scale influx of new migrants. Such changes should be tracked through monitoring processes, and the TS response should be adapted accordingly.

2.4.6 durable solutions phase

The durable solutions phase can be described, for the purposes of TS programming, as the period when the displacement has ended because sustainable and permanent settlement and shelter have been achieved for the displaced population.

UNHCR defines three possible options for durable solutions for refugees, asylum seekers, and other persons of concern within the UNHCR mandate:

- repatriation to their homeland, if conditions are suitable
- integration in the country of asylum
- resettlement in a third country.

We adopt these options, but we apply them to the cases of all displaced persons. So 'integration in the country of asylum' could also be 'integration within the area of displacement'.

All durable solutions described above have implications for the end-state of TS programmes. At the onset of displacement, it is usually not possible to predict with any meaningful certainty what the likely durable solution (or solutions) might be. Nevertheless, it is important to develop scenarios and plans based on various end-states for transitional settlement, and to anticipate any developmental goals that may follow the emergency phase of assistance.

2.4.7 exit-strategies phase

The exit-strategies phase can be described, for the purposes of TS programming, as the period after durable solutions have been achieved for the displaced populations.

Once durable solutions have been reached for the displaced population, there remains the need for exit strategies for the programmes that dealt with their TS needs. Organisational and physical assets must be either handed over locally or recycled within humanitarian organisations. Scenario planning of exit strategies, at strategic, programme, and project levels, will make this process easier and will assist in developing the following:

- the transfer of capacities and skills, both locally and within the aid community;
- the tracking of assets within the aid community, so that capital items such as heavy equipment can be recovered for later operations;
- possible developmental objectives for the period after the TS programme is completed: for example, the objective of supporting local primary health care by the construction of a permanent clinic, combined with finding staff and resources to run the clinic following final handover to local authorities.

In the case of dispersed settlement, such as accommodation with host families, handover might mean that resources previously used to support displaced persons, such as housing and agricultural resources, are retained by the host population on a family-by-family basis. In the case of grouped settlement, infrastructure and facilities might be handed over to the previous owner of the facility; for example, a gymnasium used as a reception centre might be refurbished and returned to the local authorities.

It is important that future alternative uses for TS facilities and assets are identified at the project-planning stage. It may be possible to include the handover of facilities and capital assets in negotiations with local authorities; but if the outcome cannot be predicted, care should be taken not to raise expectations that cannot be met. In addition, it is possible that local groups might put pressure on displaced groups to return prematurely, so that the facilities created for them can be handed over.

When assets cannot be handed over, programme facilities will simply have to be closed and the assets recovered. This might be the case because the facilities provided for the displaced population are too large for sustainable use by the local population.

2.5 general planning considerations

Factors such as security (2.5.1), gender and age (2.5.2), the environment (2.5.4), and funding (2.5.6) affect the planning of transitional settlement at the strategic, programme, and project levels. This section presents general considerations that should inform the planning process.

2.5.1 protection and security

The protection and security of displaced populations and their hosts must remain the central focus of national and international support for transitional settlement. The choice, form, and location of TS programmes will affect the protection and security of the displaced, local, and regional populations, both as communities and as individuals. In particular, displacement increases the vulnerability of individuals and populations, often disproportionately affecting some social groups, such as ethnic minorities and elderly people (2.5.2). Poor strategic planning may lead to communities living under threat from armed groups (a question of external security), or to individuals living under threat of physical or sexual violence (a question of internal security). There are also threats which are not man-made, such as natural hazards, and, in the context of transitional settlement, there are risks arising from construction methods.

Consequently, TS strategies based on an accurate and current understanding of protection and security can determine the survival and livelihoods of displaced and local populations, and therefore the success of national and international support operations.

The successful provision of protection and security within transitional settlement depends largely on three factors, all of which will change continually over the duration of a displacement:

- the reduction of the vulnerability and exposure of individuals and groups to internal and external threats;
- the visibility of individuals and groups to protection and security enforcers and witnesses;
- levels, quality, and degrees of impartiality of protection, security enforcement, and systems of justice, whether provided by the police or the military, and on national or international levels.

external security

Displaced populations and their hosts require protection from external threats, including threats from those groups that may have caused the displacement. Such threats can range from military action by armed forces to violent attack by armed factions. Therefore, TS strategies should begin by supporting the transit of the displaced population away from threats that might compromise their protection (8.2).

All TS programme options should be located at a considerable distance from areas of risk. UNHCR, referring to the OAU Convention, has adopted as policy the requirement that refugee camps should be set back 50 km from any international border (UNHCR 2000). Similar concerns apply to internally displaced persons, who may benefit from TS options set back from a front line or hostile group.

The security situation should be evaluated for all settlement options before choices between them are made. For instance, displaced people living with host families may be at greater risk from military incursion than those living in camps, which may be more easily defensible; in that case, grouped settlement should be supported.

internal security

Displaced populations and their hosts require internal security, including protection from aggressive political, religious, and ethnic groups within both populations. Internal threats may range from organised inter-communal violence to sexual violence. Following transit, TS strategy should support a range of TS programme options which minimise such threats.

The proximity of displaced populations to local communities should be considered, especially when the populations are of very different sizes, or when ethnic or religious tensions are likely. In some circumstances, segregation of certain groups within TS options, or segregation from local population groups, may have to be enforced. However, segregation may increase tensions by removing opportunities for communication, and by making the segregated group an easier physical target for hostile action.

Where armed factions exist within displaced populations, dispersed TS options may weaken the control of the armed factions over the populations. On the other hand, the occupants of grouped settlements are aware of strangers, a fact which enables informal control and provides a warning system to identify risks to security.

In well-planned group settlements, vulnerable groups are located in visible areas, away from the edges and close to services. Risks of sexual violence may be reduced, for example through the provision of adequate lighting at night. If their situation permits, vulnerable groups should be housed in such a way as to be well integrated into their community structures. In dispersed settlement, vulnerability may be increased, so individuals or families accommodated with host families must have constant, easy, and confidential access to advisers who can take action on issues such as abuse and sexual violence.

It is important to consider privacy, security, and safety in combination with each other. For instance, while personal spaces in a collective centre should be lockable to increase personal safety, safe evacuation in the event of fire must still be guaranteed.

risk from natural hazards

As explained in detail in section 6.3, areas at risk from natural disasters or hazards should be avoided when selecting a site for the construction of TS options. When such risk cannot be avoided, mitigating measures should be taken. For example, in flood-prone areas, early-warning mechanisms should be supported, and appropriate areas on high ground or in high buildings should be prepared for emergency shelter and evacuation.

safe materials and construction techniques

When possible, all building materials and construction techniques should be safe to use and should comply with national and international standards and building codes. Observing appropriate building codes is a complex technical matter, so specialist assistance should be sought. For example, the use of building materials containing asbestos should in general be avoided. But it might be extremely difficult to avoid such use. Materials containing asbestos vary in their degrees of toxicity and brittleness; a specialist could advise whether a particular type is safe to use in particular circumstances where there is no reason to suspect that asbestos-fibre dust might be released. However, there is no way of knowing how the material will be finally used or disposed of, so a specialist should assess whether its use would constitute a safety hazard.

Take particular care to ensure the safe handling of carcinogenic (cancer-causing) materials, such as diesel and waste engine oil, which are used to protect timber against termites in some countries. The safe use of building materials is addressed in detail in chapter 6.

2.5.2 gender and age

Displacement requires populations to live in unfamiliar circumstances where they may find it hard to maintain social structures and coping strategies. The traditional cultural roles of women, men, the young, and the elderly may be challenged and may have to be adjusted. For example, women might have been responsible for preparing food and carrying water in the original settlement. In a camp, these activities might be more difficult and might require the involvement of men. Such changes in circumstances and shifts in traditional roles often create social problems and barriers to community development.

Traditionally, women and men of different ages may undertake different roles in the construction and maintenance of shelter. In such circumstances, particular attention should be given to the needs of families or individuals if a woman or man able to undertake some of these roles is not present. Support may be required if, for example, a female-headed household is constructing a shelter but there are no appropriate men available to build the roof, which may be considered a male role.

The planning and implementation of transitional settlement affects both sexes and all ages, and equitable representation should be sought when forming teams and committees. Respect for the dignity, culture, and religion of displaced groups must be maintained at all times, while ensuring that particular elements of the community are not pressured into undertaking too many activities; that they are offered equal access to support and services, and equal opportunities for employment; and that they are equally represented when decisions are taken.

demographics

The proportions of men and women and of young and old people in a displaced population are likely to be different from those that prevailed in their home settlements. There are several possible reasons for this. There may be fewer young men, because they have volunteered for or have been conscripted into military service, or they have been killed, or they may have fled. There may be more female-headed households, because (although women are the usual target of gender-based violence) in general fewer women than men are killed in armed conflict. There may be fewer old and young people, because they are particularly vulnerable to hardship and disease, and many may have died, especially during transit. In longer-term displacements, however, better health care may reduce mortality rates, thus reversing this effect.

gender-based violence

Among displaced persons who have self-settled, vulnerability to gender-based violence (GBV) may either increase or decrease. In host families, for instance, vulnerability may be reduced because the family network offers social controls. On the other hand, opportunities for abuse may be increased because the displaced family feels obligated to the host family, or is under its control. Mechanisms should be in place to assess and monitor vulnerabilities and risks effectively.

Changed physical or social circumstances in grouped settlements can also leave certain groups vulnerable to GBV or exploitation. For instance, single men, if not integrated in wider family groups, may harass unaccompanied women. The risk is increased if women have to travel long distances to collect firewood or water because natural resources have been consumed (2.5.4).

When planning and implementing TS strategies, programmes, and projects, it is important to take into account the existing (and possible future) gender-related and age-related roles within a displaced population. For instance, there is little point in supporting primary education if the children are needed by families to collect water from a remote source.

planning to avoid GBV risks

People-Orientated Planning (POP), discussed in section 4.5.5, offers a useful assessment tool. 'People-Oriented Planning at Work: Using POP to Improve UNHCR Programming' (Anderson 1994) offers useful advice on how to take account of gender roles in the planning of grouped settlements, such as refugee camps:

> The layout of shelter in a refugee camp can either provide suitable protection or exacerbate the likelihood of unsafe conditions. In particular, people vulnerable to sexual attack (both women and young children) must have access to well-lighted, nearby toilet facilities as this is one area that has often proved dangerous for unaccompanied users. In addition, placement of vulnerable people in outlying camp sections increases their risk of physical sexual assault. [...]
>
> If tradition dictates that women should be secluded within household compounds, housing styles and latrine locations must be designed to respect these traditions. In addition, the locations of wells and food or other service distribution points must take account of women's mobility, if women are to be ensured access to them.
>
> Shelter arrangements for women without husbands in situations where women are usually secluded must also take into account the tradition of seclusion. Two possible approaches include:
>
> • providing shelter that 'pairs' women who do not have men with families where men are present
>
> • building and reserving special areas for groups of single women and their dependents.
>
> Anderson (1994)

table 2(a): lessons learned from UNHCR experience of programming for shelter

	problems	possible solutions
1	Materials provided to refugee families to build their own houses cannot be used by families where the person who builds is absent (sometimes men, sometimes women).	Identify the families who do not have anyone who can build their house; provide extra assistance.
2	Provision of resources and services is linked to the completion of self-build homes; if families (usually female-headed households, FFHs) lack a traditional builder, they are further disadvantaged.	Unlink provision of resources from housing; provide help to families who do not have a traditional builder; if there are no cultural taboos, teach women to construct their houses.
3	Unaccompanied women refugees absorbed into asylum-country families have been sexually exploited by men of the host families.	A difficult problem. On-the-ground monitoring of safety is the first step. Provide ways to report abuse; and offer alternative living arrangements (possibly with asylum-country FHHs).
4	Overcrowded shelter conditions can put unaccompanied women at special risk of sexual violence.	Identify the families for whom this is an issue. Consult with refugees on appropriate traditional systems for protection. Group single women in well-guarded places and establish a refugee committee (of male and/or female elders, possibly) for oversight and enforcement of their protection.
5	Location of residences in relation to water points, food-distribution points, or latrines may involve long and sometimes dangerous trips for women and children.	Consider the location of essential services and who will be using them. Minimise danger. Provide guards. Ensure use during daylight and safe hours.
6	Lighting may be inadequate in camp areas (e.g. latrines) increasing risks, especially for women.	Increase lighting.

(based on Anderson 1994)

2.5.3 vulnerable groups

Vulnerable groups include, but are not limited to, elderly people, unaccompanied minors (UAMs), the sick and infirm, disabled people, and those suffering from chronic diseases such as AIDS. Within a displaced population, such groups have special settlement requirements which may require that standard plans have to be adapted. For example, UAMs may be in need of special accommodation which is different from the type of housing provided for a family. It is also particularly important that site planning should take into account and support the internal social support given to vulnerable groups by their own communities.

Vulnerable groups must be offered equal access to community services and other resources available to non-vulnerable people. In addition, they should be given enhanced access to resources of which they are in greater need. For example, the physical assistance of building teams should be offered to assist vulnerable groups with shelter construction and maintenance.

Community services offer a mechanism with which to identify and support vulnerable groups. They also allow these groups to express their needs and priorities. Their needs should inform not only the TS response, but also the support provided by other sectors.

2.5.4 environment

The physical environment provides both displaced and local populations with essential resources with which to maintain their livelihoods: water for drinking, cooking, washing, laundry, and sanitation; fuel for cooking; materials for construction; and food from agriculture and animal husbandry. The management of these resources is essential to development and must be considered in the TS response. Great care must be taken to ensure the sustainable use of natural resources, and to prevent conflicts arising from competition over access.

natural-resource management

Natural-resource management (NRM) must be considered at every level of planning, because damage to the environment and to relations with local communities is difficult to repair. Currently, most environmental programmes in the field must aim to mitigate avoidable damage, because environmental considerations were not taken into account in the planning process. Forward-looking environmental programmes need not be complex or costly. They can be designed to encourage local policies and practices to include environmental considerations, in addition to defining or enforcing new practices. It is also important to include environmental considerations in contractual agreements from the outset, to ensure that they are part of the overall environmental strategy.

The UNHCR Environment Unit has developed, along with other bodies, considerable practical advice on NRM by refugees. Most of the advice is relevant for all displaced populations (UNHCR 1996; 1998 a/b/c/d/e; 2002a). The Unit recommends that all stakeholders should be involved from the emergency phase onwards, in particular the local and displaced populations and local authorities. The aim of such co-ordination is to enable the stakeholders to discuss the various options and measures to be taken, and to agree to the following initiatives.

- Strengthen or establish NRM co-ordination committees, such as local forestry departments and agricultural co-operatives, ensuring the inclusion of representatives from both the local and displaced populations.

- Involve local and displaced populations in measures to protect local environmental resources and support NRM, in the interests of achieving sustainability.

- Develop clear policies on access and user rights to natural resources, defining the roles and responsibilities of all stakeholders.

- Raise awareness among displaced populations of the environmental rules and regulations of the locality, by means of organised meetings and possibly the display of signs and posters.

Establishing ownership of and user rights to environmental resources is essential for effective and sustainable NRM, as well as successful rehabilitation. Access to environmental resources, and rights to use them, may act as incentives for displaced populations and local communities to take part in environment-protection activities. For instance, if a displaced family are given responsibility for managing a patch of fruit trees, in return for benefiting from the harvest, they will naturally be more inclined to protect the trees. When user rights are not made clear, people generally have little interest in managing natural resources.

It is essential to protect environmental resources strictly, and to monitor their use. This includes regulating the harvesting of wood, grasses, wild foods, and wild animals, perhaps zoning different areas for use on a rotational basis. It also involves the strategic designation of no-cutting zones, to promote their use as genetic banks for eventual regeneration. Particularly sensitive ecological zones might need to be closed off completely in order to protect them. Possible ways to reduce the consumption of natural resources include attaching either a monetary value or an in-kind exchange value to them. These methods may be more effective than enforcing the protection of natural resources through regulatory means, or they may be combined with regulation and the deployment of forest guards.

Deforestation can be discouraged by marking certain trees which it is permitted to cut, or marking sites from where materials are permitted to be collected, and appointing guards to direct and control activities. When there has been deforestation on public land, it is usually most effective to promote regeneration and managed harvesting. This is likely to make a much more significant contribution than tree planting, even when planting is on a large scale. When trees are planted or protected, as part of a damage-mitigation or environment-rehabilitation strategy, it is imperative to establish the ownership rights of the eventual users of the trees clearly at the outset.

In later phases, environment protection and rehabilitation should aim to restore the capacity of the local community to derive a sustainable livelihood from their natural-resource base. At the same time, the displaced populations should be offered the environmental resources to sustain a livelihood over the period of their displacement, regardless of the form of their durable settlement solution. This dual aim should be pursued because sustainable livelihoods will bring advantages to all stakeholders, creating increased social and economic autonomy (UNHCR 2002e).

The UNHCR Environment Unit offers a series of guidelines on NRM in refugee situations (www.unhcr.ch). CARE has developed a Rapid Environmental Assessment (REA) tool (Kelly 2001).

planned and self-settled camps

Much of the existing literature on environmental issues is focused on the negative impacts of high-density grouped transitional settlement, such as planned camps, and ways to mitigate them. Perhaps the most important lesson to learn is that high-density settlement should be avoided whenever possible.

Where high-density settlement is unavoidable, planning for environmental sustainability is often the key to the sustainability of the settlement itself. There is evidence, for example, that severe environmental degradation has influenced decisions of certain countries not to grant asylum to refugees and other displaced persons.

Small plots limit the opportunity for tree planting and create an imbalance between supply and demand for natural resources. An area of 200–300m² per plot is the current recommended compromise for ensuring appropriate social control and protection, maintaining vegetation, and avoiding the spread of camps over an area so large that infrastructure and maintenance become unsustainable for the aid community or host government.

The larger the plot, however, the greater the area over which a displaced family is able to take some management responsibility, and over which it can exert control. Effective NRM in displaced settlements is more likely where family plots are large. Tree planting and the protection of existing vegetation is practical only on household plots, because common areas within a settlement are difficult to protect. Thus the larger the plot allocated to a family, the greater the area that benefits from some form of assured management.

Planting within camps, particularly on household plots, normally achieves high survival rates and is of immediate social benefit. Seedling production to supply such programmes should be decentralised to local community groups and displaced groups as early as possible.

An alternative to planting on private plots is to establish independent plantations. While plantations may help to respond to host governments' concerns that tree cover has been damaged, the provision of new trees may be inappropriate, for several reasons. If previously uncultivated land is opened up by displaced populations, there is a chance, particularly where the supply of land is short, that it will continue to be cultivated by locals if the displaced leave the area.

It is unrealistic to expect that transitional settlement will not result in any negative environmental impact, however closely it is monitored and supported through the different phases of response (2.4). It is therefore necessary to plan and budget for the environmental rehabilitation and recovery of an area or site after its temporary occupation by a displaced population. Clean-up work should begin well in advance of the closure of the operation.

In many cases, activities to mitigate environmental impact will be undertaken by a local or international organisation, which in rare cases might in turn supervise a contractor. Such activities might include the following:

* repairing damage to local vegetation by promoting replanting schemes, especially if the damage contributes to erosion gullies or the silting of water courses;

* creating or repairing other erosion-control measures, such as surface-water drainage channels;

* aerating any compacted soil, for example on former footpaths, in order to reduce water run-off and risks of erosion, and to increase water infiltration so that the land can be used for agriculture;

* other measures to regenerate land for agriculture or livestock, for example the safe disposal of inorganic wastes, including the cleaning-up of oil spills from the ground or water sources;

* making pit latrines safe, for example by adding lime and back-filling them;

* the permanent safe disposal of medical wastes, for example by incineration at high temperatures.

Additional programmes should be considered in support of the regeneration of the wider landscape, assuming that environmental impacts are unlikely to be localised. These programmes should focus on general developmental support, such as agro-forestry or agriculture, based on an understanding of local land ownership and developmental priorities.

global environment

The impact of a TS programme on the global environment is less direct than its impact on the local environment. It is complex to define, and even harder to quantify or measure. Furthermore, in

---

most cases it is likely that the priority will be to safeguard the local environment before any issues of global environmental sustainability are considered. In recent years, however, the issue of both local and global environmental accountability has become of increasing importance to all stakeholders. So it is important to understand how to judge the impact of transitional settlement on the global environment.

For the purposes of these guidelines, the effect of transitional settlement on the global environment may usefully be approximated to the energy cost of a settlement (UNHCR 1998a). There are three main contributions to the energy cost: the embodied energy of building materials and the energy used in their transportation on the one hand, and the energy cost incurred during the running and maintenance of the settlement on the other.

embodied energy

'Embodied energy' is the amount of energy required to fabricate a given material. In the context of transitional settlement, many important imported construction materials, such as plastic sheeting and fired bricks, contain significant embodied energy through their manufacturing processes.

energy for transporting materials

Often transitional settlement makes use of materials that have been imported regionally or internationally. This involves transportation, which carries an environmental cost as well as an economic cost.

maintenance costs

The fuel required for cooking and heating by the displaced persons and relief workers may be significantly greater than the amount that can be harvested sustainably on a local scale, or even on a regional scale. This may result in deforestation and soil erosion, which may, over time, have a negative impact on the global environment.

2.5.5 seasonal climate changes

Knowledge of local seasonal climate changes and their likely impact is vital for successful strategic, programme, and project planning in a particular locality. For instance, an on-coming monsoon or winter will affect patterns of displacement and the settlement options chosen by displaced populations.

livelihoods The season of the year influences the ability of both the displaced and local populations to provide for their own needs. The climate may also affect decisions and actions taken, with an impact on their protection, security, and health. For example, displaced farmers may not want to move too far from their land before the harvest. This would affect their protection, as well as the choice of TS options supported by local governments and aid organisations.

construction seasons

Implementing TS programmes is complicated by the need to work within the local 'construction season': the periods when construction work is made impossible by winter or a monsoon. The climate affects site access, the availability of local materials and labour, and the viability of employing local construction methods, such as making mud bricks in hot climates.

2.5.6 funding cycles

The timing of emergencies and the funding cycles of donors rarely match local construction seasons. Therefore care should be taken when scheduling works to ensure that funds are available when required.

Many emergencies happen in places where international agencies are already present, and similar emergencies sometimes recur in the same locations. Such agencies will have acquired considerable experience in that particular locality. They may be able to offer valuable advice on financial management matters when new staff and additional capacity arrive on the ground: their assistance should be sought where possible. Some concerns relating to financial management in the various phases of operation (2.4) are noted below.

financial management: early phases

International bilateral and multilateral funding mechanisms are essentially reactive. This means that even activities undertaken in the preparedness, contingency, and transit phases which might prevent or mitigate displacement can usually be financed only by using limited core funding from certain organisations.

In the emergency phase, donors may be willing to fund initial non-recurring expenses of a shelter programme. In the care and maintenance phase, however, they may be less willing to fund on-going or recurrent works, such as the maintenance of buildings.

Uncertainty concerning the availability of follow-up funding has an impact on the type of emergency settlement strategy which is selected in the early phases of an emergency. If it seems that the chances of securing funding to upgrade shelter at a later date are low, it may be appropriate to select a TS strategy which will deliver durable solutions already in the emergency phase.

During the emergency phase, the delivery of settlement objectives can be delayed by a number of factors.

- Often, funds cannot be released because programme funding comes from abroad, while national purchases have to be made in local currency. Importing foreign currency and establishing accounts within national and local banking structures is often a long and bureaucratic process. In addition, there may be concerns about security, because there are often no banks operating in conflict areas, and so cash must be carried by hand.

- When a contract exceeds a certain financial value, agencies or local governments may require implementing agencies to conform to local tendering processes. This may add to the time taken to complete a project.

- Emergencies often happen in places where no purchases can be made, so relief items have to be imported. In some situations, however, settlement and shelter requirements may dictate significant local purchase. In such cases, the transfer of funds to local suppliers may prove problematic, if local suppliers do not have recognised financial systems in place to enable secure purchasing. Local suppliers also sometimes cannot undertake purchasing for international agencies.

- There may not be many, or any, local contractors and builders with suitable capacity to undertake large infrastructural and settlement programmes, particularly in remote locations. In this case, local contractors may require a large portion of a contract fee to be paid in advance, to purchase equipment and materials. However, it is the policy of many agencies and donors to restrict up-front and initial payments to contractors before work has begun.

financial management: maintenance phase

In the care and maintenance phase, funds for programme development and unforeseen circumstances should be available from emergency appeals processes. However, in practice it can be difficult to attract funding for activities such as the expansion or re-planning of camps and infrastructure improvements, even if it is demonstrated that they will improve efficiency in the longer term.

When agreeing the terms and conditions of funding for the care and maintenance phase of TS activities, the funding cycles of the relevant organisations should be taken into account. In many cases, money has to be spent by a given date, regardless of local operating conditions. This may delay the completion of a building project, if the required funding is not allocated before the end of the donor's financial year.

In longer-term operations, currency fluctuations can be a major concern. International and local exchange rates should be monitored to ensure that international and local financial commitments can be met.

financial management: durable solutions and exit phases

Planning for the management or handover of residual materials should be integrated into financial management from the outset. Asset management, asset recovery, and cost recovery are not so well developed in aid organisations as they are in many commercial organisations, but some progress is being made.

2.5.7 sectoral considerations

Choices about transitional settlement always have an impact on other sectors of humanitarian response, and may affect their effectiveness. Sector professionals should help the team to define the requirements for infrastructure to support the delivery of their services, such as a clinic or a water-supply system. The planning of transitional settlement should integrate such services into wider strategic and programmatic responses, such as planned camps or support for self-settled displaced households in urban areas.

Where possible and where politically expedient, existing services should be reinforced in a sustainable manner. It is not advisable to create parallel infrastructures when some already exist, both because this may undermine the existing infrastructure, and also because the parallel infrastructure may not be sustainable. Primary health care, for example, may be impossible to provide if dispersed rural self-settlement is supported in an area where there is no local population and thus no health-care infrastructure. Conversely, supporting dispersed rural self-settlement may present an opportunity to upgrade a local health-care system permanently.

Listed below are some representative examples of how TS responses may affect other humanitarian-aid sectors.

health Contaminated water and many insects are a source of disease, such as malaria, bilharzias, and sleeping sickness. This is one of the reasons why flood-prone areas should be avoided as sites for planned camps or self-settlement (6.3.11). The risk of disease may be reduced through a variety of measures which can be integrated into shelter design, such as eliminating the breeding areas of mosquitoes (6.3.5) or using insecticide and netting (7.6.4).

water and sanitation

One of the main factors which should be considered when planning water and sanitation schemes is population density, because it determines individuals' access to sanitary and waste-disposal services. It may also be necessary to take into account traditional hygiene practices, for instance when choosing between the construction of family or communal facilities.

nutrition In cold climates, the body requires more food in order to keep warm, especially if shelter support is poor. So it is necessary to ensure that family shelter and heating strategies are consistent with the calorific value of the food distributed to displaced persons. Foodstuffs must be appropriate to the cooking options and cultural traditions of the displaced community.

education Education is important for social cohesion and child welfare. Infrastructural support must be made with the full participation of sectoral specialists and all stakeholders, based on an understanding of the educational systems and traditions of the displaced and host communities.

3 options

3 options

The alternatives open to displaced individuals for finding shelter following conflict and natural disaster have been categorised into six transitional settlement programme options: dispersal in host families, rural self-settlement, urban self-settlement, collective centres, self-settled camps, and planned camps. The options can be viewed as three dispersed options and three grouped options, or as four self-settled options and two planned options.

This chapter introduces the six transitional settlement (TS) options open to displaced populations:

3.1   **overview of TS options** compares the dispersed and grouped options to aid understanding of how to combine them.

3.2   **dispersed in host families**: this option involves sheltering the displaced population within the households of local families, or on land or in properties owned by them.

3.3   **dispersed in rural self-settlement**: displaced families settle on land in a rural context owned collectively, rather than privately.

3.4   **dispersed in urban self-settlement**: displaced populations settle in an urban environment, occupying unclaimed properties or land, or settling informally.

3.5   **grouped in collective centres (mass shelter)**: these are usually transit facilities located in pre-existing structures, such as community centres, town halls, gymnasiums, hotels, warehouses, disused factories, and unfinished buildings, where a large group of displaced people find shelter.

3.6   **grouped in self-settled camps**: a displaced community settles in a camp, independent of assistance from local government or the aid community.

3.7   **grouped in planned camps**: accommodation on purpose-built sites where a full services infrastructure is provided.

The overview makes important general points. It should be read in conjunction with any of the TS options, which are stand-alone. Each of the six TS options is structured consistently, according to the phases of operation introduced in section 2.4, in order to assist with comparison and selection.

3.1 overview of transitional settlement options

The TS options may be viewed either as three grouped options and three dispersed options (3.1.1), or as four self-settled options and two planned options (3.1.2). This section compares the options in order to aid understanding of how to combine them into a settlement strategy most appropriate to the needs of all stakeholders.

combining options

It is likely that more than one option will be appropriate where there is a need for transitional settlement. It is important, wherever possible, for external aid organisations and local authorities to support a variety of settlement options for displaced population groups to choose from. In fact, it is likely that groups within a displaced population will choose more than one of the six options, irrespective of the support offered by the international aid community. In choosing between options, displaced families and groups can make best use of their own coping strategies for livelihoods, community development, and security. The more the displaced families can do for themselves, the less they are dependent on external support – and the more support can be made available to other families and for other humanitarian activities.

In most instances, populations who have been displaced will have already selected one or more of the TS options by the time that organised support becomes available. For example, a displaced population may be so much larger than the host population that they are forced into rural self-settlement while they await a response from the government and the aid community.

In general, displaced groups will move between options throughout the duration of their displacement. For example, displaced families with links to communities in the host area may choose to live with host families immediately after their flight, especially if the international aid community has not reacted fast enough to develop appropriate support. After some time, some families may decide to move on to urban areas, or to camps.

The obligation of external aid organisations and local authorities is to support the combination of TS programme options that minimises risks and maximises opportunities for both the displaced and local populations.

relocation Experience has shown that the relocation and reorganisation of transitional settlements is invariably fraught with social difficulties. It is also expensive, and it often requires a lot of work to be done with affected communities in order to avoid causing further conflict. From the very start of the settlement operation, it is better (if possible) to implement TS options which will make relocation unnecessary until the time when the displaced population has achieved durable solutions.

After displacement, individuals and communities have a great need for physical and spatial security. If displaced people have to be relocated, it is usually best to support them to move as early as possible in the operation, because significant resistance is often encountered after only short periods of inhabitation. This can occur even if the beneficiaries have made relatively small capital investments in land and shelter resources.

3.1.1 dispersed or grouped settlement

figure 3(a): six transitional settlement options

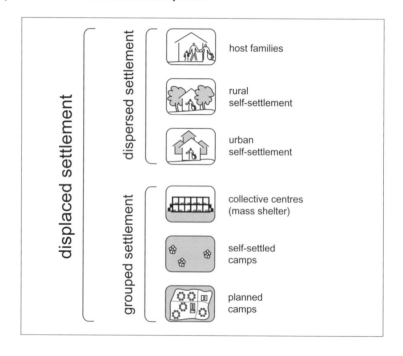

The six transitional settlement options can be viewed as three dispersed options and three grouped options. The three dispersed settlement options are: accommodation with host families (3.2); rural self-settlement (3.3); and urban self-settlement (3.4). The three grouped programme options are collective centres (3.5); self-settled camps (3.6); and planned camps (3.7).

Displaced populations frequently choose dispersed settlement, often prior to (or regardless of) the response of the aid community. This fact indicates the importance to the displaced of maintaining their independence and their ability to sustain themselves. Support by the aid community for dispersed settlement can be practical, responsive, effective, and efficient, and (compared with grouped settlement) it can offer greater developmental benefits to the local population. Dispersed settlements may also pose a lower security risk than grouped settlements, because they do not offer an obvious target for attack.

Displaced populations often spontaneously choose grouped settlement for security reasons, to support communal coping strategies, and to increase their visibility to host governments and to the aid community. Grouped settlement options require the aid community to provide centralised resources. Grouped settlements offer greater control by community leaders of both displaced and local populations. Moreover, they offer the host government and the aid community greater control over the impacts of the displaced population on security, natural resources, and the economy. There exists, however, the risk that any one of these groups may abuse the control offered by grouped settlement.

It is sometimes more difficult for displaced populations from grouped settlements to achieve durable solutions than it is for those from dispersed settlements. In dispersed settlements, families may rely more on each other than on community leaders and external assistance, and so the families can respond flexibly to opportunities. In grouped settlements, the population is often able to act only collectively, rather than in family units, and therefore people have to rely heavily on community leaders and external assistance. Grouped settlements can, however, become part of a resettlement programme, offering permanent accommodation as part of durable solutions for the displaced population. In such cases, care must be taken as soon as permanence is being considered to understand the role that settlement will play in the livelihoods of the population and their hosts: there is little point in settling a displaced population in an area where there are no opportunities for them to sustain themselves, or where they will be competing with a local population for insufficient natural resources or work.

Supporting dispersed settlement over grouped settlement is often preferable, for several reasons:

- It can be more responsive to the changing needs and circumstances of displaced groups, if it allows the displaced population more choice and better relations with the local community.

- It can be more appropriate to the needs of displaced groups, offering better use of existing coping strategies and local contacts.

- It can be more effective in offering developmental opportunities to the local population, for example by allowing the aid community to support common infrastructure and services.

- It can be more cost-effective for the aid community, requiring smaller initial investments than large-scale responses, such as planned camps.

In terms of politics and security, dispersed settlement can reduce the potential for tension and conflict between displaced and host populations, because dispersed displaced populations often fit in better with local natural-resource management (NRM) strategies, for example in the collection of fuel wood. Another environmental benefit of dispersed settlement is that it makes less intensive demands on resources, so that it remains within the local carrying capacity. Grouped transitional settlement may concentrate resource use so much that it is unsustainable, resulting in impacts such as deforestation and soil erosion. However, if dispersed settlement is unsupported, it may have similar negative effects, such as over-burdening local infrastructure, services, and environmental resources.

If dispersed settlement is the preferred option of the displaced population, it should be the preferred option for support by the aid community, in most circumstances. Consideration should be given, however, to the advantages and disadvantages of each alternative presented in the following sections. The support of grouped settlements should only be considered in situations where one or more of the following criteria are encountered. (Many of these criteria have been used inappropriately as excuses, however, and the relative importance of each criteria must be weighed against the other transitional settlement considerations presented in these guidelines.)

- The only sites available for transitional settlement are in environments where there is no local community or settlement within which to integrate displaced people.

- Political, social, and financial costs of emergency and long-term support for dispersed infrastructure are deemed too high.

- The need is so urgent that there is insufficient time to provide infrastructure for dispersed settlement.

- The local population is unwilling to accept (or is hostile towards) the integration of a displaced population.

- The host government is unwilling to allow dispersed transitional settlement for political or security reasons: for example, if the displaced population is large, and in particular if it is larger than the local population.

- The dispersed settlement would result in competition for insufficient local resources, such as water or fuel wood.

- The displaced persons require significantly greater service infrastructure and support than the local people who have always lived in that area: for example, emergency feeding centres and cholera hospitals as well as food distribution.

- The local environment is fragile, and the impacts caused by the migrant population can be better contained in a grouped settlement, compared with dispersed settlement. The use of natural resources and communal facilities should be managed sustainably, with the development of the local population in mind.

Aid organisations risk undermining community structures by taking over many of their roles: for instance, by making decisions that should be made by community committees. Community development activities (8.5), often run by agencies' social services departments, seek to minimise the negative impacts of emergency interventions. Although such activities are usually initiated in support of grouped TS options, such as camps, displaced communities face their own challenges if they have opted for dispersed transitional settlement, such as accommodation with host families. It is important to devote attention to initiating community development activities appropriate to their needs.

problems of dispersed settlement

Given the usual field constraints of limited personnel and access, it can be more difficult for the aid community to understand and support the needs of dispersed displaced populations than it is to address the needs of grouped populations. Protection and security concerns, particularly relating to vulnerable groups, may prove more difficult to identify than they are in grouped settlement options.

- Displaced populations usually self-settle close to a border area or the front line of a conflict, which may encourage insurgency by armed factions. This not only increases the vulnerability of the displaced population, but it could also place the host population at risk.

- Security might be compromised if displaced and host populations are of different ethnic or political groups with a history of hostility towards one another.

- Dispersed settlements pose problems for aid agencies when trying to estimate population numbers and register beneficiaries. In turn, this makes the assessment of needs difficult and may result in inappropriately designed assistance programmes.

- Limited physical access to a dispersed population can present logistical difficulties, which can affect the speed and the efficiency of the assistance.

- Displaced persons, especially those who are vulnerable, must be assured maximum access to essential services. Their dispersal over a large area will stretch the resources of the aid community and local authorities, given the time and effort needed to deploy sufficient resources.

- In some circumstances, security and stability can more easily be improved by the local authorities and the aid community when displaced populations are concentrated into groups and not dispersed.

- In some circumstances, the local environment is so fragile that it is better to contain, rather than disperse, the impacts caused by the displaced population.

[...] whilst dispersed settlement might be the preferred option (for displaced individuals, which should make it the preferred option for consideration by the aid community), it is not without risk. The challenge facing the aid community is then how to ensure that the needs of the displaced and local populations are best understood and met when such settlements are supported.
Mellander (1988)

problems with grouped settlement

Grouped settlements are associated with a number of risks, including the following:

- risks to security, because they constitute a clear target, especially if they are located close to a border area or the front line of a conflict, which may encourage insurgency by armed factions, thus increasing not only the vulnerability of the displaced population, but also that of the host population;
- concentration of demand for natural resources, and hence the risk of natural resources being harvested beyond the sustainable limits of the area;
- the segregation of displaced and local populations, which, combined with the disparity in support offered to each, may create tensions or conflict;
- de-skilling and increased dependency among the displaced population over the longer term, if there are fewer opportunities for the displaced population to work, especially with the local population;
- a high initial capital investment, without any certainty about the duration of the displacement.

3.1.2 self-settlement or planned settlement

The six transitional settlement options can be viewed as four self-settled options and two planned options. The four self-settlement options are accommodation with host families (3.2), rural self-settlement (3.3), urban self-settlement (3.4), and self-settled camps (3.6). The two planned settlement options are collective centres (3.5), and planned camps (3.7).

figure 3(b):   self-settlement or planned settlement

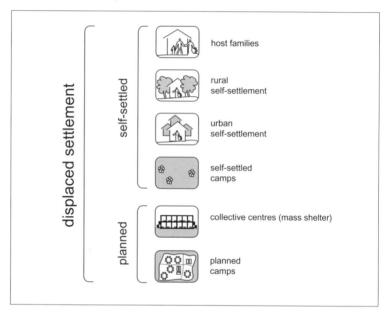

Whether displaced groups choose self-settlement or planned settlement is determined in part by the point in time when each option becomes available to them. This section does not, therefore, seek to compare them as alternatives, because the alternatives may not be available either to the displaced population or to the planner. Planned camps, for example, are usually not available to displaced populations until some time after their displacement, because camps take time to construct. In many circumstances, particularly in the early phases of displacement, self-settlement may appear to be the most appropriate option to the displaced population. The lack of options available to that population, and the poor conditions of their self-settlement, may mean, however, that self-settlement is appropriate only for a certain period.

When seeking to self-settle, displaced populations consider many factors, including the following:

- access to sufficient land for settlement and agriculture;
- access to water, fuel wood, and construction materials;
- protection and security, either from external forces or from groups within the displaced populations, especially if displaced populations self-settle near a border or conflict area;
- access to food aid until agricultural self-sufficiency might be expected (typically six months to two years), and especially during the emergency phase;
- access to services, such as health centres and schools.

The concerns and priorities of various groups within a displaced population should be assessed and monitored, as part of the strategic planning process (chapter 2). It is important to remember that the factors that led displaced families to select a particular TS option are likely to change during the course of their displacement. It is therefore vital that the aid community maintains an understanding of these changing factors, because they will determine whether displaced families are likely to move between options.

External aid organisations and local authorities should identify existing self-settled populations as soon as possible. They must then determine whether a particular form of transitional settlement should be supported, or whether the displaced population should be moved: for example, if they are at risk from incursion, or if their presence in that location is a risk to local security.

Planned settlement is often the only form of transitional settlement supported by the aid community. There are two main scenarios, however, in which self-settlement by the displaced populations should be supported in preference to planned settlement (when security, local relations, and resources permit):

- The decision was made by the displaced people themselves, who usually have a better understanding of their needs and circumstances than those who wish to support them – although sufficient assessment must be undertaken immediately to form an understanding of these needs and circumstances relative to those of other stakeholders, such as the local population.

- The displaced populations have made commitments when selecting their options: for example, by investing time and effort in building houses or cultivating land, or in developing constructive relations with the local host population.

problems with self-settlement

Self-settlement typically poses numerous problems.

- Displaced populations usually self-settle close to a border area or the front line of a conflict, leading to the same sorts of risk that were identified for grouped settlement in 3.1.1 above.
- Sometimes there is no significant host population in the area, and there is therefore no infrastructure to use or for aid organisations to improve.
- Often the displaced population is much larger than the local population, meaning that the required infrastructural improvements would become redundant in the longer term.
- Displaced populations need service infrastructure immediately after their arrival, and it may be difficult to undertake appropriate improvements to existing infrastructure in time to meet those needs. In some cases, an emergency provision concentrated in a few centres may be more feasible.
- Displaced populations who have recently arrived in an area have certain needs for service infrastructure which differ from the needs of the local people who have always lived there, such as emergency feeding centres and cholera hospitals; so additional provision has to be made.
- In order to maintain relations between the displaced population and their hosts, self-settlement needs to happen in such a way that the displaced population is distributed in approximately the same density pattern as the local population: for example, a local village should not have a large displaced population settling around it while a large town hosts only a small population, otherwise improvements to services and infrastructure will be inequitable.
- The closer relationship usually implied and required between the displaced and local populations in self-settlement may be a cause of stress, or may be simply unfeasible, if the populations belong to different ethnic or political groupings, or if there is a history of hostility between them.

Chambers summarises the possible negative effects of unsupported self-settlement on the host and displaced populations:

> An examination of evidence suggests seven points on self-settlement. They are: instant impoverishment; mixed reception; cheap labour, dear food; poor access to land; political and legal vulnerability; the first to suffer, the last to gain; costs to the poorer hosts.
> Chambers (1979)

problems with planned settlement

Planned settlement is often the only form of transitional settlement supported by the aid community, in spite of the inherent problems associated with it:

- Planned camps and collective centres rarely offer the same level of support for family coping mechanisms and flexibility for livelihoods activities as self-settled options do.

- Because planned facilities are expensive and time-consuming to prepare, and expansion cannot usually keep pace with large influxes, there are rarely sufficient facilities available for a displaced population.

- Planned settlement often involves the provision of some services parallel to those that exist for the local population, which creates unsustainable duplication.

3.2 dispersed in host families

This settlement option involves sheltering the displaced population within the households of local families, or on land or in properties owned by them.

Displaced people may have the opportunity to live with relations, friends, or strangers who act as host families for a period of time. They may be allocated a place to stay in the house where the host lives, or in a different house or outhouse owned by the host, or on the host's land. The displaced person may be allowed to stay without payment or on a rent-paying basis, paying either in cash or in kind, for example by offering labour.

Compared with other options, this presents more opportunities for positive interaction with the local population. It facilitates a wider social support network, benefiting the displaced population.

Another advantage is the fact that existing coping strategies, especially for vulnerable individuals, can be supported by keeping families together and within a stable household environment. The length of the period of hosting is likely to be crucial, however, both for the displaced and the host families. A prolonged period of hosting is likely to cause considerable stresses, socially and financially.

The displaced family may decide to move to a different TS option as external conditions change, or because the period for which hosts are prepared to offer hosting has changed.

vulnerabilities

Dispersal stretches the capacity of aid organisations and local authorities to assess and support displaced populations: constraints on access and limits on logistics capacity mean that reaching one family takes longer in a dispersed settlement than it would in a more concentrated settlement. Conversely, a displaced population which is dispersed usually has much better contact with the local population. This can mean that the displaced population has more direct access to resources, work opportunities, support mechanisms, and infrastructure, such as local clinics. This access can greatly reduce their vulnerability, as long as the relations with the local population are sustainable. It is important to assess the impacts of the displaced population on the local population, in order to decide how external support might best be targeted to mitigate any negative impacts, while increasing the local capacities sustainably.

Transitional settlement with host families can increase the vulnerability of either or both parties in several respects:

- the risk of external attack on the host families, resulting from their close proximity to the hosted families;

- opportunities for physical or sexual abuse, or for financial exploitation, by either the host or the hosted;

- resentment of the hosted families by their hosts, leading to rejection or violence, if the assistance offered to them is perceived to be unfairly generous;

- environmental vulnerability, resulting from the needs of the displaced population for natural resources, such as water and cooking fuel, in addition to the requirements of their hosts, which may disrupt established patterns of natural-resource management (2.5.4) and even lead to violence or the termination of hosting;

- risks to security posed by local groups, as well as displaced and insurgent groups;
- more difficult access to local and aid-supported communal services, such as health care, especially for vulnerable groups;
- more difficult access to distributed aid, such as food, especially for vulnerable groups.

Any one of these vulnerabilities may make living with a host family impossible for a displaced family, for an entire displaced community, or for their host families. Vulnerability may be reduced if the host families and hosted families know each other: if there are relationships to build on, then displaced families are likely to be able to rely on support from the host population as well as from the displaced population.

All vulnerabilities may be reduced to some extent through negotiation based on regular face-to-face contact between the populations. This in itself may result, however, in the dependence of displaced individuals upon hosting individuals, which may constitute an increase to certain vulnerabilities.

livelihoods Assessing the livelihoods of host and hosted families is important, in order to identify opportunities for the hosted family to become more or less self-sufficient. It is important to ensure that support offered to the displaced population does not raise their standard of living beyond that of the local population, who may be living in circumstances far below international standards for displaced populations. Standards should be developed that are appropriate to local circumstances, based firmly upon international standards. Support should be offered to both local and displaced populations in order to prevent tensions and support positive relations.

The host families may offer opportunities for the hosted families to find work. They may want the hosted family members to be employed in order to bring more money into the household, so that rent can be charged. Opportunities for both host and hosted families to do domestic work, such as small-scale manufacturing, may be constrained, however, by lack of space in host-family houses. Other constraints may include competition for local resources, such as land for cultivation.

The presence of displaced workers may increase competition for casual labour opportunities. The local population may see the displaced population as a threat, because the latter may be able to undercut labour markets, possibly because of the support that they receive from the aid community.

If assistance is provided to both host and displaced families within the same assistance programme, aid agencies should consider promoting income generation for both beneficiary groups as a method of defusing potential tensions over resources or support of the displaced. Livelihoods can be supported, for example, by involving both populations in all construction activities.

 ## 3.2.1 contingency phase

assessment of capacity

Early consultation with all stakeholders will help agencies to estimate the potential capacity for hosting displaced families. They should take into account ethnic and religious compatibility, livelihoods, and overall numbers of families, rather than attitudes towards hosting, which are likely to vary considerably before an influx of displaced people takes place.

Consultation will maximise co-ordination and co-operation, and minimise potential disputes between local and displaced populations. Consultation should include meetings with the local administrations and relevant community representatives, developing options for parallel systems of support for the host and the hosted, with long-term benefits for the host-family household, but without raising expectations in any group.

assessment of feasibility

An assessment should be made of previous displacements and migrations from and into the area of displacement, in order to increase understanding of the common history of the local and displaced communities. Take account of the presence of economic migrants and cross-border mixed marriages. A high presence of migrants implies a greater chance that displaced populations will integrate with local communities. It is also important to assess the composition of the local population, and to consult the displaced group to ensure compatibility of ethnicity and religion.

The following factors, particularly important for settlement with host families, should be assessed by use of the tools presented in Chapter 4:

- border entry points or routes to the locality of displacement: these will affect the hosting pattern, because displaced families often look for hosts close to the border that they have just crossed, potentially putting themselves and the host families in danger of being involved in hostilities;

- the condition of transport infrastructure for access, such as roads, bridges, and paths, including all-year, all-weather access options;

- possible improvements to the existing water, sanitation, health, transport, and education infrastructure;

- the density and dispersal of potential host populations, which will determine the pattern of support in terms of distribution and infrastructure support.

awareness and information

Explore with the national and local governments the need for and possible impacts of an information campaign aimed at the local populations who are most likely to be affected by displaced populations. Consider whether a separate information campaign is required for the displaced population. Concentrate on providing information and increasing awareness, rather than raising expectations over future benefits that cannot be guaranteed.

Be aware that information about a possible influx of displaced people may have negative impacts on the local population. These impacts may be of different types, such as panic or suspicion of 'foreigners', and they may be expressed in a variety of ways, such as further displacement or violence.

 ## 3.2.2 emergency phase

influx management

Monitor variations in the influx rates of the displaced. Establish methods of assessment appropriate to their dispersed settlement. If the displaced people are so difficult to reach that it is very hard to help them, consider increasing operational capacity or discussing with beneficiaries options for relocation.

As described in chapter 2, a programme plan should be formulated, in consultation with other stakeholders and within a continually up-dated framework of appropriate assessment, monitoring, and evaluation. The contents and assumptions of the contingency plan should be reviewed and integrated, as appropriate, because the people who drafted it cannot have anticipated every aspect of the opportunities that will be available to specific displaced populations and their host families.

The needs of and opportunities for displaced populations and their hosts should be considered separately, with further disaggregation in order to understand the needs of specific groups, differentiated by sex and age. Note, however, that the resulting programme plan should integrate support to the displaced and their hosts. It is likely that part of the programme plan will be reactive, mapping hosting patterns and exploring support options, while part of the plan may be proactive, identifying and making available additional hosting capacities.

Once the emergency has started, the following responses are important.

- Provide information to all the stakeholders, and keep up-dating it.
- Wherever possible, help to ensure good relations between hosts and hosted households by accommodating people of similar ethnic or religious background within the same household.
- Provide assistance to vulnerable individuals if they cannot receive appropriate assistance from their families or from their host families: for example, if pre-emergency social support has been disrupted as a result of displacement and hosting.
- Provide assistance to vulnerable individuals, families, or groups who have no access to any income-generation opportunities; take care to avoid ethnic or personal conflicts of interest , especially if local government is involved: for example, government officials of a particular ethnicity may be accused of favouritism if they are charged with assisting a displaced population that includes a group of the same ethnicity.
- Agree and meet standards for support, such as the Sphere standards, including the provision of a minimum floor area per person.
- Register displaced people, employing the health and security screening processes that are essential to identifying vulnerable civilians, combatants, and other groups within the displaced

population (important also as a first step for those seeking asylum under international refugee law).

- Reduce mortality and morbidity by setting up an emergency health-care infrastructure for screening and treatment: for example, by building therapeutic and supplementary feeding centres.

implementation options

There are three main accommodation-support options for host-family programmes:

- sub-dividing, up-grading, or expanding existing accommodation within the host-family household, provided that there is sufficient living space for hosts and hosted, and provided also that the sub-division will be of long-term relevance for the host family;
- up-grading an existing outbuilding or barn;
- building a new structure on the land of the host family.

The extent and type of assistance offered to host families will depend on the living standards of the host population. The lower the local living standards, the greater the needs of both the displaced and the host population.

family agreements for works

Negotiate agreement on the rights and responsibilities of the host and hosted households regarding the accommodation to be provided, in both the short term and the long term. This understanding may require a consideration of the lifestyles of the local and displaced populations, such as the need to partition the house into separate male and female sections. It might also need to include agreement on the final ownership of any additional accommodation provided with external support.

Where possible, formal agreements should be reached, ideally involving the hosts, the displaced population, the local authority, and the implementing agency. However, formal agreements can be difficult to negotiate and implement. In some cases it may be preferable to limit the signatories to the host and hosted parties, as far as possible obtaining the approval of the implementing agency and the local authority. In this case, the onus for addressing future issues should be placed on the individual households themselves, rather than including agencies which may well have departed, or local authorities who may not have the resources or inclination to act. Local authorities must be supported in drafting or implementing policy, and integrating international laws and standards, because they may be unwilling to make a formal acknowledgement of major population movements.

If a four-way agreement is to be adopted, ensure that all parties understand it. The agreement should be translated into the relevant languages and signed by all parties.

Ensure that the host family is in legal ownership of the property to be up-graded. In the case of rented properties, a different agreement should be drafted, and it should include the owner. Where customary rights to use land are commonly recognised, such rights should be included in any formal agreements between host and hosted families.

compensation and payment options

Options for the compensation of host families include the following:

- up-grading or expansion of an existing house
- access to improved or up-graded infrastructure, such as water supply, sanitation, and health-care facilities
- opportunities for cash-for-work during the construction or rehabilitation of infrastructure
- opportunities for skills training through the construction or rehabilitation of infrastructure.

Another method of compensating host families is payment in cash or in kind, such as food items or non-food items (chapter 7), depending upon an assessment of livelihoods (UNHCR 2002e). In addition to receiving rent, host families might be offered help to pay local taxes or the costs of utilities, such as water, electricity, or gas. Many donors, however, do not support direct cash payments, and this option is often inappropriate or difficult to achieve. For materials distribution, nominal beneficiary cards may be used, similar to the ones used for the distribution of food items, so that the provider can monitor the distribution and use of the materials. Beneficiary cards are an established tool in distribution systems; they usually record details of the beneficiary family and details of the items that have been distributed to them.

livelihoods Displaced families may have brought livestock with them, which will require water and grazing. Or they may wish to farm land, to generate income or diversify their diets. Finding water and grazing for livestock is an urgent imperative, because livestock often constitutes the main wealth of a displaced population, and its final opportunity for recovery. Agricultural land may be an urgent concern, depending on the local cycle of planting and rains. Discussions with the local authorities and communities will determine the availability of suitable land, the options for the transitional use of common land, and local traditions of natural-resource management. It may be necessary to provide emergency supplies of fodder, or water troughs, or seeds.

labour-management options

All three main labour-management alternatives presented in chapter 5 should be considered, including combinations of them. It should be remembered that women, and especially single females or female-headed households, may be vulnerable to exploitation when they seek help in constructing shelters.

Consideration should be given to the constraints and opportunities present in each situation, including the following factors:

- the possibility of training additional skilled labour
- improving access to trained and existing labour resources
- the availability of tools and plant
- seasonal work patterns
- the distance from other host families or supporting organisations.

upgrading communal infrastructure

The presence of the displaced population will have an impact on the wider local community, and not merely on the host families. Care must be taken to prevent tensions and to ensure that local services can be maintained. In addition to supporting family accommodation, some up-grading of infrastructure might be considered, such as improvements to the following:

- transport, including roads and bridges
- health care, including clinics, hospitals, and dispensaries
- water and sanitation, including water supply, surface-water drainage, and sanitation in communal areas or for communal services

- schools, including crèches, and primary, secondary, and tertiary institutions, where available
- the generation and transmission of power
- food production and food security, such as grain stores
- police stations, prisons, and courts.

Consider giving support to public meetings involving both the local population and displaced populations. Offer activities to both groups, such as training courses or social events. This will help the local population and the displaced communities to become familiar with each other, opening channels of communication which will help to prevent misunderstandings and can be developed into means of resolving disputes.

3.2.3 care and maintenance phase

The care and maintenance phase of the hosting option is reached when the rate of arrival of the displaced people diminishes, and consolidation and up-grading activities can begin. The needs of the displaced and local populations change after the emergency phase, as basic levels of health are restored and community development begins.

timeframe Hosting may result in social complications, so accommodation with host families should be limited to a maximum length of time, agreed in a programme plan. This time limit should be reviewed regularly during the care and maintenance phase, and contingencies should be put in place to offer alternative TS options to the hosted displaced families.

livelihoods It is important to appraise the abilities of displaced households to support themselves through work. As time passes, it is also necessary to monitor the changing circumstances which may have both positive and negative impacts on their livelihood opportunities. Consider offering skills training and related income-generating activities, in order to provide the displaced population with at least a basic livelihood – and do it as soon as possible, in order to reduce their dependency. With social-services professionals, consider the physical support that is required by displaced adults if they are to make the most of income-generating opportunities. Whenever possible, if offering training courses, invite the participation of the local population. This will promote integration of the two groups and at the same time will constitute a form of compensation for the local community. Income-generating activities in general should take into account the relations between host and hosted labour.

Consult education professionals to determine how best to support the access of the displaced children to the local school system, and to provide extra support or provision to the built infrastructure, as appropriate. Also consider with education professionals the physical support required for unofficial schooling among the displaced population, to enable teaching in their own language.

up-grading communal infrastructure

The presence of the displaced population will have an impact on the wider local community, so action is required to ensure that local services can be maintained and tensions are prevented. In addition to supporting dispersed families, consider up-grading infrastructure such as transport, health care, water and sanitation, and power. Similarly, support might be offered to communal services, such as schools and clinics.

 ### 3.2.4 exit strategies

for the local population

In general, host populations should have benefited from the hosting programme, either through improvements in housing or infrastructure, or from new job opportunities or training courses.

If any inputs are to be handed over to the host families, consider asking each head of household to sign a document recording their acceptance. Handover is an opportunity to assess the impacts of the programme (although a structured evaluation for every family is not always necessary). The organisation responsible for the programme must ensure that each host family understands that the programme has been completed. Ideally, each family should agree that no negative impacts have resulted from it.

for the displaced population

The usual three options open to displaced families are return, resettlement in the host country, and resettlement in a third country. The host-family TS programme option offers no specific advantage, although there have been cases where IDPs have converted their initial hosting arrangements into durable solutions on the same parcel of host land, including the transfer of land-use rights.

3 options

Attention should be given to reviewing any agreements entered into with families and local authorities, ensuring the transfer of outstanding responsibilities as appropriate. Part of this review should include appropriate programme evaluation.

3.3 dispersed in rural self-settlement

Rural self-settlement takes place when displaced families settle on rural land that is owned collectively, rather than privately.

Displaced people may cross a border, stop at the first village that they reach, and negotiate the use of land on which to settle temporarily, often with their animals. This option offers opportunities for degrees of self-sufficiency, if agriculture or animal husbandry are possible. It promotes integration with the local population and facilitates a wider social-support network, with benefits for the displaced population. However, if the displaced population grows, or if there is unforeseen competition for resources, the local authorities may refuse to allow transitional settlement, and people may find themselves re-displaced.

If agricultural land is available, this form of settlement, although it often complicates aid agencies' access to beneficiaries, allows a quicker integration with the local community and provides self-sufficiency options. Rural self-settlement often involves a high degree of population movements, as some of the family may remain self-settled in a rural environment, while other family members move away to look for work. This fluidity may, however, be seen as a direction expression of choice by the displaced population.

vulnerabilities

Dispersal stretches the capacity of aid organisations and local authorities to assess and support displaced populations: constraints on access and limits on logistics capacity mean that reaching one family takes longer in a dispersed settlement than it would in a more concentrated settlement. Conversely, a displaced population which is dispersed usually has much better contact with the local population. This can mean that the displaced population has more direct access to resources, work opportunities, support mechanisms, and infrastructure, such as local clinics. This access may greatly reduce their vulnerability, as long as the relations with the local population are sustainable. It is important to assess the impacts of the displaced population on the local population, in order to decide how external support might best be targeted to mitigate any negative impacts, while increasing the local capacities sustainably.

In the case of rural self-settlement, the main source of vulnerability is proximity to the border or an area of conflict. If the rural self-settlement is near an insecure border or front line, it is likely that the protection and security of the displaced and local populations will be compromised. In such circumstances, rural self-settlement close to a border should not be supported; instead, support should be offered for viable alternative TS options, located away from the conflict.

The following vulnerabilities are common in dispersed rural self-settlement:

- sexual or financial exploitation by a host landowner
- risks to security resulting from local as well as displaced and insurgent groups
- more difficult access to local and aid-supported communal services, such as health care, especially for vulnerable groups
- more difficult access to distributed aid, such as food, especially for vulnerable groups.

livelihoods Assessing the livelihoods of displaced and local populations is important, in order to identify opportunities for the displaced to become more self-sufficient. It is important to ensure that support offered to the displaced population does not raise their standard of living beyond that of the local population, who may be living in circumstances far below international standards for displaced populations. Standards should be developed that are appropriate to local circumstances, based firmly upon international standards. Support should be offered to both local and displaced populations in order to prevent tensions and support positive relations. Livelihoods may be supported, for example, by involving both communities in all construction activities.

While negotiating with the local population to obtain land for transitional settlement, it may be possible also to negotiate access to land for grazing, allowing normal livelihood strategies to continue. However, these strategies may not be sustainable, except in the very short term. Competition for resources between the local population and the displaced population is an important factor to consider in programme planning.

By settling in close proximity to the local population, displaced people have the chance to offer services and sell goods in local markets. The proximity of the populations may create interdependence, a factor which might put social and cultural pressures on the displaced population to behave in accordance with the customs and traditions of the local populations. One positive result might be improved management of natural resources.

In some cases, under very specific security conditions, the displaced population may be able to continue cultivation on their own land, if they are near enough and able to withdraw to the transitional settlement at night.

3.3.1 contingency phase

assessment of capacity

It is useful to assess potential sites for rural self-settlement and verify the capacity of the local community and region to absorb the influx. Water supplies and water sources may be scarce and may need improvement, in order to meet the needs of the local community as well as those of the displaced. If there are several displaced families from a single area of origin, it is likely that they will try to self-settle in close proximity to each other, in an attempt to maintain their community and its coping mechanisms.

A quick indication of the practicality of large-scale rural self-settlement can be obtained by assessing the size of the local population and comparing it with the size of the displacement that is likely to take place. If the displaced outnumber the local people, rural self-settlement is unlikely to be acceptable to the local population and authorities. In any event, it may be difficult to support such an imbalance in practical terms, because local settlement density is usually based on the carrying capacity of the local environment.

assessment of feasibility

An assessment should be made of previous displacements and migrations from and into the area of displacement, in order to increase understanding of the common history of the local and displaced communities. Take account of the presence of economic migrants and cross-border mixed marriages. A high presence of migrants implies a greater chance that displaced populations will integrate with local communities. It is also important to assess the composition of the local population, and to consult the displaced group to ensure compatibility of ethnicity and religion.

 ### 3.3.2 emergency phase

influx management

Monitor variations in the influx rates of the displaced, and establish methods of assessment appropriate to their dispersed settlement. If the displaced people are so difficult to reach that it is very hard to help them, consider increasing operational capacity or supporting the beneficiaries to move to a different location.

programme planning

As described in chapter 2, a programme plan should be formulated, in consultation with other stakeholders and within a continually up-dated framework of appropriate assessment, monitoring, and evaluation. The contents and assumptions of the contingency plan should be reviewed and integrated, as appropriate, because the people who drafted it cannot have anticipated every aspect of the opportunities that will be available to specific displaced populations.

Once the emergency has started, the following responses are important.

- Provide information to all the stakeholders, and keep up-dating it.

- Provide assistance to vulnerable individuals, families, or groups who have no access to any income-generation opportunities; take care to avoid conflicts of interest (ethnic or personal), especially if local government is involved.

- Agree and meet standards for support, such as the Sphere standards, including the provision of a minimum floor area per person.

- Register displaced people, employing the health and security screening processes that are essential to identifying vulnerable civilians, combatants, and other groups within the displaced population (important also as a first step for those seeking asylum under international refugee law).

- Reduce mortality and morbidity by setting up an emergency infrastructure for screening and treatment: for example, by building therapeutic and supplementary feeding centres.

site location Although rural self-settlement implies that support will be essentially reactive, before offering support it is necessary to determine whether the TS programme option is appropriate and safe for all stakeholders. Assess whether the sites selected by the displaced populations are appropriate in terms of security from attack and risk from natural hazards, such as flooding or the presence of standing water that breeds mosquitoes (6.3.5). If the sites are not appropriate, consider recommending transfer to a safer or vector-free area.

identifying beneficiaries

The identification of beneficiaries is difficult in a rural self-settlement, because families may be located far away from one another, and the local community may not have any registration mechanism in place.

Monitoring influx and registration are important mechanisms to gain an early impression of the size of the influx, because numbers may be more difficult to verify later. The identification of vulnerable beneficiaries should be integrated into any registration process, and improved by direct assessments on the site where the displaced have settled.

communication with community representatives

One mechanism for maintaining contact with a dispersed population is to engage with community representatives. Committees for activities such as food distribution offer other opportunities. Care must be taken to ensure that the representatives do not misuse their power to manipulate the displaced population or aid community: for example, if the representatives are also the leaders of displaced armed factions, they may be able to extort and divert supplies of food for their own benefit.

distribution centres

Because the beneficiary families are scattered, providing adequate assistance may be unfeasible or time-consuming, so attention should be given to finding options to overcome this problem.

In some circumstances, it is advisable to create distribution centres where beneficiaries can receive rations, and where vulnerable beneficiaries can be given special assistance to collect relief items.

support for local health-care systems

Health-care options should be assessed by sectoral professionals, but it is generally better to support the local health-care structure or system, rather than creating a parallel infrastructure for the displaced population. If a permanent structure is not required and the local population already has access to some form of health care, a transitional or mobile system may be used to raise levels of provision. Creating permanent structures may be a waste of resources, if the local authorities or communities cannot maintain such structures in the future.

livelihoods Displaced families may have brought with them livestock, which will require water and grazing. Or they may wish to farm land, to generate income, or diversify their diets. Finding water and grazing for livestock is an urgent imperative, because livestock often constitutes the main wealth of a displaced population, and its final opportunity for recovery. Agricultural land may be an urgent concern, depending on the local cycle of planting and rains. Discussions with the local authorities and communities will determine the availability of suitable land, the options for the transitional use of common land, and local traditions of natural-resource management. It may be necessary to provide emergency supplies of fodder, or water troughs, or seeds.

upgrading communal infrastructure

The presence of the displaced population will have an impact on the wider local community. Care must be taken to prevent tensions and to ensure that local services can be maintained. Some up-grading of infrastructure might be considered, such as improvements to the following:

- transport, including roads and bridges
- health care, including clinics, hospitals, and dispensaries
- water and sanitation, including water supply, surface-water drainage, and sanitation in communal areas or for communal services
- schools, including crèches, and primary, secondary, and tertiary institutions, where available
- the generation and transmission of power
- food production and food security, such as grain stores
- police stations, prisons, and courts.

Consider giving support to public meetings involving both the local and displaced populations. Offer activities to both groups, such as training courses or social events. This will help the local and the displaced communities to become familiar with each other, opening channels of communication which will help to prevent misunderstandings and can be developed into means of resolving disputes.

 ### 3.3.3 care and maintenance phase

The care and maintenance phase of the rural self-settlement option is reached when the rate of arrival of the displaced people diminishes, and consolidation and up-grading activities can begin. The needs of the displaced and local populations change after the emergency phase, as basic levels of health are restored and community development begins.

livelihoods It is important to appraise the abilities of displaced households to support themselves through work. As time passes, it is also necessary to monitor the changing circumstances which may have both positive and negative impacts on their livelihood opportunities. Supporting the livelihoods of a rural dispersed population might include the distribution of seeds and tools, or fodder through a dry season, but support should not be considered unless security conditions allow.

Consider offering skills training and related income-generating activities, in order to provide the displaced population with at least a basic livelihood – and do it as soon as possible, in order to reduce their dependency. Together with social-services professionals, consider the physical support that is required by displaced adults if they are to make the most of income-generating opportunities. Whenever possible, if offering training courses, invite the participation of the local population. This will promote integration of the two groups and at the same time will constitute a form of compensation for the local people.

Consult education professionals to determine how best to support the access of the displaced children to the local school system, and to augment the built infrastructure, as appropriate. Also consider the physical support required for unofficial schooling among the displaced population, to enable teaching in their own language.

3.3.4 exit strategies

for the local population

The local community should be left with improvements to their communal facilities, such as water sources and improved health and educational infrastructures. If they took part in skills-training programmes, they should be left with increased capacities.

for the displaced population

The usual three options are open to the displaced families: repatriation, local settlement in the host country, and local settlement in a third country. Rural self-settlement offers a specific advantage to displaced families, as a durable solution, if such families are allowed to settle permanently on or near the land that they have been occupying. In this case, developmental assistance programmes designed to sustain and develop livelihoods may follow on from transitional settlement. It is important to define an acceptable standard of living which will constitute an 'end state for settlement', in order to determine when to cease support and hand over to development organisations.

for the aid organisation

If the aid organisation built any collective infrastructure as a response to the emergency, it should be handed over, either to the local authorities or to the local population. Similarly, if agency infrastructure is purchased and not rented, it could be handed over to local and international NGOs dealing with development programmes within the same area.

3.4 dispersed in urban self-settlement

 Displaced populations from an urban background may decide to settle in a town, occupying unclaimed properties or land, or settling informally.

If a displaced family is living in a property or on land that has been claimed rightfully by an owner, that family is considered as living with a host family. Urban self-settlement is the alternative option, when the property has not been claimed, or where the land is owned communally or by the state. Displaced people may be moving to a different area of the city than the one that they previously occupied, or they may occupy unclaimed properties in a city to which they have fled for safety or to find work.

Although the displaced population will not generally own the property or land where they live, there may be a need to rehabilitate or weather-proof part of the property. Depending on the form and state of emergency, agencies providing assistance may need to define a strategy with the local government to provide support, regardless of the ownership of the properties or land.

Displaced people often increase the size of existing informal settlement areas in the periphery of cities, living on land that they do not own. Programme planning and assistance in such circumstances should be undertaken in full consultation with formal and informal local authorities, because it is likely that plans already exist for informal, illegal, or 'slum' settlements. It is also likely that the existence of such settlements will be politically sensitive, a fact which might in turn have politicised their inhabitants and neighbours. Care should be taken to ensure that any support offered takes into account or integrates any existing inhabitants and their neighbours, in addition to the displaced population.

In some instances, aid organisations have ignored displaced people who have self-settled in urban areas, concentrating instead on planned provision, on the grounds that they must make effective use of the limited resources available. However, the support of the local government and aid community, such as offering protection through transitional shelter, must be extended equitably across the entire displaced population and their hosts. If urban self-settlement is an option that confronts aid organisations when they arrive, it must be assessed and, if appropriate, supported within a co-ordinated transitional settlement strategy.

vulnerabilities

Dispersal stretches the capacity of aid organisations and local authorities to assess and support displaced populations: constraints on access and logistics capacity mean that reaching one family takes longer in a dispersed settlement than it would do in a more concentrated settlement. Conversely, a displaced population which is dispersed generally has much better contact with the local population. This can mean that the displaced population has more direct access to resources, work opportunities, support mechanisms, and infrastructure, such as local clinics. This access can greatly reduce their vulnerability, as long as the relations with the local population are sustainable. In this case, external support should aim to mitigate any negative impacts of the displaced population on the local population, while increasing the local capacities in a sustainable manner.

The following vulnerabilities are common in dispersed urban self-settlement.

- Urban settlements, and particularly dense urban settlements, can prove very difficult to up-grade to meet minimum standards of humanitarian response.

- Access to local and aid-supported communal services, such as health care, is more difficult, and especially so for vulnerable groups.

- It is more difficult to access distributed aid, such as food, and especially so for vulnerable groups.

In urban conditions, especially, there is almost always an existing community of informal or 'squatter' settlers which offers the easiest self-help model for an urban self-settled population to follow. Informal settlement is usually not wholly legal, so settlers often intentionally avoid contact with local authorities. The displaced will tend to follow the same pattern as the local informal settlers with whom they live, in order to maintain good relations with them and to take advantage of the self-help methods that they have developed. If the displaced do not wish to be recognised by local authorities, it is difficult for aid organisations to assess their needs or offer support. Successful support for dispersed urban self-settlement therefore needs to be based on an understanding of the needs of both the displaced and the local informal settlers.

Care must be taken to ensure that the opportunities enjoyed by parts of a displaced population who choose urban self-settlement does not increase the vulnerability of other groups within the population, such as children and minorities. For example, it is common to find a disproportionate number of children and older people in planned transitional settlement, such as refugee camps, when the less vulnerable in the displaced community disperse in urban self-settlement in order to maximise their opportunities for paid work. This can fracture communities, or result in vulnerable individuals moving into inappropriate urban environments in order to maintain family structures.

livelihoods There are a number of advantages for displaced people who move to urban areas: cities and towns tend to be wealthier, local markets are larger, and opportunities for continuing or developing new livelihood strategies are generally greater for the displaced population, which has no land to farm. However, if people enter an urban area from a rural area, they are unlikely to be able to continue any livelihoods that involve cultivation or animal husbandry. This is likely to increase their vulnerability, so it is essential to consider the consequences of this when providing shelter and settlement support.

Care must be taken that support offered to the displaced population does not raise their standard of living beyond that of the local population, who may be living in circumstances much below international standards for displaced populations. Standards should be developed that are appropriate to local circumstances, based firmly upon international standards. Support should be offered to both local and displaced populations to prevent tensions and support positive relations. Livelihoods can be supported, for example, by involving the displaced and local populations in all construction activities and facilitating access to local markets.

 3.4.1 contingency phase

assessment of capacity

Assess local population size, demographics, patterns of dispersal, and livelihoods; consider how they might be affected by the estimated influx of displaced people. Assessment should continue as long as new groups of displaced people arrive. Previous displacements, cultural practices, religion, ethnicity, politics, and land tenure may be sources of co-operation or division between displaced and local populations, and they will influence the success or failure of the transitional settlement.

While it may be possible in the contingency phase to gain an understanding of how a displaced population of various sizes might be received, great care should be taken not to create unrealistic expectations on the part of any of the stakeholders; for example, avoid making firm predictions concerning the duration of the displacement, or the speed at which certain support will be made available. The influx of a displaced population is likely to be a politically contentious event that may be manipulated, especially if such expectations become widespread.

Assess previous displacements and migrations from and into the area of displacement, in order to understand the common history of the local and displaced communities. Take account of the presence of economic migrants and cross-border mixed marriages. A high presence of migrants implies a greater chance of integration for potentially displaced populations. It is also important to assess the composition of the local population, and verify compatibility between the two groups in terms of ethnicity and religion.

In an urban context, the built environment is particularly important. To assess this, consider the following factors:

- the local built environment, especially if there is an expected influx in an area of former conflict, in which case any unsafe buildings or suspected unexploded ordnance should be visibly marked;
- potential improvements to the infrastructure of informal settlements, such as roads and water and sanitation.

It might be possible to consult an up-dated cadastre (official record of land and property ownership). If a cadastre does not exist, or it was destroyed during a conflict, establish operational rules with the emerging representatives of the local community, so that some form of assistance can be planned if displacement occurs.

 3.4.2 emergency phase

influx management

Monitor variations in the influx rates of the displaced, and establish methods of assessment appropriate to their dispersed settlement. If the displaced people are so difficult to reach that it is very hard to help them, consider increasing operational capacity or supporting the beneficiaries to move to a different location.

programme planning

As described in chapter 2, a programme plan should be formulated, in consultation with other stakeholders and within a framework of continuing assessment, monitoring, and evaluation. The contents and assumptions of the contingency plan should be reviewed and integrated, as appropriate, on the assumption that the contingency plan cannot have anticipated every aspect of the opportunities available to specific displaced populations.

It is likely that part of the programme plan will be reactive, and other parts may be proactive. Once the emergency has begun, the following responses are important.

- Provide information to all the stakeholders, and keep up-dating it.
- Provide assistance to vulnerable individuals, families, or groups who have no access to any income-generation opportunities; take care to avoid conflicts of interest (ethnic or personal), especially if local government is involved.
- Agree and meet standards for support, such as the Sphere standards, including the provision of a minimum floor area per person.
- Register displaced people, employing the health and security screening processes that are essential to identifying vulnerable civilians, combatants, and other groups within the displaced population. (This is important also as a first step for those seeking asylum under international refugee law.)
- Reduce mortality and morbidity by setting up an emergency health-care infrastructure for screening and treatment, for example by building therapeutic and supplementary feeding centres.

repair or weather-proof living spaces

As long as the building occupied by displaced people is not structurally damaged and is not a hazard to its inhabitants or neighbours, consider helping them to weather-proof part or all of the building, for example by repairing roof and walls (taking account of the ownership of the building).

distribution centres

It is important to identify structures for the storage and distribution of food supplies. Vulnerable people may need help to reach distribution centres or to carry their rations away.

livelihoods Even when they are seeking transitional settlement in urban areas, displaced families may have brought with them livestock requiring water and grazing, or they may wish to farm land to generate income or diversify their diet. Finding water and grazing for livestock is an urgent imperative, because they probably constitute the main wealth and final opportunity for recovery of the displaced population. Finding suitable agricultural land may also be an urgent concern, depending on the local cycle of planting and rains.

Discussions with the local authorities and communities will determine whether suitable land exists, and will identify options for the transitional use of common land, and local traditions of natural-resource management. Emergency provision of fodder, water troughs, or seeds may be considered.

support for basic service infrastructure

Assess and, if necessary, improve the water and sanitation infrastructure, and re-establish any electricity-distribution system for primary and public use. In cold climates, consider providing heating in hospitals and schools.

In informal settlements, consider up-grading the most critical living situations, providing sanitation and water and giving displaced people access to the local health facilities.

upgrading communal infrastructure

The presence of the displaced population will have an impact on the local community. Care must be taken to prevent tensions and to ensure that local services can be maintained. In addition to supporting family accommodation, some up-grading of infrastructure might be considered, such as improvements to the following:

- transport, including roads and bridges
- health care, including clinics, hospitals, and dispensaries
- water and sanitation, including water supply, surface-water drainage, and sanitation in communal areas or for communal services
- schools, including crèches, and primary, secondary, and tertiary institutions, where available
- the generation and transmission of power
- food production and food security, such as grain stores
- police stations, prisons, and courts.

labour-management options

All three main labour-management alternatives presented in chapter 5 should be considered, including combinations of them.

It should be remembered that women, and especially single females or female-headed households, may be vulnerable to exploitation when they seek help in constructing shelters.

Consideration should be given to the constraints and opportunities present in each situation, including the following factors:

- the possibility of training additional skilled labour
- improving access to trained and existing labour resources
- the availability of tools and plant
- seasonal work patterns
- the distance from other host families or supporting organisations.

community events

Consider giving support to public meetings involving both the local population and displaced populations. Offer activities to both groups, such as training courses or social events. This will help the local population and the displaced communities to become familiar with each other, opening channels of communication which will help to prevent misunderstandings and can be developed into means of resolving disputes.

 ### 3.4.3 care and maintenance phase

The care and maintenance phase of the urban self-settlement option is reached when the influx rate of displaced people diminishes and consolidation and up-grading activities can begin. The needs of the displaced and local populations change after the emergency phase, as basic levels of health are restored and community development begins.

existing urban management

Involve the existing urban administration, usually the local government, as much as possible in defining and implementing support measures. Consider capacity building within the existing urban administration as a programme objective. It may be that local administrators should be supported in tasks such as refuse collection and water supply.

Support for families or individuals may involve existing mechanisms: for example, government systems for distributing financial assistance might already be in place. However, additional mechanisms might be needed specifically for the programme: a system for the distribution of non-food items (NFIs), for example.

city administration

If for any reason the local administration is weak, creating a parallel administrative system is not necessarily a sustainable response. Instead, consideration might be given to building capacity in the existing system. If local administration is non-existent, it is likely that other power structures have evolved. If so, it is essential to identify and consult them before considering options.

Unless political factors or lack of skills suggest otherwise, it is often productive to involve existing or previous staff and administrators as much as possible: they have experience and are more likely to be aware of formal and informal channels for communication and management.

Try to reach agreement with stakeholders about who should be responsible for particular aspects of administration. This includes agreement on appropriate roles for the local and international aid communities; for example, they might support the development of official records of property ownership. Be aware of opportunities for corruption or political interference.

improvement of facilities

Consider improvements such as up-grading the electricity distribution infrastructure, extending the supply to private houses; or distribution systems for fuel for heating and cooking. Include possible environmental and economic impacts in the assessment process.

livelihoods It is important to appraise the abilities of displaced households to support themselves through work. As time passes, it is also necessary to monitor the changing circumstances which may have both positive and negative impacts on their livelihood opportunities. Consider offering skills training and related income-generating activities, in order to provide the displaced population with at least a basic livelihood – and do it as soon as possible, in order to reduce their dependency. Together with social-services professionals, consider the physical support that is required by displaced adults if they are to make the most of income-generating opportunities. Whenever possible, if offering training courses, invite the local population to participate. This will promote integration of the two groups and at the same time will constitute a form of compensation for the local community.

Consult education professionals to determine how best to support the access of the displaced children to the local school system, and to provide extra support or provision to the built infrastructure, as appropriate. Also consider with education professionals the physical support required for unofficial schooling among the displaced population, to enable teaching in their own language.

upgrading communal infrastructure

As described in the section above concerning the emergency phase, the presence of the displaced population will affect the local community, and mitigation measures are required to ensure that local services can be maintained and that tensions are prevented. In addition to supporting dispersed families, consider some up-grading of infrastructure such transport, health care, water and sanitation, and power. Similarly, consider offering support for communal services, such as schools and clinics.

 ### 3.4.4 exit strategies

for the local population

The local community should be left with improvements to communal infrastructure, such as water sources, and improved health and education services. If they took part in skills-training programmes, they should be left with additional capacities.

for the displaced population

The normal three options are open to the displaced families: repatriation, local settlement in the host country, and local settlement in a third country. Sometimes displaced individuals dispersed in urban environments have a higher chance of integration within the host country, because they may find better job opportunities. If they choose to be repatriated, resettled, or relocated, they should be referred to the relevant host-government depart-ments and the United Nations body mandated with their protection.

for the aid organisation

If the aid organisation built any collective infrastructure as a response to the emergency, it should be handed over, either to the local authorities or to the local population. Similarly, if agency infrastructure is purchased and not rented, it could be handed over to local and international NGOs dealing with development programmes within the same area.

3.5 grouped in collective centres

Collective centres, also referred to as mass shelters, are usually transit facilities located in pre-existing structures, such as community centres, town halls, gymnasiums, hotels, warehouses, disused factories, and unfinished buildings. They are often used when displacement occurs inside a city itself, or when there are significant flows of displaced people into a city or town.

Collective centres, or mass shelters, are usually appropriate for short-term accommodation for displaced populations while their transit to other TS options is being arranged. Collective centres should not be considered for longer-term accommodation unless they can offer appropriate support, such as conditions to ensure privacy. This is especially important if centres are being considered for vulnerable groups, such as elderly people.

The length of time during which the displaced individuals and families stay in a collective centre is likely to be crucial. As with any form of institutional accommodation, unless sufficient privacy and independence can be assured, a prolonged period of stay is likely to result in stress, possibly leading to depression, social unrest, or other individual or communal psychosocial problems.

The local government may offer a number of government-owned structures or facilities for conversion into collective centres. The main strategic issues to consider, in conjunction with the local authorities or the owner of the structure, are the following:

- Is the structure or facility appropriate to the task?
- How long will it be available? For example, will it have to return to its former use at some point?
- Who owns it?
- What is the nature of the access, services, and utilities?
- In what condition should the structure or facility should be left eventually?

It is also important to consider the livelihoods strategies of the local population. The building or site considered for use as a collective centre will have had a previous use, and great care should be taken to understand the impacts of the proposed new use. For example, if the collective centre is located in a school, consider where the local children will be educated.

There is often a high proportion of old people and individuals without families in collective centres, many of whom may be categorised as vulnerable. They may have chosen to move into the collective centre because they expect to receive more care there than they would receive in other TS options. Collective centres facilitate assistance from agencies, because they improve access to services: a health team can, for example, visit a centre and identify problems more easily than it can do when a population is dispersed.

The security of a collective centre is important, due to the high concentration of displaced people in one place. The presence of the centre may increase vulnerability to attack; it may become a focus for hostilities, or it may become a safe haven.

Fire is a constant risk, especially for vulnerable individuals for whom evacuation is difficult. The buildings used are unlikely to have been designed for dense habitation. Multi-storey buildings constitute the greatest risk.

The spread of communicable disease is more likely in densely occupied living areas with communal services such as sanitation and cooking. Discuss the risks with the appropriate health professionals.

livelihoods As with camps (3.6, 3.7), collective centres can often accommodate entire displaced communities in one place. This means that care is needed in supporting community development (8.5). Collective centres offer different livelihood opportunities from those available to dispersed populations: in general they reduce the variety of income-generating opportunities because they do not provide premises where the activities may take place, or because they constrain access to the local population and therefore to employment opportunities. On the other hand, urban, peri-urban, and rural centres can offer a base for casual labour, such as construction work. There will be a local casual labour force, so it will be necessary to consider the potential competition for job opportunities.

If accommodation is no more than a room within a building, there is probably little opportunity to use that room as somewhere to make something, to offer a service, and to sell or store goods. This will place severe limits on people's ability to continue some livelihood strategies.

If people enter an urban area from a rural area, they are unlikely to be able to sustain any livelihoods involving cultivation or animal husbandry. While the land on which the collective centre is sited may be used, access to further land may have to be negotiated, to ensure that there will be sufficient land to cultivate or keep animals on.

Support offered to the displaced population should not raise their standard of living beyond that of the local population, who may be living in circumstances far below international standards for displaced populations. Standards should be developed that are appropriate to local circumstances, based firmly upon international standards. Support should be offered to both local and displaced populations, to prevent tensions developing, and to support positive relations. Livelihoods can be supported by involving the displaced and local populations in all construction activities, and facilitating access to local markets.

 ### 3.5.1 contingency phase

assessment of capacity

Identify organisations and other resources that might be organised before the onset of an emergency. Assess the type, size, opportunities, and constraints of the capacities available, which should be compared with the contingency requirements identified for each scenario as part of contingency planning.

Consider the density and dispersal of the collective centres, and their combined impact on and interaction with the surrounding environments, both human and environmental. Take account of considerations such as security, population movements, and ethnicity.

assessment of feasibility

As in all other options, it is important to assess the composition and compatibility of ethnic and religious groups within the displaced population. Care should be taken, if security is uncertain, to shelter displaced persons of the same group together, or at least to maintain separate access to facilities such as food and water supplies.

contingency planning

Select the structures to be used as collective centres, paying regard to the safety and accessibility of their location, and the amount of renovation work that would be required before they could accommodate displaced persons. Make sure you are able to provide at least a decent minimum of comfort and privacy to each individual or family, and a place where they can safely store their belongings. Be aware of fire hazards.

In your programme plan, include the support that will be required for the infrastructure and facilities external to the planned centres for displaced populations: for example, health-care systems and water supplies. If appropriate infrastructure and facilities are not available, they are likely to be insufficient for the local populace too, so any support for the displaced population should be planned as a sustainable contribution to the well-being of the local community.

For each potential collective centre, build upon the detail of the strategic plan by assessing the possible sites. When designing an appropriate assessment, use the technical criteria offered in table 3(a).

Identify owners and make intention agreements so that the structures can be vacated for the use of displaced people in case of an emergency. Avoid using buildings which provide key local services, such as schools. It is usually easiest to reach agreement on the use of buildings and sites that are in public ownership. Be aware that UNHCR does not offer rent under such circumstances, and that other organisations should understand this policy.

Contingency preparations can be made for urgent up-grading works, involving tendering (see 5.4.3), the pre-selection of local contractors, and the pre-selection of organisations or staff to manage the facility.

formal agreements

Develop protocols of understanding or three-way agreements with the local authorities and owners, to be signed in the emergency phase. The agreements should address the following issues:

- ways in which the structure would need to be modified
- administrative authorisation for modifications
- any local or national building codes that must be met
- proposed maximum occupancy
- deadlines, if any, for the beginning and end of occupancy
- how and in what state the structure should be returned after being used.

table 3(a): technical criteria for assessing the suitability of sites for collective centres

criteria	reason	advice
structure	The building may not be strong enough to accommodate the number of people; alterations may be required, such as partition walls.	Consult a structural engineer or an architect.
layout, walls, and partitions	It must be possible to sub-divide the space to permit basic security and privacy.	Survey the building and the site; plan options; consult an architect.
water and sanitation	It must be possible to up-grade existing provision to meet the needs of high-density occupation.	Base provision on Sphere and UNHCR standards for camps, presented in section 8.4.1.
energy supply/ heating	Lighting must be safe and sufficient; space heating is required in cold climates, which is expensive to install or renovate, and to fuel.	Beware of fire risks; consult a mechanical-services engineer.
cooking facilities	Family-based cooking is rarely safe or feasible, so facilities and management are required for communal cooking.	Beware of risks from fire and smoke inhalation; develop a strategy with the organisation that will be responsible for maintaining the facility.
building and equipment safety	The building and services need to be safe: for example, fire escapes, asbestos, gas installation, electrical wiring.	Consider the safety of the building when it is returned to its original function.

3 options

If any upgrading is required, take this into account when negotiating the use of the building and site with the owner. Consider how the building will be used when it is returned to its original function, and how the planned works will affect this. Make sure that up-grading will be sustainable; for example, there is no point in installing expensive space heating, if finally there will not be sufficient funds to maintain or fuel the system.

information plan

The local community should be involved in deciding what happens in their locality, but care must be taken not to raise unrealistic expectations. It is important to formulate, as part of the contingency plan, an information plan for the local population. In the event that the centres are occupied, both displaced and local populations require regular and accurate information, and regular and accountable community meetings where representations can be made.

 3.5.2 emergency phase

influx management

Monitor variations in the influx rates of the displaced, and establish methods of assessment appropriate to their dispersed settlement. If access to the displaced population is so difficult that it becomes hard to help them, consider increasing operational capacity or supporting the beneficiaries to move to a different location.

programme planning

As described in chapter 2, a programme plan should be formulated, in consultation with other stakeholders and within a continually up-dated framework of appropriate assessment, monitoring, and evaluation. The contents and assumptions of the contingency plan should be reviewed and integrated, as appropriate, because the people who drafted it cannot have anticipated every aspect of the opportunities that will be available to particular displaced populations.

If no contingency plan has been formed, the same steps need to be undertaken during the emergency phase. Reaching agreements on ownership and use can be complex and time-consuming – a fact which limits the effectiveness of collective centres as an unplanned emergency response. A centre should not be established until ownership and use are agreed, because any lack of clarity on this matter may create problems in later phases.

It is likely that part of the programme plan will be reactive, while other parts may be proactive. Once the emergency has begun, the following responses are important.

- Provide information to all the stakeholders, and keep up-dating it.
- Provide assistance to vulnerable individuals if they cannot receive appropriate help from their families or from their host families: for example, if pre-emergency social support has been disrupted as a result of displacement and hosting.
- Provide assistance to vulnerable individuals, families, or groups who have no access to income-generation opportunities; take care to avoid conflicts of interest (ethnic or personal), especially if local government is involved.
- Agree and meet standards for support, such as the Sphere standards, including the provision of a minimum floor area per person.
- Register displaced people, employing the health and security screening processes that are essential to identifying vulnerable civilians, combatants, and other groups within the displaced population. (This is important also as a first step for those seeking asylum under international refugee law.)
- Reduce mortality and morbidity by setting up an emergency health-care infrastructure for screening and treatment, for example by building therapeutic and supplementary feeding centres.

labour-management options

All three main labour-management alternatives presented in chapter 5 should be considered, including combinations of them.

Consider the constraints and opportunities present in each situation, including the following factors:

- the possibility of training additional skilled labour
- improving access to trained and existing labour resources
- the availability of tools and plant
- seasonal work patterns.

infrastructure and facilities

Even in grouped settlement such as collective centres, the displaced population may rely to some extent on existing communal infrastructure, such as a water supply. Whether or not this is significant, the presence of the displaced population will have an impact on the local community, and mitigation measures are required to prevent tensions and ensure that local services can be maintained. In addition to supporting dispersed families, consideration might be given to up-grading some infrastructure, such as transport, health care, water and sanitation, and power. Similarly, support might be offered to communal services, such as schools and clinics.

Support for local and collective-centre infrastructure and facilities should be offered in a phased plan, to ensure that emergency provision can be achieved as soon as possible. While some support can be offered quickly, such as the distribution of medicines to a clinic, take care not to raise expectation of the local community beyond the phase and levels of support that can reasonably be guaranteed.

community events

Consider giving support to public meetings involving both the local population and displaced populations. Both groups should be offered activities such as training courses or social events. This will help the local population and the displaced communities to become familiar with each other, opening channels of communication which will help to prevent misunderstandings and may be developed into means of resolving disputes.

 ### 3.5.3 care and maintenance phase

The care and maintenance phase of the collective-centre option is reached when the influx rate of displaced people diminishes, and consolidation and up-grading activities can begin. The needs of the displaced and local populations also change after the emergency phase, as basic levels of health are restored and community development begins.

duration The population within the collective centre is likely to change over time. Families and groups will leave for or arrive from other TS options, depending on their needs. For example, those able to work

---

112

may leave, while others who are unable to work may arrive. As a consequence, the role of the centre may change: for example, from being a transit centre to serving as a centre for older people.

Targets, such as the planned duration of the collective centre, should be continually re-assessed and re-evaluated. It is common for relief workers to ignore the psychosocial impacts of a centre if no alternative TS option is available. Delaying the creation of an appropriate alternative is, however, likely to compound any negative psychosocial impacts.

Collective centres are often established as temporary measures to meet specific needs, such as transit during an influx. If such centres continue to be used after the planned need has ended, the strategic TS plan should be reconsidered.

Monitor seasonal changes, such as the onset of a cold winter; or the new school year, which may require the building that is being used as an accommodation centre to be returned to its original use.

general maintenance

Good maintenance of the centre will improve the morale of the residents and support them in other ways too, providing work and an income for some, and also increasing the confidence of the local population in the support programme. Maintenance is the most cost-effective way of ensuring that the centre will eventually be handed back to the owners in an appropriate state. Additional considerations include the need for vector control and possibly hygiene promotion.

livelihoods It is important to appraise the abilities of displaced households to support themselves through work. As time passes, it is also necessary to monitor the changing circumstances which may have both positive and negative impacts on their livelihood opportunities. Consider offering skills training and related income-generating activities, in order to provide the displaced population with at least a basic livelihood – and do it as soon as possible, in order to reduce their dependency. With social-services professionals, consider the physical support that is required by displaced adults if they are to make the most of income-generating opportunities. Whenever possible, if offering training courses, invite the participation of the local population. This will promote integration of the two groups and at the same time will constitute a form of compensation for the local community.

Consult education professionals to determine how best to support the access of the displaced children to the local school system, and to provide extra support or provision to the built infrastructure, as appropriate. Also consider with education professionals the physical support required for unofficial schooling among the displaced population, to enable teaching in their own language.

Consider continuing the upgrading of existing communal infrastructure, as in the emergency phase.

3.5.4 exit strategies

for the local population

The terms under which the centre is returned to its owners should have been agreed before beginning initial works and operation. Before making any compensation agreed under these conditions, the impact of the centre on all local groups should be assessed: it is likely that circumstances will have changed, and that some impacts could not have been predicted. The compensation package or activities should be negotiated and agreed by all parties.

for the displaced population

It is vital that displaced individuals and groups are not left in collective centres for long periods without access to alternative TS options appropriate to their needs. Support for durable solutions, such as aid packages for returnees, should take into account the level of care required and received: those living in collective centres are unlikely to have received shelter NFIs such as tents, cook sets, or mattresses.

for the aid organisation

The manner in which compensation is offered is likely to influence local people's perception of the motives and competence of the aid organisation. In turn, this may condition the attitude of the local community towards other on-going TS options.

Although collective centres should be the first TS options to be discontinued, they are often the last. As such, they have been used as opportunities to expend remaining project funds. Care should be taken to ensure that such expenditures are the most appropriate use of the resources available.

3.6 grouped in self-settled camps

A displaced community or displaced groups may settle in camps, independently of assistance from local government or the aid community. Self-settled camps are often sited on state-owned or communal land, usually after limited negotiations with the local population over use and access.

Camps replicate an entire support system, rather than simply adding the components of existing settlement that are missing for a displaced population. As a result, establishing camps involves factors such as the following:

- strategic planning
- the selection of sites
- camp management
- options for phasing, development, and expansion
- cross-cutting factors, such as gender and age
- cross-sectoral factors, such as water and health.

The guidance in this section therefore requires more detail than that offered for other TS options. In addition, building on the guidance offered in this section, detailed guidance on the physical planning and implementation of camp programmes is presented in chapter 8, section 4.

Grouped self-settlements are usually established before the arrival of aid organisations in the field. Displaced communities often choose this option because they find living in a group preferable for social reasons. Also, it makes them feel more secure, and they hope it will improve their chances of receiving external assistance.

The main strategic decision to be made by the aid community is whether the site and settlement can be supported and improved, or whether the settlement must be supported to move to a different site, or whether alternative settlement options need to be developed. The main reasons for needing to relocate a self-settled camp are related to safety and security. For example, the camp may be located too close to a border to offer the displaced population adequate protection, or the camp may be at risk from natural hazards, such as flooding.

If the location is acceptable, the settlement is likely to require some adjustments to its density, and to its water supply and sanitation infrastructure, in addition to the introduction of fire-breaks to reduce fire hazards.

vulnerabilities

Camps can make displaced persons more vulnerable to both external and internal security threats. Registration and screening are required from the outset, in order to identify combatants among the civilian population. UNHCR usually takes the lead role in the registration process in refugee situations.

It is important to assess the security threat, particularly because the local population may become a target if the displaced population have not travelled very far from the source of their displacement.

livelihoods The organisational structure of aid delivery to camp settlements, and the mechanisms for it, affect both communications with local populations and the displaced community's prospects for self-sufficiency. It is very rare, however, to find organised settlements where displaced persons have no formal or informal interaction with local populations and economies, and where settlements have no internal economies to generate a degree of self-sufficiency. At the other extreme, it is also rare to find circumstances where local economic conditions and available land allow whole migrant populations to re-settle sustainably in a self-sufficient manner, on a permanent or transitional basis. In reality, most camp settlements fall between these extremes.

The support offered to the displaced population should not raise their standard of living beyond that of the local population, who may be living in circumstances far below international standards for displaced populations. Standards should be developed that are appropriate to local circumstances, and based firmly upon international standards. Support should be offered to both local and displaced populations to prevent tensions and to support positive relations. Livelihoods can be supported, for example, by involving the displaced and local populations in all construction activities and by facilitating access to local markets.

It is important to consider the former use of communal land on which a self-settled camp is built; to ask what local population activities have been displaced by the influx of displaced people; and to find ways to compensate the local population for this loss.

3.6.1 contingency phase

assessment of capacity

It may be appropriate to identify contingency TS capacity in the form of self-settlement in camps. There is no contradiction in forming a contingency plan for self-settlement: the difference between contingency planning for self-settled and for planned camps (3.7.1) is that self-settled camps might receive little external support during the emergency phase, while planned camps should be prepared in step with, or prior to, an influx of displaced persons. It is often the case that local government and the aid community lack the capacity to prepare for receiving a large displaced population, or that a large influx is expected in only the most extreme of the scenarios considered.

assessment of feasibility

For this option, contingency planning consists of assessing whether self-settled camps are viable for a potential displaced population in a particular area. There may be, for example, a long and relatively secure border with an abundant supply of natural resources and good access, and only a small local population. In such circumstances, it may be feasible to assume that the displaced population itself can undertake settlement, while intervention by international organisations concentrates on assisting vulnerable groups within the communities by supporting other settlement options, such as accommodation with host families.

It is important to assess the composition and compatibility of ethnic and religious groups within the displaced population. Care should be taken, if security is uncertain, to shelter displaced persons of the same group together, or at least to maintain separate access to facilities such as food and water supplies.

transit and reception centres

In order to be prepared for a large influx of displaced people, identify or build structures which can serve as reception centres, where people will be registered and receive a first health check and initial assistance.

If people need to be transferred to safer sites, for instance farther away from the conflict area, consider the establishment of transit centres and the provision of transport.

contingency planning for new influxes

If the aid community is already in the field and expecting the arrival of more displaced people in the area, a fundamental task is to identify new sites for the expansion of the existing camp and to ensure that they conform to safety regulations and minimum standards.

 ### 3.6.2 emergency phase

influx management

Monitor variations in the influx rates of the displaced, and establish methods of assessment appropriate to their dispersed settlement. If the displaced people are so difficult to reach that it is very hard to help them, consider increasing operational capacity or supporting the beneficiaries to move to a different location.

programme planning

As described in chapter 2, a programme plan should be formulated, in consultation with other stakeholders and within a continually up-dated framework of appropriate assessment, monitoring, and evaluation. The contents and assumptions of the contingency plan should be reviewed and integrated, as appropriate, because the people who drafted it cannot have anticipated every aspect of the opportunities that will be available to specific displaced populations and their host families.

It is likely that part of the programme plan will be reactive, while other parts are proactive. Once the emergency has begun, the following responses are important.

• Provide information to all the stakeholders, and keep up-dating it.

• Provide assistance to vulnerable individuals, families, or groups who have no access to income-generation opportunities; take care to avoid conflicts of interest (ethnic or personal), especially if local government is involved.

• Agree and meet standards for support, such as the Sphere standards, including the provision of a minimum floor area per person.

• Register displaced people, employing the health and security screening processes that are essential to identifying vulnerable civilians, combatants, and other groups within the displaced population (important also as a first step for those seeking asylum under international refugee law).

- Reduce mortality and morbidity by setting up an emergency health-care infrastructure for screening and treatment: for example, by building therapeutic and supplementary feeding centres.

camps set up without external assistance

It often happens that camps are self-settled, because international organisations or local authorities have not had the capacity in place to organise a planned alternative. In such circumstances, determine whether the camp offers appropriate levels of security and safety to all displaced groups and to the local population: for example, is the camp too near to a border, or in a flood plain? In such a case, improvements to security and safety should be made, or the camp should be closed and its population should be supported to relocate to another site, or offered another TS option.

registration Registration is key to planning and offering TS support, as it is for other assistance activities. Aid agencies should negotiate with the mandated UN body, such as UNHCR, and with the local authorities on behalf of the displaced people already living within the self-settled camp, to recognise their rights and define a strategy for the new caseloads.

monitoring influxes and distribution

Build or identify a reception centre in order to register all new arrivals. Keep in constant touch with those working at the entry points, because they will have the most up-to-date information on the numbers of people entering. Work with the camp-management professionals and committees to identify and provide the appropriate infrastructure for food storage and distribution, considering the longer-term potential of these structures for the local population.

alternatives to self-settled camps

Negotiations should be undertaken by the lead agency with the local authorities to identify and secure additional sites for extensions to camps, in case the location of the existing ones proves to be appropriate, or to lack sufficient capacity.

health care, water, and sanitation

Liaison with health professionals is important, in order to ensure adequate health-care infrastructure. This might involve negotiations with the local authorities to allow access for the displaced population to the local health infrastructure. If such infrastructure is insufficient or non-existent, consult health professionals to determine the infrastructure required for both the displaced and local populations; for example, it might be necessary to build a new clinic.

Experts in the provision of water and sanitation should be consulted, to plan and build infrastructure with the capacity to respond in the emergency phase and the potential to be easily up-graded during the care and maintenance phase.

extending the camp

Sites for extending the camp should be identified immediately, especially if the self-settled site requires reorganisation. As described in section 3.7 on planned camps, the physical planning of extension sites should also be undertaken, in order to accommodate new caseloads and the natural population growth. Consider the phased expansion in services that will be required, such as food distribution and water supply, and decide how incremental growth can best be supported: for example, how the first and the last families will move into the planned extension.

livelihoods Displaced families may have brought livestock with them, which will require water and grazing. Or they may wish to farm land, to generate income or diversify their diets. Finding water and grazing for livestock is an urgent imperative, because livestock often con-stitutes the main wealth of a displaced population, and its final opportunity for recovery. Finding suitable agricultural land may also be an urgent concern, depending on the local cycle of planting and rains. Discussions with the local authorities and communities will determine the availability of suitable land, the options for the transitional use of common land, and local traditions of natural-resource management. It may be necessary to provide emergency supplies of fodder, or water troughs, or seeds.

labour-management options

All three main labour-management alternatives presented in chapter 5 should be considered, including combinations of them. Remember that women, and especially single females or female-headed households, may be vulnerable to exploitation when they seek help in constructing shelters.

Consider the constraints and opportunities present in each situation, including the following factors:

- the possibility of training additional skilled labour
- improving access to trained and existing labour resources
- the availability of tools and plant
- seasonal work patterns.

upgrading communal infrastructure

The presence of the displaced population will have an impact on the wider local community. Care must be taken to prevent tensions and to ensure that local services can be maintained. In addition to supporting family accommodation, some up-grading of infrastructure might be considered, such as improvements to the following:

- transport, including roads and bridges
- health care, including clinics, hospitals, and dispensaries
- water and sanitation, including water supply, surface-water drainage, and sanitation in communal areas or for communal services
- schools, including crèches, and primary, secondary, and tertiary institutions, where available
- the generation and transmission of power
- food production and food security, such as grain stores
- police stations, prisons, and courts.

community events

Consider giving support to public meetings involving both the local population and displaced populations. Both groups should be offered activities such as training courses or social events. This will help the local population and the displaced communities to become familiar with each other, opening channels of communication which will help to prevent misunderstandings and can be developed into means of resolving disputes.

3.6.3 care and maintenance phase

The care and maintenance phase of self-settled camps is reached when the influx rate of displaced people diminishes, and consolidation and up-grading activities can begin. The needs of the displaced and local populations also change after the emergency phase, as basic levels of health are restored and community development begins.

up-grading existing camps

Undertake a thorough assessment of risks, such as flooding and fire, and plan and implement provisions accordingly: for example, relocating some shelters to create sufficient fire-breaks. Relocate any shelter in the self-settled camp that is situated in hazardous areas. Consider up-grading programmes, if locations and structures are appropriate, through distributing materials and providing guidance, if required.

Determine whether the existing camps meet international standards, such as those concerning density. Decide whether action is required, such as reducing the density of occupation of the camp by locating some families in an extension area. Apply international standards (Sphere 2004 and UNHCR 2000), which have been developed from experience gained in risk management. A particular concern is the link between population density and the spread of disease. Local circumstances, however, must be considered.

Consult health, water, and sanitation professionals to determine how best to support the up-grading of services. For example, the water and sanitation infrastructure may be improved by providing family latrines and a water point for each community.

livelihoods It is important to appraise the abilities of displaced households to support themselves through work. As time passes, it is necessary to monitor the changes in circumstances which may have both positive and negative impacts on their livelihood opportunities. Consider offering skills training and related income-generating activities, in order to provide the displaced population with at least a basic livelihood – and do it as soon as possible, in order to reduce their dependency. With social-services professionals, consider the physical support that is required by displaced adults if they are to make the most of income-generating opportunities. Whenever possible, if offering training courses, invite the local population to

---

participate. This will promote integration of the two groups and at the same time will constitute a form of compensation for the local community.

Consult education professionals to determine how best to support the access of the displaced children to the local school system, and to provide extra support or provision to the built infrastructure, as appropriate. Also consider with education professionals the physical support required for unofficial schooling among the displaced population, to enable teaching in their own language.

Consider continuing the up-grading of existing communal infrastructure, as in the emergency phase.

 ### 3.6.4 exit strategies
for the local population

All communal infrastructure should be planned from the outset to be handed over to the local community and/or local authorities. Such infrastructure should therefore take into account its final use, and the sustainability of its operation and maintenance: for example, a distribution centre may finally become a school, if it is planned and located appropriately, and if funds are available to pay a teacher.

Depending on the type of camp, the handover may include roads and camp clinics, schools, wells, and other water infrastructure. Water supply and distribution systems should benefit the local/ neighbouring communities and should therefore be well designed and constructed to high standards.

If support has been offered to self-settled camps, the lead agency is responsible for ensuring that the camp site is returned to the local authorities in the manner and condition initially agreed. It is common for camp sites, once they have been closed, to contain a lot of refuse, some of which may be hazardous, such as medical sharps.

Abandoned pit-latrines and surface-water drains may constitute additional hazards if the site is to be re-used. Environmental degradation is likely to be considerable, and soil erosion may be expected. Reforestation or other mitigation programmes should have been considered since the establishment of the camp, to enable a smooth handover to the local authorities.

for the displaced population

Refer to section 8.4.8, on closing camps.

for the aid organisation

Refer to section 8.4.8, on closing camps.

3.7 grouped in planned camps

Planned camps are places where displaced populations find accommodation on purpose-built sites, and a full services infrastructure is provided, including water supply, food distribution, non-food item distribution, education, and health care, usually exclusively for the population of the site.

Camps replicate an entire support system, rather than simply adding the components of existing settlement that are missing for a displaced population. As a result, establishing camps involves factors such as the following:

- strategic planning
- the selection of sites
- camp management
- options for phasing, development, and expansion
- cross-cutting factors, such as gender and age
- cross-sectoral issues, such as water and health.

The guidance in this section therefore requires more detail than that offered for other TS options. In addition, building on the guidance offered in this section, detailed guidance on the physical planning and implementation of camp programmes is presented in chapter 8, section 4.

Planned camps are considered to be the option of last resort by organisations such as UNHCR, for several reasons: they are seen as drawing displaced away from other TS options; as promoting dependency; as requiring disproportionate support compared with other options; as more difficult to withdraw from than other options; and as posing more of a challenge to efforts to achieve durable solutions for the population. However, these problems can often be mitigated. And it is possible that planned camps are the most appropriate TS option for a given population and situation.

Camps may increase the vulnerability of displaced persons to security threats, both external and internal. Registration and screening are required from the outset, to identify combatants among the civilian population. UNHCR usually takes the lead role in the registration of refugees.

It is important to assess the security threat, particularly because the local population may become a target if the displaced population have not travelled very far from the source of their displacement.

livelihoods The organisational structure of aid delivery to camp settlements, and the mechanisms for it, affect both communications with local populations and the displaced community's prospects for self-sufficiency. It is very rare, however, to find organised settlements where displaced persons have no formal or informal interaction with local populations and economies, and where settlements have no internal economies to generate a degree of self-sufficiency. At the other extreme, it is also rare to find circumstances where local economic conditions and available land allow whole migrant populations to re-settle sustainably in a self-sufficient manner, on a permanent or transitional basis. In reality, most camp settlements fall between these extremes.

The support offered to the displaced population should not raise their standard of living beyond that of the local population, who may be living in circumstances far below international standards for displaced populations. Standards should be developed that are appropriate to local circumstances, based firmly upon international standards. Support should be offered to both local and displaced populations to prevent tensions and support positive relations. Livelihoods can be supported, for example, by involving the displaced and local populations in all construction activities and by facilitating their access to local markets.

3.7.1 contingency phase

assessment of capacity

On many occasions, camps have been built before an influx, to provide contingency capacity for reception, transit, and transitional settlement during the emergency phase – regardless of the settlement options that the population groups will choose for their displacement. Providing such contingency capacity is costly and risky, because not all factors can be predicted; for example, the actual displacement may occur across a border that is too far from the camp to make the facilities a feasible option. Contingency capacity in camps may, however, be the key to ensuring adequate provision, especially in the case of large influxes. Contingency capacity can also be created in other TS options, such as collective centres and accommodation with host families. See chapter 2 for a description of the process of developing an integrated strategy.

assessment of feasibility

The selection of appropriate sites for camps, whether in contingency or emergency phases, is described in chapter 8. Site selection is based on forming profiles of the displaced and local populations to determine what type of settlement is required, and then forming profiles of the various sites to determine which are suitable.

It is important to assess the composition and compatibility of ethnic and religious groups within the displaced population. Care should be taken, if security is uncertain, that only displaced persons of the same group are sheltered in the same neighbourhood of the camp, or at least that facilities such as access to food and water are kept separate.

 3.7.2 emergency phase

influx management

Monitor variations in the influx rates of the displaced, and establish methods of assessment appropriate to their dispersed settlement. If the displaced people are so difficult to reach that it is very hard to help them, consider increasing operational capacity or supporting the beneficiaries to move to a different location.

programme planning

As described in chapter 2, a programme plan should be formulated, in consultation with other stakeholders and within a continually up-dated framework of appropriate assessment, monitoring, and evaluation. The contents and assumptions of the contingency plan should be reviewed and integrated, as appropriate, because the people who drafted it cannot have anticipated every aspect of the opportunities that will be available to specific displaced populations and their host families.

It is likely that part of the programme plan will be reactive, while other parts are proactive. During the emergency phase, the lead agency should co-ordinate its response with those of other organisations, aid professionals, and the local authorities to achieve the following:

- Support for access and transit, such as emergency improvements to road infrastructure and the construction of way-stations and transit centres (chapter 8).

- Registration, using the health and security screening processes that are essential to identifying vulnerable persons, combatants, and other groups within the displaced population (and necessary also as a first step for those seeking asylum under international refugee law).

- Site planning and development: preparing land for use as sectors and blocks within the camp to keep pace with the influx, for example by undertaking rough clearing of trees and then marking out the plots, ensuring that healthy trees are retained as wind breaks and for shade, and space is left for economic and recreational activities, as well as infrastructure, such as surface-water drainage.

- Emergency health infrastructure for screening and treatment, in order to reduce mortality and morbidity, for example by building therapeutic and supplementary feeding centres, and preparing an area which can quickly be developed into a separate camp to isolate and treat an outbreak of cholera, or other infectious diseases.

- Emergency water and sanitation infrastructure, such as bladder-tanks and tap-stands and defecation fields.

- Emergency distribution infrastructure, including – as part of the reception process – facilities for issuing food and non-food items, such as a distribution centre or fenced area with secure storage.

- Information for all the stakeholders (which should be frequently up-dated).

- Assistance to vulnerable individuals, families, or groups with no access to income-generation opportunities, taking care to avoid conflicts of interest (ethnic or personal), especially if local government is involved.

- Agreement and implementation of standards for support, such as the Sphere standards, including a minimum floor area per person.

The provision of basic services and the development of the camp must be planned in a phased manner, even if the basic camp has been constructed in the contingency phase. The requirements and functions of a camp change over time. For example, reception facilities will be needed during the period of influx. Emergency infrastructure should be developed by all the sectors of operations involved, as part of a plan for its eventual upgrading. For example, space should be left within the plan of family plots for family latrines, washing areas, and a piped water supply with tap-stands.

site selection

The international community and host government are primarily responsible for selecting sites for camps. The host government is expected to offer land without requiring its purchase or rent. The lead agency, such as UNHCR, will discuss land-tenure issues with the host government. This might be done through consultation with local or national authorities, as well as with community leaders. Formal and informal land use should also be taken into account when selecting a site, in order to prevent any later conflict between a host and a displaced population.

rebuilding communities

During the influx, families should be allocated plots near to other families whom they know, in order to reinforce the coping strategies of the displaced population by supporting the rebuilding of their sense of community. It is common, however, for influxes to happen over a long period of time, which makes it difficult to predict how much space will be required, so it is not always possible to allocate adjacent plots to families who arrive at the beginning or the end of the influx. Predictions can be made more accurate through good influx management and through interviews with the displaced families when they arrive. It may be assumed that a period of consolidation and relocation will occur in the care and maintenance phase, when families may be assisted to exchange or relocate their plots: indeed, informal 'estate agents' operate in some planned camps. But note that external support is necessary to help to prevent corrupt practices. Families who settled at random throughout a camp during the confusion of the emergency phase can be relocated in closer proximity to each other when camps are later extended.

livelihoods Displaced families may have brought livestock with them, which will require water and grazing. Or they may wish to farm land, to generate income or diversify their diets. Finding water and grazing for livestock is an urgent imperative, because livestock often constitutes the main wealth of a displaced population, and its final opportunity for recovery. Negotiating access to agricultural land may be another urgent concern, depending on the local cycle of planting and rains. Discussions with the local authorities and communities will determine the availability of suitable land, the options for the transitional use of common land, and local traditions of natural-resource management. It may be necessary to provide emergency supplies of fodder, or water troughs, or seeds.

labour-management options

All three main labour-management alternatives presented in chapter 5 should be considered, including combinations of them.

It should be remembered that women, and especially single women and female-headed households, may be vulnerable to exploitation when they seek help in constructing shelters.

Consideration should be given to the constraints and opportunities present in each situation, including the following factors:

- the possibility of training additional skilled labour
- improving access to trained and existing labour resources
- the availability of tools and plant
- seasonal work patterns.

upgrading communal infrastructure

The presence of the displaced population will have an impact on the wider local community. Care must be taken to prevent tensions and to ensure that local services can be maintained. In addition to supporting family accommodation, some upgrading of infrastructure might be considered, such as improvements to the following:

- transport, including roads and bridges
- health care, including clinics, hospitals, and dispensaries
- water and sanitation, including water supply, surface-water drainage, and sanitation in communal areas or for communal services

- schools, including crèches, and primary, secondary, and tertiary institutions, where available
- the generation and transmission of power
- food production and food security, such as grain stores
- police stations, prisons, and courts.

community events

Consider giving support to public meetings involving both the local population and displaced populations. Both groups should be offered activities such as training courses or social events. This will help the local population and the displaced communities to become familiar with each other, opening channels of communication which will help to prevent misunderstandings and may be developed into means of resolving disputes.

 ### 3.7.3 care and maintenance phase

The care and maintenance phase of the planned-camps option is reached when the influx rate of displaced people diminishes and consolidation and upgrading activities can begin. The needs of the displaced and local populations also change after the emergency phase, as basic levels of health are restored and community development begins.

managing the camp

Care should be taken during the emergency phase to consider how the camp will be managed, ideally consulting those who will manage it. It is important to document properly the decisions made and the stakeholders involved. The development, maintenance, and administration of a camp may be undertaken by organisations different from those that built it in the emergency phase. Even if this is not the case, it is likely that staff will be re-deployed after the emergency phase has ended. The roles of the local authorities, line ministries, and local and camp committees will also change over time, so the care and maintenance of the camp should reflect these changes.

The management of a camp is often undertaken by a number of different organisations, with each taking on responsibility for a particular service, such as food distribution, water and sanitation, or health care. There is usually a lead agency or co-ordinating agency, such as UNHCR.

transfers between options

It is likely that many of the displaced population do not consider a planned camp as their preferred TS alternative. Their choices may, however, be constrained. After the emergency phase, more choices may become available, or the circumstances of the displaced persons might change: for example, a family may meet again after being separated during transit. Similarly, displaced persons living in settlement options other than camps may decide that camps offer the best alternative for them: for example, if they have been renting a room and they run out of money. Lastly, events such as a harvest, a monsoon season, or changes in security in the region are likely to result in population movements between settlement options.

As a result, it is common for camps to experience a considerable turnover of population, even if the overall population appears to be relatively constant. The demographic composition is also likely to change: for example, if young men move to the camps to avoid conscription into armed factions, or if economically active adults leave the camp to find employment in the region, leaving elderly people and children behind in the camps.

It is important to maintain an accurate profile of all groups within the displaced populations, both inside and outside the camps, in order to be able to predict (or at least expect) population movements into and out of the camps. Such movements can constitute a significant proportion of the camp's total numbers and, as such, will affect the degree of infrastructure and support required.

extending the camp

As with self-settled camps, sites should be identified to accommodate new influxes and natural population growth. Extensions can be used as part of reorganisation even in planned camps, once communities have re-formed following the emergency phase. When planning an extension, considerable care should be taken to ensure that the overall size of the camp does not place too great a strain on local resources or on relations with the local population, and that appropriate infrastructure is also extended.

livelihoods It is important to appraise the abilities of displaced households to support themselves through work. As time passes, it is also necessary to monitor changes in circumstances which may have both positive and negative impacts on their livelihood opportunities. Consider offering skills training and related income-generating activities, in order to provide the displaced population with at least a basic livelihood – and do it as soon as possible, in order to reduce their dependency. With social-services professionals, consider the physical support that is required by displaced adults if they are to make the most of income-generating opportunities. Whenever possible, if offering training courses, invite the participation of the local population. This will promote integration of the two groups and at the same time will constitute a form of compensation for the local community. Income-generating activities in general should take into account the relations between host and hosted labour.

Consult education professionals to determine how best to support the access of the displaced children to the local school system, and to provide extra support or provision to the built infrastructure, as appropriate. Also consider with education professionals the physical support required for unofficial schooling among the displaced population, to enable teaching in their own language.

 ### 3.7.4 exit strategies
for the local population

All communal infrastructure should be planned from the outset to be handed over to the local community and/or local authorities. Such infrastructure should therefore take into account its final use, and the sustainability of its operation and maintenance: for example, a distribution centre may finally become a school, if it is planned and located appropriately, and if funds are available for a teacher.

Depending on the type of camp, the handover may include roads and camp clinics, schools, wells, and other water infrastructure. Water supply and distribution systems should benefit the local community and should therefore be well designed and constructed to high standards.

The lead agency is responsible for ensuring that the camp site is returned to the local authorities in the manner and condition initially agreed. It is common for camp sites, once they have been closed, to contain a lot of refuse, some of which may be hazardous, such as medical sharps. Abandoned pit latrines and surface-water drains may constitute additional hazards when the site is re-used. Environmental degradation is likely to be considerable, and soil erosion may be expected. Reforestation or other mitigation programmes should have been considered when the camp was first established, to enable a smooth handover to the local authorities.

for the displaced population

See 8.4.8, concerning the closing of camps.

for the aid organisation

See 8.4.8, concerning the closing of camps.

transitional settlement: displaced populations

4 assessment

4 assessment

4.1 shelter assessment, monitoring, and evaluation (SAME)

This chapter presents shelter assessment, monitoring, and evaluation (SAME), a single-sector method for the assessment, monitoring, and evaluation of both the transitional settlement and shelter of populations displaced by conflict and natural disasters, and the impacts upon the populations hosting them.

It is not possible to achieve and sustain an appropriate technical response unless it is informed by appropriate and consistent assessment, monitoring, and evaluation. Section 4.1 describes how to use SAME by following the four steps presented in the following sections:

4.2 step 1: why? – agreeing why the programme is needed

4.3 step 2: when? – identifying the resources required to undertake it

4.4 step 3: what? – choosing the appropriate questions or criteria

4.5 step 4: how? – selecting ways to ask questions with available resources.

4.1.1 SAME: a single method

The SAME method for the transitional settlement of displaced populations is livelihoods-based. SAME is consistent with, and informed by, other tools in use by the major organisations that are operational in the aid community. It is appropriate for all operational stakeholders, including governments, community-based organisations (CBOs), non-government organisations (NGOs), international organisations (IOs), United Nations (UN) bodies, and donors. It can be undertaken within an emergency environment, in a limited period, with limited resources, and by non-specialist personnel who are untrained in assessment.

The method presents assessment, monitoring, and evaluation as a continuous process, maintaining an on-going relationship between stakeholders, rather than being a series of unrelated events.

Experience suggests that some previous assessments and evaluations in this sector have been undermined by being undertaken only once or twice, by using different methods, and by having minimal monitoring. Such processes have not provided the time required to achieve accurate understandings of the situation, or to assess how the situation and the priorities of the populations change over time.

SAME has been developed as a single method for the assessment, monitoring, and evaluation of transitional settlement and shelter. It spans the continuum from relief to development. Assessments and decisions made early on in a response determine the form and success of later assessments and decisions. Methods for assessing, monitoring, and evaluating situations which involve populations reconstructing their homes, following conflict or natural disaster, should be made consistent with the SAME method, building upon any previous programmes undertaken using this method.

4.1.2 SAME: design

The following four steps should be followed to develop a programme for assessing, monitoring, and evaluating a situation. The same steps should be used consistently to plan each assessment, monitoring, and evaluation activity within the programme.

step 1: why? It is essential to identify all existing assessment, monitoring, and evaluation programmes which refer to the displacement situation. From this background material, the reasons for undertaking a new programme, or programme activity, should be developed and agreed by all stakeholders. (See 4.2 for details.)

step 2: when? Programmes should be designed appropriately for each displacement situation, each placing different emphasis on activities such as monitoring, and each identifying appropriate stages in assessment and evaluation. The design of programme schedules will be determined by the human, transport, financial, and time resources available. (See 4.3.)

step 3: what? Each assessment, monitoring, or evaluation team will need to identify and agree with stakeholders the questions that are most appropriate to the displacement situation. Some questions will be so important that they will need to be verified by use of a variety of sources. Some questions will be suitable to act as indicators of change or success in the programme. (See 4.4.)

step 4: how? Finding responses to the questions, using the resources available, will require the use of a variety of tools, all based on the options of research, observation, and interview. (See 4.5.)

4.1.3 SAME: reporting

The following report structure is based on standard formats used by the UN and by donors, international organisations, and NGOs. It is appropriate for assessments and evaluations, as well as for presenting the results of completed monitoring activities. It is essential that a consistent format is agreed between stakeholders for reporting each activity within programmes of assessment, monitoring, and evaluation. Failure to agree on a format will complicate and weaken the comparison of assessments, and of assessments against monitoring activities and later evaluations. Appropriate ways of recording monitoring results should be developed for each activity.

The following sections and sub-sections provide a further level of detail, expanding on the report structure described in table 4(a).

table 4(a): **SAME report structure**

SAME report structure
title page author country, district/region of programme name/branch of organisation date report number, including revision numbers
executive summary summarise the situation, the aims of the report, and its conclusions
table of contents include list of acronyms include lists of tables, figures, and appendices
description of the situation describe the SAME framework agreement for the operation describe any wider process planned nationally or regionally
reason for the assessment, monitoring, or evaluation clear statements of the aims and objectives (4.2.2) anticipation of the form of the results

step 1: why?
describe the role of this report in these processes
describe aims and objectives of the report, including the reasons why it was
initiated, and any expectations of its conclusions (4.2.2)

step 2: when?
describe how the SAME programme was developed (4.3.1)
give a report of the timeframe for SAME programmes (4.3.2)

step 3: what?
criteria used, and why (4.4.1)
sample of information to illustrate what was done
weaknesses and challenges, problems and solutions
possible inclusion of data collected in appendices

step 4: how?
describe which analysis methods were chosen, and why (4.5.1)
describe the bias encountered during the SAME programme (4.5.7)
describe how the information was analysed (4.5.7)

results
describe the profile developed (see 2.2), summarising the results in a framework
    which can be used for future decision making
report key successes of the operation and major obstacles to it

conclusions
summary of results
lessons learned, good practices
future steps in SAME programme
further SAME activities required, in addition to those already agreed
relevance of the organisation's operations within the country and emergency
    contexts
appropriateness of process and management of interventions
sustainability of the interventions, ability to benefit from collaboration between
    agencies
partnership strategies
recommendations to the aid organisation
recommendations to other stakeholders

appendices
a list of organisations and individuals consulted
original data collected during SAME programmes
full methodologies and SAME programme design
maps and other reference material
previous relevant reports and other documents reviewed
terms of reference and itinerary for the field visits

4.2 step 1: why?

It is essential to identify all existing assessment, monitoring, and evaluation programmes that refer to the displacement situation. From this background material, the reasons for undertaking a new programme, or programme activity, should be developed and agreed by all stakeholders.

4.2.1 other assessment programmes

Previous and on-going programmes for assessment, monitoring, and evaluation should be identified, in order to inform the scope of the programme proposed. Other programmes may have been undertaken: by other stakeholders, including host governments; by professionals in other sectors, such as health; for other purposes, such as for regional economic development; and at different times, such as during a contingency planning phase.

Relevant sections from other programme reports should be included in the SAME report. All other programme reports should be referenced, and a copy kept for future reference.

4.2.2 current assessment programme

It is essential to understand the aims and objectives of the programme, and of every assessment, monitoring, and evaluation activity within it.

aims The programme aims should be a brief statement of the desired end-state within the displacement situation: for example, 'To achieve safe transitional settlement for the displaced population without a negative impact on their hosts'.

objectives The programme objectives should add detail to the programme's aims by describing specific opportunities or constraints in the particular displacement situation: for example, one objective might be to achieve security, if the displaced population appears to have settled temporarily too close to an area of conflict.

Assessment and monitoring are important, in order to elicit feedback with which to inform improvements to programmes. The results of the first assessment should be used to question its aims and objectives. Changes in the aims and objectives should be recorded and explained, to inform any later changes and the interpretation of results.

The aims and objectives may be as brief as two paragraphs, but the process of agreeing them should be as inclusive as possible. All stakeholders in the programme, including representatives from the displaced and host populations, should be presented with a proposal for the aims and objectives of the programme. The views of each stakeholder should be sought. When possible, later consultations with stakeholders – as many as is practical – should be undertaken, to agree the criteria appropriate to achieving the objectives, and to seek opinions on which tool might be most appropriate, given the operational conditions, for the gathering of information for each criterion.

Negotiating agreement with all stakeholders on the reasons why the assessment, monitoring, and evaluation programme is being undertaken will improve several aspects of the programme: participation by stakeholders; the general understanding of the assumptions behind the activities, especially by staff who were not present when the programme was established; and the clarity of design and reporting of the activities.

4.3 step 2: when?

Programmes should be designed appropriately for each displacement situation, each placing different emphasis on activities such as monitoring, and each identifying appropriate stages in assessment and evaluation. The design of the programme schedule will be determined by the human, transport, financial, and time resources available.

4.3.1 developing an assessment programme

Efficient assessment, monitoring, and evaluation programmes involve a wide variety of stakeholders, in addition to the programme team. Undertaking such a programme will affect the wider operational response, by sensitising those involved, and by creating expectations. Programmes should therefore be a conversational relationship between the programme team and all stakeholders, offering opportunities to react to new information or circumstances, and to correct any misunderstanding caused by the programme itself, or by the operational response.

list and disaggregate stakeholders

Developing a programme should begin by listing the stakeholders and their interests in transitional settlement and shelter. Each stakeholder group should be disaggregated, so that smaller groups with special interests are recognised and included. For example, groups of single mothers or single young men should be considered, because these groups may be disproportionate in size and may be affected disproportionately by later operational decisions, if they are not consulted early on, and if their specific interests are not considered. The disaggregation of assessments is part of the ninth guidance note in the Sphere Common Standard 2 on initial assessment (Sphere Project 2004).

list resources and constraints

A list should be made of the resources and constraints of the programme, and the list should be analysed to determine which elements are likely to be most important. Resources and constraints may include the people who might be involved in an assessment team, the condition of the roads, the time available, security factors, or the monsoon season.

compose the programme

A programme comprises a series of activities, usually including a number of assessments, one or more monitoring procedures, and interim and final evaluations. It is necessary to determine the number and type of activities most appropriate to the displacement situation, and the resources and constraints present. Consult or involve as many stakeholders as possible, in order to maximise the feasibility of the programme, and its appropriateness to the aims and objectives agreed in step 1.

4.3.2 scheduling an assessment programme

Once the composition of the programme is agreed, and the resources and constraints are understood, a schedule should be developed. This schedule should present each activity in detail, including a description of objectives, likely duration, the team involved, other stakeholders participating, and probable constraints.

identify milestones

The major events, or 'milestones', in a programme should be agreed by the planning team. These milestones can be used to mark out the schedule into planning steps that are appropriate to the programme. An example milestone might be the onset of a season with specific additional requirements such as winter, which may in turn lead to the question of whether the host population can host all of the displaced families over the cold period, or whether other options should be explored. These decisions are linked to the objectives identified in step 1.

develop the schedule

A number of activities may run concurrently, or may be dependent on each other or on external circumstances, such as a donor's financial year, or a cold winter. Potential conflicts may be highlighted by visualising the programme schedule, either through a 'schedule of operations' diagram, such as that proposed in 2.3.3, or through a 'schedule of works', such as that described in 6.2.1.

4.4 step 3: what?

Each assessment, monitoring, or evaluation team will need to identify and agree with stakeholders the questions that are most appropriate to the displacement situation. Some questions will be so important that they will need to be verified by use of a variety of sources. Some questions will be suitable to act as indicators of change or success in the programme.

4.4.1 selecting criteria for assessment

Different questions, or criteria, are important in different displacement situations, and in different phases and for different groups. It is important, therefore, to identify which criteria are the most important for the assessment, monitoring, or evaluation activity.

use the core criteria as the basis

The SAME method presents a list of core criteria (4.4.2) common to most displacement situations, to act as a basis for selecting criteria. To simplify comparison with other assessments, monitoring processes, and evaluations, the criteria are grouped into five categories, following 'the livelihoods approach' (1.6.1):

- social and political capital (4.4.3)
- human capital (4.4.4)
- natural capital (4.4.5)
- physical capital (4.4.6)
- financial capital (4.4.7).

In the following tables of criteria categories (sections 4.4.3–4.4.7), the core criteria (4.4.2) are included again at the top of each category table. The core criteria are likely to be relevant to every situation, while additional criteria from the other criteria in each category should be selected if they are relevant to the specific situation.

The core criteria can produce only a basic understanding of the situation. Other criteria should be added to them to make the assessment, monitoring, or evaluation more accurate and more appropriate.

Checklists of other more detailed criteria are presented in sections 4.4.3–4.4.7, based on the same livelihoods categories. These detailed criteria have been developed for different situations, for example for cold climates, for collective centres, or for the emergency phase only.

The criteria on the checklist should be used as a basis of discussion with the programme team and other stakeholders, in order to agree a list of criteria appropriate to the situation. The criteria listed are suggestions only, and they are not exhaustive: new criteria should be included, if they are more appropriate to the situation; or the suggested criteria should be modified. Other situation-specific criteria may be found in other sources, such as the following:

- standard procedures of aid organisations
- other recent assessment, monitoring, or evaluation activities in the region, especially those involving transitional settlement
- assessment, monitoring, or evaluation activities in other sectors of operation, such as health services.

It is important to identify the most important criteria and to investigate them thoroughly, rather than simply collecting large amounts of data.

Prioritisation of criteria can be made easier by considering the decisions that the assessment, monitoring, or evaluation activities should inform. But take care not to limit the scope of the activities to the extent that the results are affected: it is a mistake to design an assessment, for example, which concludes only with the results that the assessors wish to find (4.5.7).

The tools for collecting the information to respond to these criteria are presented in section 4.5 as 'step 4: how?'.

4.4.2 core criteria for assessments

table 4(b): core criteria for assessments

criterion number	core criteria: basic questions for your programme*
A	**social and political capital**
A.1	What caused the displacement?
A.2	Is the cause of the displacement still putting the displaced or host population at risk?
A.3	Is the displaced population settling at a safe distance from the cause of the displacement?
A.4	When did the displacement occur?
A.5	What are the characteristics of the displacement? How severe is the damage? What is the extent of the losses? What are the likely short-term and long-term needs? How many people are affected, and how many regions, districts, or cities?
A.6	What geographic areas and locations have been affected?
A.7	What are the cultural and religious backgrounds of the displaced and host populations? (Disaggregate the populations according to ethnicities and religions, if relevant to the displacement.)
A.8	Has there been previous contact between the displaced and host populations?
B	**human capital**
B.1	How many people are affected, and what proportion of the overall population is this? If possible, identify the sex, age, and other demographic details of the affected population.
B.2	How big is the host population, and how is it organised?
B.3	How many deaths have been attributed to this displacement? What is the source of this information?

4 assessment

continued ...

table 4(b): core criteria for assessments (cont.)

criterion number	core criteria: basic questions for your programme*
B.4	How many injuries have been attributed to this displacement? If possible, specify the sexes and ages of those injured, and the causes.
B.5	How many people are displaced or evacuated? Where they have gone? If possible, specify the sex, age, and family composition of those affected.
B.6	How many families are affected?
C	**natural capital**
C.1	Are there sufficient resources for construction materials?
C.2	Where are the nearest sources for procuring construction materials in the region?
D	**physical capital**
D.1	How many households or dwellings have been completely destroyed?
D.2	How many households or dwellings are partly damaged but not completely destroyed?
D.3	What are the immediate needs of the displaced and host population, and who will respond to them? Describe the unmet needs for shelter, water, sanitation, food, household supplies, and health. Quantify and qualify the targeted needs.
D.4	What will be needed in the longer term, and who will supply it (after the first month)?
E	**financial capital**
E.1	What resources and capacities do the local population have for responding to this disaster, and how might these resources be used?
E.2	What storage and transport facilities are available locally for immediate use? (Include commercial vehicles, and those belonging to government and the aid community.)
E.3	What is the physical and/or financial damage to other property, buildings, and infrastructure in the affected area?
E.4	What is the physical and/or financial damage to crops and livestock?
E.5	What are the expected financial damage and costs to businesses in the affected area?
	(adapted from IFRC 2000)*

4.4.3 criteria for assessing social and political capital

table 4(c): criteria for assessing social and political capital

criterion number	criteria: questions to consider including in your programme	step 4 how?
A	**social and political capital**	
A.1	What caused the displacement?	PLA …
A.2	Is the cause of the displacement still putting the displaced or the host population at risk?	POP …
A.3	Is the displaced population settling at a safe distance from the cause of the displacement?	
A.4	When did the displacement occur?	
A.5	What are the characteristics of the displacement? How severe is the damage? What is the extent of the losses, and what are the likely short-term and long-term needs? How many people are affected, and how many regions, districts, or cities?	
A.6	What geographic areas and locations have been affected?	
A.7	What are the cultural and religious backgrounds of the displaced and host populations? Disaggregate the populations according to ethnicities and religions, if relevant to the displacement.	
A.8	Have the displaced and host populations been in contact before?	
A.9	What is the distance to the border/conflict area? Do any displaced groups need relocation to a safer area?	
A.10	Is there a pattern of previous displacement and migration? Is there a history of relations between the populations? Are the cultural customs of the populations compatible?	
A.11	How does the local population react to the influx of displaced people? Are information / awareness campaigns being organised?	
A.12	How does displacement affect the displaced population's traditional support networks?	
A.13	How do the living standards of the local and potentially displaced populations compare?	
A.14	What are the issues of concern for the host community?	
A.15	Has a strategy for providing assistance been agreed with the local authority?	

4 assessment

continued ...

criterion number	criteria: questions to consider including in your programme	step 4 how?
A.16	What is the legal context of the country in which the aid organisation operates? Are there any national rules and regulations to be known and followed, such as labour laws, town-planning regulations, etc.?	
A.17	Have risks been clearly marked out and/or explained to the incoming displaced population?	
A.18	Will there be a risk to the local population in being associated with displaced families (and vice versa)?	
A.19	Can existing local administrative structures be used to identify beneficiaries?	
A.20	Can displaced communities help aid organisations to identify vulnerable beneficiaries?	
A.21	Is there positive interaction between the displaced and local populations (and within the displaced community)?	
A.22	How can external assistance be targeted to mitigate any negative impacts of displacement on local people?	
A.23	Are means of conflict-mitigation available to displaced and host populations?	
A.24	Is there a risk to the local population in being associated with displaced families (and vice versa?)	
A.25	How can the displaced population be helped to recreate their familiar living environment?	
A.26	Have representatives of both local and displaced groups been identified, and involved whenever possible in decisions affecting the communities?	
A.27	Are regular meetings held with all the stakeholder groups?	
A.28	Have all remaining responsibilities been transferred to the appropriate people/organisations?	
A.29	(host families) Can existing local administrative structures be used to identify host families and their properties?	
A.30	(host families) Are mechanisms in place to assign incoming displaced groups to host families?	
A.31	(host families) What are the options for compensating host families?	
A.32	(host families) How will support for the hosted family be accompanied by benefits for the hosting family?	
A.33	(host families) What are the expectations of the host population?	

continued ...

criterion number	criteria: questions to consider including in your programme	step 4 how?
A.34	*(host families)* Will there be a risk to the host family in being associated with displaced families (and vice versa?)	
A.35	*(host families)* Does each host family understand and agree that the programme has been completed?	
A.36	*(rural self-settlement)* Are distribution centres needed to support the displaced?	
A.37	*(rural self-settlement)* What provisions are available for vulnerable individuals who cannot reach distribution centres?	
A.38	*(rural self-settlement)* What is the most effective way to continue supporting the self-settled population?	
A.39	*(rural self-settlement)* Can representatives of both communities be identified, and involved in decision making?	
A.40	*(urban self-settlement)* Are informal or illegal settlements/slums politically sensitive? How will this affect the assistance given?	
A.41	*(urban self-settlement)* Do the local authorities (formal and informal) have pre-existing plans for informal or slum settlements?	
A.42	*(urban self-settlement)* If upgrading informal settlements, is such support provided equally to the local and displaced populations to avoid tensions?	
A.43	*(urban self-settlement)* In consultation with the existing urban administration, consider how capacity can be built.	
A.44	*(urban self-settlement)* What responsibilities (such as refuse collection) can local administrators take on/continue?	
A.45	*(urban self-settlement)* What is the most effective way to continue supporting the self-settled urban population?	
A.46	*(urban self-settlement)* Can representatives of both communities be identified, and involved in decision-making, to facilitate communication and collaboration?	
A.47	*(urban self-settlement)* What arrangements can be made to allow displaced people access to existing social services?	
A.48	*(urban self-settlement)* If existing administration is weak, how can its capacity be developed?	
A.49	*(collective centres)* How does the local population currently use the structure under consideration?	

4 assessment

continued ...

criterion number	criteria: questions to consider including in your programme	step 4 how?
A.50	*(collective centres)* What will be the densities and locations of collective centres? How will they affect and interact with the surrounding environment and local people?	
A.51	*(collective centres)* Can the local population afford the temporary loss of this structure? If the centre is a school, where will the local children be educated?	
A.52	*(collective centres)* How can the local community be involved in making decisions about collective centres?	
A.53	*(collective centres)* What are the chances of the centre becoming a focus for hostilities – or a safe haven?	
A.54	*(collective centres)* Is there a deadline when the collective centre's structure and facilities must be returned to their original use? What are the rights concerning ownership, access, utilities, and services? Is there an agreement about the end-condition in which the building must be left?	
A.55	*(collective centres)* How can the local population be compensated in the short term for the loss of the collective-centre structure?	
A.56	*(collective centres)* What work can be found for staff who previously worked at the building used for the collective centre?	
A.57	*(collective centres)* Are representatives of the displaced population involved in the functioning and maintenance of the collective centre, and are they party to agreements on its use?	
A.58	*(collective centres)* Are regular and accountable community meetings held, where representations can be made by the local and displaced groups?	
A.59	*(collective centres)* Can representatives of both communities be identified, and involved in decision-making, to facilitate communication and collaboration?	
A.60	*(collective centres)* Does living in a collective centre limit access to income-generating activities? How can this be remedied?	
A.61	*(collective centres)* Do vulnerable groups tend to settle in collective centres, and are they more isolated as a result?	

continued ...

criterion number	criteria: questions to consider including in your programme	step 4 how?
A.62	*(collective centres)* Has the collective centre been returned to its original function? If not, what provisions have been made for local population for the loss of the use of the centre? Are these provisions still satisfactory?	
A.63	*(collective centres)* Are targets for the planned life-span of the collective centre being continually re-assessed and re-evaluated?	
A.64	*(collective centres)* How do seasonal changes (e.g. the start of a new school year) affect the local needs for the structure that is being used as a collective centre?	
A.65	*(collective centres)* Has all compensation for use of the collective centre, agreed in the contingency phase, been paid? Are all parties satisfied within the handover?	
A.66	*(self-settled camps)* How can the local population be compensated for the loss of their land to the self-settled camp?	
A.67	*(self-settled camps)* How can the land be returned in better condition to the local community when the emergency is over?	
A.68	*(self-settled camps)* Can the local population be offered access to communal camp facilities (such as clinics) as a form of compensation?	
A.69	*(self-settled camps)* Whose land is being used for the self-settled camp? Have agreements on the use of land and a timeframe for its occupancy been formalised?	
A.70	*(self-settled camps)* Can existing administrative structures be used to keep a register of the displaced population? Is the local administration informed about the projects, and involved in them?	
A.71	*(self-settled camps)* In what ways can the original social / geographical organisation of displaced community be maintained if the camp is upgraded / extended?	
A.72	*(planned camps)* Have expansion sites / options been identified in case influx numbers are greater than expected?	
A.73	*(planned camps)* Can contingency capacity be created in advance of a population influx? Have the financial implications been considered?	
A.74	*(planned camps)* How can contingency and preparedness planning be co-ordinated between the agencies?	

4 assessment

continued ...

criterion number	criteria: questions to consider including in your programme	step 4 how?
A.75	*(planned camps)* Has consideration been given to how the camp will be managed? Are decisions being documented properly, for future reference?	
A.76	*(planned camps)* How can the local population be compensated for the loss of land to the planned camp?	
A.77	*(planned camps)* How can the land be returned in better condition to the local community when the emergency is over?	
A.78	*(planned camps)* can the local population be offered access to communal camp facilities (such as clinics) as a form of compensation?	
A.79	*(planned camps)* If assets are to eventually be handed over to the local community, are they being designed and constructed to high standards of durability?	
A.80	*(planned camps)* Have agreements on the use of land and the timeframe of use been formalised with the local authorities/owners?	
A.81	*(planned camps)* Are all groups in the camp represented in the decision-making process?	
A.82	*(planned camps)* Can the camp be geographically organised to reflect the original social organisation of the community?	
A.83	*(planned camps)* Or can families be allocated plots near to other families whom they knew before displacement?	
A.84	*(planned camps)* Can the displaced population be involved in construction activities and helped to access local markets?	
A.85	*(planned camps)* Can the camp be geographically organised to reflect the original social organisation of the community?	
A.86	*(planned camps)* Is an accurate profile of all groups within the displaced population being maintained?	
A.87	*(planned camps)* Are the displaced population reluctant to leave the camp at the end of the emergency? If so, are plans in place to address their concerns and support the return process?	

4.4.4 criteria for assessing human capital

table 4(d): criteria for assessing human capital

criterion number	criteria: questions to consider including in your programme	step 4 how?
B	human capital	
B.1	How many people are affected, and what proportion of the overall population is this number? If possible, also identify the sexes, ages, and other demographic details of the population affected.	
B.2	How big is the host population, and how is it organised?	
B.3	How many deaths have been attributed to this displacement? What is the source of this information?	
B.4	How many injuries have been attributed to this displacement? If possible, specify the sex and age of those affected, and the causes of their injuries.	
B.5	How many people are displaced or evacuated? Where they have gone? If possible, specify the sex, age, and family composition of those affected.	
B.6	How many families are affected?	
B.7	What are the immediate needs of the displaced and host populations? Who will respond to them? What are the unmet needs for shelter, water, sanitation, food, household supplies, and health services? Quantify and qualify the targeted needs.	
B.8	What will be needed in the longer term (after the first month), and who will supply it?	
B.9	Are both host and displaced populations at a safe distance from the cause of displacement?	
B.10	Will there be a risk to the local population in being associated with displaced families (and vice versa)?	
B.11	What is the current influx rate? How is it likely to change in the near future? How can variations in influx be accommodated?	
B.12	How is the risk of disease affected by the increase in population density?	
B.13	What are the immediate health needs of the incoming population? How can the local health-care systems be supported to cope with the population influx?	

4 assessment

continued ...

criterion number	criteria: questions to consider including in your programme	step 4 how?
B.14	What are the nature and proportions of occupations and skills within the host and displaced populations?	
B.15	Would tools and skills training be useful?	
B.16	Do the host and displaced populations speak the same language?	
B.17	What is the background and structure of the populations? Socio-economic groupings? Rural/urban proportions?	
B.18	What are the demographics of both populations? Total number; number and size of family units; sex ratios; age distribution; unusual patterns; variations over time; distribution over space.	
B.19	Which individuals are potentially vulnerable? What is the cause and nature of vulnerabilities? How can the cause of vulnerability be reduced?	
B.20	Will vulnerabilities change over time?	
B.21	Are efforts being made to reduce any physical/sexual abuse and financial exploitation within and between the populations?	
B.22	Are mechanisms in place to monitor and identify beneficiaries, including vulnerable groups, during influx?	
B.23	How can the local health-care systems be supported to cope with the population influx?	
B.24	Can knowledge of the local language by displaced individuals be harnessed to improve communications?	
B.25	How can displaced individuals be trained to help to implement the aid programmes?	
B.26	Have skills been transferred from the aid community to those permanently based in the area?	
B.27	(host families) Can displaced families/individuals be placed with host families in a manner that is culturally/economically compatible?	
B.28	(rural self-settlement) Does the self-settled population have adequate access to services for health checks and treatment?	
B.29	(rural self-settlement) Do all members of the self-settled population have access to medical advice and help?	
B.30	(urban self-settlement) Does the self-settled population have adequate access to services for health checks and treatment?	

continued ...

criterion number	criteria: questions to consider including in your programme	step 4 how?
B.31	*(urban self-settlement)* Do all the self-settled people have access to medical advice and help? Can water and sanitation infrastructures be up-graded in informal settlement areas?	
B.32	*(collective centres)* Are the displaced population uncomfortable for cultural reasons to share internal/external space?	
B.33	*(collective centres)* Is there a proposed maximum length of time for individuals to stay in the collective centre?	
B.34	*(collective centres)* How can structures be modified to support cultural norms (e.g. to ensure privacy for girls and women)? Can people of the same ethnic group/cultural background be sheltered in the same collective centre?	
B.35	*(collective centres)* What measures are in place to prevent communicable diseases? What are the immediate health needs of the incoming population?	
B.36	*(collective centres)* Do vulnerable groups tend to settle in collective centres and thus become more isolated from mainstream society? What exit plans exist to facilitate transfer of vulnerable groups to a durable solution?	
B.37	*(collective centres)* Do all occupants of the collective centre have access to adequate medical advice and help?	
B.38	*(collective centres)* For how long have individuals been staying in the collective centre? How does the population in the collective centre change over time, as families/groups leave for or arrive from other settlement options?	
B.39	*(collective centres)* Do those who formerly lived in the collective centre have support (such as tents) to make the transition to durable solutions?	
B.40	*(self-settled camps)* Can the self-settled camp be reorganised to reduce the density of occupation? Is an adequate health and sanitation infrastructure in place?	
B.41	*(self-settled camps)* If the displaced population are seeking asylum, has UNHCR been informed?	
B.42	*(self-settled camps)* How many transit or reception centres are needed to deal with incoming displaced population?	

4 assessment

continued ...

criterion number	criteria: questions to consider including in your programme	step 4 how?
B.43	*(self-settled camps)* How can displaced children best be provided with education: local school system or unofficial in-camp schooling?	
B.44	*(self-settled camps)* Do all the self-settled population have access to medical advice and help?	
B.45	*(planned camps)* Are health-screening facilities in place for new arrivals?	
B.46	*(planned camps)* What structures could be used as reception or transit centres?	
B.47	*(planned camps)* How can the camp be planned to reduce density of occupation and risk of disease? Is an adequate health and sanitation infrastructure in place? Are vaccination campaigns necessary? Should medical equipment – e.g. family bed nets – be distributed?	
B.48	*(planned camps)* If the displaced population are seeking asylum, has UNCHR been informed? Are new arrivals being registered and screened (for example, to distinguish combatants from civilians)?	
B.49	*(planned camps)* How can access to schooling for the displaced children be best supported: local school system or unofficial in-camp schooling? If the local and displaced populations share a language, can the displaced take part in local activities?	
B.50	*(planned camps)* Do all the camp occupants have access to adequate medical advice? Are existing local health-care facilities available to the displaced? If so, how can the facilities be supported to cope with the population influx?	

4.4.5 criteria for assessing natural capital

table 4(e): criteria for assessing natural capital

criterion number	criteria: questions to consider including in your programme	step 4 how?
C	natural capital	
C.1	Are there sufficient supplies of construction materials?	
C.2	Where are the nearest sources for procuring construction materials in the region?	
C.3	What are the risks from natural hazards and other extreme events?	
C.4	What will be the effect of increased population density on water, food, and energy resources?	
C.5	What are the usual weather conditions (including variations over time)?	
C.6	What are the seasonal or cyclic weather conditions?	
C.7	What are the local regulations and strategies for procuring construction materials? Does materials procurement destabilise local markets or natural-resources bases?	
C.8	What are the short-term and long-term environmental impacts of the population increase in the area?	
C.9	How can key resources (water, food, and energy) be sustained in the long term? What role can both populations, and local authorities, play in the management of natural resources?	
C.10	Can land be obtained, if necessary, for displaced people's livelihood strategies?	
C.11	What are the risks from natural hazards and other extreme events (e.g. earthquakes, fire, industrial accidents)?	
C.12	How much edible food is available and accessible? Are food supplies safe to collect? How does food availability vary over time? How sustainable is the food supply?	
C.13	What is the availability and accessibility of fuel? Are fuel supplies safe to collect? Is the fuel supply sustainable? If there is an electricity supply, what is its capacity?	

4 assessment

continued ...

criterion number	criteria: questions to consider including in your programme	step 4 how?
C.14	How much potable water is available and accessible? Is it safe to collect? What are the variations in water availability over time? Is the water supply sustainable?	
C.15	What resources can be supplied to the displaced population in order to prevent environmental degradation and the depletion of natural resources?	
C.16	Can land be obtained, if necessary, for displaced population livelihood strategies? How can the quality of the land be improved for both populations? What is the timeframe for the use of the land?	
C.17	What will be the effect of increased population density on water, food, and energy resources?	
C.18	What have been the negative environmental impacts of the programme, and how can they be reversed before the end of the programme?	
C.19	*(rural self-settlement)* What land is available for self-settlement? Who are the owners of the land, and what is the current land use? Is there an official list of land and property ownership? Are potential sites prone to security risks and natural hazards?	
C.20	*(urban self-settlement)* What land and buildings are available for self-settlement? Who are the owners of the land, and what is the current land use? Is there an official list of land and property ownership? Are potential sites prone to security risks and natural hazards?	
C.21	*(urban self-settlement)* Have unsafe buildings and roads been clearly marked as such before the displaced people arrive?	
C.22	*(urban self-settlement)* What are the risks from pollution (e.g. river effluent) in the urban area?	
C.23	*(self-settled camps)* What land is available for self-settled camps?	
C.24	*(self-settled camps)* Who are the owners of the land, and what is the current land use? Is there an official list of land and property ownership?	

continued ...

criterion number	criteria: questions to consider including in your programme	step 4 how?
C.25	*(self-settled camps)* Are potential sites prone to security risks and natural hazards?	
C.26	*(self-settled camps)* Can land be obtained, if necessary, for displaced people's livelihood strategies? How can the quality of the land be improved for both populations? What is the timeframe for the use of the land?	
C.27	*(planned camps)* What are the risks from natural hazards and other extreme events? e.g. earthquakes, fire, industrial accidents	
C.28	*(planned camps)* How can the quality of the land be improved for both populations?	
C.29	*(planned camps)* What have been the negative environmental impacts of the programme, and how can they be reversed before the programme ends?	

4.4.6 criteria for assessing physical capital

table 4(f): criteria for assessing physical capital

criterion number	criteria: questions to consider including in your programme	step 4 how?
D	physical capital	
D.1	How many households or dwellings have been completely destroyed?	
D.2	How many households or dwellings have been partially damaged but not completely destroyed?	
D.3	How many people are without any shelter, or with inadequate shelter? Where are they?	
D.4	How accessible is the area where the displaced population is? Is access affected by weather conditions?	
D.5	Who is the owner of the land where the displaced population has settled? Is there an existing cadastral record? If not, who is the current owner of the land and what is the current use?	
D.6	Is additional service infrastructure needed in order to cope with the increased population in the area?	

continued ...

criterion number	criteria: questions to consider including in your programme	step 4 how?
D.7	What possessions have the displaced population brought with them?	
D.8	What non-food items need to be provided for displaced individuals? (clothing, bedding and blankets, hygiene products, cooking and eating utensils, vector-control measures, etc.)	
D.9	What additional items are considered socially and culturally important for maintaining the health and dignity of the affected people?	
D.10	How does the community structure of the host population compare with that of the displaced population?	
D.11	What are the local regulations and strategies for procuring construction materials?	
D.12	Have reusable assets been recovered for later operations?	
D.13	Is the accommodation of the displaced population of sufficient quality (e.g. in terms of ventilation, protection from insects) to protect individuals from health hazards? Are living spaces weather-proofed? What level of security and privacy do people have? Are the levels of security and privacy acceptable to the displaced individuals?	
D.14	Do the displaced individuals have the necessary tools to earn a living and/or cope with displacement? What are the space and storage requirements for income-generating activities?	
D.15	How can communal infrastructure (schools, roads, etc.) be upgraded to reduce tensions over increased use?	
D.16	How does the community structure of the local population compare with that of the displaced population?	
D.17	What infrastructure/assets can be handed over to the local population or local authorities?	
D.18	Have reusable assets been recovered for later operations?	
D.19	*(host families)* How easy will access be to the host/hosted populations? Will access be affected by weather conditions?	
D.20	*(host families)* What means will be used to communicate with hosted families?	
D.21	*(host families)* Will additional service infrastructure be needed in host-family areas?	

continued ...

criterion number	criteria: questions to consider including in your programme	step 4 how?
D.22	*(host families)* How can displaced individuals be physically accommodated in the host- family household?	
D.23	*(host families)* What assets can be retained by the host population on a family-by-family basis?	
D.24	*(rural self-settlement)* How easy will access be to the self-settled populations?	
D.25	*(rural self-settlement)* What means will be used to communicate with self-settled individuals?	
D.26	*(rural self-settlement)* Will additional service infrastructure be needed for the self-settled population?	
D.27	*(rural self-settlement)* What are the requirements and constraints of local-authority regulations when shelters are under construction?	
D.28	*(rural self-settlement)* What basic tools for constructing, maintaining, or repairing shelters are available to the displaced people?	
D.29	*(urban self-settlement)* How easy or difficult will access to the self-settled populations be?	
D.30	*(urban self-settlement)* What means will be used to communicate with urban self-settled individuals?	
D.31	*(urban self-settlement)* What structures can be used as distribution centres if necessary?	
D.32	*(urban self-settlement)* Will additional service infrastructure be needed for the self-settled population?	
D.33	*(urban self-settlement)* What are the requirements and constraints of local-authority regulations when shelters are under construction?	
D.34	*(urban self-settlement)* Is the accommodation of the displaced population of sufficient quality (e.g. in terms of ventilation, protection from insects) to protect individuals from health hazards? Are living spaces weather-proofed?	
D.35	*(urban self-settlement)* What degree of security and privacy do people have? Can the displaced population be helped to construct shelters? Help with construction materials? Help with designs? Training in construction techniques?	

4 assessment

continued ...

criterion number	criteria: questions to consider including in your programme	step 4 how?
D.36	*(urban self-settlement)* What basic tools for constructing, maintaining, or repairing shelters are available to the displaced people?	
D.37	*(collective centres)* What are appropriate accommodation standards for the collective centre? (Consider local and international regulations and local and displaced lifestyles.)	
D.38	*(collective centres)* Are local contractors available to convert, maintain, and repair collective centres? Can stand-by agreements be formed and can tendering take place in preparation for an influx?	
D.39	*(collective centres)* Who owns the collective centre? Is it public or private? With whom should its proposed use be negotiated?	
D.40	*(collective centres)* What structures/facilities (in private or government ownership) are available for use as collective centres? Is the structure or facility appropriate in terms of size, internal/external space, etc.?	
D.41	*(collective centres)* Is the building structurally safe? Do emergency exits, gas/electricity installations etc. meet general safety regulations?	
D.42	*(collective centres)* Will additional service infrastructure be needed for the population in the collective centre?	
D.43	*(collective centres)* Are spaces reserved in the collective centre for meetings?	
D.44	*(collective centres)* Can displaced persons be employed under external contracts in the conversion, maintenance, or repair of the collective centre?	
D.45	*(collective centres)* Can local contractors be involved in conversion, maintenance, and repair of collective centres?	
D.46	*(self-settled camps)* How easy or difficult will access to the self-settled populations be?	
D.47	*(self-settled camps)* Which local businesses could be used for materials procurement?	
D.48	*(self-settled camps)* Will additional service infrastructure be needed for the self-settled population?	

continued ...

criterion number	criteria: questions to consider including in your programme	step 4 how?
D.49	*(self-settled camps)* What are the requirements and constraints of local-authority regulations when shelters are under construction?	
D.50	*(self-settled camps)* Is a particular area viable (in terms of natural resources, security, access, etc.) for self-settled camps?	
D.51	*(self-settled camps)* Can the site and settlement chosen by the displaced individuals be supported and improved? Or does the settlement need to be moved to another site? (due to proximity to conflict, risks from natural hazards etc.) Have alternative sites/settlement options been identified in case the current site becomes unstable/too small, etc.?	
D.52	*(self-settled camps)* What basic tools are available to the displaced people for constructing, maintaining, or repairing shelters?	
D.53	*(self-settled camps)* Do the existing camps meet international standards (concerning density of occupation, for example)?	
D.54	*(planned camps)* How easy or difficult is access to the planned camp site? How can the road infrastructure be improved, if access will be difficult?	
D.55	*(planned camps)* Will access be affected by weather conditions?	
D.56	*(planned camps)* How will food and non-food items be distributed? What infrastructure/centres will be needed to support this?	
D.57	*(planned camps)* Which local businesses could be used for the sustainable procurement of materials? What are the local regulations for the local procurement and harvesting of construction materials? What is likely to be the demand for materials? Can the local economy sustain this demand? Or will demand drive prices out of the reach of the local population?	
D.58	*(planned camps)* Will additional service infrastructure be needed to support the planned camp?	
D.59	*(planned camps)* What are the local housing standards? If they are below minimum international standards, can upgrading programmes for the local population be implemented after the emergency phase?	

4 assessment

continued ...

criterion number	criteria: questions to consider including in your programme	step 4 how?
D.60	*(planned camps)* What sites are available for planned camps? What are the advantages and disadvantages of each site in terms of natural resources, access, security etc.? Are contingency sites available as a back-up option?	
D.61	*(planned camps)* Have alternative sites/settlement options been identified in case the current site becomes unstable/too small etc.? Is the site being developed to keep pace with the influx rate?	
D.62	*(planned camps)* Have sites been identified to accommodate new influxes and natural population growth without straining local resources or relations with local population?	
D.63	*(planned camps)* What is the effect of materials procurement on the local economy and resource base, and on local prices?	
D.64	*(planned camps)* After infrastructure has been handed over, how might it be used by the local population?	

4.4.7 criteria for assessing financial capital

table 4(g): criteria for assessing financial capital

criterion number	criteria: questions to consider including in your programme	step 4 how?
E	financial capital	
E.1	What resources and capacities do the local population have for responding to this disaster, and how might these resources be used?	
E.2	What transport and storage facilities (commercial, government-owned, Red Cross/Red Crescent, etc.) are available locally for immediate use?	
E.3	What is the physical and/or financial damage to other property, buildings, and infrastructure in the affected area?	
E.4	What is the physical and/or financial damage to crops and livestock?	
E.5	What are the expected financial damages and costs to businesses in the affected area?	
E.6	Does materials procurement destabilise local markets or natural-resource bases?	
E.7	How important is the cash economy? Is micro-credit available?	
E.8	What is the nature of both the informal and formal economies? market places? range of goods and services? availability of credit? opportunities and constraints? illegal activities/law enforcement (in the informal economies)? How do the displaced workers affect the labour market?	
E.9	Do the displaced people incur significant debts which could lead to exploitation by local people?	
E.10	(host families) Do the financial resources of the displaced population become depleted by payment for hosted accommodation?	
E.11	Is it possible to assist the displaced population to procure shelter or construction materials?	
E.12	(collective centres) Are individual partitioned spaces within the collective centre secure? Is secure shelter available for income-generating activities or for livestock?	

4 assessment

4.4.8 checklist of criteria for assessment, monitoring, and evaluation

The criteria in this checklist are partly included in the livelihoods lists presented in the previous sections (4.4.3–4.4.7). The checklist offers a summary of likely criteria and has been compiled in order to assist the development of monitoring and evaluation activities.

table 4(h): summary of criteria for assessment, monitoring, and evaluation

criterion	criteria: questions to consider including in your programme	
	Who is accountable?	
	Which departments of the organisation have management responsibilities for performance?	
	What are the benchmarks against which the agency's performance is to be verified (inter-agency references on good practice and/or internal agency references)?	
	What evaluation mechanisms have been put in place by the agencies or donors to increase the accountability of the process?	
	Does the proposal relate to the agency's mandate (e.g. saving lives, relieving human suffering, reducing the economic impact of natural and human-caused disasters, etc.)?	
	Are the standard evaluation tools in current use by the aid organisation sufficient for ensuring accountability, or do they need improvement?	
	What is the decision trail that has been followed? Based upon what choices? Who participated in the process?	
	Is the terminology consistently used throughout the document?	
	Does the proposal link emergency work to longer-term interventions?	
	What are the outcomes of the evaluation of the operation? Strengths and weaknesses?	
A	**social and political capital** What was the quality of relationship between beneficiaries and aid agency staff? Were the terms of engagement made clear to both parties?	
	Have agencies' obligations and/or responsibilities towards the affected population been defined?	
	Have all responsibilities been handed over to the appropriate institutions/people/organisations?	

criterion	criteria: questions to consider including in your programme	
B	**human capital** Were people's needs for protection met? How many are the affected people, and how many are the beneficiaries? Who are the affected people? What in general was the beneficiaries' opinion of the quality of assistance (timely, appropriate, accessible and adequate?)? Were people's existing capacities recognised and drawn upon? How does the proposal accommodate the most vulnerable members of the displaced population, i.e. those located on hazard-prone lands, and/or poor people, squatters, young people, elderly people, disabled people? Have skills been transferred from the aid community to those who are permanently based in the area? Have both host and displaced populations been given regular information during the programme, and are they aware of its planned duration/end?	
C	**natural capital** Is the damage to the local environment being addressed during the operation and minimised? Have all possible measures been taken to reduce the consumption of fuel wood? What have been the negative environmental impacts of the programme, and how can they be reversed before closing it?	
D	**physical capital** What is the size of the total housing stock in the affected area? How was housing built in the area before it was damaged? Who built it? How long did it take to build, on average? If self-help is proposed, how will beneficiaries be assisted if they cannot perform required activities? Is a profile of damage presented which consistently categorises how each house has been affected, and has it been agreed by all stakeholders? Have opportunities for mitigation and prevention of future disasters been identified (e.g. earthquake-resistant construction)? Have they been made integral components of the analysis?	

continued ...

criterion	criteria: questions to consider including in your programme	
	Are the numbers of people receiving assistance being reported, as well as the quantity of materials distributed? What assets can be retained by the host population on a family-by-family basis? Have reusable assets been recovered for later operations?	
E	**financial capital** What is the duty-bearer accountable for? What was the quality of financing? Were enough funds timely available? Was there undue pressure to spend funds within an administrative deadline? What have been the pattern and timing of donors' grant allocations in relationship to the requests of the operational agency? And in relationship to the funding decisions of other major donors? Have the capacity and capabilities of the local homebuilding industry been assessed? What is the availability of local building materials? What are industry constraints? To what extent can the engagement of the homebuilding industry in repair activities help to stimulate economic recovery/growth? Have links to other sectoral activities (e.g. livelihoods, environmental management) been identified? Are market impacts and opportunities discussed?	

4.5 step 4: how?

Finding responses to the questions posed in the tables and checklists in this chapter, using the resources available, will require the use of a variety of tools, all based on the options of research, observation, and interview.

4.5.1 selecting tools for assessment

As with the selection of criteria (4.4.1), the selection of tools appropriate to a specific programme or activity is best undertaken in a team discussion, consulting or involving as many stakeholders as is practical. Some data-gathering tools require specific training, access, or information from specific sources, so an analysis should be made of the resources available and the likely constraints before selecting suitable tools.

There are three generic methods for collecting information:

- **researching:** studying printed material (for example, agency and government reports, maps, books, newspapers, and websites)
- **talking to people:** formal or informal interviews with individuals or groups (for example, a discussion in a market or a meeting with a local committee)
- **looking:** quantitative measurement or qualitative assessments based on personal observation (for example, surveying a site or estimating a local agricultural economy by viewing fields, equipment, and markets).

These methods have been combined into a series of information-gathering tools, used by most aid organisations. The following are summarised in this chapter:

4.5.2 Geographical Information Systems (GIS)

4.5.3 Logical Framework Analysis (LFA)

4.5.4 Participatory Learning and Action (PLA)

4.5.5 People-Oriented Planning (POP)

4.5.6 Strengths, Weaknesses, Opportunities, and Constraints (SWOC)

More tools, and more detailed guidance on each tool, will be found in the procedures of aid organisations, and in guidelines such as SCF's *Toolkits* series (Gosling 2003).

4.5.2 Geographical Information Systems (GIS)

GIS are computer-software tools which assist in the acquisition, storage, analysis, and display of a range of geographic, environmental, social, demographic, and economic data (Bouchardy 1995).

GIS can be used to bring together varied information at multiple scales on a single layered representation, such as a map. A map can be created to include, for example, the location of every host family; the registration details of each displaced family; the history of shelter non-food items (NFIs) distributed to each family; and details of access to each area, including up-to-date security information.

GIS can be extremely useful in informing every level and phase of planning and response, and especially co-ordination, supporting the assessment, and monitoring and evaluating TS strategies, programmes, and projects. GIS also offers ways of recording, analysing, cataloguing, and presenting good practice, and an institutional memory.

designing GIS activities

The reasons for using GIS should be agreed from the outset, identifying the types of decision that the analysed information will inform, and the format and regularity that analysed information requires.

An understanding should also be formed of the sources of the original, un-analysed information to maintain the GIS. Care must be taken in targeting the use of GIS, because it is possible that the technical capacities of such systems make inappropriate demands on busy field staff, if they are required to maintain sources of detailed information, without necessarily offering them any benefit. Part of the purpose of GIS is to inform operational staff and to help them to save time when conducting assessments.

opportunities and constraints of GIS

Accurate and up-to-date GIS remains an under-used resource, despite its value for planning and co-ordination. Some limited GIS services, such as identifying maps, can be accessed via the Internet and through UN Humanitarian Information Centres (HICs), when they exist.

Technical constraints and inadequate resources limit the current impact of GIS tools. The software is expensive and it needs specialists to use and interpret it; it also often requires good Internet connectivity. The systems used were not developed for humanitarian aid operations, and they have not been co-ordinated to integrate and analyse a series of information types common to aid operations.

Remote-sensing procedures, such as multi-spectral high-resolution satellite photographs, are currently not sufficiently resourced to offer real-time support during the emergency phase, except in military environments. Remote sensing may be useful in later phases, if specialist support is available.

4.5.3 Logical Framework Analysis (LFA)

LFA (also known as the Project Framework Approach, or PFA) is a method for testing the logic of an action plan, by analysing it in terms of the objectives agreed and the resources available. This helps users to clarify how their planned activities will help to achieve their objectives, and to identify explicitly the implications of the planned activities in terms of resources, assumptions, and risks.

LFA provides a structure for specifying the components of a response and the logical linkages between them. Rather than resulting in planning procedures, LFA is a means by which a response can be structured, described, and communicated.

In order to establish the objectives and action plans, a tool such as Participatory Learning and Action (PLA) is used. LFA can then be used to analyse the logic of the relationship between its aim and the proposed activities. This is done by presenting it in the matrix shown in table 4(i).

table 4(i): project framework matrix

	A: project structure	B: indicators	C: means of verification	D: assumptions and critical factors
aim/wider objectives				
project objectives				
outputs				
activities				

column A: project structure

Describe the project as a series of hypotheses which link together the aim, or wider objectives, the project objectives, the outputs, and the activities. The four levels in the framework represent the steps described in figure 4(a).

figure 4(a): project hypotheses

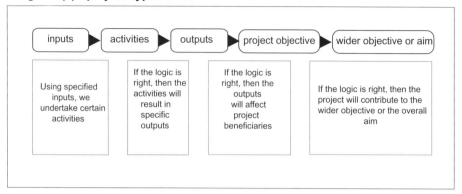

column B: indicators

Indicators enable project managers both to see whether the project has achieved what was planned at each level, and also to have a measure of this achievement, giving a clear structure for monitoring. Targets can be set to assess progress quantitatively, but note that it is important to review them regularly. LFA uses four main indicators:

- **Indicators for activities:** carrying out the activities should achieve the outputs, so the success of the activities will be measured by the indicators for outputs. Therefore there is no need to list indicators in the matrix at the activities level. The inputs required to carry out the activities should be listed instead. The inputs should include capital and current expenditure on the purchase of equipment, and a schedule for any staff training and other activities required before the project can start.

- **Indicators for outputs:** for outputs, indicators are often numerical and can usually be measured by means of existing records. The output indicators can be used as targets for monitoring and evaluation purposes, but it is important not to follow targets inflexibly: they may need to be revised as the project evolves.

- **Indicators for project objectives:** these are often more difficult to identify than output indicators. They may be quantitative or qualitative, depending on the nature of the objective. When the objective is to achieve qualitative change, it is sometimes better to use quantitative proxy indicators.

- **Indicators for the wider objective or aim:** The key indicator for the wider objective or aim of the work is likely to be an indicator measured by groups outside the immediate project team (for example, Human Development Indicators).

column C: means of verification

The method of measuring or collecting information about each of the indicators is called the 'means of verification'. It involves identifying the sources from which to gather information for the verification of indicators. The resources needed for collecting information should be considered at the project planning stage, to prevent poor attempts at verification.

column D: assumptions and critical factors

The assumptions underlying a project, and the critical factors necessary for its success, need to be acknowledged and considered at the planning stage. They signify the uncertainties that will be faced during management of the work, generally external to the project and beyond the control of the project. Generally, the significance of assumptions and the degree of uncertainty increase as you move along the framework. Uncertainties about whether the inputs will lead to the outputs are fewer than uncertainties about whether outputs will result in achieving the objectives.

issues to consider

A team approach to project planning is now generally emphasised by users of the LFA. There is also a recognition of the importance of the pre-planning research and survey work required, to ensure that problems are properly identified and that their causes and effects are related to the real experiences and needs of individuals and groups of people. These problems can then become the basis for agreeing objectives, and hence for programme design.

when to use LFA

- When structuring and describing a project in a logical fashion.
- To aid logical thinking.
- For analysing the relationship between activities and objectives.

advantages of LFA

- Checking the internal logic of a project plan links strategies, objectives, and aims; identification of indicators enables monitoring and evaluation.

- Stating assumptions and identifying critical factors for success stimulates discussion about feasibility.
- Key information, including project objectives, is compiled in one document.
- LFA encourages consideration of expectations and how they can be achieved.

disadvantages of LFA

The LFA process has some inherent disadvantages.

- The construction of the framework is time-consuming.
- Use of the project framework can be complicated and requires conceptual training.
- Summarising complex ideas or relationships in simple phrases may be meaningless.
- The Western logic of 'cause-and-effect' may be alien to many cultures.
- Focusing on 'problem analysis' may appear negative, whereas livelihoods analysis may provide a more positive approach.

The application of LFA may also pose problems.

- There is the danger of rigidly focusing on targets or indicators, obscuring the aims of the project.
- Unrealistic targets may lead to disappointment.
- The approach is intended for large-scale projects, where each level is monitored by a different level of management. This makes it less suitable for a project run by a small team.
- Indicators are generally quantitative and may not sufficiently reflect subtleties or complexities.

4.5.4 Participatory Learning and Action (PLA)

PLA – also known as PRA (Participatory Rapid Appraisal or Participatory Rural Appraisal) and RAP (Rapid Appraisal Procedures) – grew out of rapid assessment methods such as RRA (Rapid Rural Appraisal). The overall aim of the PLA is to empower a community to analyse its own situation, reversing the hierarchies between communities and those perceived as outside experts. The design and control of the programme should be the remit of the communities affected, rather than that of outside agencies, and the findings should be translated into meaningful action. The research team is a mix of external researchers and community members.

Figure 4(b) presents the essential features of PLA, in the sequence in which they should be carried out.

figure 4(b): features of PLA

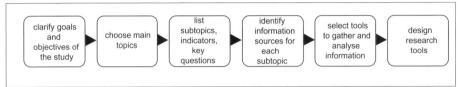

PLA is usually carried out in a workshop, and then followed by field work to gather information. Each round of information gathering is based on findings from previous rounds. The information is analysed throughout the study and in a group session at the end.

The final analysis is done by the whole team, immediately after the field work. The results can be presented in different ways for different audiences, which should include the community, project staff, and programme managers.

when to use it

PLA is most suitable when participation by all stakeholders is essential for the success of the work being proposed: for example, when setting up community space within a transitional settlement.

PLA techniques may also be suitable if 'community' is defined more loosely to include a professional community, such as construction workers in a district, all government officials concerned with a particular problem, or staff in a particular team or office. With such stakeholders, it can be used in the following situations:

- when planning, monitoring, or evaluating a programme concerned with social change;
- when you need a thorough understanding of a topic in a particular context;
- when you need to know what people think about their situation or a problem, and what their priorities are;
- when you need to find meaningful indicators for qualitative change.

advantages of PLA

- It helps everyone involved in the assessment to understand a community, its capacities, and its problems.
- It gives community members greater influence over work that affects them.
- Community members are more committed to projects if they understand them and are actively involved in them.
- Local priorities and perceptions of different problems, opportunities, and constraints are taken into account.
- Results are produced rapidly, and in a form available to the local community.
- It is useful for identifying indicators for qualitative change that are locally relevant.
- You learn as you go, rather than waiting to analyse the data at the end.
- It is potentially quicker and cheaper than a more formal quantitative survey.
- PLA and related methods often produce unexpected but essential information.
- It is less intrusive than formal interviews that use questionnaires.

disadvantages of PLA

- Results apply only to the particular communities visited. Wider generalisations cannot be made.
- It can be time-consuming for all concerned, including members of the community.
- A false picture of the situation may emerge if the team is not aware of crucial factors such as gender issues.
- It is difficult for people outside the team and area to verify the results.
- Direct observation reveals only what is immediately visible: much may be hidden from view.
- If it is not done systematically, results may be impressionistic and potentially inaccurate.
- The findings may not carry the same weight with decision makers as quantitative data do.

- PLA does not work unless the people involved maintain a positive approach and are suitably trained.

4.5.5 People-Orientated Planning (POP)

The People-Oriented Planning (POP) tool was published by the United Nations High Commissioner for Refugees (Anderson 1994). It presents standard data-collection tools, but concentrates on forming an understanding of each part of a refugee community, including vulnerable groups, emphasising risks of abuse and sexual violence. The POP tool is useful in forming an understanding of all displaced communities, and not just refugees.

UNHCR literature offers three steps to People-Oriented Planning, expanded below:

- refugee profile and context
- activities analysis
- resources analysis.

refugee profile and context

The profile is defined in POP as 'Composition of the refugee group before they became refugees and changes in that composition under the conditions of being refugees or, later, returnees'. Context is defined as 'Factors that affect this refugee situation. The two factors that are most important for programming are: the reasons that these people became refugees; the cultural mores that influence how these refugees act.'

activities analysis

Activities analysis is described as including identifying the division of labour, and identifying when and where the assessed group do the activities.

resources analysis

Resources analysis is described as including identifying the resources available to the assessed group, asking who has which resources, and deciding what resources should be provided to the refugees.

The following text is quoted directly from the publication 'People-Oriented Planning at Work. Using POP to Improve UNHCR Programming' (Anderson 1994). Further quotes from the text are included in the 'gender and age' section of chapter 2 (2.5.2).

> The layout of shelter in a refugee camp can either provide suitable protection or exacerbate the likelihood of unsafe conditions. In particular, people vulnerable to sexual attack (both women and young children) must have access to well-lighted, nearby toilet facilities as this is one area that has often proved dangerous for unaccompanied users. In addition, placement of vulnerable people in outlying camp sections increases their risk of physical sexual assault. ...
>
> Shelter arrangements for women without husbands in situations where women are usually secluded must also take into account the tradition of seclusion. Two possible approaches include: 1) providing shelter that 'pairs' women who do not have men with families where men are present; 2) building and reserving special areas for groups of single women and their dependents.
>
> (Anderson 1994)

when to use POP

- On its own, or in addition to other tools, in order to form a more accurate understanding of disaggregated groups within refugee populations. But note that, if employed, it should also be applied to host and IDP populations.
- When gender issues or the needs of vulnerable groups are likely to be of specific concern.
- When UNHCR is involved, given the familiarity of UNHCR with the assessment format.

advantages of POP

POP is particularly useful for the following purposes.

- Assessing cultural and socio-economic contexts before and after displacement – essential for understanding the TS programme options selected by and supported for displaced populations.
- Identifying the skills and human resources available in the refugee population, and encouraging their coping mechanisms.
- Disaggregating the refugee population through assessment, enabling the identification of the needs of vulnerable groups.

- It focuses on refugee camps, rather than the six TS programme options considered in these guidelines (although mention is made of refugee groups absorbed into communities).

- It assesses only the displaced population, rather than including the host population too.

- It concentrates on the needs of refugees, rather than those of all displaced populations, including IDPs.

- It assesses physical risks to women, minors, and elders, rather than assessing wider security and protection threats to communities, including risks to men, for example from the presence of armed groups within or close to a transitional settlement.

4.5.6 Strengths, Weaknesses, Opportunities, and Constraints (SWOC)

SWOC (also known as SWOT – Strengths, Weaknesses, Opportunities, and Threats – analysis) provides a framework for group analysis of a given situation. It encourages input from many people, helps people to brainstorm potential solutions (opportunities) and constraints, and is a way of gathering information that can be useful in problem analysis, monitoring, and evaluation.

The idea is to brainstorm under the following headings:

- **strengths**: what has worked, why it worked; lessons learned for the future

- **weaknesses**: what has not worked very well; times when things could have gone better

- **opportunities**: ideas for how to overcome weaknesses and build on strengths

- **constraints**: the constraints that reduce the range of opportunities for change.

when to use it

SWOC should be considered in simple contexts when speed rather than rigour is required, or in combination with other tools.

advantages of SWOC

- It is simple to use, communicate, train others to use, and understand.
- It can be used in conjunction with other assessment tools.
- It is easily transferable to strategies and reports as a tool to present background and summary material.

disadvantages of SWOC

- It is not a rigorous assessment methodology: for example, the assessors' interpretation of a strength may differ from that of the assessed group.
- It is difficult to incorporate into consistent monitoring and evaluation.

4.5.7 analysis and bias

analysis The method of analysing the information collected can be simple, such as writing a report based on discussion within the team; or more complex, such as structuring and quantifying results. The purpose of analysis is to form an understanding based on a large amount of information which can be communicated clearly, and which may be useful to planning.

This section describes three general approaches to understanding and communicating the information:

- quantitative statistical analysis
- drawings and diagrams
- weighted matrix.

quantitative statistical analysis

It is common for statistics to be misinterpreted or misused. Quantitative statistics should not be used or reported unless there is an understanding of what the value actually means in practical terms, and the assumptions behind the value. To find a typical, or average, value of a variable, it is often wrongly assumed that the arithmetical mean is appropriate. The arithmetical mean sums up all the values and divides by the number of values, thereby averaging the value. Instead, the median should be used to find a typical or representative value.

Quantitative statistical analyses are based on collecting significant data from a significant variety of sources and creating an average. Many methods for quantitative statistical analyses exist, for both single variable analyses and multivariate analyses. Standard quantities, which can be calculated, include mean, mode, median, standard deviation, error, and correlation coefficient between two variables. Most spreadsheet software includes facilities to calculate these and many other values.

The median is found by putting all values in numerical order and finding the value in the middle. If you have an even number of values, then two numbers form the middle of the set, and the arithmetical mean of these two numbers gives the median. See table 4(j).

table 4(j): example of quantitative statistical analysis

values	mean	median	comment
2, 2, 4, 7	3.75	3	both forms of analysis are reasonable
2, 2, 4, 16	6	3	the median is a more representative value

drawings and diagrams

Drawings and diagrams are powerful quantitative methods for discovering patterns and trends, and for communicating them clearly.

Maps are useful for finding out information about an area and how different groups use it, and for quickly communicating large amounts of information.

Mobility maps record, compare, and analyse the movements of different groups in a community, and are a useful indicator of social networks.

Transects are diagrams of the main land-use zones in an area. They compare the main features, resources, uses, and problems of different zones. Transects can be constructed by walking in a line through an area, talking to people or observing.

Seasonal calendars are ways of representing seasonal variations, such as variations in climate, crop sequences, agricultural activities, and income-generating activities. They can help to identify times when resources will be scarce, and the best times of the year for certain activities.

Graphs compare how one variable changes with respect to another: for example the number of displaced people living with host families over time. Time graphs are particularly useful for showing the rate and direction of change of many variables, such as crop yields, livestock population, prices, and population size.

Time lines are flow charts, showing the sequence of different events.

Daily routine diagrams compare the daily routines of different groups of people, and seasonal changes in the routines. They can help to identify suitable times for meetings, or changes in household roles over time.

Livelihood analysis diagrams interpret the behaviour, decisions, and coping strategies of households with different socio-economic characteristics. Variables for livelihood analysis may include the following:

- household size and composition
- number of labour migrants in the household
- livestock and land ownership
- proportion of income by source and credit and debt
- expenditures
- seasonality.

Flow diagrams are charts showing causes, effects, and relationships between key variables; for example:

- relationships between economic, political, cultural, and climatic factors that cause environmental degradation
- flow of commodities and cash in a marketing system
- effects of major changes or innovations (impact diagrams)
- organisation chart.

Venn diagrams are graphic representations, usually circles, showing key institutions and individuals in a community, and their relationships and importance for decision making. When the circles are separate, no contact exists between them. When they touch, information passes between them. The extent of the overlap indicates, for example, the extent of co-operation in decision making.

weighted matrix

A weighted matrix is used to compare options for which the same criteria have been measured. The steps for creating a weighted matrix are as follows.

- Choose the criteria to be used.

- Assign each criterion a weighting of relative importance: for example, between 1 and 10, with 10 being highly important and 1 being irrelevant.

- Examine each criterion and assign it a value on the same scale, say between 1 and 100: high values indicate that the criterion is positive for the option, while low values indicate that the criterion is negative.

- Multiply each criterion value by its weighting to produce an overall 'score' for that criterion.

- Add all the scores together.

- Compare the final score for each option. The option with the highest final score wins.

Some considerations to be borne in mind when developing a weighted matrix:

- Some criteria may be veto criteria: for example, if selecting sites for a refugee camp, any site within 50 km of a border might be excluded.

- Negative criteria could be given a negative score or a negative weighting.

- If some options yield scores that are similar, judging which option is best becomes more subjective.

- A lack of information could mean that values or weightings have to be estimated.

Weighted matrices are proposed as part of site selection in other guidelines (Lambert and Davis 2002). An example matrix from a fictitious situation is presented in table 4(k).

criterion	W	option A		option B		option C		option D	
		V	M	V	M	V	M	V	M
legal issues	5.5	85	467.5			28	154.0	52	286.0
potential for growing food	7.5	45	337.5			60	450.0	81	607.5
access	2.0	35	70.0			45	90.0	60	120.0
environmental health	6.0	21	126.0			45	270.0	92	552.0
fuel-wood availability	6.0	59	354.0			89	534.0	48	288.0
security	8.5	36	306.0	12	veto	37	314.5	60	510.0
water sources	9.0	85	765.0			70	630.0	12	108.0
robust environment	3.0	15	45.0			11	33.0	0	0 .0
flora and fauna	4.0	35	140.0			35	140.0	80	320.0
topography	6.5	28	182,0			84	546.0	65	422.5
natural hazard safety	8.0	19	152.0			60	480.0	63	504.0
total (summing up values in M column)			2945		vetoed		3641.5		3718

V=value; W=weighting (same for all options because it refers to each criterion); M= VxW; veto criteria: security below 25, water resources below 10

In table 4(k), Option A is clearly inferior to options C and D. More detailed analyses or sensitivity checking might be prudent for options C and D; or, if there are no other concerns, then either could be chosen.

bias It is important to make clear to each member of the assessment, monitoring, or evaluation team that assumptions and uncertainties are inevitable, but must be recorded. The intention of the activity is to find out what is not known, and to question what is not normally questioned, rather than to confirm what is known. Ignoring or suppressing results that are not understood completely undermines the purpose of the activity. The International Federation of the Red Cross and Red Crescent has identified the following forms of bias in assessment.

spatial bias: issues of comfort and ease for the assessors determine the assessment site. Rather than travel into an area, the assessors conduct a 'windshield' survey, never leaving the comfort of their truck.

project bias: the assessor is drawn towards sites where contacts and information are readily available and which may have been assessed before by many others.

person bias: key informants tend to be those who are in a high social position and have the ability to communicate in a language known to the assessor. They may or may not be conscientious, insightful, or respected by those whom they purport to represent.

season bias: assessments are conducted during periods of pleasant weather; or areas cut off by bad weather are not assessed. Thus, many typical problems go unnoticed.

mandate or specialism bias: the specialism or mandate of the assessor blinds him or her to needs beyond his or her specialty. For example, a shelter specialist may focus on assessing needs for shelter, neglecting needs for nutrition and water.

political bias: informants present information that is distorted by their political agenda. Assessors look for information which fits their own political or personal agenda.

cultural bias: incorrect assumptions are made, based on the assessor's own cultural norms. Assessors do not understand the cultural practices of the affected populations.

class/ethnic bias: the needs and resources of different classes of people or different ethnic groups are not included in the assessment. This bias can be in the minds of local assessors; or the key informants may represent only one social class or ethnic group.

interviewer or investigator bias: assessors may have a tendency to concentrate on information which confirms preconceived notions and hypotheses, causing them to seek consistency too early and overlook evidence that is inconsistent with earlier findings. Assessors may also tend to favour the opinions of elite key informants.

key informant bias: biases of key informants are carried into assessment results.

gender bias: assessors speak only to men; or interviewers survey only women.

time of day or schedule bias: the assessment is conducted at a time of day when certain segments of the population may be over-represented or under-represented.

sampling bias: respondents are not representative of the population.

Being aware of different types of bias is the first step towards minimising its impact on your assessment.

(International Federation of the Red Cross and Red Crescent 2000)

chapter 5 labour

5 labour

5 labour

This chapter offers an overview of options for contracting and managing labour for construction and engineering works for transitional settlement projects. The possible methods of selecting and paying labour are described. Explanations of the different ways of engaging labour are given.

In construction and engineering works for TS projects, appropriate labour must be selected from the local and displaced populations. There are various possible methods of payment: incentives, 'food-for-work', salaries, or contracts. Labour may be employed under a self-help scheme, or as direct labour, or via a contractor. Local and international contracting and labour laws are complex, so specialist advice should be sought. Organisations should have in place their own policies and procedures for directly engaging and managing labour, as well as for contract management; advice in the following sections of this chapter should be used only in support of these policies and procedures.

This chapter is organised as follows:

5.1 **selecting and paying labour**

5.2 **self-help labour:** families undertake the required work themselves

5.3 **direct labour:** the aid organisation hires and manages individuals

5.4 **contracted labour:** a contractor is engaged to undertake the works.

5.1 selecting and paying labour

5.1.1 selecting labour

Before any project design is carried out, the availability of skilled and unskilled labour in the local and displaced populations should be assessed, as should the availability of building or engineering contractors, who are usually registered with local authorities.

Assessment criteria should include organisational and local requirements. Most organisations have their own policies and guidelines on engaging contractors and the direct recruitment of labour: for example, concerning the importance of offering equal employment opportunities to men and women. Co-ordinating structures and local authorities may have their own procedures and standards, especially concerning pay scales.

Assessments should include requirements for tools and equipment, including plant, such as bulldozers. Care should be taken to ensure that tools and equipment are in good working order, that transport is available to move them to site, and that they are not committed to other works or other contractors.

selecting the right way to engage labour

Self-help, direct labour, and contracted labour each have their own advantages and drawbacks, described in sections 5.2, 5.3, and 5.4. In general, self-help projects tend to be supported by direct or contracted labour to assist vulnerable households who are unable to undertake the work themselves. Direct labour is often used when there are no contractors present; or during the emergency phase when displaced persons are not in a position to help themselves, and contracting processes would take too long. Contractors are often engaged for complicated works requiring specialist skills or equipment.

The different ways of engaging labour can be combined within the same programme, or even within the same project. For example, some families may build their own shelters; vulnerable families may be supported by direct labour hired by the aid organisation; and infrastructure for all families might be improved by using contractors.

community participation

Both the displaced and local communities should be involved in planning from the outset (2.2, 2.3). Discussion with the leaders of the communities, as well as discussion with the communities themselves, can often identify individuals who have the necessary skills to manage or lead projects. Management skills and leadership skills are essential to the success of projects, especially when security is poor or the works are complex.

Even if contractors are used for all works, it should be possible to employ labour from both the displaced and local communities.

A displaced population is likely to contain a large potential workforce. Labour from the displaced community can be used as self-help (5.2) or hired as direct labour (5.3) by aid organisations; or hired via contractors (5.4); or used as contractors (5.4), provided that the contracting firms meet local laws. Attention must always be given to offering equal opportunities to vulnerable groups. Incentives (5.1.2) should be considered, even in self-help construction projects, because time spent on construction reduces the time available to support other livelihood activities.

Employing local labour can stimulate the local economy and improve relations with both the displaced population and aid organisations. Involving local contractors, small local construction companies, and other local organisations may also increase the contracting organisation's understanding of local natural-resource management procedures, such as the harvesting of construction materials.

Ideally, an appropriate combination of labour from the displaced and host populations should be employed, in order to avoid tensions between the two groups. In longer-term projects, apprenticeships or formal training could be offered, to build up developmental capacities within both communities.

A substantial distinction should be made between workers employed within the local community and those employed within the displaced community (5.1.2). For example, local workers will be subject to local and national regulations, which may require a salary to be paid. Workers from the displaced population are likely to be receiving support such as food aid and shelter and may therefore require a smaller salary or fewer extra incentives.

skilled labour Technical skills are usually to be found in displaced and local communities for self-help (5.2) and direct-labour (5.3) projects, as well as within contracting companies. Discussion with the leaders of the communities, as well as discussion with the communities themselves, can often identify appropriate individuals. Identifying the skills available may determine the nature of the works: for example, knowledge of how to fix reinforcement for concrete. Skilled construction workers are often highly respected within a community, and care should be taken to recognise their contributions. Skilled workers often own their tools, although displaced workers may not, and this limitation will affect their livelihoods.

In most societies, it is usual for both women and men to undertake roles in the construction and maintenance of family shelter (2.5.2). However, traditional roles may be challenged by different circumstances in displacement, by different construction materials and methods, or by the loss of family members. Consider providing or supporting accessible and appropriate crèche facilities if the role of women envisaged in the construction activity compromises child care, and if families and communities cannot offer the necessary assistance unaided.

5.1.2 paying labour

Section 2.5.6 discusses some aspects of the financial management of TS support in various phases of aid operations. Such support usually requires significant disbursements of funds. Some other points to consider when paying labour are listed below.

- Handling large amounts of cash in the field is a security risk; in the absence of banks, this may present problems for aid organisations.

- Delays in payments to labourers may undermine their livelihoods and also create security risks.

- Co-ordination among aid organisations operating in the same area is important, in order to ensure consistency: labourers may move between jobs if different payments or benefits are offered.

- Records must be kept of all disbursements, including payments in cash or in kind to workers, who should be asked to sign receipts.

There are four ways in which to pay labour for construction works:

- **incentives:** paying less than a minimum wage when other support is offered

- **'food-for-work':** payment in kind, with goods rather than money

- **salaries:** regular payments, with associated rights and obligations in law

- **contracts:** a scheduled number of payments with associated rights and obligations in law, often including penalties and additional incentives.

5 labour

payment through incentives

Incentive payments may be made to displaced self-help labour (5.2) and direct (5.3) labour instead of a salary in the following circumstances:

- if normal salaried employment would not be legal under local law, but incentive payments are legal;

- if local law requires the payment of a minimum wage, but incentive payments below this minimum may be made, because the displaced population is receiving other support, such as food aid and shelter;

- if skilled and unskilled labour need to be treated differently: for example, skilled labour engaged in roofing all the shelters in a displaced community might receive a salary, while those engaged in unskilled work on their own shelter might receive an incentive.

Aid organisations should co-ordinate their policies, to agree a consistent scale of incentive payments.

It is essential to keep records of every disbursement; this includes requiring all daily paid labourers to sign or make their mark on receipts for incentive payments, and giving copies of the receipts to the workers.

payment through 'food-for-work'

In-kind rewards may be used as payment for self-help labour (5.2) and direct (5.3) labour. If the rewards consist of essential commodities, such as food, such distributions should be additional to normal rations.

Projects adopting food-for-work as a method of payment should take special care to consider groups who cannot undertake the work: vulnerable groups, for example, or those who have other responsibilities. It may be counterproductive to offer food-for-work activities exclusively to women, with the intention of empowering them, if the same women are expected by the community to cook the food and collect water and fuel; the result may be that they do not have enough time to complete all activities satisfactorily.

It is essential to keep records of every disbursement; this includes requiring all daily paid labourers to sign or make their mark on receipts for in-kind payments, and giving copies of the receipts to the workers.

---

payment through salaries

Salaries usually offer the greatest benefit to displaced households when there are family members able to act as self-help labour (5.2) and direct labour (5.3), because they are free to use the salary as they see fit. Employers should understand the local, international, and organisational regulations and responsibilities governing employment, including employment rights and conditions, such as liability for breaches of health and safety rules.

Salaries should be paid in local currencies wherever possible. The regular transport and disbursement of cash salaries constitutes a security risk. It is essential to keep records of every disbursement; this includes requiring all daily paid labourers to sign or make their mark on receipts for payments, and giving copies of the receipts to the workers.

payment through contracts

Some circumstances may require individual contracts to be made with each labourer, such as skilled workers and those who own particular tools. Some aid organisations have standard contract forms and job descriptions according to functions, such as building-site foreman, truck driver, mason, and labourer. If a standard contract form is not available, a simple contract should be drawn up, as appropriate, between the aid organisation and the worker.

In cases where a contractor is engaged to undertake the works, an appropriate contract should be drawn up between the aid organisation and the contractor. Section 5.4.4 presents basic guidance on drafting and managing such contracts, including agreeing a schedule of payments, and incentive and penalty clauses.

5.2 self-help labour

Self-help labour, whereby families themselves undertake the required work, is managed by aid organisations directly.

Different aid organisations have different guidelines on the employment of beneficiaries when they are constructing their own shelters. However, it is generally considered acceptable for the agency to provide construction materials and some supervision, while the adult and non-vulnerable beneficiaries provide voluntary work. Self-help may also be rewarded by in-kind or incentive payments.

The responsible agency requires a considerable capacity for local management, and local and specialist knowledge of construction. Consider hiring consultants, sub-contracting aid organisations with the appropriate capacities, or using project-management companies if the project is large, and especially if town planning, architectural, or engineering skills are required (5.4.2).

It is usual for self-help labour to be used in combination with at least one of the other two types: direct or contracted labour.

5.2.1 advantages and disadvantages of self-help labour

advantages Because the beneficiaries themselves are doing the construction, it is likely that the quality of the work will be good. It is important to design sufficient flexibility into the project, so that the household can make their own modifications, if necessary. If any remuneration is made, it is paid to the beneficiary household, rather than to external groups or contractors, thus increasing the developmental benefit.

If a component of self-help labour is included in projects involving direct or contracted labour, it is likely that the beneficiary household will have more opportunities to have a positive influence on the other workers.

If the project design is good, using self-help labour can empower beneficiary households, by offering them more choices. Offering skills training and tools will broaden livelihoods opportunities.

disadvantages

Beneficiary householders may not have the time, skills, or equipment necessary to undertake all projects.

Self-help projects may divert key householders from other more urgent priorities. Displaced populations must retain choice in their lives, because they are best placed to determine their own priorities. For example, if there is only one able-bodied adult in a family, that person should decide whether he or she should be engaged in constructing shelter, looking after livestock, or assisting other families.

Special provision must be made to assist vulnerable households who cannot participate in self-help projects. There are different levels and causes of vulnerability, so each case should be treated individually and monitored to ensure that an appropriate level of support is maintained.

The local population will not benefit from any projects directed exclusively at the displaced population.

The aid organisation must have the skills, local experience, and resources to undertake the necessary co-ordination and management of the project.

5.2.2 managing self-help labour

documentation

The objective of each activity within a self-help project should be agreed publicly or officially by the beneficiary household. This may involve a contract between the aid organisation, the head of household, and the local authorities. Any remuneration and NFIs in the form of shelter materials should be disbursed in phases which reinforce the achievement and monitoring of the agreed project activities.

work attendance

A phased schedule of works should be agreed and recorded in the documentation. The schedule should include sufficient flexibility to allow labour within the beneficiary household to undertake other activities, and for beneficiary households to involve their wider social group in undertaking works.

5.3 direct labour

Direct labour, where the aid organisation hires and manages individuals to undertake a project, may draw upon both displaced and local labour forces.

The responsible agency requires a considerable capacity for local management, and local and specialist knowledge of construction. Consider hiring consultants, sub-contracting aid organisations with the appropriate capacities, or using project-management companies if the project is large, and especially if town planning, architectural, or engineering skills are required (5.4.2).

The co-ordination and management of direct labour is very important. It often depends on identifying experienced and trusted supervisors. Master craftspeople in various trades should also be identified and supported.

One method of scaling up unskilled direct labour is to ask a number of known individuals to arrive on site, each with a small labour team of approximately ten workers. Then identify the best-performing individuals in these teams and ask them to arrive the next day or week with their own teams.

Care should always be taken to involve labour from all groups within displaced and local labour forces, in order both to prevent suspicions of favouritism or bias, and to prevent the control of the labour force by a particular political or ethnic grouping.

5.3.1 advantages and disadvantages of direct labour

advantages Any remuneration will be paid to the local and displaced populations, rather than to external contractors, thus adding to the developmental benefit and reducing tensions that may result if local populations resent assistance being given to the displaced. Benefits are spread more equitably among both populations.

Projects are likely to support communal facilities, rather than the family shelters and very localised projects that are more appropriate to self-help projects.

If the project design is good, direct labour can empower beneficiary communities, by building their capacity for collective action. Projects which also offer skills training and tools can broaden livelihoods opportunities.

disadvantages

Beneficiary and local communities may not have the time, skills, or equipment necessary to undertake all projects.

Direct labour projects can divert key community resources from other more urgent priorities.

Take care to prevent dominant groups within the community, for example particular ethnic or political groups, controlling direct labour projects, their communal benefits, and any remuneration.

The aid organisation must have the skills, local experience, and resources to undertake the necessary co-ordination and management of the project.

5.3.2 managing direct labour

documentation

Leaders of local and displaced communities should be involved in public or official negotiations to agree the objective of each activity within a direct labour project. A contract may be drawn up between the aid organisation, the community leaders, and the local authorities.

Direct labour sometimes requires contracts (5.1.2) to be made with individual workers, such as skilled labourers or those who possess specific tools.

Any remuneration and NFIs in the form of shelter materials should be disbursed in phases which reinforce the achievement and monitoring of the agreed project activities.

work attendance

A phased schedule of works should be agreed and recorded in the documentation.

A system should be introduced to record work attendance for each worker on the building site. The system should also include records of recruitment, the pay roll, evaluation, any warnings, and any dismissals. Ideally, to maximise capacity building within communities, this system should be managed by community representatives, monitored by representatives of the aid organisation.

5.4 contracted labour

Contracted labour, whereby a contractor is engaged to undertake the works, may also involve local and displaced labour, within local employment regulations. The use of a contractor means that the aid organisation does not have to deal directly with individual workers.

Using contracted labour usually involves a process of tendering in order to choose a suitable contractor. Preparing tender documentation and the process of bidding for contracts for construction and engineering works are discussed in section 5.4.3, while drawing up contracts is discussed in section 5.4.4.

5.4.1 advantages and disadvantages of contracted labour

advantages Contracted labour, whereby a contractor is engaged to undertake the works, may be used when projects are large and complex, when specialist skills or equipment are required, or when the local and displaced populations have more urgent priorities than engaging in construction work.

Contracted works are often completed faster than those undertaken by self-help or direct labour, especially if the contractor has specialist equipment available. Contracted works may be undertaken more reliably and to higher standards of quality.

Contractors can be required in the contract with the aid organisation to engage skilled and unskilled labour from local and displaced communities, if employing displaced labour is legal. This ensures that some of the funds are distributed locally through wages, and – if training and apprenticeships are provided – it develops skills.

disadvantages

Unless the contractor involves local and displaced labour, the contract sum is paid to the contractor, rather than to the local and displaced communities.

If the contractor is not required in the contract to include skills training and apprenticeships, there is little likelihood of capacity building within local or displaced communities.

Large contract sums may attract unscrupulous contractors, and contractors may become involved in disputes with local authorities.

Using contractors does not guarantee that works will be undertaken more reliably and to higher standards of quality.

Whether the contractors are local or international, links with political parties, politicians, and local community leaders are common. This may delay works if it creates opportunities for political interference and corruption. 'Cartels' may form, where the bidders for a contract engage in secret negotiations to decide among themselves which company will submit the most attractive bid, and at what price (5.4.3).

5.4.2 managing contracted labour

For larger construction and engineering projects, project management will be required. This may be done by the aid organisation itself, or by consultants hired directly by the aid organisation; or by sub-contracting to other appropriate aid organisations; or by engaging commercial project-management capacity from firms of architects, engineers, or town planners.

Some aid organisations have standard forms for contracting work to architects, engineers, builders, and site managers, who are often hired locally. Using local professional services is important in order to ensure the overall effectiveness of the aid organisation in transitional settlement support.

Architecture and engineering firms can be selected on the basis of a public tender (5.4.3), an invited tender (5.4.3), or an invited competition: practices vary in different countries, and for different sizes of project. In an invited competition, several architectural or engineering firms are invited to conduct pilot studies of the work proposed. A panel appointed by the commissioning aid organisation judges the competition. It may be necessary to pay a fee to firms that have submitted the required material and are not selected.

When projects must be begun quickly, it may be possible to appoint an architectural or engineering firm directly without tendering or competition, depending on local laws and the policies of the commissioning aid organisation. The appointment of a contractor may be made on the basis of recommendation, or reputation, or the strength of earlier works already carried out. The chosen contractor should be registered and authorised by the local authorities to undertake the scope of works required.

If the works are very small in scale, it may also be possible to appoint the contractor, rather than submitting the job for tender. Local law or policies within aid organisations usually offer guidance on the sum above which an appointment is not appropriate and tendering is required.

5.4.3 tenders and bids

Tendering is the process by which bids for a contract are made. Tenders may be required by the policies of aid organisations, donors, or local authorities. They are often required above a certain contract sum, determined by local law or aid-organisation policy (5.4.2).

Tendering is useful to the commissioning aid organisation, because terms and conditions can be stipulated, to increase the likelihood that the project is completed on time, to national and international standards, using appropriate materials, and within the budget available. The primary purpose of tendering may not be to minimise costs. The reliability of the potential contractors is an important factor. This information should be sought from other aid organisations or contacts.

Tendering is useful to potential contractors, as well as to donors and aid organisations, because it offers a transparent and accountable system of selection, in which every eligible contractor has an equal opportunity to make a bid for the works.

In some cases, and generally for large-scale works, public tendering is required and must be carried out according to the legislation of the country where the agency is working. In other circumstances, an invited tender, whereby the aid organisation invites particular contractors to bid, is often used, especially if the commissioning organisation maintains a list of approved contractors. Other aid organisations should be consulted about the reputations of local contractors.

Local or national tendering is often difficult in emergencies, due to the temporary lack of existing procedures and the changing nature of the local markets. International tendering is used when large quantities of shelter items (for example, plastic sheeting) need to be purchased for a specific emergency or for stockpiling. This type of tendering is usually managed by the agency's head office. Relations between in-country offices and their head office, and the procedures governing national and international tendering, are regulated by internal guidelines and differ depending on the organisation.

The following 12 points describe the various steps of a typical process of tendering to award a contract for construction and engineering works for TS projects, from the identification of a brief to the award of a contract to the contractor chosen for the implementation of that brief. The process described here is not completely rigid: it may be adapted as necessary, according to the situation. Section 5.4.4 defines the documentation that should be included in the construction contract.

step 1: define a brief

The project brief is a clear description of the phased functional, social, physical, and developmental requirements of the project, as well as performance specifications. The process of defining a brief should involve assessments of the needs of the aid organisation, the displaced community, and local groups who will use the project. It should identify the individuals or teams who will manage and maintain the project, and representatives from the local authorities.

step 2: commission outline drawings

All formal documentation should be prepared by architects or engineers registered in the locality where the project will be undertaken. Hiring a local consultant or professional firm allows the design to be compared with local standards, ensures that the designs are understood, and provides a contact with the local authorities and builders which will be useful if problems arise later. It may be useful, before putting the project out to tender, to obtain independent estimates of the likely costs of the works, for comparison.

Local permissions, such as planning permission, must be obtained before putting the project out to tender. Title deeds to land and other documentation should be in order, and the local authorities should be consulted about other local procedures.

step 3: prepare tender documents

Tender documents should include the following elements:

- master plans and execution plans
- specifications sheets, including the contract and contracting details, such as the required registration, experience, and organisation of the contractor, and the deadline by which the bids must be received
- the method of paying the contractor
- the bill of quantities (BOQ): the list of materials and activities required to undertake the works, based on the outline drawings, which each potential contractor will use to prepare proposals for pricing and undertaking the works
- any factors for the selection of contractors, other than price, that are important to the aid organisation
- any additional documentation required under local or international law, or by the commissioning aid organisation or donor.

Each complete set of tender documents should be put in an envelope, numbered, and recorded in a 'Tender Book', before being issued.

step 4: advertise the contract

The contract should be advertised so that all the potential contractors eligible to make a bid have the opportunity to see it, to avoid accusations that one contractor has been given preferential treatment. Legal requirements for advertising contracts usually vary with the size and type of job; they often include advertising on the notice boards outside the offices of the local authority and commissioning aid organisation, and in the local or international press.

Care should be taken to avoid cartels, where the bidders for a contract engage in secret negotiations to decide among themselves which company will submit the most attractive bid and at what price. Methods to avoid cartels include widening the geographic range of places where the tenders are advertised and accepted; negotiating with other contracting organisations to agree piecework prices for common works; and dividing large contracts into smaller ones, with a number of different contractors working in parallel on similar activities.

step 5: issue tender documents

All the contractors who wish to apply should be given copies of the tender documents at the same time, to avoid accusations that one contractor has been given preferential treatment.

Some aid organisations recommend that contractors who already have a contract in progress with the organisation should be automatically excluded from further tendering.

Numbered copies of the tender documents should be issued. The details of each contractor should be recorded in the Tender Book.

step 6: meet with all contractors

All contractors should attend a meeting with the aid organisation, to allow them to ask questions regarding the tender, and the conditions and activities of the contract. Each contractor should receive the same information. It is important that each contractor should visit the future building site before bidding, to gain an understanding of the work to be done.

---

step 7: bids are submitted

Contractors return their bids in sealed envelopes by the specified deadline.

step 8: bids are registered

All the bids should be registered in the Tender Book. Depending on local regulations, a minimum of three returned bids is usually required in order for the contract to proceed, except in exceptional circumstances and when the national law and the aid organisation's procedures allow it.

step 9: bids are opened

All the contractors should be invited to the opening of the bids. Usually at least two people from the aid organisation should be present. All documents should be entered in the Tender Book, which should then be signed by all those present.

step 10: bids are examined

The bids should be examined and discussed by the representatives of the aid organisation, usually in private, and a decision should be reached.

Factors that may influence the selection of the contractor include the way in which the contractor proposes to undertake the works; the resources, labour, and equipment available to the contractor; the quality of previous work of a similar type; the relevant experience of the contractor; and whether the rates quoted by the contractor are realistic. In commercial environments, the contract will usually be awarded to the contractor who quotes the lowest price. The contractors will expect this commercial approach, so any likely overriding factors should be explained publicly to all contractors from the outset, ideally as part of the tender documentation.

step 11: detailed discussions

A meeting should be arranged between the successful contractor and the architect or engineer representing the aid organisation, to discuss the bid in detail. These talks will include the contractor's proposals for carrying out the work, and any outstanding clarifications or negotiations.

step 12: contract is awarded

The contract is awarded when it is signed by the contractor and the aid organisation. Each aid organisation has its own policies concerning who within the organisation should sign the contract, usually depending on the sum of money involved, and the line management of the project.

5.4.4 contracts

This section does not present a standard contract or standard clauses, but offers basic guidance on contract management.

Care should be taken when applying a general format when negotiating contracts for construction works or materials supply. It is usually necessary to adjust contracts to fit the specifics of the job, and the law in the country in which it is being carried out.

contract documents

Contract documents must include the following elements:

- present conditions of the contract, including contract language(s) and insurance
- actual text of the contract, including a copy of the bid form (if a tender process was used)
- contract drawings
- specifications
- bill of quantities (BOQ) (5.4.3)
- working plan: including completion period, schedule of payments, incentive and penalty clauses, skilled labour and key equipment, variation orders, dates of preliminary handover and final handover.

All the above documents are essential, and must be precise. To avoid conflict or misunderstanding, which can arise when a single document is read out of context, all the documents forming the contract should be read together.

The laws of the country of operations govern the contract, its meaning and interpretation, and the relations between the parties. National law may not be clearly defined for situations of emergency.

agree conditions of contract

The terms of the contract should be set out, in a manner that is legally binding, for both parties to agree. They should define the legal responsibilities of the aid organisation in question, its consultants, and the contractor and any sub-contractors.

The languages of the contract are usually the organisation's language and the local or operative language. The contract should be translated and presented in both forms to both parties, with both copies signed. If there are any differences between them in meaning or interpretation, the language version of the aid organisation should prevail. This should be made clear in the contract.

insurance It should be made clear in the contract that the contractor must meet all the insurance costs associated with the risks that the contractor will face. This includes, but is not limited to, the following:

- loss of or damage to material or equipment
- personal injury or death during performance of the works
- damage to the works.

The insurance must extend from the starting date of the contract until the end of the warranty period (the period after the end of the construction works during which a contractor guarantees the quality of the work and its maintenance).

bid form The bid form is the document submitted by the contractor to the client aid organisation for participation in the tender. It includes the bill of quantities, namely the volume of works and materials to be used, with prices. It forms part of the contract. If a contractor was directly appointed, instead of tendering for the work, that contractor should still supply the client aid organisation with a form containing information equivalent to that on a bid form. Quantities included on the bid form are estimates only: payment will relate to the actual quantities used. As the work progresses, the aid organisation's supervisor should verify the actual quantity of materials used. The contractor is then paid for what has been used, at the rates shown on the bid. Any variations or additions to the contract are calculated on the basis of the rates shown on the bid, if applicable, or at rates mutually agreed between the organisation and the contractor, if market prices of materials have fluctuated significantly. The bid form includes a calculation of the amount of labour required to complete the works, and its cost.

An independent verification that contract prices are realistic should have been performed when the bids were examined (5.4.3). Ideally, the aid organisation should independently and periodically gather data about market prices for common materials, allowing for the fact that prices fluctuate considerably in unstable economies.

5 labour

specifications

The specifications cover the minimum standards of workmanship and materials required by the conditions of contract. All works should be carried out to the approval of the aid organisation's architect or engineer. Any items that do not meet the requirements of the specifications should be repaired, or demolished and re-built at the contractor's expense. The contractor should be liable for any delays to the project caused as a result of repairing or rebuilding defective work. Any items of work not described in the specifications but forming part of the works should meet the minimum standards of workmanship and materials which can normally be expected locally. Where there is conflict between local standards and the specification, the specification should take precedence. The specifications form part of the contract, and should be read in conjunction with the other contract documents.

contract drawings

The contract drawings define exactly what will get built: they are a legal document and they form part of the contract. They should be fully annotated and drawn to scale, with full dimensions given; they should describe materials and should always be numbered and signed. They should contain detailed construction information.

working plan: completion period

The completion period is the number of working days necessary to carry out the works. It is based on the contractor's bid (if a tender process was used) and is recorded in the contract. The completion period may be revised and changed by the client, who should issue notification of a time extension after agreeing it with the contractor. The completion date defined in the contract is the day on which the contractor shall complete the construction works.

working plan: schedule of payments

A schedule of payments should be established, to reflect the phases of construction. It may be appropriate to pay a proportion of the total amount at the beginning of the contract to cover costs incurred by the contractor in bringing equipment on site or in procuring sufficient materials to begin the works.

The contract should contain a retention clause, ensuring that a significant proportion of the total contract amount is paid only after satisfactory completion of the works and final handover (see below).

This is to ensure that final activities are carried out in accordance with the contract.

working plan: incentives and penalties

Consider including incentive clauses and penalty clauses in all contracts, to control the delivery time and quality of a project. Incentives are paid in addition to the agreed contract sum. The conditions of incentives and penalties should be stated within the contract itself. Local legal mechanisms may not be sufficiently robust to guarantee the timely enforcement of penalties. However, the effect of a penalty clause can be maintained if the works are divided into short small contracts, with the award of the next contract dependent on the satisfactory completion of the previous one.

working plan: skilled labour and equipment

When certain skills or equipment are in demand, it may be useful to identify specific payments within the contract: the names of skilled labourers and the serial numbers of specific equipment might be included. To increase the likelihood of the required labour and equipment being available on time, specific incentive and penalty clauses could be attached.

working plan: variation orders

A variation order (VO) should be used when there is to be a change from the original contract in respect of quantities or costs; or if a time extension is required. For example, if the aid organisation decides during the execution of the contract that the length of road being constructed should be extended, a VO is used to specify this. The contractor prepares the VO and provides information on costs. The aid organisation authorises the VO. Two copies should be made, one for the contractor and one for the aid organisation.

working plan: preliminary handover

After completion of the works, the contractor should invite the client in writing to attend the preliminary handover of the works. The contractor and the client aid organisation usually make an inspection of the works and agree a list of remaining activities, sometimes referred to as a 'snagging list'. After the remaining activities have been carried out and inspected by the aid organisation, the client should issue a certificate of the preliminary handover of the works. Both the aid organisation and the contractor should sign this document. If local authorities are involved in the handover, this document may require a third signature.

working plan: final handover

Final handover may occur at the end of the construction process, or at the end of a warranty period defined in the contract. At the end of the warranty period, the contractor must repair any defects which are due to the contractor's errors or bad execution. After any repairs, the aid organisation should issue a certificate of the final handover of the works, signed by both the aid organisation and the contractor. The aid organisation should consider who has liability for any defects in workmanship or materials, or for any claim resulting from the works. The aid organisation is not normally liable, but specific mention of whatever liability is required should be included in all agreements made. Liability must be described in the contract. If the local authorities are also involved, these documents may require a third signature.

chapter 6 construction

6 construction

6 construction

This chapter offers an overview of construction-related considerations for organisations that support transitional settlement programmes. They are presented in general terms, concentrating on the physical processes common to the planning and implementation of all building works.

The chapter consists of the following sections:

6.1 profile and planning process: the necessary steps in a successful construction activity

6.2 implementation: considerations and best practice in the management of a construction activity

6.3 risks: information and advice to inform design and site-selection for transitional settlements in areas subject to hazards (natural and otherwise)

6.4 climatic design: the effects of climate on shelter needs, with general guidance on climate-related design for transitional settlements

6.5 site management: issues such as on-site safety, storage, and security

6.6 electrical services

6.7 materials procurement, storage, and use: information on common construction materials

6.8 construction from foundations to roof: the key concepts, varieties, and materials associated with foundations, walls, and roofs.

A significant reference literature exists to inform most construction activities, such as books dealing with the details of field engineering (Davis and Lambert 2002) and materials use (Stulz and Mukerji 1981). Labour and contract issues are discussed in chapter 5 of the present book, while the distribution of material and household shelter non-food items (NFIs) is discussed in chapter 7.

6.1 profile and planning process

The following subsections (6.1.1 and 6.1.2) focus on the context in which the construction activity is to be undertaken. Risk (6.3) and climatic design (6.4) can be used as indicators when assessing the current circumstances of the displaced population, and the hazards that a construction programme may encounter.

6.1.1 strategic, programme, and project plans

All construction should be considered within the framework of strategic, programme, and project planning (chapter 2), regardless of the TS option that a construction activity is intended to support. The planning framework in chapter 2 offers construction-relevant guidance on the following tasks:

- technical or social assessments, to inform the planning of a construction activity (2.2.1)
- setting objectives to determine the reasons why a construction activity should be undertaken, and what it should achieve (2.3.1)
- defining how the construction activity relates to other project activities, including producing a brief for the work (2.3.2)
- co-ordinating the schedule of works for the construction activity with the schedule of operations for all TS support for a displaced population (2.3.3)
- scheduling works within local construction seasons (2.5.5)
- scheduling works within the funding cycles of donors and within local finance-management constraints (2.5.6).

6.1.2 surveying

Surveying is the first act in the implementation of a construction activity. It identifies the opportunities and constraints presented by the site for the design of the structure, and ensures that an accurate record of the activity can be maintained. The survey plans should be used in tendering procedures and in negotiations with the land-owner or local authority, making reference to any cadastral records of property ownership.

electronic surveying tools

In addition to traditional surveying equipment, electronic tools may be available, including hand-held Global Positioning Systems

(GPSs). These work by receiving signals from a series of satellites, making it possible to triangulate the site's position accurately to within a few metres, which is sufficient for some large sites. Differential GPSs (DGPSs), which use a ground beacon to increase accuracy, are rarely used by aid organisations, due mainly to their higher cost.

GPS and DGPS can be used in conjunction with Geographical Information Systems (GISs), or databases offering a variety of information about an area (4.5.2). GISs can be extremely useful in combining assessment, planning, and operational information: for example, changes in transit routes, paths, and roads can be mapped next to the positions of landmines and unexploded ordnance (UXO) and updated in the daily security briefing.

The use of a GPS and the building of a GIS should be considered when initiating complex construction programmes, such as supporting camps (3.6, 3.7, and chapter 8).

siting and marking out

Siting key facilities and marking out the site (8.4.2 for camps) should be undertaken with great care and accuracy, ideally with the support of specialists. Local surveying companies, when available, might be engaged to undertake surveys and marking out.

6.2 implementation

The following sub-sections (6.2.1 and 6.2.2) explain key concepts and list documents that are essential for successful and safe construction activities. The implementation of a construction activity is illustrated through sections on site management (6.5), plumbing and electrical services (6.6), procuring, storing, and using materials (6.7), and construction from foundations to roof (6.8).

6.2.1 schedule of works and project implementation

The project brief (2.3.2) describes the requirements (functional, social, physical, and developmental) of the project activity. It should form the basis of a schedule of works, in which each activity is phased and co-ordinated. The schedule of works for the project activity should be co-ordinated with the schedule of operations for the programme (2.3.3), to avoid competition for key resources and labour.

Schedules of works are usually presented in the form of a table, or Gantt chart, which shows the time that each activity should take and the sequence in which the tasks should be undertaken. It is necessary to agree this schedule with the contractor or labour force, a process which includes agreeing the time required for each activity and the deadline by which they will be completed. To be legally binding, such a schedule needs to form part of more detailed contractual documentation (5.4).

Project-activity implementation should continually monitor the following factors:

- health and safety on site (6.5.1)
- on-site management of security, labour, tools, and materials (6.5.2, 6.5.3)
- supply and logistics chains (7.3), to ensure the prompt arrival of the correct materials, with the minimum of transit losses
- materials-sourcing (7.4.2), to ensure high quality and to meet ethical, environmental, economic, and development criteria
- construction methods and quality standards. (This might require the services of an independent professional supervisor or clerk of works.)

6.2.2 drawings and documentation

It is important to maintain a consistent, accurate, and up-to-date set of drawings and documentation describing the construction work, in order to ensure the following results:

- Stakeholders, such as the proposed users, understand the final outcome.
- Local permissions, such as planning permission, are obtained before any works are initiated.
- Any contractors, clerks of works, and self-help or paid labour have the correct working drawings with which to undertake the works.
- The procurement and logistics chain, including manufacturers and suppliers, is supported by the documentation needed to source and deliver the appropriate materials at the appropriate times.
- Staff responsible for strategic planning remain aware of the activity on the ground, including progress and any alterations.

Similar to the elements of a tendering process (5.4.3), documentation that should be prepared and maintained by managers of construction work should include the following items:

- a schedule of works
- any local permissions and additional documentation required under local or international law, or by the commissioning aid organisation or donor
- correspondence with local authorities, local community representatives, contractors, clerks of works, managing aid organisations, and donors
- contractual documentation, such as the Tender Book, the bid accepted, and the method of paying the contractor or other labour
- master plans, containing details of the construction(s) in question within a survey plan
- execution plans, including technical working drawings detailing every part of the construction and specifying each material
- the bill of quantities (BOQ): a list of the type, source, and quality of materials to be used, and activities to undertake the works, based upon the technical working drawings
- health and safety measures taken on the building site, and responsibilities in case of accidents
- site preparation required, including levelling, vegetation clearance and protection, marking out, utilities connections, and storage of topsoil
- site completion required, including the disposal of construction wastes, vegetation, hard surfacing, landscaping, drainage, and utilities connections.

6.3 risks

These guidelines are not intended for transitional settlements and shelter provided during or after natural disasters, unless the survivors have been displaced and have no option to return home. Nonetheless, we include basic information and advice which may be used to inform design and site selection for transitional settlements in areas subject to hazards, natural and otherwise.

The prime source of information on all risks and hazards is the knowledge and experience of the local population; but remember that memories are often short, and past experience will not include everything that might happen in the future. Conducting wide-ranging assessments and monitoring (4.2) is essential.

In most TS environments, a combination of hazards occurs. Often, sites for settlement are limited, and the local population are already living in the least hazardous sites. As a result, hazardous sites might be the only alternative, so TS planning and design must allow for some risks.

6.3.1 risk assessment

Before any construction activity is undertaken, a basic risk assessment must be completed. The result should be a hazard map of the area, including the sites of any transitional settlements, and access to them. This assessment will indicate the natural and artificial hazards (**hazard mapping**), such as security threats from armed incursions, as well as the vulnerabilities of the people, their livelihoods, and their communities (**vulnerability assessment**).

Chapter 4 deals in detail with the processes of assessment, monitoring, and evaluation. Participatory Learning and Action (PLA) (4.5.4) and surveys are liable to be the most appropriate tool for vulnerability assessment. PLA, combined with investigations of environmental criteria (4.4.5), will tend to produce the best hazard assessments. However, no tool or set of criteria is ideal. Overall, local knowledge would be the best guide to frequent hazards; but local knowledge should be supplemented by national and international data, if available. Your own creativity, open mind, and acceptance of unusual or unexpected conditions are the most essential tools.

Hazard mapping records a hazard as a time / space / severity process. Ideally it would include information of the following types:

- the nature of the hazard: for example volcanic, seismic, or related to water, temperature, or wind
- the meaning of 'extreme' for the hazard
- the frequency of extreme hazard events
- the duration of the hazard: for example, how long flood waters are likely to remain, or the duration of a volcanic eruption

6 construction

- the specific location of the hazard, and the area affected
- the severity of the hazard, as measured on agreed scales, such as the Modified Mercalli scale for earthquakes, or the probability of a certain flood depth
- the characteristics of the hazard, for example its potential impact on lives, property, and the environment.

Maps of certain hazards are sometimes produced by national or inter-government authorities.

6.3.2 combination of hazards

The hazard assessment must consider not only individual hazards, but also combinations of hazards. Hazards may occur both simultaneously and in sequence. **Simultaneous hazards** occur when two separate events, such as a volcanic eruption and a cyclone, occur in the same place at the same time. **Sequential hazards** occur when two separate events occur in the same place in sequence, or when one hazard event leads to another, such as an earthquake causing landslides which block roads and change drainage patterns, leading to flooding in unexpected areas. Common sequences include the following:

- Earthquakes lead to fires, floods, landslides, and volcanic activities.
- Volcanic activity can lead to fires, floods, landslides, and earthquakes.
- Tropical cyclones lead to coastal flooding, followed by inland flooding.
- Floods may expose or redistribute mines and unexploded ordnance.

6.3.3 security, conflict, and ordnance

Aid organisations should maintain security guidelines and security plans specific to each operation, besides offering some training in recognising threats and so reducing risk. Training should be far more comprehensive than the notes in this section. It should be designed to give people the confidence to cope with any eventuality as safely as possible.

Security threats vary in all conflicts, in post-conflict contexts, and with the passage of time. Some threats are specific to building transitional settlements, while others apply to all activities undertaken in the region. As a result, this section can only provide some general rules as guidance. Specialist advice and instruction should be sought whenever possible.

security Section 2.5.1 offers guidance on the protection and security of displaced populations and the siting of transitional settlement.

At its most basic, security for displaced people is provided (in visual terms at least) by a locally built family shelter or a canvas tent, which prevents those outside from knowing whether the shelter is occupied.

Warehousing and infrastructure have specific security needs: additional walls, fencing, or boundary markers may be required, ranging from a plastic netting fence to barbed wire – depending on available materials, as well as the local security situation.

The security of the occupants and their goods depends not only on the materials and design of their shelters, but on the placement of a structure in a settlement. For example:

- Street lighting provides security, especially near communal facilities used at night, such as latrines; but maintaining electricity supplies is not always feasible in transitional settlements.

- Reducing vegetation that casts shadows and creates hiding places can contribute to security in some areas; but vegetation can also provide a barrier, inhibiting entry to a property.

Exit routes from areas and buildings should always be planned and marked, so that people can leave quickly in case of attack or fire.

mines and ordnance

Transitional settlements should be sited away from minefields and areas known to contain unexploded ordnance (UXO), to prevent people entering them by accident. Any site where armed conflict has taken place, or where combatants have been camped, is likely to contain hazardous munitions and UXO. In many regions, it can be assumed that a previous military camp will have been defensively mined.

When a transitional settlement must be sited in an area that includes minefields and areas with munitions and UXO, the suspect areas must be well marked. This may be hard to achieve if the materials used for marking have a resale value. When possible, the local and displaced populations should be involved in the marking or in preparing the marking materials, to increase awareness of the dangers. Every member of both populations should be sensitised to the threat and the consequences of handling or stepping on explosive devices.

When there is a risk of continued conflict, glass in buildings should be covered with sticky tape on the inside, or on both sides, to prevent injuries from flying glass caused by explosions. Bags filled with sand or earth are often used outside buildings to deflect blast and prevent fragmentation. They provide some protection to the occupants, and to key machinery or goods, but they should not be considered as offering complete protection. Depending on the risk assessment, underground bomb shelters may be appropriate, if they provide safety from bullets and fragmentation.

Both during and after armed conflict, it is wise to be suspicious of unoccupied and damaged buildings, and abandoned military positions and military hardware. They may contain unexploded munitions, and/or they may have been mined defensively or booby-trapped to prevent others using them.

When attempting to identify likely mined areas, whether in a transitional settlement or along a transit route, it may be useful to understand the reasons why minefields are used. Most anti-personnel mines placed around buildings and on sites and routes were put there to defend something, although it may have been a line of confrontation that has long since disappeared. Typically, defensive minefields are used to defend settlements, military posts, power-lines, dams, roads, bridges, and any item of essential infrastructure. Larger anti-vehicle mines may be laid in long belts to restrict the movement of armoured attackers. These large mines may be surrounded by small anti-personnel mines, to prevent attempts at clearance. When a conflict targets a civilian group, mines and improvised explosive devices (IEDs) may be used to deny people access to their homes and property, or to essential utilities such as a water source.

The threat from munitions other than mines and booby-traps should not be underestimated. In some areas, half of all civilian casualties are caused by other explosive remnants of war, whether unexploded ordnance, or ordnance that has been fused and fired but has not exploded, or munitions that have not been used. The latter may not have been fused, but if they are close to fused munitions they can still present a severe threat. In general, 15–20 per cent of all munitions fired do not explode as intended. This means that battle areas are often strewn with UXO. Many are inactive, but others may be sensitive to any movement. Unfortunately, UXO fascinates children and young people. They must be discouraged from collecting them or playing with them.

If there are people living in the area who were present during the conflict, they may be the most reliable source of information about the threats in the area. It is often appropriate to approach their leaders and ask for advice on whom to consult. It is always useful to promote good relations with local people, and this is often achieved by working through the recognised local leaders and hiring local labour to help to identify and mark hazardous areas.

It is always wise to avoid areas that local populations avoid. These may be obviously abandoned and overgrown. While identifying dangerous areas, always follow well-used paths. If the path takes a detour, do not be tempted to take a short cut – even if it is a matter of only a few paces.

Whether or not there are local sources of information, all other sources should be investigated. Threats can be better identified and evaluated if you understand the history of the conflict in the region, the troop movements, and the battles. It may be useful to consider, like a soldier, what natural features might be used to conceal approach during attack: if mines were used in the area, the predictable concealed approaches will almost certainly have been mined.

During conflict, dangerous areas are usually unmarked, although occasionally they are clearly fenced. More often, they are sporadically marked by local people to warn each other of a known danger. Improvised marking systems are rarely durable. Common examples are crossed sticks, piles of stones, and unexpected barriers of brush or twisted grass. The local leaders may indicate any such signs that have been used.

6 construction

Immediately before and during mine clearance, danger areas are usually marked by the responsible de-mining group. The most common marking system involves mine-warning signs placed at regular intervals around the perimeter of a suspect area. The signs are usually red, with the symbol of a skull and crossbones, and some writing – which may be in a local script but is usually also in English. The signs may be linked with striped plastic tape, but this is rare. In rocky areas, red-painted stones may be used as markers; in areas with bush, red-painted sticks may be driven into the ground. Consult any de-mining teams who are working in the region to discover the marking system that they use. Maintain up-to-date information on areas of risk and areas that have been cleared, including any marking that the teams may have left behind.

Settlements and military camps are often sited on high ground. Note that mines and ordnance can be moved by heavy rain or landslips, and always look for evidence of ground movement in areas of known danger.

6.3.4 toxic environments

Local knowledge is critical for understanding toxic threats and sources of dangerous pollution. Here are some examples of risks to look out for:

- contamination of ground water by arsenic
- contamination of surface or ground water by chemical fertilisers and pesticides, sewage, and waste materials
- accumulations of carbon monoxide emitted by vehicles, generators, or stoves
- lead-based paints and glazes
- abandoned gem mines or mineral mines
- depleted uranium weapons
- dust raised by wind or vehicles
- acid from leaking batteries, particularly from vehicles
- oil leaking from vehicles, machinery, and storage facilities
- burning vegetation on the land, in yards, or in stoves for heat and cooking (7.6.8, 7.6.9).

Further information on health and safety issues will be found in section 6.5.1; section 6.7 contains information on construction materials and finishes.

settlements Industrial areas pose a particular risk of hazardous pollution, so care must be taken before siting transitional settlements on an abandoned industrial site, or near an active one. During armed conflict, storage tanks are often ruptured, toxic substances are abandoned, and monitoring and clean-up cannot take place. Topography and climate may trap pollution, such as smog, vehicle emissions, generator emissions, or dust. Previous development or disaster-response work might create a toxic hazard.

buildings Some materials, such as some types of asbestos, some paints, and formaldehyde, should be avoided because they are toxic. Asbestos poses the greatest risk to health when it is friable, fragmenting into small pieces due to wear or degradation.

6.3.5 vector control

Site selection plays a fundamental role in reducing or increasing the impact of vector-borne diseases on a population.

settlements Two main categories of vector need to be considered:

- insects, including mosquitoes, black flies, fleas, ticks, and sand flies
- small animals, including rats, birds, monkeys, and bats.

figure 6.3(a): site selection for disease-vector control

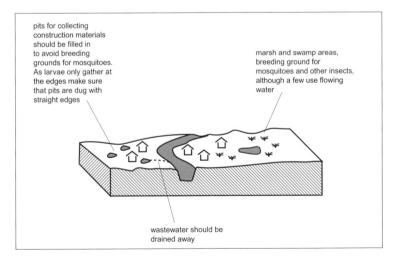

pits for collecting construction materials should be filled in to avoid breeding grounds for mosquitoes. As larvae only gather at the edges make sure that pits are dug with straight edges

marsh and swamp areas, breeding ground for mosquitoes and other insects, although a few use flowing water

wastewater should be drained away

6 construction

The dangers of malaria and other insect-borne diseases, including sleeping sickness, dengue fever, yellow fever, leishmaniasis, and encephalitis, should be considered when selecting sites for transitional settlements. Mosquitoes, for example, tend to breed in stagnant or still water; so site managers are advised to fill in pits, remove discarded tyres and tins which could collect water, cover water-collection and storage facilities, and fill in potholes in roads and tracks. Mosquitoes can travel 3km or more from their breeding site, so you need to take into consideration a large area around the settlement.

Flies and rodents, such as rats, which can carry leptospirosis, can be tackled by proper management of waste and sanitation. Appropriate personal hygiene will reduce the risk of lice, fleas, and ticks taking hold in a settlement; this in turn will help to prevent diseases such as plague and rickettsial infections. Similarly, soil-borne diseases and parasites, such as anthrax, tetanus, ascariasis, and trichuriasis, cannot be eliminated from a settlement or area, but they can be avoided by paying attention to personal hygiene and proper food preparation.

Dust can become a disease vector: for example, by carrying faeces from fleas which have typhus. Planning for transitional settlement should consider how to reduce the spread of dust by wind, vehicles, and pedestrians.

Other vectors require more careful planning, or simply efforts to increase awareness of risks among the population. Monkeys are known to enter settlements and steal fruit or other food; they can carry hepatitis and possibly haemorrhagic fever viruses, such as Ebola or Marburg. Mammals such as monkeys and bats can carry rabies.

Due to the wide variety of diseases, vectors, and other threats, local knowledge is usually essential in order to identify the most prevalent threats and techniques of dealing with them (Thomson 1995).

buildings Treated mosquito nets (7.6.4) effectively protect sleeping people against mosquitoes. Additionally, mosquito nets or fine wire mesh can be stretched over windows and door frames to keep insects out. Some sprays are toxic to humans and other animals, so spraying should be conducted with care.

Making food stores rodent-proof is particularly important. Buildings can be protected by closing all holes greater than 6mm in diameter: this is the smallest hole that a young mouse can enter. The holes should be blocked with strong material such as cement, mortar, or metal plates. Rats can chew through rope or light wire such as chicken wire.

A rodent-proof building will probably be monkey-proof as well, but primates are highly intelligent and, like racoons and a few birds, have been known to open doors and undo zip fasteners.

figure 6.3(b): rodent-proof building

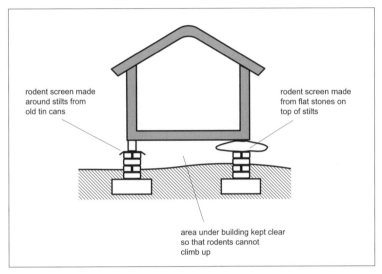

rodent screen made around stilts from old tin cans

rodent screen made from flat stones on top of stilts

area under building kept clear so that rodents cannot climb up

Diesel is sometimes poured on the ground around the outside of tents to keep snakes at bay, but it needs to be reapplied frequently.

6.3.6 fire

Fire is a common hazard in transitional settlements. The risk is particularly high in dry areas where forest fires or wildfires are common, and in cold or temperate climates where cooking and heating stoves are used inside shelters.

Fires inside a building are generally started by people acting carelessly: for example, using a poorly designed stove, dropping a

6 construction

cigarette butt, failing to keep watch on burning embers or candles, not mending faulty electrical supplies or goods, and improperly using or storing flammable or combustible substances such as gasoline. Risk prevention and risk awareness are vital. External fires, such as wildfires, can be started by people, either through carelessness, or by trying to burn vegetation or rubbish; but they can also be started naturally by lightning.

Fire needs oxygen, fuel, and a high temperature to propagate itself. Removing any one of these ingredients will stop a fire. Oxygen can be removed by smothering the blaze: for example, by placing a specially treated fire blanket over a burning pot of grease. The temperature could be reduced by dousing the flames in water (depending on the type of fire).

settlements Planning transitional settlements with firebreaks helps to stop fires from spreading. Designing and locating settlements to reduce the impact of wind (6.3.10) can also help to reduce the spread of a large fire. Large settlements will require fire-fighting teams to be based within each compound. Consider providing water points and fire beaters at strategic points. Firebreaks alone generally do not stop a fire spreading: they merely slow it down and give time for fire-fighting teams to respond and for people to be evacuated.

As a rough guide, buildings should be twice as far apart as they are tall, in order to prevent fire from spreading from building to building (UNHCR 2000). Wind, however, can cause fire to jump large distances, particularly when flying embers are produced.

figure 6.3(c): recommended width of a firebreak

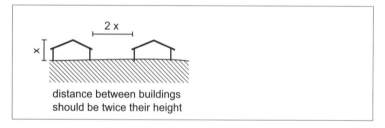

distance between buildings
should be twice their height

define firebreaks

The need for firebreaks should be taken into account in all camp planning, and they should be installed in any self-settled camps as soon as possible. UNHCR standards for 'Fire prevention' are as follows.

66. As a rule of thumb a firebreak (area with no buildings) 30 m wide is recommended for approximately every 300 m of built-up area. In modular camps firebreaks should be situated between blocks. This area will be ideal for growing vegetables or recreation. If space allows, the distance between individual buildings should be great enough to prevent collapsing, burning buildings from touching adjacent buildings. The distance between structures should therefore be a minimum of twice the overall height of any structure; if building materials are highly inflammable (straw, thatch, etc.) the distance should be increased to 3 to 4 times the overall height. The direction of any prevailing wind will also be an important consideration.
UNHCR (2000), chapter 12, p.143

buildings For all transitional settlements, basic fire safety in building design needs to be observed. The longest distance to a fire escape should be no greater than 18m. This standard is based on average escape times from burning buildings. Extra time is required for vulnerable groups, and in buildings such as hospitals and schools. Fire exits should be planned, kept open, and clearly marked. Assembly points well away from the building should be identified and made known. Consider locating disabled people on the ground floor whenever possible.

figure 6.3(d): recommended (maximum) distance to a fire escape

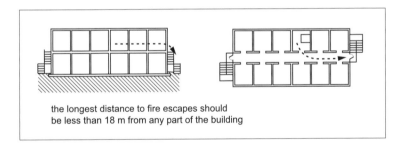

the longest distance to fire escapes should be less than 18 m from any part of the building

Heat and flames kill and injure, but smoke and toxic gases are equally dangerous. Smoke and toxic gases can cause casualties outside the building as well.

Smoke from fires is dangerous not only in an emergency but in day-to-day activities, such as the burning of vegetation and dung in a building for cooking.

6 construction

Warwick and Doig (2004) list the effects of daily exposure to smoke as follows:

- reduced effectiveness of the immune system
- increased rates of respiratory infections, including pneumonia, particularly in children
- increased rates of other lung diseases, including lung cancer, tuberculosis, and asthma
- low birth weight and increased infant mortality
- increased incidence of cataracts of the eye.

Reducing exposure to smoke should be a major goal when designing buildings in transitional settlements. Responses include the following (adapted from Warwick and Doig 2004):

- providing improved cooking devices, such as chimneys or chimneyless, improved, biomass stoves
- providing alternative fuels for cooking, such as kerosene, liquid petroleum gas, solar cookers, or electricity
- reducing the need for fire as a heat source, by providing more efficient housing or using solar energy
- improving ventilation
- improving kitchen design and stove placement
- ensuring that stoves work appropriately, by maintaining them properly
- encouraging people to avoid the smoke, for example by keeping children away from it.

6.3.7 earthquakes

Earthquakes can shake the ground severely in any direction. The soil may become almost liquid, undermining the foundations of buildings. Earthquakes may result in tsunami, landslides, floods, fire, and other hazards, so the potential impact of combinations of hazards (6.3.2) should be considered.

Earthquake zones are generally well known and well mapped, but not all specific fault lines are known, and many moderate earthquakes occur in locations with no known faults.

settlements In earthquake zones, settlements should avoid alluvial plains, unstable slopes, steep slopes, unstable soils, or reclaimed areas where the ground has not been properly engineered. In earthquake zones it is important to be aware of areas liable to landslide, rock slide, avalanche, and liquefaction. Buildings should be spaced so that if one collapses it will not destroy another one. Such a layout will also help to avoid the spread of post-earthquake fires.

buildings Several techniques can be used to make buildings withstand earthquakes better or, at least, to provide the occupants with a chance of escaping from the building or finding cover before it collapses:

- Stones should be used to tie walls together in rubble-masonry construction.
- The building should be strongly secured to its foundation.
- For masonry, the building should be reinforced with timber or concrete belts at different heights. Lintel levels are the best location for these.
- If the floor and roof are constructed of timber, it is good to provide similar reinforcing bands at floor level and eaves level as well.
- Column lengths should be similar, so do not mix tall and short columns.
- Do not use asymmetrical designs, such as ones that incorporate wings or T-shaped, L-shaped, or H-shaped buildings.
- Buildings whose length is less than three times their width are preferable, to keep the plan as square as possible.
- Avoid large and numerous openings; do not design openings near to wall junctions.
- Long walls should be buttressed at intervals.
- Strong connections should be made where walls meet, especially at corners: for example, by using vertical and horizontal reinforcement.
- Walls should be strongly connected to the foundation.
- Floor components should be strongly tied to each other; floor joists should be strongly secured to walls.
- Roof components should be strongly tied to each other.

6 construction

- Heavy roof tiles may be dislodged and may hurt or kill people even if the building survives, so tiles should be avoided, or strongly tied to the roof purlins.
- Roof rafters should be strongly secured to the walls.
- Storey heights should be similar to each other.
- Tall chimneys should always be secured to the structure.

In order to make constructions resistant to earthquakes, simple forms and simple plans are recommended. Certain shapes of buildings are very vulnerable to cracking when the ground shakes.

figure 6.3(e): good and bad design for earthquake zones

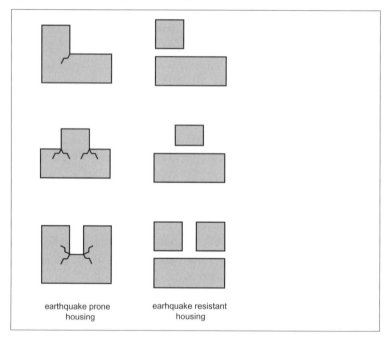

It is recommended that where a structure has to be built with a number of units, the units are connected through non-structural sections, and the buildings are structurally built of separate elements.

If the production of earthquake-resistant housing would be too expensive, consider up-grading traditional housing.

6.3.8 volcanoes

Volcanoes pose various types of hazard, including rapidly moving clouds of hot ash and dust (pyroclastic flows or surges), mudflows (lahar), lava, fire, flood, landslides, rock slides, avalanches, poisonous gases, tsunami, and ballistics (rocks thrown into the air). Each volcano is usually capable of producing only some of these hazards.

Local knowledge might not help, because volcanoes can erupt without any precedent in recorded history. Fortunately, most areas where volcanoes could occur are known and mapped. If an area is labelled as volcanic, the specialist knowledge of geologists or volcanologists will help to determine possible hazards and their relative dangers, even if there is no recorded evidence of active volcanism in the area. Seek advice from relevant geological authorities or government departments.

Volcanism yields unpredictable and complex hazards, so caution and proper assessments are essential, to protect the occupants of transitional settlements. In the past, large settlements have been destroyed by volcanic tsunami, explosive eruptions, mudflows, and pyroclastic flows, which have killed people and animals in their thousands.

settlements If there is a risk of active volcanism in an area, it is best to avoid putting a settlement there. The size of the exclusion zone varies with the volcano. If the volcano erupts explosively, a danger zone should probably exceed 100km from the summit, particularly if rapid evacuation is difficult. If a volcano is not prone to explosive eruptions, the danger zone might still be large, in order to avoid mudflows or lava, but it could also be highly localised: for example to avoid landslides or poisonous gases. Specialist knowledge would be needed in order to determine the possible hazards and danger zones.

General considerations include the following:

- If flowing lava is typical of a volcano's pattern of eruption, site the settlement at least 5km away from the edge of the largest lava field. However, bear in mind that changes in topography and eruption characteristics make this guideline far from secure.

- Do not site settlements in locations liable to be hit by pyroclastic flows; they can occur with little warning, can have temperatures in excess of 100°C, can travel at speeds of more than 100km/h, and can jump over topographic obstacles. There is little chance of escape from a pyroclastic flow.

- Volcanic ash has short-term and long-term health effects, including increases in asthma and silicosis; ash infiltrates machinery and vehicles, ruining engines and electrics, and stops jet engines. Avoiding areas of continual or dense ash fall is essential.

- Volcanoes can throw large rocks several kilometres; if a volcano has a history of explosive eruptions, take advice from volcanologists or appropriate experts.

- Flying any aircraft near an erupting volcano is extremely dangerous; runways and helipads should be sited well away from an active volcano, as should transitional settlements.

buildings The design of buildings must be informed by awareness of the specific volcanic hazards in the area. If buildings are sited near active volcanoes, it may be important to consider the risk of fires (6.3.6), earthquakes (6.3.7), landslides (6.3.9), and floods (6.3.11). Other possible effects of volcanism are extremely difficult to predict in advance.

General considerations for humanitarian agencies include the following:

- Large openings in walls should be situated on the side of the building away from the volcano, to provide some protection against blasts, ballistics, and pressures from the volcano.

- In order to leave an escape route open, do not put doors in walls facing the volcano.

- When designing roofs to withstand ash fall, always calculate the load by assuming that the ash will be completely saturated and thus extremely dense.

- Objects such as timber planks and sheets of metal should not be left lying around, in case they become missiles.

6.3.9 landslides

The term 'landslide' includes rock slides, rock falls, tree slides, mud slides, debris flows, and avalanches. The technical term is 'mass movements', but we will use the word 'landslide' in these guidelines.

settlements The best protection against landslides is the careful choice of a site: people should never build or settle in areas that are suspected of being prone to landslides. Landslides tend to occur on steep slopes, or where the land is undercut by water: for example at river bends, narrow beaches, or coastal cliffs. Deforestation and overgrazing can also reduce the stability of slopes and increase the risk of landslides. Heavy rainfall is often the event that triggers a slide. Areas recently affected by wildfire are particularly prone to landslides.

Considering the immense power of landslides and the low survival rate of people caught in them, it is best to avoid vulnerable sites. Landslides can be highly localised, so seek local information about the suitability of a site before beginning to establish a settlement. Look out for clues from the environment about landslides in the past: signs such as recently fallen rocks, vegetation-free areas running down a slope, and piles of debris. Scour-marks from past landslides may be visible.

Properly draining the settlement can prevent landslides. Saturated soil should be drained, and surface run-off should not be permitted to enter the soil of the slide-prone area.

figure 6.3(f): landslide risk to settlement

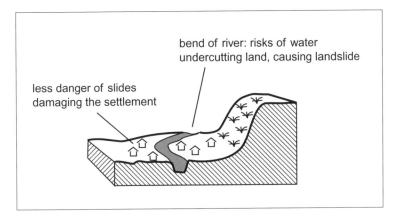

buildings Although solid foundations or raft foundations will improve stability on unstable soils (6.8.2), if the soil is moving in a landslide the building will still go with it, unless the foundation extends well below the region of soil movement.

6.3.10 storms

The term 'storm' includes a wide variety of phenomena:

- wind, including tropical cyclones, tornadoes, downbursts, and extreme wind speeds
- precipitation, including intense rain, driving rain, snow, sleet, ice, and hail
- lightning
- sand and dust storms
- extreme temperatures, involving heat, cold or humidity (6.4).

settlements The orientation, siting, and layout of settlements influence the ways in which they are affected by wind, precipitation, sand, dust, and other storm phenomena. Local topography can also have a big impact, and can create intense local variations in the storm climate. For example:

- Gaps in hills or mountain ranges can funnel wind, as can valleys.
- Complex topography can cause complex wind patterns.
- Peaks are a major barrier to moisture-holding air. Sites a few kilometres apart may experience widely varying patterns and intensities of rainfall.

Wind has both desirable and undesirable characteristics: it can clear snow and sand, and provide cooling in the summer; but it can also cause snow and sand to drift and can create chilling draughts. When locating and designing settlement sites, try to incorporate the favourable factors while reducing the negative influences of the wind.

Wind barriers, the shape and layout of a building, and the surrounding landscape and vegetation are all factors that can control the flow of air around a settlement.

Proper grouping of buildings can create a protected microclimate within the community, by buffering dwellings from winds and controlling the accumulation of sand or dust.

figure 6.3(g): storm risk to settlement

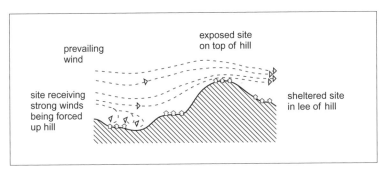

buildings The orientation, materials, and surroundings of a building affect its vulnerability to extreme storms, including the wind, rain, snow, or dust that might accompany the storm. A building can be made more resistant to wind by designing it to resist the force as an entire structure, not as an assembly of bits and pieces. Some solutions also pose risks. For example, orienting a building to increase wind resistance might expose a larger surface area to driving rain, abrasive sand, or missiles. Note also that although trees generally act as buffers against wind, in extreme events they could be blown over on to buildings or uprooted; or branches could be torn off, thereby striking buildings as missiles. Consider using a buffer of vegetation without thick branches or trunks, such as bushes. Expert judgement and local conditions will determine the most appropriate solution in each case.

figure 6.3(h): reducing wind damage

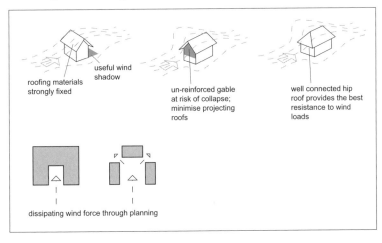

One of the primary mechanisms by which wind causes damage is 'uplift'. The roof should be tied down on to the walls, and these upward loads should then be transmitted all the way through to adequate anchorage in the foundations. It is important to ensure that the roof stays down when subject to the wind-uplift loads. Roof trusses need to be bolted to the load-bearing columns through in-cuts or straps. (See figure 6.3(i).)

figure 6.3(i): fixing roof trusses

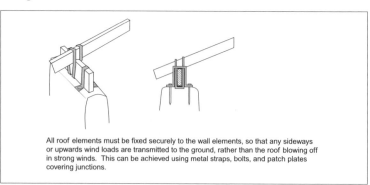

All roof elements must be fixed securely to the wall elements, so that any sideways or upwards wind loads are transmitted to the ground, rather than the roof blowing off in strong winds. This can be achieved using metal straps, bolts, and patch plates covering junctions.

A well-anchored roof will prevent water entering during rain storms or tropical cyclones. If roof shingles (wooden tiles) are used, a simple preventative measure is to use eight nails per shingle, rather than four.

Iron sheeting should not be nailed straight into supports, because it will be lifted straight out in strong winds. Connections, brackets, anchors, or tie-straps should transmit wind-uplift loads adequately to the foundation.

Hipped roofs are less vulnerable than gable roofs, because they are braced in all four directions. Good design and connections between the roof and the walls can overcome the weaknesses inherent in gable roofs. Low roofs create increased uplift, and steep roofs create increased lateral loads, so both should be avoided. Check what the local people do, because they have probably learned how to live with the hazard.

Ensure that objects that can easily be picked up by a strong wind are not left lying around. Keep flammable, explosive, and combustible materials away from buildings, and keep them well secured. If a storm is coming, especially a tropical cyclone, cover openings, especially windows, with sheets of wood or plastic.

Structures with fewer storeys are less vulnerable to wind and the impact of missiles. Metal ties, screws, and nails may corrode in humid environments, or in areas near the sea, because of the salt in the air.

Figure 6.3(j) shows how steeply pitched roofs receive a high wind loading and may blow in as a result.

figure 6.3(j): roofs and wind loads (1)

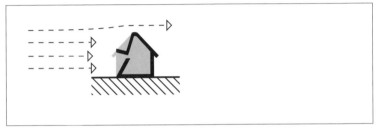

Figure 6.3(k) shows how low-pitched roofs receive a high suction and are likely to blow off as a result.

figure 6.3(k): roofs and wind loads (2)

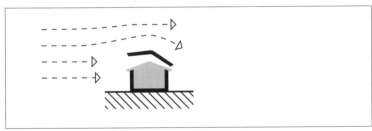

Figure 6.3(l) shows that a roof angled at 20°–30° receives the least wind stress.

figure 6.3(l): roofs and wind loads (3)

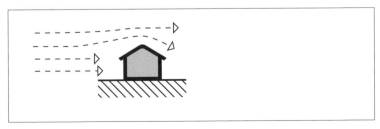

Figure 6.3(m) shows how buildings which are not properly anchored to their foundations may overturn.

figure 6.3(m): roofs and wind loads (4)

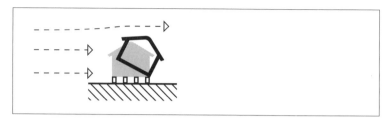

Figure 6.3(n) shows that the frame of buildings without appropriately connected and stiffened joints may distort as a result of a strong wind.

figure 6.3(n): roofs and wind loads (5)

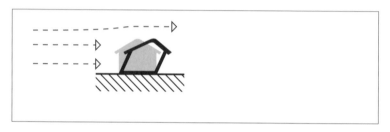

Figure 6.3(o) shows that a building that is shielded from wind, located at a safe distance to avoid trees falling on it, and built on a plinth, if correctly constructed, is well protected against winds and floods.

figure 6.3(o): roofs and wind loads (6)

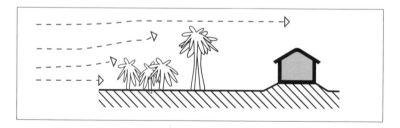

6.3.11 floods

'Floods' is a general term which includes flash floods occurring after sudden rainfall or snowmelt, or when rivers break their banks or spread out over the floodplain; surges in sea levels caused by low atmospheric pressure and severe wind; and rises in ground water due to a sudden influx of water upstream. In addition to the dangers of damage and drowning from the water, saturated ground allows mosquitoes and other insects to breed (6.3.5); food and fresh water become contaminated; and debris or waves can cause structural damage or injuries.

Contact with flood water should always be avoided, because it is usually contaminated with oil and sewage, which can compromise health and safety. Floods may also disrupt animals' normal locations and behaviour patterns, bringing poisonous snakes or crocodiles into the area.

Settlements should not be built in areas that are frequently flooded. Floodplains are usually simple to identify, although flash-flood areas are less easy to note. Specialist assistance should be sought. If building in floodable areas is absolutely necessary and completely unavoidable, seek local advice and follow local practice.

Note, however, that many populations live permanently in flooded areas, and flooding is a constant and natural feature of their lives. Some of these people adapt to the conditions by living in boats, or in structures on raised platforms, or on stilts above the water. Flooding, if poorly prepared for or unexpected, can be catastrophic and highly dangerous; but when livelihoods depend on seasonal or near-permanent flooding, water can be used to improve transport and to support livelihoods, such as fishing or rice farming.

Always ask local people for advice about flooding, and look at a site for evidence of seasonal flooding, such as cracks in the earth, deep footprints in dried earth, and marsh grasses.

6 construction

6.4 climatic design

Different designs are appropriate for different climates (7.5.1). Family shelters and other constructions should be designed and supported to meet the worst local weather conditions. Shelter and NFI needs vary, depending on the climate: see figure 6.4(a).

figure 6.4(a): shelter and NFI priorities

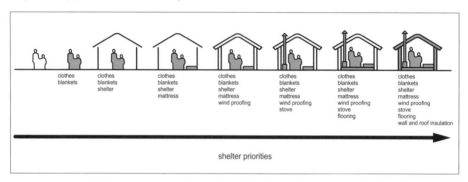

This section explores the effects of climate on shelter needs and offers general guidance on climatic design for transitional settlements. A discussion of general climatic considerations is followed by advice for specific climate types: cold climates (6.4.1), wet climates (6.4.2), and hot dry climates (6.4.3).

Climatic conditions can threaten people's health and their chances of survival. Shelter can protect against climatic threats. Seasonal variations have considerable impact on the type and cost of shelter that is needed. In cold climates most daily activities will take place indoors, so the area required will be larger, because external space cannot generally be used.

Awareness of the season is critical when planning a project and choosing the materials to be used. Many areas have a combination of climate types: temperatures may fall to −10°C in winter, while averaging more than 30°C in summer. Sometimes the difference between day and night temperatures could be 20–30°C, particularly if wind is involved.

The average skin temperature for human well-being is generally 32–34°C, particularly in cool weather or in a light breeze. For a healthy person at rest, normal core body temperature is 36–37°C. A room temperature considered to be comfortable varies between 15° and 18°C.

6.4.1 cold climates

Cold can affect people's health and therefore have an impact on their livelihoods. Death rates in most communities tend to rise in winter, but a victim of hypothermia (extremely low body temperature) might never have complained about the cold or understood the potentially fatal implication. One can feel colder on a rainy and windy day, if temperatures are above zero, than on a still dry day when temperatures are substantially below zero. Wind and moisture increase cooling. Wind causes warm air to be removed away from the body. Moisture, particularly on the skin and clothes, leads to evaporation, which removes heat.

Cold climate, especially if accompanied by malnourishment, leads to a rise in respiratory diseases and acute respiratory infections (ARIs), such as pneumonia. The risks are greater when people are gathered together in confined spaces, and when their physical resistance is reduced by working to keep warm. Keeping warm by means of adequate clothes and bedding, but also through improved living spaces, is crucial in reducing mortality and morbidity.

In cold weather, people require more energy, so they burn more calories. The increase in energy requirements due to the cold further increases the requirements for vitamins and minerals. An initial estimate of food needs should be based on the target figure of 2,100 kilocalories per person per day, but remember that this figure assumes a mean daily temperature of 20°C. An additional 100 kilocalories per person per day is needed for every five degrees below 20°C, down to 0°C. Malnutrition can cause people to shiver to death, even in hot dry climates, if the nights are cold.

If heating is not available, sufficient clothing and blankets should be distributed to keep people warm, especially while sleeping. Insulation from the ground, through mattresses, is another effective measure: heat conducts quickly from the body into the cold ground, and also the warm air in the transitional shelter will rise, making the floor area the coldest.

settlements Local climatic variations should be considered when siting a settlement: for example, wind may be funnelled through gaps in mountains, or the site may be shaded from the sun in deep valleys. Particularly at high altitudes, it can be significantly colder in the shade than in the sun. Water-supply pipes must be buried underground to prevent freezing (6.6.1).

buildings Stoves and heaters are an essential part of the heating strategy for a shelter in a cold climate. An adult human body at rest produces up to 100 watts of heat, about the same as a bright light bulb. Children produce less heat and lose it faster, because they have a larger surface area compared with their volume. A basic wood stove with extremely limited fuel will produce about 1,000 watts: the equivalent of an electric kettle. Therefore, even in a well-insulated room, a stove will release significantly more heat than the body-heat generated by most families (7.6.8 and 7.6.9). Big rooms should be partitioned in order to reduce the air volume to be heated.

Once the room has been heated, it is important to ensure that the heat does not escape. In cold climates, insulation and draught reduction are the keys to keeping houses warm. Designing a warm room with a thermal buffer zone is a common approach to the problem (see figure 6.4(b)). Some level of air infiltration must be permitted, which means that the infiltrating air must be warmed, possibly by body heat or by artificial sources. Ventilation is necessary to prevent respiratory diseases caused by cooking or heating smoke.

Houses with thick walls and insulated roofs can be very cold if they have leaky or broken windows or doors. Plastic sheeting (7.5.2) is often used for temporary repairs, and it can be used for windows (translucent plastic sheeting) or to create thermal buffer zones. In the case of windows, two sheets are significantly better than one, because they have the effect of double-glazing.

figure 6.4(b): cold-climate building principles

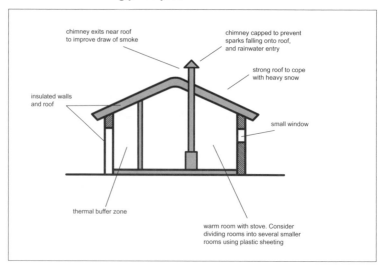

chimney exits near roof to improve draw of smoke

chimney capped to prevent sparks falling onto roof, and rainwater entry

strong roof to cope with heavy snow

insulated walls and roof

small window

thermal buffer zone

warm room with stove. Consider dividing rooms into several smaller rooms using plastic sheeting

6.4.2 wet climates

For further information on building in flood-risk areas, see section 6.3.11.

settlements In wet environments, the chosen site should be above the flood plain, and in particular it should be out of the way of seasonal rivers or the highest annual tide.

The ideal slope for a site should provide adequate drainage during the wet season; but it should not be so steep as to threaten the stability of the buildings.

In hot and humid climates, settlements should be open, with individual dwellings sited far apart from each other, to increase air flow. Trees and foliage should be kept wherever possible, to provide shade.

buildings Roofs should have a sufficient pitch for rainwater drainage: above 30° for normal tiles and thatch, and above 20° for well-lapped corrugated iron sheeting. Generous overhangs help to protect the openings from water penetration during rainy seasons.

Provide sufficient openings for good ventilation and air convection, both in the walls and on the roof.

Take care that materials do not suffer from dampness and rot. Canvas can decay very rapidly in hot and humid climates. Clothes, blankets, and metal components of stoves can also be damaged by humidity.

figure 6.4(c): wet-climate building principles

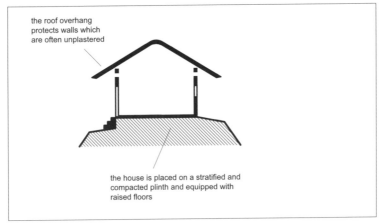

the roof overhang protects walls which are often unplastered

the house is placed on a stratified and compacted plinth and equipped with raised floors

6.4.3 hot dry climates

In hot dry climates, shade from the sun is a primary consideration during the day. Heat exhaustion and exposure are common health problems. In hot climates, people need more drinking water than in cold climates. Dust is also a problem, so shelters should be designed to be closed during sand storms. Cold is also a concern in hot dry climates, because the nights can be surprisingly chilly, especially in arid areas.

settlements Narrow streets and enclosed settlements maximise the shade created by buildings; they use the thermal mass of buildings to keep the settlement cool, and reduce the dust blown by wind. But if buildings are sited close together, fire might spread more easily, especially if the buildings are made from easily flammable materials.

figure 6.4(d): hot-climate settlement principles

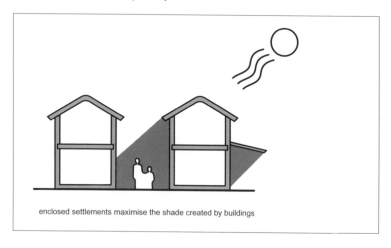

enclosed settlements maximise the shade created by buildings

buildings Thermal mass in buildings should be ensured by constructing thick walls and insulating roofs, making them cool in the day and not too cold at night. In areas prone to earthquakes, the use of concrete blocks should be considered.

If building with plastic sheeting, provide double-skinned roofs with ventilation between the two layers, to minimise heat radiation.

Position doors and window away from the direction of the prevailing winds, which are likely to be very hot. Traditional houses are often placed in compounds, which offer protection, shade, and fencing for livestock. Consider the possibility of providing external shade for outdoor activities, depending on the climatic and cultural contexts.

figure 6.4(e): hot-climate building principles

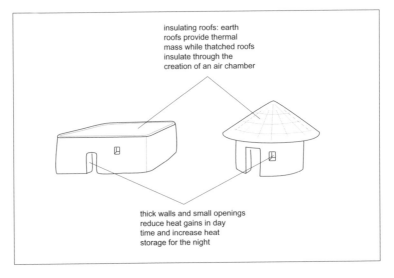

insulating roofs: earth roofs provide thermal mass while thatched roofs insulate through the creation of an air chamber

thick walls and small openings reduce heat gains in day time and increase heat storage for the night

6.5 site management

Site management is a key component of project implementation (6.2).

6.5.1 health and safety

Health and safety measures should be in place to safeguard the well-being of the workers, and to respect their rights. They are important for other reasons too: organisations need to maintain a good reputation, and local employment laws assign responsibility and liability for health and safety to the employer.

National regulations on health and safety should be observed, and possibly improved upon. Where they do not exist, aid organisations should introduce their own regulations, or actively define acceptable practices. In any case, organisations should define their own minimum standards for preventative measures, and their general policy in case of accidents.

An agreement should be negotiated with the representatives of each group of workers, to identify the measures that will be taken in case of accident or injury, and in order to prevent them happening. These matters should be discussed at the project-planning stage.

The local best practice on building sites should be considered as a minimum standard. On-site health and safety practices should take into account what is locally possible and what will be understood by workers.

If the organisation is working through a contractor, health and safety and insurance coverage will be the contractor's own responsibility and liability. This fact needs to be made clear to the contractor.

table 6(a): hazards on construction sites

hazards	how to prevent them
digging trenches/ foundations	In unstable soil, trenches and general excavations deeper than 1.5m require reinforced support to prevent landslides. Staff should be required to wear reinforced boots.
working aloft	Construction sites higher than 2m should be protected to prevent workers from falling. All scaffolding must be safe and secure; if appropriate, someone should be made responsible for checking the quality of scaffolding.
falling objects / transit under overhangs	Transit under overhangs should be avoided, in order to prevent casualties from falling objects; the transit of people around and in buildings should be controlled by sectioning off dangerous areas with striped plastic tape. Staff should be made to wear safety helmets.
splinters	Protective glasses should be worn when cutting splintering materials.
electrocution when using generators / pumps	The metal parts of low-tension plants should be earthed if they are located in a wet environment or near a big metal mass.
vehicle accidents	Mark out the limits of the areas for manoeuvre.
handling hazardous materials	Make staff aware of the hazards and train them to deal with them; supply masks, gloves, boots, or additional protective clothing as appropriate.

A first-aid kit should be available on site, and staff who are trained to give first aid should be present. Consider organising a training programme if necessary. For larger projects, a vehicle to evacuate injured casualties should be available.

Allow sufficient breaks within the working day, and limit the amount of overtime worked by staff. Where possible, works should be carried out in daylight. Locally hired labourers usually apply their own self-preserving measures, and they usually work in cycles and rhythms appropriate to the local culture and climate.

Project managers should include health and safety issues, such as the time required for breaks, in project plans. If a contractor is employed, health and safety clauses should be imposed in the contract.

6.5.2 layout and security of building sites

building-site layout

Efficient construction practices and safety considerations require that building work should take place on a site where there is ample physical space. The precise area needed depends upon the type of building and materials, the experience of the work crew, and the physical terrain; as a general rule, building work requires two–three times as much space as the building itself.

In addition to the space where the building is being erected, an adjoining area will be needed for the following:

- road access
- storing materials
- staging work
- construction waste.

Road access for the delivery of materials is often provided via the main thoroughfare. Because this road may be congested at times, a separate access for trucks delivering materials should be considered. A secure gate with a lock is recommended, to prohibit pedestrian or vehicular traffic outside working hours.

Construction schedules are more efficient if materials are stored for the shortest possible time before use. The longer construction

6 construction

materials are stored, the greater the likelihood of losses due to bad weather or theft. Delivery schedules should be revised as necessary to avoid early deliveries. (See sections 6.7.1–6.7.6 for information on the storage of specific construction materials.)

Staging work involves the preparation of building materials before use in construction. Masonry work requires large volumes of water, large quantities of blocks/bricks, and large amounts of sand and gravel to be stored and mixed. Timber needs space to be cut and perhaps assembled before use. Unseasoned, green timber must be dried before it can be worked, so space for air-drying is required. Staging areas are also needed for assembling and storing scaffolds, ladders, and sawhorses.

Construction waste can demand a great deal of space, which may be better used for other needs. Before initiating any building activities, consider how the construction waste is to be removed. If an off-site location is not available, waste materials should be separated, to make their eventual disposal or re-use easier.

Toxic materials such as paints or petroleum products should be left in their original containers and securely sealed. Nails pose a hazard to people and vehicle tyres if left lying on the ground, so they should be collected and stored for proper disposal.

security concerns

Thefts of tools, equipment, and materials can be a major problem at building sites. Understanding how and why theft at building sites occurs will help to inform the type of security plan needed.

Most construction theft can be attributed to workers or other people in the building trades. Construction workers need construction goods for income generation, and they have a professional knowledge of the use, value, and potential market for tools, equipment, and materials. Workers at building sites also have a detailed knowledge of the job site, and thus a better understanding of the security risks involved. As most construction work in transitional settlements is low paid, and financed by international donors, workers may feel a sense of entitlement which can lead them to steal supplies or equipment.

Various preventative measures can be taken to reduce theft by construction workers:

- Establish a 'zero tolerance' approach to theft, and favour local workers when hiring labour when possible, because stolen goods may be more difficult to hide in communities where workers are known.
- Reduce opportunistic theft by maintaining tidy worksites and installing prominent surveillance measures. Tools and equipment should be securely stored, and their whereabouts should be verified by the use of sign-in/sign-out sheets.
- Restrict access to building sites during non-work hours to all but essential personnel; keep the building site well lit at night; and hire trained security personnel for round-the-clock surveillance.

Building work often attracts on-lookers, who may unintentionally distract workers, interfere with the construction work, or steal items if they get an opportunity. Physical barriers, such as fences, or psychological barriers, such as roped-off construction areas, can help to keep non-essential persons out of the work site and improve safety.

Construction materials often constitute a very precious good which has a market value and often therefore becomes a target for thieves. On-site and off-site stores need to be guarded, and the guards need to be properly paid, to reduce the chances of corruption.

6.5.3 labour and tools management

labour management

Construction work is a labour-intensive process in which progress is greatly determined by the efficiency and effectiveness of workers. In turn, the productivity of workers is influenced by many factors, such as the following:

- availability of tools and materials adequate for the tasks
- favourable weather
- skill levels and training
- wages
- motivation and motivating influences, such as recognition, bonuses, job security, and participation in decision making
- effective management.

Because a number of these factors are outside the control of contractors or site managers, sound labour management must dedicate itself to reducing their impact. Adequate planning and scheduling of tasks can ensure that necessary construction goods are available when needed, and help to minimise the impact of bad weather.

Most construction workers are employed on a casual basis when work is available. Learning on the job is how most workers acquire construction skills, but the sporadic nature of the work does not encourage the development of skills. Providing all workers with opportunities to learn new skills should be a standard labour-management practice. Using higher-skilled workers as mentors is often effective as a training method, but these mentors should be hired according to their willingness and ability to teach, as well as their practical knowledge.

Low wages are the most common complaint of construction workers. They can significantly affect relations between labour and management. Contractors should be required to pay at least the legal minimum wage to workers for all building work. Delays in paying for work completed must also be avoided.

Workers in the construction industry are more effective on sites where clear communication exists between supervisors and workers. Skilled and unskilled workers alike need to know what must be accomplished – not only on a daily basis, but on a weekly level as well. Displaying work schedules where workers can see them will help them to plan their labour and see how their work fits into the bigger picture.

Setting construction goals, with rewards attached, can help to motivate labour. Providing monetary rewards or bonuses may not be possible, but other forms of remuneration may be effective, such as food stuffs, meals, hand tools, or paid time off.

Contractors often divide workers into two categories: unskilled and skilled labour. Workers often see contractors appointing unqualified staff, such as family members, to key positions as bosses or managers. This can lead to unskilled people being in charge of more skilled workers, which may create conditions in which materials wastage, poor workmanship, and resentment occur. Labour management is a professional job, and professionals should be recruited to fill such positions.

Management of tools and equipment at building sites has three main aims:

- ensuring that appropriate tools for all tasks are available
- keeping tools well maintained, clean, and sharp
- preventing theft.

Determining the types of tools needed for construction work depends on the building materials being used, the skill level of workers and tool operators, and budget limitations. Priorities should be given to tools that improve efficiency of labour, reduce risks to health and safety, and can be easily maintained and repaired in the field.

Monitoring the use of tools on a daily basis is the most effective way to ensure that they are available and in good condition, and to prevent theft or misuse. All tools should be secured in a locked storage area at the end of the working day, and signed in and out by the worker who uses the tool. Simple card-based systems can be used for inventory purposes, and any damages to the tools should be dated and recorded, to enable future repair and monitoring. Tool-room personnel should be adequately trained and receive salaries appropriate to the responsibility and their qualifications.

Motor-driven machinery, electrical generators, pumping equipment, and vehicles should have regular maintenance schedules. Spare supplies for these machines (filters, bushings, belts, etc.) should be kept, to minimise down-time. Saws, chisels, and cutting equipment should be inspected on a regular basis and sharpened as needed. Ladders and scaffolding equipment should be checked for loose connections which may affect their safe use.

Workers are often given responsibility for looking after their own personal safety equipment, such as protective headgear, eyewear, gloves, and boots. Preventing the loss of these items may best be achieved by requiring their use on the construction site.

If the aid organisation provides the tools on site for the daily construction work, it will have to ensure the following:

6 construction

- guarded overnight storage of tools
- collection and counting of tools on a daily basis
- maintenance and replacement of broken or missing tools.

If the aid organisation purchases the construction materials directly, it will have to find answers to the following questions.

- Who will transport the materials to the site?
- Who will provide the means of transportation?
- Who will load/unload the truck?
- Who will be responsible for guarding materials overnight?

If the aid organisation directly organises the harvesting of construction materials, such as grass for roof thatching, it will have to manage the following:

- transport of people, tools, and materials to and from the place of harvesting
- the harvesting process itself, monitoring compliance with agreed natural-resource management procedures, and the amount of time required for harvesting the quantity of materials needed.

If a contractor is hired to implement a project, the responsibility for procuring construction materials and construction tools and providing transport and storage will have been defined and included in the contract of agreement (5.2.1). Disputes arising from the loss or damage of tools or materials are regulated by the contract. If the contract does not clearly identify who is responsible for such loss or damage, responsibility should be taken directly by the aid organisation, or the contract should be altered as soon as possible.

6.6 plumbing and electrical services

It may not be feasible to provide plumbing and electrical services in all aspects of transitional settlement programmes. It is likely, however, that the programme will contain at least some buildings with piped water and electricity supplies, and these must be installed and maintained properly.

6.6.1 plumbing and pipes

Plumbing systems are concerned with the distribution of water to points of use throughout the building, and the discharge of water-borne waste from the building.

cold-water distribution

In areas where a municipal or private water-distribution service exists, water is distributed under pressure through pipes laid under streets, roads, or pavements. Individual buildings are then connected to the mains via a supply pipe. Water is supplied to individual points of use in the building either by mains pressure alone (direct supply), or by gravity from a storage cistern located in the roof space (indirect supply), via distributing pipes.

plastic pipes Polyvinyl chloride (PVC) pipes are commonly used in water-supply connections throughout the world. PVC is inexpensive to manufacture and distribute. Lengths of it can easily be joined together via couplings and solvent cement. Proper care must be taken to ensure that the pipe surfaces have been suitably abraded and cleaned before cement is applied, and to ensure that sufficient curing time is given before use. Alternatively, push-fit connections are available which use locking collars and water pressure to hold connections. PVC pipes are available in standard 6-metre lengths, and in widths ranging from 15mm (0.5 inch) to 28mm (1 inch) outside diameter (OD).

Polyethylene (PE) pipes are highly flexible yet strong, retaining their ductility even in freezing temperatures. This makes them highly suitable for use as underground water-supply pipes. The preferred method of joining PE pipes is by fusion welding, in which pipe ends are heated until molten and then pushed together and allowed to cool. Push-fit connections are also available.

As with PVC pipes, coloured PE pipes are susceptible to ultraviolet radiation and should not be exposed for long periods of time to sunlight. Black-coloured PE pipes should be employed for above-ground use.

metal pipes Tempered copper tubing is the most widely used material for water pipes in many developed countries. The comparatively high strength of copper enables pipes to be thin-walled and lightweight. Its ductility facilitates cold bending, and pipes can be joined easily and securely by soldered connections. In freezing temperatures,

6 construction

copper pipes may burst, unless protected by insulation or installed in heated rooms. Copper pipes come in 3-metre lengths in widths ranging from 15mm (1/2 inch) to 28mm (1 inch) outside diameter.

Galvanised iron (GI) pipe is commonly used where high strength and durability is needed, as in exposed pipe-works at tap-stands and storage tanks, or where livestock is present. GI pipes are usually supplied with tapered piped threads at both ends for making mechanical joined connections.

hot-water distribution

Hot water in buildings is usually supplied by three different types of heater:

- an instantaneous water heater, which heats cold water as it flows around a heat exchanger, fired by gas or electricity, to supply a single basin

- a single-point water heater, where a small volume of water is heated by an electrical immersion heater in an insulated tank, and used to supply a single basin

- a hot-water storage cylinder, which contains water supplied under pressure from a storage cistern and heated via a heat exchanger fired by electricity or gas; hot water is then distributed via copper tubing to each basin, bath, or shower fixture.

Gas-supplied systems must be vented to permit a proper air intake and exhaust for the gas flue, and they must be connected to a regulated gas supply. Electrically operated systems require dedicated wiring sufficiently sized to provide the necessary high amperage, and they must be protected by fuses or circuit breakers. Over current protection devices are recommended at the supply board or main circuit box, to prevent potential damage through overheating caused by excessive currents.

sewage Mains-supplied water is also used for the discharge of water-borne waste from the building. The terms 'soiled water' and 'foul water' refer to wastes that come from toilets and urinals; 'waste water', or 'grey water', originates from sinks, washbasins, baths, showers, and laundry facilities.

Soiled water must be discharged to sewers, cesspools, or septic tanks to avoid contaminating ground-water supplies. Grey water may also be sent to sewers or cesspools; or to soakaways lined with gravel and sand, which allow sediments in the waste to collect at the bottom, as the water percolates through the soil. Separate pipes are usually used to send soiled and grey water from the building to cast-iron or PVC discharge pipes.

Vent pipes that project above the sanitary fitting or at roof level are used to avoid the build-up of odours in drains leading from basins, sinks, and baths.

Cesspools are underground chambers or containers which receive and retain all soiled and grey water. When full, the contents are emptied by pumps to a tanker truck, which then delivers the material to a treatment plant. Cesspools must be watertight, to prevent the loss of water from inside and the entry of ground water from outside. Materials used in cesspools include brick with a cement and sand rendering, or glass-reinforced fibre plastic (GRP) sealed tanks.

Septic tanks differ from cesspools in that they separate solid matters from liquid sewage. Inside the septic tank a series of baffles slows the flow of liquid waste from the inlet, to permit the settlement of larger sewage particles. The liquid content is thus partly separated and runs to a series of perforated or porous land drains, from which it soaks into the ground. Periodically, the solid waste must be pumped from the septic tanks and sent to appropriate treatment plants.

Sewers take foul and grey water from buildings to a sewage-treatment plant, where a sedimentation tank permits solid sewage to settle. The liquid outflow is exposed to air to accelerate the purification process before the water is discharged into streams, rivers, lakes, or oceans.

6.6.2 electrical supply and generators

Electrical supply to buildings typically comes from connection to the utility grid, or through the use of electrical generators. In grid connections, alternating current (AC) flows from the grid through a low-voltage supply cable to the building. Generators use diesel-fuel motors to power a small electrical generator which produces an AC power supply.

utility grid Utility grids distribute AC electricity at a low voltage (240–480 volts) through a three-phase supply cable, which has three separate phase wires and a neutral connector. The neutral connector serves as a return path to complete the electrical circuit.

Connection to the grid is made to any two of the three phase wires and the neutral to provide a three-phase supply of 240 or 415 volts; or connection is made to any one of the three phase wires and the neutral for a 120/240 volt single-phase supply. Most buildings that do not have motor-driven appliances or machinery, and which use electricity only for lighting and to power small appliances, will have a single-phase connection.

generators Generators produce either single-phase AC power at 120 or 120/240 volts, or triple-phase AC power at 120/208 or 277/480 volts. Their power output ranges from 8,000 watts (8kW), suitable for residential power requirements, to 500kW, which is needed for industrial applications.

Generators typically use diesel fuel or natural gas for the motors, and a 12-volt battery and charging alternator to start the motor. Most generators are operated periodically according to demand, or as back-up systems to supplement electricity supplied by the utility grid.

demand for electricity

The demand for power that each electrical appliance or fixture needs is measured in watts. To calculate the correct size for a generator and/or the wiring needed to supply the devices with electrical power, add up the wattage needed for each appliance and fixture and multiply this load by the time during which the unit will be in operation.

Appliances with motors, such as refrigeration or tools, may use three or four times the operating wattage to start up the motor, a fact which must be included in the calculations.

Energy-conservation measures are equally important for electricity supplied by the utility grid and for generator-supplied electricity. Lighting loads can be reduced by using low-energy fluorescent lamps, which have the added advantage of a longer operating life than incandescent lamps.

distribution and circuits

Electrical power from the utility grid or generators typically is sent to a distribution terminal panel, which then distributes electricity to individual circuits throughout the building. The length of each circuit is limited, to minimise electrical resistance in the cable, as well as limiting overload current created by numerous connections. Each circuit is protected by circuit breakers or fuses in the distribution panel.

Two types of circuit are commonly used in buildings: ring and radial circuits. Ring circuits are typically used for socket outlets that provide electrical supply to portable equipment and appliances. They run in loops or rings from one outlet to the next, before terminating at the main distribution panel. Using 2.5mm-diameter cable, ring circuits are suitable for up to 100m² of floor area and are generally protected by a 30-ampere fuse or circuit breaker.

When a socket outlet cannot be conveniently fed by a ring circuit, a spur outlet may be wired, using electrical supply from a ring-circuit socket. Radial circuits are commonly used for lighting; they run from the distribution panel to the receptacles and back again. A 1.5mm-diameter cable, protected by a 5-ampere cable, should be used to connect to lighting, as each light usually requires much less power than socket outlets. To limit current flow and cable sizes, circuits are usually segregated by floors.

electrical safety

The flow of electrical current is facilitated by objects and materials that offer little resistance (conductors), and is impeded by those that have high resistance (insulators). Because the human body has only a small amount of resistance, the risk of electrical shocks is high when people are exposed to electrical current.

There are two ways of receiving an electrical shock: through direct or indirect contact. Direct contact occurs when a person has contact with exposed electrical connections that carry a live load, such as cables, sockets, fittings, or distribution panels. Indirect contact is the result of contact with exposed conductive parts that are made live by faults. The best way to prevent electrical shock by direct contact is to ensure that the following measures are taken.

- Any electrical maintenance or installation must be undertaken by skilled workers, and the electrical supply to the device or fixture must be disconnected at the main distribution panel.

- All electrical circuits and devices must be protected by circuit breakers or fuses, and all cables must be insulated and protected.

Protection against indirect contact is ensured when the following conditions apply.

- An uninterrupted earth bond is made from each device, fitting, or fixture, through the circuits and main distribution panel to a subterranean bond. This is usually a connection to a galvanised-iron water-mains supply pipe, or via a copper rod buried several metres underground.
- Automatic disconnection of power supply to a circuit is installed, through the use of residual current devices (RCD), which detect a disruption to the normal current flow produced by faults.
- Electrical appliances are double-insulated to prevent accidental faults

6.7 materials procurement, storage, and use

This section contains information on materials that are commonly used in construction and shelter programmes for displaced populations. It is not meant as a comprehensive guide: it should be supplemented with construction-technology literature.

6.7.1 timber and bush poles

Hard woods come from deciduous broad-leaf trees; soft woods come from coniferous, evergreen, fast-growing trees. Consider using bush poles, which are the trunks of small trees, rather than sawn timber: sawing timber can produce a lot of waste; also, bush poles are relatively strong, because their structural cross-section is intact. Take care when making any structural calculations for timber sizing: the strength of timber is affected seriously by the species of timber used, by the presence of any flaws, and by moisture levels and storage; in some countries all of these factors may be highly variable.

procurement Poles are generally ordered by quantity, specifying the diameter size (for example, 100mm or 150mm) at the base, which will reduce along the length of the pole, which is typically 3–4m long.

Construction poles should be cut or bought from controlled harvesting sites, possibly managed by the local administration. In countries where Forest Stewardship Council certification is in place, wood should be bought from registered sources (for further information, see www.fscoax.org). Sawn timber is ordered from the timber yard in cut sizes and standard lengths: for example, 100 x 50mm or 150 x 75mm, in 5m lengths.

storage   To prevent it from twisting and splitting, wood needs to be seasoned, or well stored for a long period in a protected and well-ventilated place to reduce its moisture content. This involves allowing the sap to dry out slowly (for three or more months), with the timber sections stacked under cover and supported by spacers to prevent sagging.

volume/transport

The wood should normally be transported into the settlement by truck in standard lengths or sections, to be cut on site. On occasions, wood may be pre-cut and machined in a timber yard, brought to the site, and assembled there. Lengths need to be fully supported on the lorry; overhang should be avoided.

health and safety

Workers should wear solvent-resistant gloves when handling wood treated with wood preservatives.

uses   Timber is often a rare and expensive resource. Reduce the size and length of sections required by reducing the span and spacing between beams (joists) or rafters. Use it in the strongest and most effective sectional plane.

Timber boards or plywood (layers of thin wood, glued together in alternate grain directions) are useful for walling and roof covering.

Figure 6.7(a) shows methods of protecting timber posts from termites.

figure 6.7(a): protecting timber posts from termites

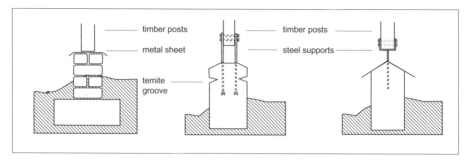

6.7.2 bamboo

Bamboo is one of the plants most widely used for construction around the world. It grows in a huge number of varieties at different latitudes. Depending on its section, it can be used for load-bearing structures or as a flexible support to thatching on roofs.

procurement Bamboo is one of the fastest-growing plants in the world. Some varieties grow more than one metre a day, and bamboo canes are ready for use in construction after five years, on average. After cutting, it starts growing again, because it reproduces through its roots.

Bamboo intended for structural works needs to be dried for two–three months after harvest, until about 90 per cent of the water content has dried out. It should be harvested at dawn, when the plant is at its most dry. Sometimes bamboos are laid out in streams, with the root end of the stem facing up-stream to wash out sap before drying.

storage The growth of fungus on bamboo can be prevented by controlling dampness in buildings. Chemicals are usually used to control insects. In developing countries a mix (2:1) of waste engine oil and diesel is often employed. Consider fumigation if the relevant expertise is available.

volume/transport

Bamboo is generally procured locally and transported over small distances, either by truck or by animal traction. Fifty per cent of the volume is air, due to the circular cross-section of the bamboos and the space left between them when they are stacked.

Workers should wear gloves while impregnating the bamboo with insecticides.

uses Bamboo can be used in the same ways as timber for structural purposes in a building. It is used as whole canes, halved canes, slats, beading, strips, and boards. It is commonly used to build roofs or parts of roofs, which are then covered in plastic sheeting and thatching. It is also often replaces wood in the structure of 'wattle and daub' constructions.

fixing Given that bamboo is hollow, nails and screws should not be used, because of the risk of splintering. Bamboo should be drilled and bolted or bounded or lashed with rattan, bamboo, or wire. Where it is used as a traditional construction material, bamboo is often bound, so that it can be loosened or tightened if necessary.

figure 6.7(b): fixing bamboo

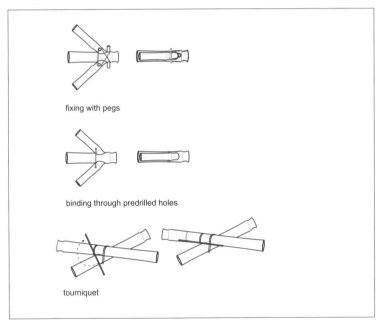

fixing with pegs

binding through predrilled holes

tourniquet

6.7.3 clay bricks and concrete blocks

Bricks are normally made of fired clay, and a good brick will ring when struck. A typical size is 215mm x 102.5mm x 65mm. Sizes may vary from country to country, but generally they are proportioned for bonding. Fired bricks are produced in a kiln, sited near suitable clay deposits. If bricks are not available, consider using concrete or adobe blocks, produced on or close to the construction site.

figure 6.7(c): typical fired-brick dimensions

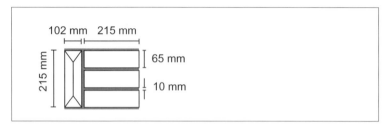

A typical mix for concrete blocks is 1:6 cement to aggregate/sand of <10 mm diameter.

Blocks should be well cured for at least 3–7 days, covered in damp sacking or sprinkled with water.

procurement Often procurement and transport can be difficult. In emergencies, consider re-using bricks from destroyed buildings, if kilns are a long way from site (but first check the ownership of the buildings).

storage Bricks can be stored in the open, but anti-theft measures should be considered. Adobe or mud-brick blocks will weather and deteriorate, unless protected from rain.

volume/transport

Normally bricks are sold per thousand. The merchant may deliver them to the site if access is adequate. Two thousand bricks weigh approximately two tons. They can be stacked loosely on a lorry, or banded, or put on pallets, or wrapped.

health and safety

Use gloves to handle bricks, and do not lift more than a handful at a time.

uses Bricks are particularly useful for building low walls, 500mm high, around temporary shelters. Such walls will prevent people and animals from crawling under tarpaulin floors. They will also keep the space warmer, by preventing the wind blowing between the sheet and the ground. Bricks provide thermal mass and keep occupants warmer, especially when sleeping on the floor. They prevent dampness. They provide permanence and they establish the footprint of the shelter for future development. Consider using bricks or blocks for more permanent structures, such as clinics and schools.

fixing When laid, bricks should be coursed, with each course, or row, overlapping by half a brick. They should be jointed with a 10mm mortar joint (sand and cement in a 1:4 mix).

Brickwork can be reinforced with expanded metal mesh laid in the mortar joint every fourth course. Brickwork needs thickening at the ends and at 3-metre intervals along the walls. Walls become unstable if they are more than 3m high without lateral restraint.

Brick walls can be made safer in earthquake areas if concrete columns are tied to the walls at intervals.

6.7.4 mud block making

Various names, listed below, are given to blocks made from clay-like earth. Such blocks differ from the previously mentioned clay bricks in that they are not fired in a kiln.

Pise or **rammed earth** consists of clay and a little water, rammed into a wall of formwork/shutter.

Wattle and daub consists of pats of clay, moulded by hand into balls and pressed into a background wall made of timber or bamboo in woven strips.

Adobe is a mud-like clay mixture formed in wood moulds. Depending on the composition of the clay, straw may be required to prevent shrinking and cracking while drying.

Cob is similar in composition to adobe, but cob is used by pressing the mixture into hand-sized balls, which are then pressed together.

A block can be made stronger by stabilising it with cement or lime. Typically 1:10 (cement/lime to clay) is a good proportion, but the precise mix depends on the type of clay. The clay can be mixed 1:4 with 10mm (or less) stone aggregate, to provide a stronger block.

Blocks can be manufactured in a hand mould, made of wood and fixed on a board: see figure 6.7(d). Or they can be compressed in a machine, typically a 'Cinva-Ram' block press, as illustrated in figure 6.7(e).

figure 6.7(d): wooden mould for clay bricks

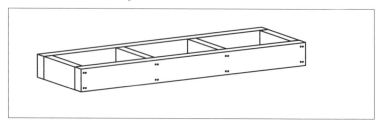

figure 6.7(e): 'Cinva-Ram' block press

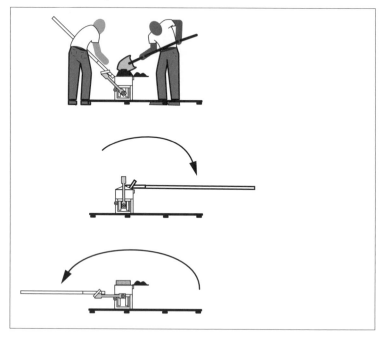

procurement Rely on local knowledge for the choice of clay and mix. Normally a pit will be dug close to the point of use. A team of four or five people may be able to produce more than 300 blocks per day.

Mud construction requires significant quantities of water, particularly in the initial construction phase. An adobe building with a 20m² ground plan is likely to require approximately 1–2 tonnes (or metres cubed) of water during construction.

storage Normally blocks are left to bake in the sun. In the case of stabilised blocks containing cement, it is important to keep the blocks moist while the cement cures sufficiently to be moveable without breaking, for use in construction. If the blocks are kept wet and the mixture is of good quality, blocks should be ready for moving and use in small structures after 15 days.

volume/transport

When transport is difficult, production should be as close to the point of use as possible.

health and safety

Bugs that transmit the chiagas disease live in mud walling. To prevent this, the internal walls should be smooth or white-washed.

Digging for clay creates pits, which collect water and can become a breeding ground for mosquitoes. After the material has been excavated, the pits should be refilled. If located on family plots, they could be used as refuse pits or for compost. In the latter case, the pit should be kept covered with a 10cm layer of earth, to control vermin.

uses A wall 500mm high is often built around the inside of tented shelters, to ward off dust and draughts. Constructions made of mud bricks may replace tents and plastic sheets, but the usefulness of mud is not always appreciated, and more permanent and expensive concrete blocks are often used instead.

If mud blocks are to be used for camp construction in the emergency phase, it is necessary to train groups of displaced people in the production of mud bricks, and to regulate from the start the harvesting of construction poles or bamboo. One way to motivate workers is to show them a demonstration shelter. Moulds need to be provided, and special assistance must be given to vulnerable members of the community. It is often a good idea to organise people into teams, to ensure sufficient production.

fixing The mortar is a clay mix, 10mm thick, which can be reinforced with straw. Adding a rendered face to the wall will prevent water penetration. The render should be a mixture of cement, lime, and sand, in a ratio of 1:1:4. It should be no more than 12mm thick, to prevent it from becoming detached from the wall.

Figure 6.7(f) shows how to protect a mud-brick wall from rain and from water infiltrations from the ground.

figure 6.7(f): protecting a mud-brick wall from water-logging

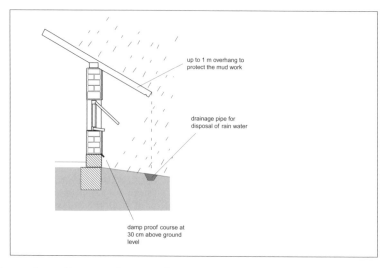

up to 1 m overhang to protect the mud work

drainage pipe for disposal of rain water

damp proof course at 30 cm above ground level

6.7.5 mortars, lime, and cement

Mortars are the binding agent for bonding bricks and blocks together. Typically a strong mortar will be a 1:3 mixture of cement and sand. A mortar mixed with sharp or coarse sand will produce a render which, when applied in a 12mm layer on a rough surface with a firm background, will provide a waterproof face to a wall.

A more practical mortar is cement, lime, and sand in a 1:1:6 mix. Lime is a base material and is available in many situations, but it is often neglected in favour of cement, which is more expensive and harder to procure. Lime is limestone of various degrees of purity, fired in lumps in a kiln at 900°C (slightly hotter than a strong barbeque heat). The lime from the kiln is 'quick lime'. This is very volatile, and is usually available in bags of powder (sometimes sold in local markets), to be used to sanitise latrines or corpses. If the lime from the kiln is slaked in a pit with plenty of water, the result will be hydrated lime, which is sold in bags. This can be used as a weak cement for mortar, or plaster (applied to internal walls), or render (applied to external walls). Mortar made with lime is better than pure cement for use with mud bricks or backgrounds that can move. Lime takes at least three weeks to harden when exposed to the air. In comparison, cement continues to harden over many years, but can be sufficiently strong to move in 3–7 days, and usually achieves 80 per cent strength in 30 days.

Ferro-cement is a render reinforced with chicken wire or wire mesh. It is very useful for making water tanks for rainwater harvesting.

procurement Cement and hydrated lime are commonly available in 50kg bags. Slaking of lime is carried out in a pit on site, or close to the construction works. Local experience should be considered if it is planned to produce lime locally.

figure 6.7(g): lime-use cycle

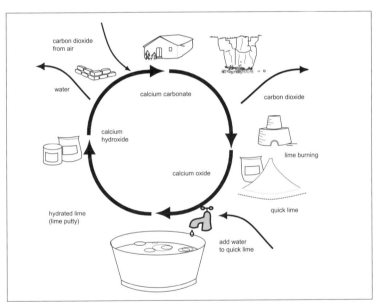

carbon dioxide
from air

water

calcium carbonate

carbon dioxide

calcium
hydroxide

lime burning

calcium oxide

quick lime

hydrated lime
(lime putty)

add water
to quick lime

storage Cement bags should be stored in a dry place, no more than six bags high, and they should be used on a first-in/first-out basis.

volume/transport

Cement is usually sold as 20 bags/ton. Bags need to be tightly packed, because they break easily. They need to be covered with tarpaulins while transported.

Portland cement is a hydraulic cement. It is used as a binding agent in mortar and concrete. Contact between cement powder and body fluids, such as sweat or eye fluid, may cause irritation. Cement dermatitis can be avoided by using appropriate clothing to prevent repeated and prolonged skin contact.

Quick lime is dangerous: it will burn the skin. It is essential to store it in a dry place, because a chemical reaction will take place when it comes in contact with water, releasing a great deal of heat.

uses Both lime and cement can be used for binding bricks and blocks, rendering external walls, plastering internal walls, and (mixed with clay) for making stabilised blocks and a flooring surface. Lime wash is often used as a paint-sealer for walls, especially in clinics and hospitals.

6.7.6 aggregates (sand and gravel)

Sand is either fine/soft or sharp/coarse, with a particle diameter of under 5mm. Beware of the silt (organic matter) and clay content, because it will weaken mortars or concrete. As an initial test, spit on the palm of your hand and rub in a sample of sand, then watch for excessive staining. As a more detailed test, half-fill a jar with a sample of the sand and some salty water. Shake it and leave it to settle. If you get more than 5mm of silt, consider washing the sand to remove the silt, or use a cleaner source.

Aggregate is coarse, 20mm or graded 20mm down to 5mm or all-in (often as dug) ballast 20mm down. Use 20–40mm+ in large volumes of concrete which will not have unusual loading, such as making level the ground under a strip foundation. These large volumes are often termed 'mass concrete'. Rounded pebbles tend to be more workable when used in concrete. Angular pebbles are better for locking particles together.

figure 6.7(h): use of aggregates in concrete

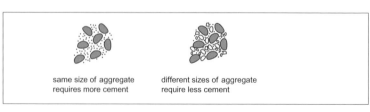

same size of aggregate
requires more cement

different sizes of aggregate
require less cement

Hardcore is crushed or broken stone, possibly recycled from concrete or bricks. Roughly fist-sized, hardcore is used for sub-bases to concrete work.

procurement As damp sand has more volume than dry sand, allow 25 per cent more damp sand than dry sand when calculating the volume proportions for mixing sand as part of a batch of concrete. This also has to be taken into account when ordering by the truckload. Wadi (dried-up riverbeds) and banks of rivers are good sources of sands / aggregates, most commonly on the inside of bends; but suitable material may also be found in layers beneath the dry riverbeds.

Ask about local procurement from quarries. Where there is no local aggregate, fired bricks or concrete may be broken and crushed to suitable sizes. Use a flattened-out sheet of corrugated iron, with handles and nail holes, to grade fine aggregates. A screen propped at an angle can also be used: when aggregate is thrown at the screen, the fine dust passes through, while coarse stones fall down on the face of the screen.

When procuring sand and gravel, take care to prevent soil erosion. If erosion gullies are formed, they need to be repaired by making check-dams with stones at regular intervals along the gully.

storage Aggregate is stored in piles of sorted sizes or, to prevent wastage, in bins (low wooden frames). The aggregate should be covered, to prevent infiltration of organic matter.

figure 6.7(i): aggregate storage

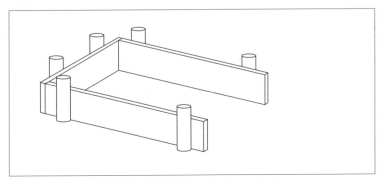

table 6(b): approximate weights for sand and aggregates

material	kg per m³
sand	approx.1600 with average moisture
gravel	approx. 1650 if 20mm
brick hardcore	1197

uses Aggregates are used in concrete (6.7.7). Hardcore is used in a sub-base for concrete, 150–250mm thick, and in the beds of roads.

6.7.7 concrete

Concrete is a mix of cement, coarse sand, and 20mm stone aggregate. A mix for general use is 1:3:6. For simple reinforced columns and beams, a 1:2:4 mix is used. For mass concrete, in foundations of small buildings for example, a 1:4:8 mixture is generally acceptable. The water should be clean and free of organic matter. Salt water is acceptable where reinforcement is not being used. Good concrete cannot be produced unless the proportions of fine and coarse aggregates and the water:cement ratio are controlled.

Outlined below are the steps involved in mixing concrete. They should be regarded as only a guide, not as a prescription, because many variables (such as the quality and size of the aggregates, and the volume of water) can affect the outcome of the mix.

mixing concrete

Add just enough water to the mix to make the concrete workable, at the point when the mix will pour off a shovel more easily. Adding too much water may leave voids in the concrete when the excess water evaporates. Too much water can also wash the cement out of the mix, especially if it is mixed on the ground, rather than using a misting board or area. A cone test is often made for workability: see figure 6.7(j). A good workable mix will result in a 50–100mm slump, or drop in height, after the cone is removed and the concrete mix is standing alone.

figure 6.7(j): slump test for concrete mix

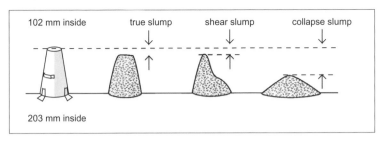

When mixing concrete by hand, do it on a clean surface and not directly on the ground. Use boards, or make a concreted area that will be used for mixing the concrete.

figure 6.7(k): mixing concrete by hand

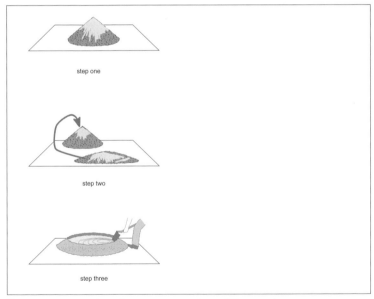

Step 1: start pouring the cement on top of the sand.

Step 2: mix and turn it over at least four times, and then add more cement and repeat.

Step 3: once the dry mix is ready, make a hole in the middle and pour in water. Remember that too much water will weaken the concrete.

Combine the dry mixture with water, starting from the outside and stirring towards the inside. When the entire dry mix has been heaped up in the centre of the pool, it should have taken up all the free water. As in the beginning, turn the mass over and back again at least four times. Thorough mixing is essential for making good concrete.

Step 4: now add the measured quantity of stone. You will need to judge whether the stone needs to be dampened slightly before it is added, depending on the mixture that you already have. In order to know how much stone to add, remember that all the interstices between stones must be filled with mortar when the concrete is finally in place.

table 6(c): materials required for one cubic metre of concrete

proportion	water (litres)	sand (m³)	coarse aggregate (m³)	water (litres)
1:3:6	203kg or 4 bags of 50kg	0.54	0.83	116
1:2:4	291kg or 6 bags of 50kg	0.55	0.79	119

compacting concrete

The purpose of compacting is to expel voids and air bubbles that have become trapped in the concrete mass during mixing. Full compaction is essential, because the strength of the concrete is reduced by voids.

Thorough compaction can be achieved only by using the correct proportions of the ingredients and water, and the appropriate amount of compaction, whether hand compaction or vibration compaction. Good compaction ensures that there are no air bubbles in the mix, and that all of the corners and other less accessible areas are properly filled.

curing concrete

It is important to prevent water evaporation before the chemical reaction has occurred – a process which takes between three and seven days. This is especially important in hot countries. The concrete should be covered with a plastic sheet, or damp sack, or damp sand, or sprinkled with water.

Concrete should also be covered in cold conditions where there is a risk of frost. Avoid curing concrete in conditions where it could freeze, and take precautions to prevent this: warm water should be used in the mix, and insulation should be laid over the concrete to be cured, a process which is aided by the chemical reaction of cement with water, producing heat; note that in some conditions even blow heaters should be used. Alternatively and when available, chemicals called accelerators can be added to the mix, to shorten the curing time.

formwork Concrete is poured into a temporary mould or wooden formwork or shutter. This must be strong enough to withstand the weight of wet concrete; external reinforcement may be required. The mould should be painted on the inside with a de-bonding agent, such as light oil, to prevent the concrete adhering to the wooden shutter.

figure 6.7(l): process for making concrete blocks

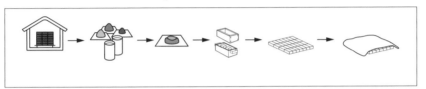

procurement In urban areas, concrete may be produced at a ready-mix concrete-batching plant, and brought to site within 30 minutes from mixing, in a 5m³ concrete-transporting wagon.

In remote situations, concrete must be batched on site to the correct proportions, either in a rotating drum/mixer (mixed dry for two minutes, then mixed with added water for a further two minutes), or by hand on a prepared surface or on a board.

Pre-cast concrete sections can be produced in formwork and lifted into position once cured. This method is often used to produce lintels (horizontal cross-members).

volume/transport

A concrete wagon carries 5m³ of concrete. The capacity of a site drum/mixer is 0.5m³.

health and safety

Contact between cement powder and body fluids, such as sweat or eye fluid, may cause irritation. Cement dermatitis can be avoided by

6 construction

using appropriate clothing to prevent repeated and prolonged skin contact. People working with concrete should wear boots and gloves.

uses Concrete is used for foundations, floors, columns, and beams. Reinforced concrete may be required; it contains steel rebar (see 6.7.8) and should be designed by specialists.

Concrete is frequently used in transitional settlements to make latrine slabs. In this case, the concrete should be reinforced. If of appropriate size (approximately 1m in diameter), these slabs do not require an additional secondary wood slab, and easy hygienic cleaning of the latrines is ensured.

6.7.8 steel reinforcement

This section refers to ferrous metals and the harder type of steel that is used for reinforcing concrete. With its great tensile strength, steel has major structural uses.

The two main grades of steel are G43 (S355) – mild steel – and G50 (S275) – high-tensile steel. Reinforcements (rebar) for concrete consist of either smooth round bars of mild steel, or bars of tensile steel, deformed through twisting or ribbed indents, so that the steel bonds to the concrete. Their diameters vary. A 10mm diameter is appropriate for light loading, and a 20–40mm diameter is needed for more structural work. A construction specialist is needed to calculate the appropriate diameter for the particular piece of work.

procurement Steel needs to be ordered well in advance. In an emergency context, second-hand sections might be used, or material from destroyed buildings might be re-used (but first check the ownership and availability of the material). As a general guide, check the use of steel in existing buildings. Arrange transport and obtain lifting equipment.

Reinforcement is generally sold in 10–12m lengths, or in rolls for smaller diameters. Often it is pre-cut to length, or made up into cages for use in concrete.

storage Steel will rust in the open air, so it needs to be stored under cover. Other metals are precious and liable to theft, so they too should be stored securely. Heavy sections should be placed on timber battens, so that chains/ropes can be secured. Stack them in order, so that the first to be used are the last to be stacked. Sheets can be stacked, but should be supported on battens to prevent bending.

volume/transport

Steel reinforcement is sold by sectional size and length. It should be secured with wedges and straps when it is transported on lorries. Consider how heavy sections will be lifted. Often rebar is cut and shaped, then brought to site in bundles.

health and safety

Lifting steel sections needs careful preparation, especially where there are poor or unchecked lifting appliances. Keep workers away from lifting appliances. Tie rope to the ends of sections to guide the steel into place. Check that chains/ropes can carry the required load. Pack timber pieces against chains to stop slipping.

uses Rebar is used for beams and columns. It is placed where concrete will be in tension, typically in the lower section of a beam.

fixing Steel should be supplied with a means to cut, place, and fix it. Welding is normally done in a fabrication shop, and bolted connections are used on site. Cutting can be done by gas burning or with a mechanical saw. Columns need to be secured to foundations on base plates with holding bolts.

Rebar needs to have continuity, by running through steel at beam/column junctions. Cages are constructed with tie wire. The long sections of steel are made into a full cage by using wire to tie together shorter sections of steel, bent to the shape required. These shorter sections are termed 'stirrups'. They are used structurally to carry shear loads, which are loads that, for example, would break a beam rather than allowing the long steel to transmit all the forces to the ends of the beam.

6.7.9 roofing tiles

Locally made roofing tiles vary in shape and size. Tiles are heavy, so roof structures must be constructed appropriately to ensure that they can carry the load.

procurement Tiles can be generally procured locally. They are usually made of clay, although concrete or stone are sometimes used. A production system for fibre-reinforced concrete tiles is easy and cheap to set up, and the result is considered a satisfactory alternative to corrugated metal sheets. The equipment required is usually very simple and can be made locally.

storage Tiles can be stored in the open. As with most construction materials, measures should be taken to prevent theft.

volume/transport

A loss of 10 per cent for breakage should be calculated when transporting tiles. Additional losses are to be expected if road conditions are bad.

health and safety

In areas prone to earthquakes, smaller tiles are preferable, because they will cause less damage if they are dislodged. In areas prone to cyclones, bigger and heavier concrete sheets are less likely to be lifted.

uses Tiles are used as roof covering. Beware of their heavy weight when loading a structure. Ten square metres of tiles will weigh between 400 and 600kg, excluding the weight of the battens and the nails.

fixing Tiles should be distributed with sufficient nails to fix them in place. It is not necessary to nail each tile individually, but at least every third course should be nailed, in order to resist winds of medium strength. Appropriate procedures should be applied in cyclone-prone areas.

Tiles are generally shaped so that they can be hooked to the battens. Holes should be drilled beforehand in concrete tiles, to take nails or bolts. Nibs with wire loops can be cast in during moulding, thus avoiding the need for drilling.

figure 6.7(m): fixing roof tiles

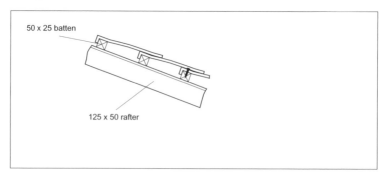

50 x 25 batten

125 x 50 rafter

6.7.10 roof thatching

Roof-thatching materials include palm leaves, banana leaves, straw, grass, and reeds. The choice depends on the geographical area of use.

procurement Local knowledge of where to procure thatch is needed. Remember that the type and quality of thatching material will vary.

storage Vermin will ruin stored thatch, and damp conditions will decay it.

volume/transport

Thatching material is normally brought to site in bundles: thatch is lightweight but bulky. For transport, draught animals or a truck will be required.

uses Thatch can be used to cover pitched roofs, to a maximum thickness of 300mm. A better use is to fix it over a sheet of plastic or corrugated iron. Thatch is a good insulator, preventing heat loss in cold climates and heat gain in hot climates. The pitch of the roof should be more than 40 degrees, to prevent water soaking into thatch. The same materials that are used for roof thatching can be woven into mats and used for walling, flooring, doors, and window screens.

fixing Ensure that the thatch is securely fixed to the roof structure with string or twine. Overhang the thatch by 300mm from the wall faces. Ten square metres of grass thatch can weigh up to 300kg; the roof structure needs to be designed accordingly.

health and safety

Thatched roofs are very flammable. Treatments are sometimes available to protect them from both fire and decay.

6.7.11 corrugated metal sheets

There are two types of galvanised sheeting, which is sometimes called corrugated iron sheeting, or CIS: thin gauge is used for walling, and thicker sheets (G32–24SWG) for roofing. Ordinarily, 22-gauge (0.80mm thick) sheets are used for roofs.

When painted silver grey, corrugated metal roofs are cooler by 5°C than they are when left in their natural state.

procurement Check the sheet for damage to the galvanised layer. Ensure that the profile is compatible with other sheets that you may want to use.

6 construction

If considering the use of galvanised sheeting, remember that it is imported in most developing countries.

storage Metal sheeting should be covered to protect it from rain when stored for a long period of time. Do not stack the sheets too high, because profiles will flatten out. (Twenty sheets in a pile is the maximum number advisable.)

volume/transport

Eighty sheets/ton is an average. Sheets should be transported vertically in order to prevent flattening.

health and safety

Workers should wear gloves when handling corrugated metal sheets. Beware of fixing sheets on a windy day.

uses Roofing and walling are the most common uses of corrugated metal sheets. Consider the noise produced by heavy rainfall. In windy or storm-prone areas, make sure that the sheets are well fixed.

These roofs are not generally laid at a slope flatter than 1 in 5. A slope that is frequently adopted is 1 vertical, 2 horizontal. A 40° slope may be preferable in areas of heavy rainfall.

Corrugated metal roofs are cooler by 5°C when painted silver grey than they are when left in their natural state.

fixing Wooden or steel purlins are fixed over the principal rafters. The spacing of purlins should be determined by the size of the panels, to avoid cutting, but it should not exceed the values in table 6(d), which depend on the thickness of the material.

table 6(d): spacing of purlins for a given thickness of CGI sheet

thickness of CGI sheets	spacing of purlins
0.63mm – 24 gauge	1.60m
0.80mm – 22 gauge	1.80m
1.00mm – 20 gauge	2.00m
1.25mm – 18 gauge	2.40m
1.60mm – 16 gauge	2.80m

Wind ties should be made of 40 x 6mm flat iron, fixed just above at the eaves ends of the sheets in continuous lengths, bolted down every 1.2m. The fixing should be done with the same hook bolts that secure the sheets to the purlins.

Ridges and hips should be covered with the ridge and hip section of plain 20-gauge GI sheet, with a minimum of 22.5cm overlap on either side over the sheet.

Holes should be drilled (not punctured) in the ridges of the corrugation. Drilling should preferably be done on the ground.

Sheets can be secured to wood framing by screws or jagged nails 65–75mm long, at intervals not exceeding 30cm on every bearer.

figure 6.7(n): securing corrugated metal to a roof structure

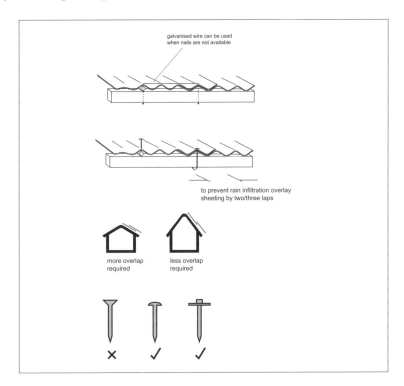

6.7.12 paints and treatments

There are two types of paint: emulsion (distemper/water-based) and gloss (spirit-based or turpentine-based). Numerous treatments can be applied to materials to deter insects and vermin and to protect them from wear and tear.

procurement Paint is normally available in 2.5-litre and 5-litre cans. Typically one litre of paint will cover 10m².

storage Some paint products are flammable. Large stores need to be well ventilated and should be sited away from other buildings.

health and safety

Paints and treatments should always be applied in a well-ventilated space.

insecticides for treating soil against termites

Products containing dieldrin or aldrin are not safe. Potentially safer products include those based on permethrin and chlorpyriphos. Termiticides are best absorbed and retained by dry permeable soils. Applications should be avoided during or immediately before rain.

uses Paint and chemical treatments can be used to protect materials in various ways. Red lead/oxide paint protects metal from rusting. Linseed-oil creosote, and diesel + waste engine oil in a 1:2 mix, protect wood from decaying. Timber is treated with solignum and permethrin to prevent attacks by termites. (Waste engine oil and diesel in a 1:2 mix may also be used.) Special intumescing paints can be used to protect wood from fire. The wood may also be impregnated with large quantities of chemicals such as ammonium diphosphate, sodium arsenate, or sodium tetraborate.

This is a typical sequence in the painting of timber:

• Stop the resin from the knots.

• Apply primer to the bare wood.

• Apply undercoat, and then a gloss finish.

A mix for whitewash (useful for creating hygienic washable surfaces in health centres and hospitals):

• 50kg of lime

• 6.5kg salt in 20 litres of hot water

• 3.8kg rice boiled to a paste

• 0.7kg of glue (animal/casein)

A 50mm-thick sand and cement screed or granite chippings, applied to the surface of floors, prevents dusting of the concrete. An epoxy/polyurethane paint can be applied to a dry surface as a floor finish.

6.8 construction from foundations to roof

Do not attempt to build structures of any size or complexity without professional advice. All construction activities involve risks. Managing these risks requires an understanding of built structures, knowledge of the characteristics of building materials, and a careful assessment of available skills.

6.8.1 building structures and loads

The function of a building's structure is to transfer loads safely from the roof to the foundations. Basic structural considerations for all buildings include the following principles:

- Buildings should be capable of carrying their own dead weight.
- Foundations should remain stable under load.
- Wind forces should not cause buildings to collapse.
- Walls, floors, and roofs should not deflect unduly when loaded.

figure 6.8(a): transferred loads

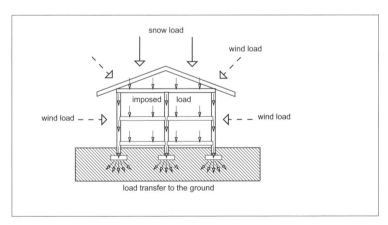

types of load The primary loads that all buildings must be able to carry or resist are as follows:

- the total weight of the building itself (dead loads)
- loads which act on a structure during its use, such as people, machinery, furniture, etc. (imposed / live loads)
- pressures produced by winds. Forces involved in wind loads are those that push against a building (positive pressure), and/or create suction on different areas of a building (negative pressure).

Snowfall collecting and resting on a roof can also add a considerable load to a building.

Secondary loads on buildings include the following:

- temperature changes, which can cause shrinking or expansion in building components;
- in regions of seismic activity, pressure from earth movements, which can create dynamic loads and stresses on buildings.

The elements of a building which carry structural loads and are used in most constructions are foundations (6.8.2), floors (6.8.3), walls (6.8.4), and roofs (6.8.5).

6.8.2 foundations

The function of foundations is to carry the loads of a building and distribute them over the ground in such a way that movement of the building is minimal. Different types of foundation are used, depending on the following factors:

- building load
- structural form of building
- soil condition and types
- climate and geophysical factors (such as cyclones, earthquakes, etc.).

All foundations should be constructed on solid subsoil that is not prone to settling, expansion, or subsidence. They should be protected against frost heave, rain, surface-water run-off, and erosion.

There are four main types of foundation:

- strip foundation
- pad foundation
- raft foundation
- pile foundation.

figure 6.8(b): four main types of foundation

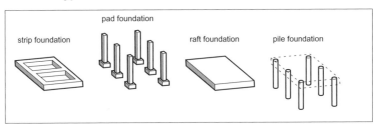

strip foundations

Strip foundations are long continuous footings which run the length of the main load-bearing walls. Depending upon ground conditions and the loading involved, concrete or compacted stones are used as the foundation bed. For concrete strip foundations, a minimum thickness of 150mm is needed. Iron reinforcement bars in the poured concrete may be needed for additional strength in the foundation.

If the upper layers of topsoil are loose or porous, the sides of the trench may require formwork, to provide temporary support for the concrete. On sloping sites, it is critical that the bottoms of the trenches are cut level, because substantial changes in bearing depth will cause differential settlement. For naturally sloping sites, vertical steps are cut, in order to maintain a level bottom to the trenches.

Strip foundations are suitable for lightweight masonry and other structures. Their construction requires basic building skills.

A variation of a strip footing is the trench-fill foundation. Trench-fill foundations are deeper than strip foundations. They enable the surrounding soil to help the building to support loads by providing frictional resistance at the side. Concrete, with or without reinforcement, is filled in the trench to approximately 150mm of ground level; once the concrete has cured, soil is added to reach ground level. Stones may also be used, with larger flat stones placed on the trench bottom, interspersed with smaller stones tightly compacted. Trench-fill foundations are suitable for lightweight masonry structures on clay soils. Basic building skills are required for their construction.

figure 6.8(c): strip and trench-fill foundations

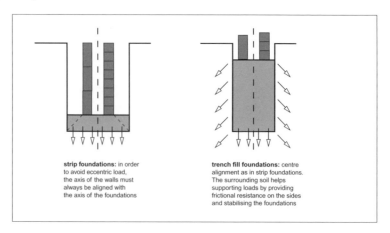

strip foundations: in order to avoid eccentric load, the axis of the walls must always be aligned with the axis of the foundations

trench fill foundations: centre alignment as in strip foundations. The surrounding soil helps supporting loads by providing frictional resistance on the sides and stabilising the foundations

pad foundations

Pad foundations are designed to support high loads over a limited area: for example, in buildings where the structural form brings loads to the ground via columns. An excavation directly under the column is filled with concrete, and the column itself is attached securely to the concrete. Methods used for attachment include the following:

- hold-down bolts and column base plates for timber and steel columns

- L-shaped reinforcement bars inside poured-concrete columns and linked with horizontal bars in pads

- concrete grout, used to hold pre-cast columns inside a pocket in the pad to receive the bottom end of the column.

Pad foundations are suitable for lightweight structures of steel, masonry, or timber where columns are used. Basic building skills are required for proper construction.

282

raft or slab foundation

Raft foundations consist of poured-concrete slabs, cast with a reinforced thickened edge around the building perimeter, to distribute loads over poor soils. The slab itself is often reinforced with pre-formed steel mesh, and the concrete used is a higher-strength grade than that used in other types of foundations.

Raft foundations are suitable for soft ground, to spread the building load; on made-up (back-filled) soil, to bridge across weak areas; on soils where differential settlement is likely to be extreme; or where the soil is susceptible to excessive shrinking and swelling. The concrete raft is often formed on a hardcore gravel fill, to further limit the potential for foundation damage from ground swell.

Raft foundations require an engineered design. They are most often used to overcome a particular problem caused by back-filled land, clay soil, or trees growing excessively close to the building. Advanced building skills and additional materials are needed for construction.

figure 6.8(d): **building loads on a raft foundation**

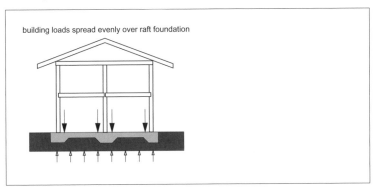

building loads spread evenly over raft foundation

piled foundations

Piled foundations involve the insertion of structural columns below ground, to transfer structural loads to the substrata that are capable of bearing the loads. Due to the heavy machinery needed for drilling and supporting the piles, this type of foundation is limited to heavier and multi-storey structures.

In simpler structures such as pole buildings, timber piles are used as pile foundations by inserting them into holes in the ground and backfilling either with compacted earth or concrete. Diagonal bracing between poles and floor joists helps to distribute the loads more effectively. Pole buildings with piled foundations are common in coastal areas or regions prone to flooding. In areas where termites are prevalent, the timber should be treated with creosote or used motor oil, to limit infestation.

table 6(e): foundation types for given soil and site conditions

soil and site conditions	possible type of foundation
rock (requiring pneumatic pick for excavation)	shallow strips or trenches; pads
solid chalk, sand, and gravels	shallow strips; pads
compact and contained clay	all types
firm stiff clay with trees close to building	trench fill; rafts or piles with ground beams
sand / silt / loose clay	strip / raft
peat / back-filled sites / flooded areas	piles

6.8.3 floors

Floors are categorised as solid or suspended. The ground itself provides the support in solid ground floors. Suspended floors are those that span between supporting floors.

All floors must be able to carry loads and resist excessive deflection. A variety of materials is used for floor structures, and an even greater variety for floor coverings. Typical materials used for floor structures include the following:

- earth
- reinforced concrete
- timber beams or joists, covered with decking or sheet materials
- concrete beams and infill blocks with a floor screed.

earth floors Earth floors are built of several layers of compacted earth, built up over a carefully prepared site that is free of all organic materials. To avoid the risk of rising ground moisture, a waterproof barrier is first set down. Common waterproof barriers include a 10cm layer of clay and earth, bitumen and earth, or lime-stabilised sandy soil; and plastic sheeting (1000g polythene), resting on a layer of dry sand.

The final layer of compacted earth should be raised 15cm above ground level to avoid rainwater infiltration. A drainage channel around the perimeter of the building, with an overhanging roof, will

284

help to keep the floor area dry. Durability of compacted earth floors can be improved through the addition of stabilising agents (clay, lime, oil) to the upper layers of soil.

reinforced-concrete ground floors

A more durable floor structure is made with reinforced concrete. To ensure stability, the concrete is cast on top of a 150mm bed of uniform-sized gravel (hardcore). Damp-proof membranes (polythene sheeting) are placed beneath the hardcore to prevent the passage of ground moisture into the slab.

Wire mesh embedded in the slab helps to increase the durability of concrete floors and minimise settlement and expansion cracks. Applying wet burlap, moist sawdust, or straw helps to control evaporation and reduce shrinkage cracks. Polythene sheeting may also be used, if care is taken to ensure an air space between the sheet and slab as it cures.

Concrete floors are often finished with a sand and cement screed, concrete sealers, or paint.

suspended floors

Suspended floors are elevated above ground level. They usually consist of timber floor joists, covered with wood boards, plywood, or matting. Support for the floor joists is provided by blocks or beams placed under the joists, or by hanging the joists off a ledger board attached to the walls.

Because the space below the joists provides an ideal area for rodents and other vermin, consider sealing off the air space under the joists, but do not obstruct the flow of air. In order to prevent dry rot, wall vents are used to ventilate the air space.

figure 6.8(e): two types of suspended floor

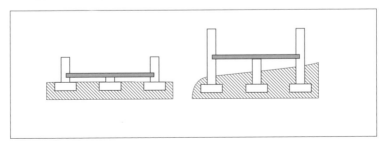

6.8.4 walls

Walls serve to transfer building loads to the foundation, which then transmits them safely to the ground. Walls also provide protection from the elements, security, and privacy for the building's occupants.

load-bearing walls

Loads acting on walls produce two main types of stress:

* compressive stress, produced when walls are being compressed by dead and live loads acting upon them;

* tensile stress, when the wall is being stretched by loads acting upon them.

To resist these loads, structural wall components must be stiff, dense, and stable.

masonry Masonry walls must be able to resist compressive stress created by dead and live loads. By alternating each course of blocks or bricks, a bond is created to help to distribute compression loads throughout the wall. Tensile stresses, which occur as the length of a wall increases between support columns, can produce buckling and make the wall collapse.

Lateral stability can be provided by adding piers and/or buttresses to masonry walls. Piers are columns along walls which increase the thickness of the wall at periodic points. Buttresses are supports formed by internal walls which pass through the external walls, or at corners as returning wall ends. Buttresses and piers act as braces to stiffen walls and help them to transfer tensile stress to the foundation. Adequate foundation support for piers and buttresses must also be considered.

timber Timber used in load-bearing walls resists compressive stress by its ability to behave elastically. Corners and columns in timber-framed walls are made of thicker pieces of timber, which distribute the loads over a wider area. Intermediate vertical wall supports (studs) may be narrower, but cladding material, such as plywood or boards attached horizontally between studs, is needed to improve wall shear strength.

steel Steel has high-tensile strength and stiffness. It is used in both masonry and timber structures as support beams, braces, and fastening plates. Lightweight galvanised steel studs are available as an alternative to timber in many places.

concrete Concrete is a strong material for resisting compression loads, but weak in tensile strength. Adding steel reinforcement bars to concrete improves its tensile strength, making it suitable for use as load-bearing columns and beams.

structural reinforcements: connections

Load-bearing walls should have solid connections to roof structures, foundations, and adjoining walls. In framed walls where timber, tree trunks, or bamboo are used as columns and beams, nails, bolts, wire, and rope can be used as connectors. For walls where steel columns and beams are used, bolts and/or welded connections are favoured. Reinforced concrete columns should be integrated into horizontal structural supports in beams and foundations, either by casting in place, or through wire ties linking the horizontal and vertical steel bars.

In areas where high winds, heavy rainfall, or seismic activity are prevalent, additional connectors should be used. Metal brackets ('hurricane ties') are added to roof members and wall plates in both timber and masonry constructions. Plywood gussets, forming triangle shapes and connecting rafters or trusses, may also be used to provide additional support to wind loads.

In rural Central America, barbed wire is looped around roof rafters and wall plates in timber-framed houses, to provide added reinforcement. As the wire is pulled taut, the barbs are nailed into the timber to further strengthen the connection.

structural reinforcements: horizontal ties

Masonry and earth walls often have horizontal reinforcement (wire, steel bars, or bamboo) set between wall courses to help to distribute compression loads evenly across the wall lengths. A horizontal ring beam running the full perimeter of the walls helps to reduce the effects of dead loads, wind loads, and shrinking and expansion in masonry buildings.

structural reinforcements: bracing

Diagonal bracing set in walls from the roof level to the foundation can help walls to resist tensile forces and transfer loads effectively. This is especially important in platform-framed timber walls, to avoid buckling. Metal strapping attached at a diagonal from the top

6 construction

(roof) wall plate to the bottom (foundation) plate is commonly used. Knee braces made of timber set at a 45° angle from the foundation plate to corner columns, or corners to roof plates, also provide a degree of structural reinforcement for timber walls.

non-load-bearing walls

While not subject to the same degree of stresses as exterior walls, internal walls that divide interior spaces often serve to provide complementary support to load-bearing walls. Well-constructed internal walls can provide lateral support to outer walls, and help to support ceiling joists.

A common form of non-load-bearing wall is a lightweight framed structure attached securely to floors and ceiling joists, over which plastic sheeting, corrugated iron sheets, plywood, or gypsum wall panels are applied. Internal walls in masonry structures made of blocks or bricks must be adequately supported by the foundation, because their weight creates a high load.

openings: windows and doors

Window and door openings can weaken the structural integrity of walls, unless care is taken to ensure that the load above the openings is adequately transferred to other structural components.

Lintels are horizontal beams set above wall openings to support the wall above. They are supported by columns/posts on the immediate sides of the openings, which transfer the loads to the foundation. Materials used for lintels include wood, concrete, stone, or brick. The correct size for lintels is determined by the type of building materials, the width of the wall opening, and the load above the opening.

Lintels for both doors and windows should be set at a uniform height along exterior walls to help to distribute loads evenly throughout the building. In masonry buildings, a continuous lintel along the entire length of the building can also serve as a ring beam to help to ensure structural stability.

Arches are used in masonry buildings to transfer loads to the sides of the opening. To prevent arches from spreading, they are sometimes inset and flanked by vertical restraining walls, which function as piers to improve the tensile strength of arched walls.

Windows must be spaced at an adequate distance (typically 600mm) from the building corners and doors, to avoid compromising the ability of walls to transfer the loads and stresses. In small masonry buildings, avoid locating doors and windows in the same wall section, unless some form of intermediate support is used.

6.8.5 simple roof structures

The main function of a roof is to protect walls, floors, and occupants from infiltration by rain and snow. Roofs also help to control heat loss and condensation.

Winds produce areas of pressure and suction on roofs and walls, which can seriously damage a building or its occupants. In areas of high winds, it is essential that the roof is designed and built according to engineering standards to resist these pressures.

The type of roof used is a function of climate, culture, and design. There are three types of roof structure: flat, pitched, and vaulted.

flat roofs The simplest roof structure is a flat roof with a slight gradient (3cm per metre), to allow water to be drained off. Flat roofs are common in hot dry regions, but are less suitable for areas of tropical cyclones/hurricanes, due to the danger of pressure differential that may tear the roof away.

Materials used for flat roof structures include timber, steel, and bamboo. There is a wide range of roof coverings: organic materials such as grass, thatch, or earth; tiles of earth, slate, or cement; bitumen-based products (asphalt rolls, shingles); metal coverings (corrugated-iron sheeting); plastics (polythene sheeting; polycarbonate sheets); and concrete.

pitched roofs Pitched roofs are common in temperate climates, owing to their ability to drain water from rain and snow. They are common also in tropical cyclone regions because (with a minimum gradient of 30°) they are less susceptible to wind forces than flat roofs are.

After a flat roof, a gable roof, consisting of two slopes (pitches), is the easiest type of roof to construct. In a gable roof, rafters extend at an angle (generally 25–45°) from the walls to meet a centre ridge board. The lower ends of the rafters typically extend 25cm from the walls as eaves, to protect foundations and walls from rainfall.

Gable roofs require two rectangular walls to support the rafter ends, and two A-shaped (gable-end) walls, which meet the ridge line. The construction of gable-end walls consumes more time and materials than rectangular walls, and it often requires scaffolding to ensure efficiency and the safety of workers.

Gable roofs can be built with prefabricated trusses consisting of roof triangles lifted on top of the walls, instead of rafters and ridge boards assembled in place piece by piece. Trusses have the advantage of using less material to carry the roof load, stronger connections (welded or nail plates) between each individual piece, and the ability to span longer building widths. Cranes may be needed to hoist large truss sections on buildings.

Hip roofs offer better protection against high winds, because their four slopes offer bracing in each direction. As each face of a hip roof exposes a smaller surface area to the wind, the effects of wind loading and uplift (thrust) are limited. Because hip roofs rest on four rectangular walls, wall construction is often easier and requires less material (but the savings may be negligible, because of the additional complexities involved in framing a hip roof).

Vaulted roofs are barrel-shaped or dome-shaped structures, typically found on earth and masonry buildings. They utilise the same building materials as the walls. In brick buildings, bricks are set curving upwards from the wall to the roof apex and held in place on temporary formworks until the mortar dries. As concrete has a high compressive strength, relatively thin vaulted roofs can be built, using concrete mixture with reinforcement steel bars and wire mesh.

Vaulted roofs are best suited to dry climates, because rainwater can infiltrate through surface cracks unless adequate damp-proof renderings are applied and maintained.

Engineered and well-constructed vault roofs have a moderate resistance to earth tremors, but note that the ratio of span to width in earthquake zones should not exceed 1.5 for single spans. Longer spans may be covered by a series of small transverse vaults.

roof drainage The ability of roofs to shed water efficiently depends on their shape, the exposure of the building to prevailing winds, and the effectiveness of roof drainage systems.

Drainage channels (gutters) made of plastic, fibreglass, light metals, or wood are attached to the eave edges of roofs to carry water to downspouts and away from foundations.

Thin sheets of rolled metal (aluminium, zinc, or lead) or bitumen-based sheets are used as flashing, to prevent wind-driven rains from entering penetrations in roof coverings such as chimneys, vents, or skylights.

ceilings Ceilings, attached to the underside of roof substructures or on separate joists, can increase the comfort of occupants by trapping air between the ceiling and roof. This restricts heat loss in cold climates, and heat infiltration in hot climates. Ventilation is needed to prevent the build-up of condensation and to permit adequate air exchange. It can be provided though the use of vents inserted at eaves level and on roof tops.

Materials used for ceilings include plastic sheeting, gypsum sheets, timber boards, plywood, cardboard, and woven panels of straw, bamboo, or reeds.

chapter 7 distribution

7 distribution

7 distribution

This chapter discusses the design of distribution projects and systems. 'Distribution' in this context refers to selecting, procuring, and distributing shelter non-food items (NFIs) to a displaced population. The final two sections of the chapter provide specifications for typical shelter items.

The design and distribution of shelter NFI packages, whether of household items such as blankets and cooking utensils, or of construction materials, is a continuous process. Once items have been sourced and purchased, their journey from the supplier to each population group requires a distribution system. The system must be carefully managed within a distribution project to minimise breakage, cost, environmental wear and tear, and theft.

The scale of the logistics required to support a transitional settlement (TS) programme means that the design and effectiveness of the programme are often directly proportional to the size and type of the logistics capacity available. Consequently, logisticians should be involved from the outset in programme design, as well as in project implementation.

Support for TS programmes must not, however, be limited to achieving efficient distributions. When assessing, monitoring, and supporting distributions, extension work is required to ensure that, for example, construction materials distributed in a cyclone-prone area are used by beneficiaries to build a suitable shelter in a manner appropriate to the circumstances, helping the affected population to adapt their traditional construction methods to reduce hazards.

This chapter covers the following topics:

7.1 distribution projects: what to distribute, and how to do it

7.2 shelter NFI packages: how to design them

7.3 distribution systems: maximising their effectiveness

7.4 procurement: finding and buying items for shelter NFI packages

7.5 shelter-material items: specifications for tents, sheeting, and other items

7.6 household shelter items: specifications for day-to-day items such as kitchenware and bedding.

This chapter does not present or replace specialist standards, policy, or guidance on logistics; instead it adds considerations that are specific to the support of TS programmes.

7.1 distribution projects

Each of the six TS programme options described in chapter 3 requires a series of projects to implement it. At least one of these projects will probably deal with the distribution of shelter NFIs, such as construction materials, blankets, and cooking utensils, to a displaced group or to the local population. This section presents guidance and reference for selecting and distributing shelter NFIs appropriate to the needs of each displaced population group.

7.1.1 distribution within a project plan

Planning a distribution project should follow the same process as any other project plan. The steps involved in project planning are presented in section 2.1. They include forming a profile of the displaced persons to be supported, and a plan of how to respond, integrated within programme and strategic plans.

The purpose of the distribution project should be constantly reviewed. Projects, programmes, and strategies should all work towards achieving objectives identified during the planning process.

Four factors are central to the success of planning and implementing shelter NFI distribution:

- **Secure all-weather access**, which must be provided not only to the TS options, but also from the areas where natural materials are harvested, and from the railheads, ports, and airports where materials will arrive.

- **Procurement capacities** (7.4): it will be necessary to purchase large quantities of materials during the emergency phase, when procurement systems are often at their weakest.

- **Logistics capacities** (7.3.3–7.3.4), such as numbers of staff and transport vehicles, as well as local and regional commercial haulage capacities. Shelter NFI distribution projects require a larger procurement and logistics capacity than other sectors of operations, except those for food and fuel supplies. Thatching materials, for example, are much more voluminous and heavy than supplies for primary health-care services. For this reason, the logistics capacity of the organisations involved may become the key constraint in the development of a project plan.

- **The co-ordination of distribution activities:** it is important to avoid the duplication of distribution systems and double handling that may result if (for example) shelter NFI distribution is managed separately from food-item (FI) distribution. Shelter NFI distributions should be co-ordinated with non-shelter NFI and FI distributions. Similarly, assessments and monitoring for non-shelter NFI and FI distributions should inform shelter NFI distributions.

When starting a distribution, it is very important to agree with the beneficiaries **what** will be distributed, **how** it will be distributed, and **why** it will be distributed. Care should be taken not to raise false expectations or to make promises that cannot be kept. The distribution of inappropriate or excessively expensive items can destabilise local markets, as well as attracting displaced persons who do not actually need the aid.

7.1.2 combining packages and distribution systems

The assessment and monitoring of distributions that support transitional shelter are often the most detailed processes in any sector of operations. For this reason, consideration should be given to informing and integrating other sectoral components, such as protection, health care, and water and sanitation. Distribution to a family rarely happens only once, and the distribution of TS materials should take account of existing distribution programmes for food items and non-food items. In the case of shelter materials in particular, it is often useful to undertake a series of phased distributions, in order both to ensure that the materials are used for the activity agreed, and to monitor and inform progress. This continuous monitoring process offers an important opportunity to discuss key concerns, especially with more isolated beneficiaries in circumstances where access is difficult. Such discussions should include the impact of vulnerability or skills shortages on their ability to make use of the support offered.

A project plan should therefore consider using the distribution system for the following extension activities:

- assessment of the livelihoods and environment of the local and displaced populations
- assessment of capacities and options for procurement and construction
- assessment of the local availability of skills, labour, and tools
- assessment of shelter NFI needs
- identification and support of vulnerable individuals and groups, for example those unable to build or maintain their own shelter
- monitoring the degree to which the distribution of shelter NFIs is achieving the project objectives, and identifying operational changes that might make it more effective.

7.2 shelter NFI packages

There are five common types of shelter NFI distribution 'package' (7.2.1), each involving a combination of shelter NFIs which should be developed (7.2.2) for each displaced population group.

Section 7.5 offers an overview of shelter-material NFIs that contribute to the physical sheltering of a family, such as tents and plastic sheeting. Section 6.7 of the previous chapter gives an overview of other material NFIs that may be distributed as part of a shelter package, such as timber and cement. Section 7.6 offers an overview of household shelter NFIs used inside a family shelter, such as blankets and cooking utensils.

7.2.1 types of shelter NFI package

During the emergency phase, all five common types of shelter NFI package are usually in great demand, as shelters are built and occupied. Later supplementary distributions tend to be responses to specific circumstances, such as the onset of winter or further population movements.

family-shelter NFI packages

As the family fled, they may have lost or sold the basic items necessary for their survival, such as blankets and water containers. It is essential to assess and maintain the package of basic items for each family, and to monitor how it should change in different seasons and in different phases of their displacement.

family-shelter support packages

Most displaced families build and maintain their own shelter, whatever TS options they choose. Often they lack essential tools and materials. Often the harvesting of a particular material creates unsustainable environmental damage, or conflict with the local population over competition for these resources.

Family-shelter support packages offer the construction tools and materials that families cannot obtain for themselves on a sustainable basis. Packages may include thatch, plastic sheeting, nails, and drums of water for the manufacture of mud bricks.

family-shelter provision packages

The lack of local materials, the speed, unpredictability, or scale of an influx, the vulnerability of a beneficiary group, or the time of year may (singly or in combination) prevent displaced families building their own shelter. In such circumstances, the shelter provided should offer the maximum opportunity for adaptation to their changing needs and livelihoods, and it should be easily repairable.

Family-shelter provision packages may include tents, mattresses, flooring, stoves, and lamps, constituting a complete set of shelter items required for survival with dignity.

communal-shelter support packages

Shelter NFI support is also required by displaced persons living with host families, or in vacant urban buildings or communal dwellings. Support may take the form of materials to upgrade a space in use by the displaced family, or a contribution to the communal-shelter needs of the displaced and/or their hosts.

family-shelter return packages

Displaced families may require material assistance to move from their chosen TS options to their chosen durable solution, which may range from reintegration in their country of origin to local settlement. Material assistance in this process often includes shelter NFIs, such as tools, water containers, and cooking sets.

7.2.2 developing shelter NFI packages

Combining or selecting the five NFI packages to create a distribution project should be undertaken within the processes of project, programme, and strategic planning presented in chapter 2.

This section considers the identification of appropriate items to be included in the five types of shelter NFI packages.

objective It is important to consider the design and distribution of shelter packages as part of a sheltering process, seeking to achieve an agreed objective, rather than regarding it as an end in itself. The project plan will have identified the purpose of the distribution of shelter NFIs: for example, the objective may be to maximise the number of available host families. Other activities within this same project might include offering cash to hosted families for the improvement of their shelter in ways that contribute to the development of the homes of the host family.

selecting items for a shelter package

Selecting the contents of one of the five types of NFI package (7.2.1) involves the following steps:

- Assess the livelihoods of the beneficiaries, and group them according to families' specific material needs.

- Consider, if buying materials (such as blankets), the likely impact on the local market.

- Take into account the likely impact on the local environment if material (such as firewood) is to be harvested.

- Develop a distribution system appropriate to the frequency, volume, sources, and destinations of the packages (7.3). If distribution is to be made to a distribution point, rather than to the family shelter itself, the weight and volume of a shelter package must be transportable by the beneficiaries. Support should be made available to vulnerable households who are unable to transport or use the materials.

7.2.3 maintaining shelter NFI support

The role of support staff is key to the distribution process, because the distribution of shelter packages is part of a sheltering process. Activities of the support staff, whether from a national or international aid organisation or local authority, include the following:

7 distribution

- undertaking on-going assessments, monitoring, and evaluation
- identifying vulnerable households and groups, and managing support for them
- maintaining capacities for local storage and local distribution.

The distribution strategy will depend in part on the capacity of the support staff available (2.2.1), the size and dispersal of the beneficiary population, and access to that population, given the types of item to be distributed. For example, a large staff would be required to manage the distribution of roofing thatch to a rural displaced population dispersed over a large area with poor roads during a rainy season.

Support for vulnerable households may require labour assistance: for example, managing teams of thatchers to cover the roofs of shelters.

7.3 distribution systems

Distribution and logistics capacities often determine the success or failure of the TS response. Developing an appropriate distribution system for a project is important. It should have the following aims:

- to support the wider project objectives
- to ensure fair provision of supplies
- to ensure support for vulnerable families
- to maintain assessment, monitoring, and evaluation processes.

For shelter NFI packages, this may involve a significant logistics component: for example, distributing thatch for 1,000 households every year would require harvesting, transport, and storage on a significant scale, besides support for vulnerable households.

reducing donor visibility

Some beneficiaries may consider receiving aid as shameful, because it implies to them that they are incapable of meeting their own needs or the needs of their family. There have been instances when plastic sheeting was put over a roof the wrong way up, because it had the name of an aid organisation printed on one side. (Such marking is termed 'visibility' by some organisations.) To respect the sensitivities of such beneficiaries, and to ensure that the shelter NFIs are used in an appropriate manner, consideration might be given to marking shelter NFIs in a way that is not obvious, especially when they are in use.

As an alternative to printing large logos on shelter NFIs, consider marking the transport vehicle, or spreading the marking over a number of items: for example, a logo might be stencilled over the end-pieces of pallets of sawn timber, so that after transport, when the pallet is broken up for distribution and use, only a part of the logo remains on each end-piece.

7.3.1 types of distribution system

There are three dimensions to consider when designing a distribution system:

- whether distribution takes place through representatives or via heads of households
- the frequency of distribution, and the final number of distributions
- the size and contents of the shelter NFI packages.

distribution channels

UNHCR lists three channels through which distribution may take place (UNHCR 2000):

- **Group leaders:** commodities are given in bulk to a community representative, who then distributes them to heads of households. This channel is often employed in the emergency phase, even before ration cards are introduced. It requires self-regulation by the displaced population and their representatives. High commodity costs, however, put pressures on community leaders and increase the likelihood of exploitation and corruption. Sample monitoring may be used to assess the effectiveness of coverage.

- **Groups of heads of extended families:** the family head distributes the commodities to heads of households. This option is the one most open to exploitation for personal or financial gain.

- **Individual heads of households:** either men or women.

7 distribution

When shelter NFIs are being distributed, it may be possible to get members of the wider group to support vulnerable households, especially with help to transport materials to their shelters.

It is possible to combine the benefits of all three channels by giving shelter NFIs directly to the individual heads of households, while involving group leaders at all community levels within all community groups.

frequency of distribution

Distribution projects must consider how to use the distribution process to contribute to the wider objectives and needs of the distribution project, beyond simply giving items to families.

One method to achieve this is by identifying what shelter NFIs should be distributed, at what phase of operations (2.4). Multiple distributions may be phased, in order to support a shelter activity or to respond to changing needs. For example, in the emergency phase, distributions to support urban displaced populations may start with plastic sheeting, to create a waterproof space. In the care and maintenance phase, roof tiles may be distributed, to upgrade the shelter. If roof tiles are distributed too early in the process, tiles will be broken in storage, commandeered by other groups, or sold on to generate funds to meet other needs. The second distribution should not be undertaken until it is demonstrated that the commodities in the first distribution have been used for the purpose originally agreed with the beneficiaries. This form of conditionality should be highly flexible, because the intent is to support families: if the first distribution has not been used in the way intended, it is likely that further assessment is required, in order to understand why. Circumstances may have changed, requiring the shelter package and distribution project to be reconsidered. In this manner, phased distribution supports the implementation of the project, while allowing on-going monitoring and evaluation.

Phased distribution may not be possible unless the shelter package contains many commodities, and unless the distribution is repeated regularly, and unless there are sufficient support staff with sufficient access to beneficiary families to undertake the project.

size and contents of NFI packages

The contents of a shelter NFI package (7.2.2) depend on project objectives and the capacities and resources available. Bulky packages

---

transitional settlement: displaced populations

should be delivered to a point as close as possible to individual families, and there should be sufficient support staff or volunteers available at the point of delivery to unload items at the doorsteps of families. Alternatively, smaller packages might be delivered to distribution points, and people might be asked to collect their package – in which case, consideration should be given to the needs of vulnerable beneficiaries.

7.3.2 developing distribution systems

Developing a distribution system within a project plan (2.3) combines the following elements:

- project objectives (2.3.1)
- shelter NFI package design (7.2.2)
- transport capacities and access (7.3.3)
- storage capacities (7.3.4)
- support-staff capacities (7.2.3, 2.2.1).

It is essential that the impacts of the distribution on all population groups are understood, and that all groups are involved in the design of the distribution system, including men and women, individuals of different ages, and every ethnic and social group. For example, the project objective might be to support immediate TS capacity in rural self-settlement, as part of a wider programme involving support for water-supply infrastructure and other communal services. Assessment to determine who will use the infrastructure and shelter might lead to a decision that the shelter NFI package should include water-storage containers and materials to support the construction of family shelter, such as a bucket with lid, nails, plastic sheeting, and a hammer and shovel. Commercial haulage may be available; however, vehicular access may be limited to one road only, with families self-settled on either side of the road, within walking distance. So storage for imported and local goods should be provided in warehouses, with satellite warehouses located along the access road. Support staff would need to ensure that the commodities reached each family; to do this, they would need to involve group leaders in the distribution from the satellite warehouses, while the support staff walked off the road to undertake monitoring of the process.

7 distribution

figure 7(a): distribution chain

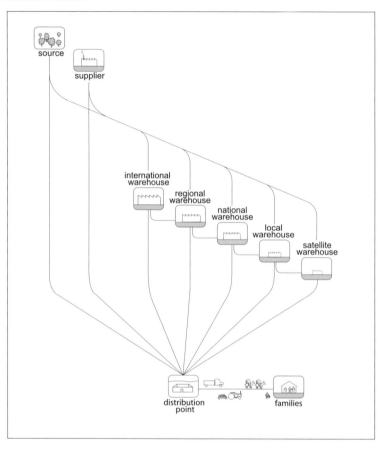

After harvesting, procurement, or manufacture, commodities are transported from the source or supplier to the beneficiary families, via a series of warehouses. The distribution chain should minimise the number of warehouses involved, and the amount of double handling required; but it should also offer the necessary opportunities for commodities to be compiled into distribution packages.

7.3.3 transport

Specialist and organisational guidelines (UNHCR 2000) offer detailed information on transport logistics, such as the capacities and restrictions of various modes of transport, including cargo aircraft and lorries.

access to beneficiaries

The displaced populations, the areas that they harvest, and the airstrips, ports, and rail-heads at which their resources arrive all need secure, all-weather access. Different commodities from different sources, required in different phases of operation, will require different access in different seasons, using different modes of transport: for example, distributing bush poles sourced locally in the emergency phase along tracks during a monsoon may be best achieved by using pack animals, while trucks might be more appropriate when sustainable sources can be found in a wider area later.

availability and capacity

Shelter-material NFIs, such as timber, often have high volume and weight relative to food items and other non-food items, and they often need to be distributed quickly, at an early stage in an aid operation. Other demands on transport capacity, such as the delivery of food aid, may conflict with the need for shelter NFIs. In such circumstances, consider co-ordinating distribution in order to increase efficiency, and using different modes of transport more appropriate to the specific commodities, such as trains and carts rather than aircraft and ships.

transport management

Aid organisations, governments, military forces, and commercial companies all have transport capacities. Each mode of transport has its own impacts, and care should be taken to anticipate these. For instance, if military vehicles are used, the shelter NFI project and the implementing organisation might be linked with the armed forces concerned.

Care should be taken to consider the potential impact of large transportation contracts on the local economy and transport capacity.

7 distribution

potential damage

Large transport operations involving some modes of transport may damage local infrastructure. For example, rural roads may not be appropriate for convoys of trucks, and the resulting damage may, unless repaired, have a bad effect on local relations.

losses in transit

Some materials, such as ceramic roof tiles and glass, are fragile; breakages in transit should be expected, especially over bad roads. Such losses should be factored into project planning, and additional materials should be ordered. Mitigation measures include improving packing, such as packing loads on pallets and protecting them with sandbags; and improving handling procedures and equipment (because many losses occur during loading and unloading). Tarpaulins might be specified or distributed, if the items are vulnerable to damage by rain or sun.

Valuable materials may make transport operations vulnerable to hijack or theft. Additional security measures should be considered.

handling commodities

Commodities with high volumes and weights may put a strain on transport capacities, because the loading and unloading required is labour-intensive. High-value commodities are a greater temptation to thieves if they are stored for long periods; so they should ideally be ordered and distributed on demand. A lack of handling equipment, such as forklift trucks, will slow down unloading. Palletised loads can speed loading and reduce loss in transit, provided that appropriate handling equipment is available. Sufficient labour should be made available, and additional support should be arranged to ensure distributions to vulnerable groups (7.2.3).

7.3.4 storage

There are two main considerations when planning the storage of shelter NFIs: the need for a storage strategy to support distribution systems; and requirements for the storage of specific shelter NFIs.

developing a storage strategy

For efficiency, shelter NFIs are usually distributed to each family in packages containing various commodities – so that, for example, a truck-load of nails is not followed immediately by a truck-load of hammers. This process requires materials from a variety of sources to be brought together for distribution, although each family's package may be compiled at a local distribution point rather than in a remote warehouse.

The storage strategy should seek to minimise double handling (the unloading, storage, and re-loading of materials), which wastes time and labour, and increases the probability of breakage and theft. Consider negotiating direct deliveries with the supplier, or short-term storage, or the maintenance of a stock of a specific commodity.

requirements for storing shelter NFIs

Section 6.7 presents guidance on the storage of the most common shelter-material NFIs, such as timber and cement. This is extremely important, because inappropriate storage can lead to considerable losses, both from material degradation and from theft.

7.4 procurement

This section discusses the procurement of shelter NFIs, in the following stages:

- **specification:** performance and technical specification (7.4.1)
- **sourcing:** identifying a sustainable supply and appropriate supplier (7.4.2)
- **purchasing:** locally or internationally (7.4.3).

This section assumes that aid agencies and government organisations have their own logistics standards and procedures, and catalogues of equipment and materials. These guidelines are not intended to replace specialist logistics guidance.

7.4.1 specification

When shelter NFIs are to be distributed, it is important to specify the items carefully, to ensure that the materials will be of the appropriate quality and the right type for use with other shelter NFIs, and to ensure that their weight, size, and packing volume will match the expectations of the logistics chain.

Items should be procured either in accordance with a performance specification, which describes the **function** that the item is to undertake, or in accordance with a technical specification, which describes the **quality** of materials and fabrication. Performance specifications are often used for rapid local or regional procurements, when it is not possible to undertake detailed multi-stage tendering processes (5.4.3). Technical specifications or design specifications are often used for common items included in equipment catalogues, if similar items have been purchased in bulk over many years and detailed descriptions can be developed.

Technical and performance specifications of common shelter-material items are presented in section 7.5, while common household shelter items are presented in section 7.6. The specifications follow standards laid down by Sphere (Sphere Project 2004) and UNHCR (UNHCR 2000), which contain more details about the function of each item, as part of support for transitional settlement.

7.4.2 sourcing

Aid organisations, the donors supporting distribution projects, and local authorities may have policies and procedures concerning the sources of materials and commodities procured. Basic considerations are listed below:

- **ethical concerns**, including the question of whether child labour was used in harvesting, or whether the human-rights record of the manufacturing country is deemed unacceptable;

- **environmental concerns**, including the potential impact of a large-scale order on the local environment and on natural-resource management (2.5.4): for example, whether timber is harvested from sustainable forests, or whether production involves ozone-depleting chemicals;

- **economic issues**, including the potential impact of a large-scale order on the local economies, both formal and informal: for example, whether the donor country has negotiated trade agreements with the supplier country which might reduce costs, or whether tariffs are in place which might increase costs;

- **developmental factors**, including opportunities for relief-aid projects to offer sustainable local development: for example, whether procurement in a particular region might help to stimulate economic growth.

Local, national, regional, and international market sources should be evaluated to identify those that have the capacity to supply the commodities to the quantities and qualities required, reliably over the period required; and those that can provide emergency or back-up capacities, or offer alternative commodities.

local sourcing

It is preferable to purchase materials locally, because this can stimulate the local economy, build on local capacities, and reduce tensions between displaced and local communities by spreading the benefits of aid beyond the displaced population.

Large-scale procurements may have significant impacts on the local markets, forcing the costs of the commodities up beyond the reach of the local inhabitants and beneficiaries. For example, it is often the case that local disadvantaged communities rely on the same commodities that are being purchased to support the displaced population. Local purchase may therefore create unacceptable problems for local people, even to the extent of forcing them to seek the support that is offered to displaced communities.

The needs of displaced populations are by their very nature hard to predict. Large orders may be placed locally, and capacity may be increased in response (in part through local specialisation and investment), but after the response is completed the increased capacity may be unsustainable.

Furthermore, large orders may have serious and adverse impacts on the local environment. The environmental impacts are particularly noticeable in the case of wood harvested for construction or fuel. Many other materials, such as thatches and gravel extraction, also have an impact on the local environment. Phased procurement may reduce negative local impacts. Where appropriate, tree re-planting schemes or other environmental reparation measures should be considered (UNHCR 1998).

The Sphere Project offers guidance on construction standards:

Sourcing of shelter materials and labour: livelihood support should be promoted through the local procurement of building materials, specialist building skills and manual labour. Multiple sources, alternative materials and production processes, or the provision of regionally or internationally sourced materials or proprietary shelter systems are required if the local harvesting and supply of materials is likely to have a significant adverse impact on the local economy or the environment. The re-use of materials salvaged from damaged buildings should be promoted where feasible, either as primary construction materials (bricks or stone masonry, roof timber, roof tiles, etc.) or as secondary material (rubble for foundations or levelling roads, etc.). Ownership of or the rights to such material should be identified and agreed (see Shelter and settlement standard 6, guidance note 3 on page 228).
Sphere Project (2004), chapter 4, p 225

national and regional sourcing

If there are insufficient local sources of materials (perhaps because of concerns for the local environment and effects on the local market, or for reasons of cost), it may be necessary to source materials nationally or regionally. Transport costs will be higher, and supply will be slower. If the goods must cross a national border, customs requirements should be considered.

There may be regional stockpiles and items pre-positioned in anticipation of an emergency. Stockpiling is a crucial part of contingency planning. It should be noted that some materials do not last indefinitely, and old materials from some stockpiles may be in poor condition, especially materials that have been badly stored and those which have short shelf-lives, such as cement and tents.

international sourcing

Some shelter equipment may need to be sourced internationally: items that do not exist regionally, or have long lead times, or need to be stockpiled, or those for which significant savings can be made if ordered in bulk.

Aid organisations should consult head-office procurement staff, because they are likely to have guidance notes on sourcing, and records to indicate whether individual suppliers and manufacturers can deliver satisfactorily.

7.4.3 purchasing

It is important to make sure that the appropriate commodities have been properly specified (7.4.1), sourced (7.4.2), and selected before purchasing. Selection should take the following factors into account:

- whether beneficiaries are familiar with the commodities, and whether they know how to use them;
- the reparability and maintenance of the commodities, including parts, tools, and skills required;
- options for the replacement or substitution of the commodities – because sustainable support is an important objective, and because all materials commodities have a limited design life.

Some aid organisations and donors have policies which require different procedures to be adopted for single procurements over a certain cost: for example, tendering may be required (5.4.3), or approval by staff at headquarters. Such policies might apply to the purchase of a large quantity of a single NFI commodity.

Other financial constraints and opportunities relevant to purchasing (concerning, for example, the maintenance of a cash flow) are offered in section 2.4.2.

quotations It is very important to understand what a quotation includes: for example, does it cover the costs of packing goods on to pallets, loading them, and maintaining additional stocks? The same is true when tendering for labour and building contracts. It is important to take into account the costs of transport, loading, unloading, and storage, especially when procuring bulky shelter materials, because these costs can exceed the costs of the actual materials. It is important to determine whether the supplier or the transport company will pay for losses in transit; such losses are commonly as high as 10 per cent, or even higher for fragile items such as tiles or glass.

frame agreements

'Frame agreements', in which an aid organisation agrees to use a certain supplier first, in exchange for purchasing a commodity at a guaranteed price, may be made or may already exist.

ordering Having decided where and from whom to buy materials, next you need to develop a list of required conditions and specify them in the contract: for example, conditions might include delivery times, the material and packing specifications, liability for losses in transit, and responsibility for costs of transport, loading, and unloading. Consider including penalty clauses or incentive clauses to increase the likelihood of commodities arriving on time.

quality control

It is important to maintain quality control, to ensure that specification and sourcing standards are maintained. The purchasing organisation should undertake regular inspections and 'spot' inspections, when the inspection is not announced to the supplier. In some cases, a reputable private inspection company may be employed instead. It is particularly important to check the quality of materials at their source, if the materials have to travel a significant distance. In most cases, the cost of maintaining quality control through regular and impartial inspections will be far less than the losses incurred when suppliers seek to avoid their obligations.

7.5 shelter-material items

This section gives an overview of shelter-material NFIs that contribute to the physical sheltering of a family, such as tents and plastic sheeting. Section 7.6 gives an overview of household shelter NFIs used inside a family shelter, such as blankets and cooking utensils. Other material NFIs that may be distributed as part of a shelter package (7.2), such as timber and cement, are considered in section 6.7.

The following shelter-material NFIs are considered in this section:

7.5.1 tents

7.5.2 plastic sheeting

7.5.3 prefabricated shelter and containers

7.5.4 materials and tools for construction.

Once the need for a distribution is established, and the role of each item in the livelihoods of the beneficiaries is understood, close monitoring is recommended. Monitoring may, for example, identify a need for instruction or safety training if the beneficiaries are not familiar with certain items, such as tents.

standards This section includes relevant entries from standards for shelter-material items developed by the Sphere Project (2004), UNHCR (2000), and the United Nations Development Programme and the Inter-Agency Procurement Services Office of the United Nations Development Programme (UNDP / IAPSO 2000). Thanks are due to these agencies for permission to reproduce their copyright material.

From *Humanitarian Charter and Minimum Standards in Disaster Response* (Sphere Project 2004), references are made to the standards, key indicators, and guidance notes sections.

From *Handbook for Emergencies* (UNHCR 2000), references are made to chapters 12, 13, 17, and 18.

From volume 1 of *Emergency Relief Items – Compendium of Generic Specifications* (UNDP / IAPSO 2000), excerpts are reproduced from the specifications sections, with details of criteria such as weight, size, and packing volume.

The extracts presented here are intended to give an overview of the kind of information that is available, and to aid general understanding. They do not include the preambles and introductions necessary for a detailed specific understanding of any of the items. The original publications should always be consulted before any standards are used.

7.5.1 tents

Table 7(a) presents the six types of tent in general use by the aid community, summarising and comparing their properties and range of uses.

table 7(a):   six types of tent in general use by the aid community *

	ridge	centre pole, tall wall	centre pole, low wall	tunnel	frame	warehouse
use	family shelter	family shelter	family shelter	family shelter; small facilities, e.g. stores, clinics, transit and feeding centres	family shelter; small facilities, e.g. clinics, transit and feeding centres	warehousing; reception and distribution centres; medical services
positive points	traditional relief tent: proven design; large production capacities	proven design; good headroom; can use bunk beds; large production capacities	proven design; single-fly versions lightweight; large production capacities	rot-resistant; lightweight; modular; good use of external space; headroom	proven design; robust; modular; good headroom; some can be winterised; synthetic types resist rot	proven design; robust; rot-resistant; modular; good head-room; some can accom-modate vehicles; floor can be cast
negative points	canvas rots; inflexible; draughty; limited head-room; good types are heavy	canvas rots; inflexible; draughty; heavy; may be unstable in high winds or heavy snow	canvas rots; inflexible; draughty; limited headroom; good types heavy	technology under devel-opment; unproven production capacity, buildability, and flexibility	expensive; heavy; canvas-covered types rot	expensive; heavy
use in different climates	hot and temperate, if double-fly; winterisation limited to flue hole	hot and temperate, if double-fly; winterisation limited to flue hole	hot and temperate, if double-fly; winterisation limited to flue hole	hot and temperate; winterisation proven in one type only	hot and temperate; in some types winterisation is by flue hole, double fly, hot-air heater holes	hot and temperate; in some types winterisation is by flue hole, double fly, hot-air heater holes

continued ...

* Adapted from Ashmore 2004

	ridge	centre pole, tall wall	centre pole, low wall	tunnel	frame	warehouse
structure	2–3 vertical poles, one ridge pole	single or double centre poles with high side walls, held up by more poles	centre pole and low walls, without additional poles	hoops in a tunnel shape; new-generation relief tent	rigid frame, usually from flat poles: common for military use	rigid frame, usually from flat poles, usually covered by synthetic materials
covering	usually canvas or poly-cotton	usually canvas or poly-cotton	usually canvas or poly-cotton	usually synthetic materials, such as nylon or polyester	varies: canvas, poly-cotton, nylon, polyester	usually synthetic materials, such as nylon or polyester
weight	75–120kg	120kg	50–100kg	40–80kg, more for winterised types	100–120kg, more for winterised types	over 250kg, depending on type

international performance standards

Currently, few of the tents specified as standard by the major aid organisations conform to internationally agreed shelter standards, such as that which specifies the covered area required per person (UNHCR 2000). For tent performance standards, see Ashmore (2004). The standards provided by the International Organization for Standardization (ISO) and similar organisations have not been developed with tents in mind, although some standards have been adapted subsequently by some aid organisations for the specification of tent fabrics.

field adaptation by families

When developing tent specifications, remember that, although most tents are designed to be assembled in one way only, in reality most are adapted to meet local circumstances. In addition, replacement tents or repair materials are often not available when required. Most tents continue to be used until they are dismantled, and are then re-used as component parts for other shelter.

As the beneficiary family spends longer in the tent, and as the tent degrades, adaptations and repairs are made to meet family needs and local environmental circumstances: for example, more guy ropes may be used in areas where there are high winds.

7 distribution

Aid organisations often have specifications for their preferred standard tents, although many include a number of types for different uses. Standard tents should be used whenever possible, because they are tried and tested, and because the procurement chain has been optimised.

The procurement and distribution of tents should be undertaken only as part of a project involving assessment, field support, and a complete package of shelter NFIs.

Specifying and sourcing tents should begin with defining a brief for the use of the tents, as part of project planning (2.3). Tents can be used for a variety of purposes, from family shelter to warehousing, and can be specified to meet a number of criteria. Bear in mind the following factors:

- Does the design under consideration meet international standards, such as the covered area required per person (Sphere 2004, UNHCR 2000)?

- Is the outside space around the tent flexible enough to allow for activities such as child care, cooking, and surface-water drainage, all of which may be constrained by entry points and guy ropes?

- Can the tent be easily adapted by its users?

- Is it easy to assemble? Are clear instructions supplied?

- Is there a repair kit, with spare materials?

- What will the tent be used for?

- How long should it last?

- In what climatic range will it be used? Can it be weather-proofed for winter conditions?

- What range of household shelter NFIs will be supplied with it?

- What is the weight, and what is the packing volume?

- How long is the lead-time to delivery?

- What is the supplier's production capacity?

- Are national and international stockpiles maintained by aid organisations and suppliers?

- Is the material fire-retardant? If it is, does the design help to prevent the fire moving across the tent, and has this flame

---

316

spread been tested to agreed standards? In the event of fire, can the doors be opened and the tent evacuated quickly?

- Are there valences or 'mud-flaps' around the bottom of the tent, big enough to be buried to increase stability in high winds? Are they made from a material that does not rot?

materials and manufacturing

Specialist guidelines, such as those presented by Ashmore (2004) and Howard and Spice (1989), offer detailed information about the specification, materials, and manufacturing of tents, including general guidance on the use of plastic sheeting.

second-generation tents

New tents made wholly from synthetic materials, such as plastic sheeting and nylon, are being developed by several aid organisations and companies. They add to the available range of traditional, standard, canvas-covered tents.

Most of the new second-generation tents are tunnel-shaped, made from a series of hoops, and covered with plastic sheeting or nylon. Some types of second-generation tent have been deployed in quantity, but the design is still being refined. There are several advantages in using second-generation tents, including the following:

- Long-term storage is possible, enabling an emergency shelter capacity to be maintained at a more reasonable cost than is the case with canvas-covered tents, which rot.
- Weight and volume are reduced, cutting transport costs and enabling more to be carried by a single airlift or vehicle.
- The design can be more easily refined, to improve modularity, flexibility, adaptability, and reparability.
- Draughts are reduced, improving internal climatic control, and making the development of winterisation options easier.

standard canvas tents

Figure 7(b) illustrates the component parts of a traditional canvas-covered ridge tent, as used in similar forms by most major aid organisations.

7 distribution

figure 7(b): parts of a tent *

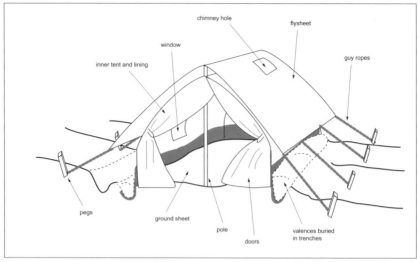

*Adapted from Ashmore 2004

The UNHCR standards for generic tents are as follows:

81. Tents may be useful and appropriate for example when local materials are either not available at all or are only seasonally available or for refugees of nomadic background. The life-span of an erected tent depends on the climate and the care given by its occupants; it may be as long as 2 to 3 years. Where tents are used, repair materials should be provided to the occupants. A group of tents may also serve as transit accommodation while more appropriate shelter is constructed. Standard specifications for tents can be found in Annex 1 to chapter 18 on supplies and transport.

82. Tents should be covered with an outer fly to shade and protect the tent below. The tent should provide free standing height all over the floor area. Tents are difficult to heat as canvas walls and roof cannot provide insulation against heat loss. However, it is possible to some extent to heat a good, well sealed tent, if enough heat is produced in a tent stove. This stove needs fuel (usually wood or kerosene) around the clock to maintain a comfortable temperature. The fuel cost will be high. Therefore tents are not suitable as cold climate shelters, but if there is no choice, they can save lives and bridge the time until more suitable shelters are established.

UNHCR (2000), chapter 12, p145

The UNHCR standards for double-fly, double-fold, centre-pole, family-sized tents are as follows:

external dimensions:	4.4m x 4.4m (outer fly), surface area 19.36 m², centre height 3m.
internal dimensions:	4m x 4m, floor area 16 m², centre height 2.75m, side wall height 1.8m (25cm distance between outer and inner fly).
material:	Cotton canvas; 100% cotton yarn (10/2 x 10/2 twisted in warp 42/44, weft 24/26 threads per inch, plain weave); 15-16 oz/m². Canvas to be free of weaving defects and finishing faults adversely affecting strength, waterproofness and durability. Water proofing/resistance to water penetration by paraffin wax emulsion and aluminium acetate to withstand 20–30cm hydrostatic head. Stabilization against decomposition of the fabric (rot-proofing) with copper napthanate.
poles/ropes/pegs:	4 aluminium or bamboo poles for roof corners (2m x 22mm diameter); heavy duty sectional steel tube (or aluminium or bamboo) centre pole, plastic clad or galvanized (3m x 50mm diameter). Complete with ropes made of 9mm 3 strand polypropylene; 24 T-Type bars 40mm x 40mm, 50cm long; 12 iron pegs (25cm x 9mm diameter), one iron hammer of 1kg; one repair kit with one straight and one curved needle with 20m of suitable thread for tent repair, illustrated assembly instructions with list of contents.
ground sheet:	Reinforced PVC groundsheet 250g/m².
packing:	All rolled into a canvas bag. Weight 100–130kg, dimensions: 2m x 50cm diameter (0.4 m³).

UNHCR (2000), chapter 18, annex 1, p. 26

7.5.2 plastic sheeting

Polythene plastic reinforced sheeting is often distributed in the early stages of an emergency. Sometimes plastic sheeting is distributed as part of a shelter NFI package which includes ropes and materials such as bamboo or bush poles, to build a structural frame for a shelter.

Plastic sheeting used for shelters should meet standard specifications, such as those presented below. Three basic types of plastic sheeting are produced, each to different qualities and standards:

- **multi-purpose plastic sheeting** (white, or white with reinforced coloured stripes), such as the UNHCR types specified below
- **heavyweight or roofing sheeting** (sometimes orange and grey), which is often used under roof tiles or as a damp-proof membrane for tanking
- **window sheeting** (translucent), used for temporary repairs to windows in damaged buildings .

cutting and fixing

Considerable care should be taken when cutting and fixing plastic sheeting, in order to increase the effectiveness of its use and the length of time that it can be made to last without replacement, and in order to minimise waste. It might be appropriate to include tools and materials for cutting and fixing the plastic sheeting as part of the shelter NFI package. Cutting should ideally be done from a roll, rather than from pre-cut tarpaulins, because this produces less waste through off-cuts. It is preferable to distribute plastic sheeting in a single piece, so that the beneficiaries can cut it to meet their needs. Four factors are important when fixing plastic sheeting:

- Prevent tearing from the fixing points: this can usually be achieved by spreading the loads created by point fixings, such as by using nails or battens, or by rolling over the edge of the sheeting to be secured one or more times before fixing through all of the folds.

- Stop the sheeting flapping about and degrading, by fixing it so that it is tight, like a drum-skin; but not too tight, if temperature changes are large between day and night: sheeting may shrink when temperatures fall, for example in the evening after fixing, and this can cause tearing.

- Prevent tearing by ensuring a minimum number of wear points under the plastic: for example, plastic sheeting will degrade quickly if it continually rubs against a tree branch.
- Prevent the ponding of rainwater on roofs, because the weight of the water may overload the roof structure.

figure 7(c): two ways to fix a plastic sheet to a wooden support

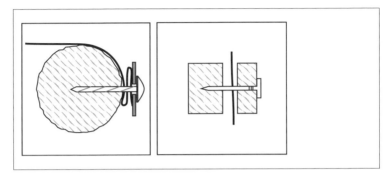

Using washers or thin pieces of wood as battens to attach the sheet can reduce tearing, but this should be done with care, because timber can have sharp edges.

The UNHCR standards for plastic sheeting are as follows:

> 79. Plastic sheeting has become the most important shelter component in many relief operations. In urban areas roofs can be repaired with specialized UV-resistant heavy duty plastic sheeting. Windows can be repaired with translucent reinforced panels. Tents and emergency shelters can be covered with highly reflective UV-resistant woven plastic tarpaulins.
>
> 80. Wooden support-frames and stick skeletons for these shelters, if collected from surrounding forests, can harm the environment considerably. It is therefore important to always supply frame material (which is sufficient to support plastic). The frame material should come from sustained, renewable supply sources. Bamboo is ideal, if available. Standard specifications for plastic sheeting can be found in Annex 1 to chapter 18 on supplies and transport.
> UNHCR (2000), chapter 12, p. 145

7 distribution

The UNHCR standards for reinforced plastic tarpaulins in sheets are as follows:

Sheets are 4m x 5m each.

Material:	Made of woven high density polyethylene fibre; warp x weft (12/14 x 12/14 per inch); laminated on both sides with low density polyethylene with reinforced rims by heat sealing on all sides and nylon ropes in hem; 1000 denier min. Stabilized against ultra-violet rays and excess heat for long outdoor exposure (1.5% loss of strength in yarn and in lamination); provided with strong aluminium eyelets or equivalent on four sides of the sheet at 100 cm centre to centre.
Dimensions:	Thickness: 200-230 microns; weight 190g/m²; density 0.9–0.95kg/cubic decimetre.
Tensile strength:	Min. 600 N both directions of warp and weft (BS 2576, 50mm grab test or equivalent).
Tear resistance:	100 N Min. both directions (BS 4303 wing tear or equivalent).
Heat/cold resistance:	Flammability: flash point above 200°C.
Colour:	Blue one side, white on reverse; UNHCR logo.
Weight:	4.8kg per piece, packed in bales of five, weight per bale 22.5kg; volume per bale 0.045m³.

UNHCR (2000), chapter 18, annex 1, p. 263

7.5.3 prefabricated shelter and containers

There are few circumstances in which prefabricated hard-walled shelters or containers should be used in support of the transitional settlement of displaced populations, either as part of family shelter, or as part of facilities for aid organisations. In most instances, building permanent or semi-permanent structures, mainly from local materials, is quicker and cheaper. The results are more flexible and easier to maintain, and may offer more opportunities for follow-on uses locally, for example after handover to local authorities.

Prefabricated hard-walled shelters can sometimes be used for semi-mobile, high-specification facilities, such as clinics. Shipping containers, when available, may be used as secure stores for expensive items, or to keep out rodents, but they should be shaded and ventilated in hot climates.

The UNHCR comments on the merits of prefabricated shelter as follows:

> Neither pre-fabricated building systems nor specially developed emergency shelter units, even winterised shelter units, have proved effective in large scale refugee emergencies. Reasons include:
>
> i.   High unit cost;
>
> ii.   Long shipping time;
>
> iii. Long production time;
>
> iv.   Transport problems including cost of transport;
>
> v.   Inflexibility.
>
> Usually emergency shelter arrangements will have been made before these systems can arrive.
> UNHCR (2000), chapter 12, p.145

7.5.4 materials and tools for construction and maintenance

Other shelter-material NFIs that may be distributed as part of a NFI shelter package (7.2), such as timber and cement, are discussed in section 6.7 in the construction chapter.

A list should be compiled of the tools required to use and maintain the shelter-material NFIs under consideration. The list might include some or all of the following items:

- health and safety equipment, such as helmets, boots, and harnesses
- marking string, tapes, and measures
- spirit levels and set squares
- shovels, spades, and picks
- buckets and wheelbarrows
- machetes, axes, and saws
- trowels and floats for cement and plasterwork

7 distribution

- nails, screws, and other fixers
- hammers, screwdrivers, and drills
- jemmies and crowbars.

7.6 household shelter items

This section gives an overview of household shelter NFIs used inside a family shelter, such as blankets and cooking utensils. Section 7.5 deals with shelter-material NFIs such as tents and plastic sheeting. Other material NFIs that may be distributed as part of a shelter package (7.2), such as timber and cement, are considered in section 6.7.

The household shelter NFIs overviewed in this section are:

7.6.1 blankets

7.6.2 clothing

7.6.3 lighting: lamps, torches, candles

7.6.4 vector control

7.6.5 mattresses and rugs

7.6.6 sets of cooking utensils

7.6.7 water containers

7.6.8 fuel types

7.6.9 stoves and heaters

After the need for a distribution has been agreed, and the role of each item in the livelihoods of the beneficiaries has been established, close monitoring is recommended. Monitoring may, for example, identify a need for instruction or safety training in the use of items with which the beneficiaries might not be familiar, such as pressure cookers.

references made to standards

As in section 7.5, this section includes (with permission) relevant entries from standards, in this case for household shelter items, developed by the Sphere Project (2004), UNHCR (2000), and the United Nations Development Programme and the Inter-Agency Procurement Services Office of the United Nations Development Programme (UNDP / IAPSO 2000).

From *Humanitarian Charter and Minimum Standards in Disaster Response* (Sphere Project 2004), extracts are quoted from the standards, key indicators, and guidance notes sections.

From *Handbook for Emergencies* (UNHCR 2000), excerpts are quoted from chapters 12, 13, 17, and 18.

From volume 1 of *Emergency Relief Items – Compendium of Generic Specifications* (UNDP / IAPSO 2000), excerpts are taken from the specifications sections, listing criteria such as weight, size, and packing volume.

The extracts presented here are intended as an overview of the kind of information that is available, and to aid general understanding. They do not include the preambles and introductions necessary to gain detailed specific understanding of any of the items listed. The original publications should always be consulted before any standards are used.

7.6.1 blankets

Blankets are a key component of most shelter NFI packages, not only in cold climates but also in hot climates where temperatures drop at night. Blankets are a valued resalable commodity, used for bedding, flooring, and dividing spaces to reduce draughts.

The Sphere Project standards for clothing and bedding include the following:

The people affected by the disaster have sufficient clothing, blankets and bedding to ensure their dignity, safety and well-being.

key indicators

[...] Infants and children up to two years old also have a blanket of a minimum 100cm x 70cm.

People have access to a combination of blankets, bedding or sleeping mats to provide thermal comfort and to enable separate sleeping arrangements as required.

Those individuals most at risk have additional clothing and bedding to meet their needs.

[...] blankets and bedding materials meet the most personal human needs for shelter from the climate and the maintenance of health, privacy and dignity [...]

7 distribution

appropriateness: [...] Bedding materials where possible should reflect cultural practices and be sufficient in quantity to enable separate sleeping arrangements as required amongst the members of individual households.

thermal performance: Consideration should be given to the insulating properties of clothing and bedding and the effect of wet or damp climatic conditions on their thermal performance. An appropriate combination of clothing and bedding items should be provided to ensure a satisfactory level of thermal comfort is attained. Provision of insulated sleeping mats to combat heat loss through the ground may be more effective than providing additional blankets.

durability: Clothing and bedding provided should be sufficiently durable to accommodate typical wear and likely prolonged usage due to the lack of alternative items.

special needs: [...] Infants and children are more prone to heat loss than adults due to their ratio of body surface area to mass, and may require additional blankets, etc. to maintain appropriate levels of thermal comfort. Given their lack of mobility, older people and the ill or infirm, including individuals with HIV/AIDS, may also require particular attention, such as the provision of mattresses or raised beds.

Sphere Project (2004), chapter 4, pp. 230–1

The UNHCR specifications for woven dry raised blankets for warm climates are as follows:

composition:	woven, minimum 30% wool. Balance of new cotton/synthetic fibres
size:	150cm x 200cm, thickness 4mm
weight:	1.5kg
thermal resistance of garment:	TOG value: 1.2–1.6
packing:	in compressed watertight wrapping in pressed bales of 30 pcs. Each bale of 30 pcs would be about 0.3 m³ volume and weight approx. 48kg

UNHCR (2000), annex 1, p. 262

The UNHCR specifications for woven dry raised blankets for cold climates are as follows:

composition:	woven, minimum 50% wool. Balance of new synthetic fibres
size:	150cm x 200cm, thickness 5mm
weight:	1.5kg
thermal resistance of garment:	TOG value: 2.0–2.4
packing:	in compressed watertight wrapping in pressed bales of 30 pcs. Each bale of 30 pcs would be about 0.35 m³ volume and weigh approx. 50kg.

UNHCR (2000), annex 1, p. 262

7.6.2 clothing

Clothing can be essential to survival, and is sometimes a higher priority than blankets in cold climates. It is essential to maintaining cultural practices and personal dignity.

Consider providing appropriate clothing to all population groups, including pregnant women and infants. Care should be taken when accepting donated and second-hand clothing, to ensure that it is appropriate in climatic and cultural terms. Stored clothing should be protected from parasites.

The Sphere Project standards for clothing and bedding include the following:

The people affected by the disaster have sufficient clothing, blankets and bedding to ensure their dignity, safety and well-being.

key indicators

Women, girls, men and boys have at least one full set of clothing in the correct size, appropriate to the culture, season and climate. [...]

Those individuals most at risk have additional clothing and bedding to meet their needs.

Culturally appropriate burial cloth is available when needed.

guidance notes

changes of clothing: Individuals should have access to sufficient changes of clothing to ensure their thermal comfort, dignity and safety. This could entail the provision of more than one set of essential items, particularly underclothes, to enable laundering.

appropriateness: Clothing should be appropriate to climatic conditions and cultural practices, separately suitable for men, women, girls and boys, and sized according to age. [...].

thermal performance: Consideration should be given to the insulating properties of clothing and bedding and the effect of wet or damp climatic conditions on their thermal performance. An appropriate combination of clothing and bedding items should be provided to ensure a satisfactory level of thermal comfort is attained. [.....]

durability: Clothing and bedding provided should be sufficiently durable to accommodate typical wear and likely prolonged usage due to the lack of alternative items.

special needs: Additional changes of clothing should be provided where possible to people with incontinence problems, people with HIV/AIDS and associated diarrhoea, pregnant and lactating women, older people, disabled people and others with impaired mobility. [...].
Sphere Project (2004), chapter 4, pp. 230-1

The UNHCR has this to say about the provision of clothing:

32. Used clothing is often offered in emergencies but is generally an unsatisfactory way of meeting a need for clothing and should be discouraged. It often arrives in poor shape, dirty or badly stored and will frequently be inappropriate for the customs of the refugees. Consider the alternative of purchasing, particularly locally made clothes, and ensure that what is provided is culturally acceptable.
UNHCR (2000), chapter 18, p. 255

7.6.3 lighting: lamps, torches, candles

Safe lighting is essential for personal security, child care, and maintaining livelihoods, as well as for human dignity. Lighting which involves naked flames, such as kerosene lamps, can greatly increase risks from fires, especially when used by people unfamiliar with that specific type of lighting. If a safe source of light is not offered to beneficiaries, they have no options but to improvise, using less safe sources. As an approximate indication of fuel use, kerosene lamps consume one litre of kerosene for 30 hours of light.

The Sphere Project standards for stoves, fuel and lighting include the following:

> Each disaster-affected household has access to communal cooking facilities or a stove and an accessible supply of fuel for cooking needs and to provide thermal comfort. Each household also has access to appropriate means of providing sustainable artificial lighting to ensure personal security.
>
> **key indicators**
>
> Each household has access to sustainable means of providing artificial lighting, e.g. lanterns or candles.
>
> Each household has access to matches or a suitable alternative means of igniting fuel or candles, etc.
>
> Sphere Project (2004), chapter 4, pp. 234-5

7.6.4 vector control

Bed nets impregnated with insecticides offer the best immediate measures to control vector-borne diseases, such as malaria. Section 6.3.5 discusses vector control, in particular how to eradicate the breeding areas of mosquitoes and other insects, and how to choose an appropriate site location. The same section describes specific measures for making food stores proof against rodents.

The Sphere Project standards for individual and family protection against vector-borne diseases include the following:

> All disaster-affected people have the knowledge and the means to protect themselves from disease and nuisance vectors that are likely to represent a significant risk to health or well-being.
>
> **key indicators**
>
> All populations have access to shelters that do not harbour or encourage the growth of vector populations and are protected by appropriate vector control measures.
>
> People avoid exposure to mosquitoes during peak biting times by using all non-harmful means available to them. Special attention is paid to protection of high-risk groups such as pregnant and feeding mothers, babies, infants, older people and the sick.
>
> Bedding and clothing are aired and washed regularly.

Individual malaria protection measures: if there is a significant risk of malaria, the systematic and timely provision of protection measures, such as insecticide-treated materials, i.e. tents, curtains and bed nets, is recommended. Impregnated bed nets have the added advantage of giving some protection against body and head lice, fleas, ticks, cockroaches and bedbugs. Long-sleeved clothing, household fumigants, coils, aerosol sprays and repellents are other protection methods that can be used against mosquitoes. It is vital to ensure that users understand the importance of protection and how to use the tools correctly so that the protection measures are effective. Where resources are scarce, they should be directed at individuals and groups most at risk, such as children under five years old, non-immunes and pregnant women.

Individual protection measures for other vectors: good personal hygiene and regular washing of clothes and bedding is the most effective protection against body lice. Infestations can be controlled by personal treatment (powdering), mass laundering or delousing campaigns and by treatment protocols as newly displaced people arrive in a settlement. A clean household environment, together with good waste disposal and good food storage, will deter rats and other rodents from entering houses or shelters.

Sphere Project (2004), chapter 2, pp. 76-8

UNHCR advice on the control of pests and vectors such as insects and rodents states as follows:

Physical screens are the best immediate measure.

Preventive action to eliminate or limit breeding areas and conditions favourable to the vectors is the best long-term solution.

Specialist supervision of all chemical measures is necessary, as is local knowledge of resistance.

Avoid chemical control where possible.

general considerations

66. The environment in a refugee emergency is typically favourable to the proliferation of disease-carrying insects and rodents ('vectors'), which can also destroy or spoil large quantities of food.

67. Flies tend to breed in areas where food or human excreta are present, mosquitoes where there is stagnant water, and rats where there is food, garbage and cover. As a result of overcrowding and inadequate personal hygiene, lice, fleas, mites, ticks and other arthropods may also cause health problems. [...]

68. Reducing the numbers of flies, mosquitoes and rodents quickly in an emergency is difficult and physical screens may be the best immediate measure. Over the longer term, the most effective method of controlling insects and rodents is preventive: to improve personal hygiene, sanitation, drainage, garbage disposal and food storage and handling practices and thus make the environment less favourable for the vectors. Examples of practical measures are the removal of stagnant waste water, regular garbage collection, use of oil in latrines and provision of soap and sufficient water for washing. The recommended monthly supply of soap is 250 g soap per person per month. The programme should provide for regular inspection and be integrated with other public health measures.

69. The problems should be discussed with the refugees and education given on the significance of vector control. Where solutions unfamiliar to the refugees are employed, these must be carefully explained.

70. Whatever the nature of nuisances and pests, one should avoid having systematic recourse to chemical control by means of pesticides (insecticide, rodenticide, molluscicide, etc.). Such products are costly and toxic to both human beings and the environment. There is a risk of poisoning during transport, storage, handling and of course spraying the chemicals. Also, pests can develop resistance to the chemicals.
UNHCR (2000), chapter 17, pp. 240–41

The UNHCR standards for physical pest control are as follows:

71. Measures described in this chapter to deal with excreta and waste disposal will also help control pests (flies and rodents particularly).

72. The elimination of stagnant water and other breeding and resting sites for mosquitoes through drainage is important and the drainage network must be maintained.
UNHCR (2000), chapter 17, p. 241

The UNDP / IAPSO specifications for mosquito screens to be placed on windows or doors for insect screening are as follows:

material:	knitted polyester, plastic-coated or impregnated fibre-glass yarn
size:	90 to 120cm wide 100m per roll
denier:	75 or 100 (weight in gms of 9000mtrs of thread)
mesh:	156 (i.e. 12 x 13 holes per square inch) or 196 (14 x 14)

shipping weight:	5kg/100mtr.roll
shipping volume:	0.01m³
packaging:	20 to 25 rolls per pallet

UNDP / IAPSO (2000), p.196

The UNDP / IAPSO specifications for insecticide-impregnated bed nets are as follows:

material:	knitted polyester, plastic coated or impregnated fibre-glass yarn shipping
weight:	35kg/100 nets
size:	single 70 x 180 x 150cm
denier:	75 or 100 (weight in gms of 9000 mtrs of thread)
mesh:	156 (i.e. 12 x 13 holes per square inch) or 196 (14 x 14)
features:	sheeting border (reinforcement at the bottom of the net for increased life span) slit door for easy access into the net, with overlap of approx. 60cm; optional kit for impregnation including basin, bucket, gloves and instructions
shipping volume:	60 x 60 x 65cm
packaging:	pressure baled into small packs, wrapped in water resistant PE bags

UNDP / IAPSO (2000), p.196

7.6.5 mattresses and rugs

Mattresses and rugs prevent conductive heat loss to the ground. They can be essential to survival when beneficiaries sleep on the floor in climates where temperatures are low, especially at night in a cold period.

Mattresses are bulky and should be procured locally, whenever possible. Bed rugs can substitute for them if they are culturally acceptable. Rugs take a long time to produce and are harder to find than mattresses, unless they are already produced and stocked in sufficient quantity. Hammocks may also be used when they are common, and where beneficiaries are living in rigid shelters other than tents.

The Sphere Project standards for clothing and bedding include the following:

The people affected by the disaster have sufficient clothing, blankets and bedding to ensure their dignity, safety and well being.

key indicators

People have access to a combination of blankets, bedding or sleeping mats to provide thermal comfort and to enable separate sleeping arrangements as required.

Those individuals most at risk have additional clothing and bedding to meet their needs.

guidance notes

appropriateness: [...] Bedding materials where possible should reflect cultural practices and be sufficient in quantity to enable separate sleeping arrangements as required amongst the members of individual households.

thermal performance: consideration should be given to the insulating properties of clothing and bedding and the effect of wet or damp climatic conditions on their thermal performance. An appropriate combination of clothing and bedding items should be provided to ensure a satisfactory level of thermal comfort is attained. Provision of insulated sleeping mats to combat heat loss through the ground may be more effective than providing additional blankets.

durability: [...] bedding provided should be sufficiently durable to accommodate typical wear and likely prolonged usage due to the lack of alternative items.

special needs: [...] Infants and children are more prone to heat loss than adults due to their ratio of body surface area to mass, and may require additional blankets, etc. to maintain appropriate levels of thermal comfort. Given their lack of mobility, older people and the ill or infirm, including individuals with HIV/AIDS, may also require particular attention, such as the provision of mattresses or raised beds.

in cold climates: [...] The loss of body heat through the floor should be minimised by ensuring that the floor is insulated and through the use of insulated sleeping mats, mattresses or raised beds.

Sphere Project (2004), chapter 4, pp. 230-31

7 distribution

The UNDP / IAPSO specifications for mattresses are as follows:

material:	polyurethane foam
shipping weight:	approx. 2kg
volume:	approx. 0.5m³
size:	200 x 80 x 10cm
density:	23–25 kg/m³
cover:	removable non-woven spun bounded synthetic covering material (min. 100 g/m³) with zip fastener or 100% cotton
colours:	preferably dark colours
packing	10/12 pieces to be vacuum packed in strong polyethylene material

UNDP / IAPSO (2000), p. 58

7.6.6 sets of cooking utensils

 Culturally appropriate cooking pots and utensils are essential to maintain hygiene and minimise fuel required for cooking.

Providing displaced families with cooking facilities and equipment makes a very important contribution to the re-establishment of their dignity and identity. Moreover, the items can be easily transported once the emergency is over.

Communal cooking can be supported in two ways: through the distribution of big pots with lids that fit, and through camp planning which allows the grouping of extended families (for example, for the preparation of those foods that require longer preparation time).

The Sphere Project standards for cooking and eating utensils include the following:

Each disaster-affected household has access to cooking and eating utensils.

key indicators

Each household has access to a large-sized cooking pot with handle and a pan to act as a lid; a medium-sized cooking pot with handle and lid; a basin for food preparation or serving; a kitchen knife; and two wooden serving spoons.

Each person has access to a dished plate, a metal spoon and a mug or drinking vessel.

guidance notes

appropriateness: items provided should be culturally appropriate and enable safe practices to be followed. Women or those typically overseeing the preparation of food and the collection of water should be consulted when specifying items. Cooking and eating utensils and water collection vessels should be sized to suit older people, people with disabilities and children as required.

metallic goods: all cutlery, bowls, plates and mugs should be of stainless steel or other non-ferrous metal.

infant feeding: infant feeding bottles should not be provided, unless exceptional circumstances require the provision of breast milk substitutes.

Sphere Project (2004), chapter 4, pp. 233–4

The UNDP / IAPSO specifications, which comply with UNHCR standards, for family-sized kitchen sets are as follows:

shipping weight:	approx. 5kg
shipping volume:	0.04m³
contents:	item 1: 1 no. cooking pot
	item 2: 2 no. cooking pots
	item 3: 5 no. bowls
	item 4: 5 no. plates
	item 5: 5 no. cups
	item 6: 5 no. knives
	item 7: 5 no. forks
	item 8: 5 no. tablespoons
	item 9: 1 no. kitchen knife
	item 10: 1 no. bucket
set combinations:	set A consists of items 1–10
	set B consists of items 1, 2, 3 or 4, 5, 6, and optionally 9
	set C consists of items 1, 3 or 4, 5, and 6
set for 250 people:	shipping weight: 90kg
	shipping volume: 0.5m³
set for 100 children:	shipping weight: 80kg
	shipping volume: 0.5m³

UNDP / IAPSO (2000), pp. 59–62

7 distribution

7.6.7 water containers

 Cleanable, culturally appropriate water containers for each household are essential for maintaining hygiene, and to reduce pressures on water-collection time and water-supply infrastructure. The practical and cultural use of water containers within transitional shelter should be understood in order to maximise benefits and minimise risks. Water containers need lids and regular cleaning to prevent contamination. The water distributed should, in most cases, retain a residual level of chlorine to reduce such contamination.

Generally, large quantities of stackable items are procured, in order to make transport more efficient. It is important to consider distributing durable items, so that water containers can be taken home by the displaced population.

The Sphere Project standards for cooking and eating utensils include the following:

> Each disaster-affected household has access to cooking and eating utensils.
>
> **key indicators**
> Each household has access to two 10- to 20-litre water collection vessels with a lid or cap (20-litre jerry can with a screw cap or 10-litre bucket with lid), plus additional water or food storage vessels.
>
> **guidance notes**
> All plastic goods (buckets, bowls, jerry cans, water storage vessels, etc.) should be of food-grade plastic.
> Sphere Project (2004), chapter 4, pp. 233–4

The UNDP / IAPSO specifications for non-collapsible plastic jerry cans are as follows:

description:	white transparent stackable plastic jerry can
use:	for storing and carrying water
material:	high molecular LDPE
shipping weight:	0.5kg
shipping volume:	0.3m3
size:	10 litres
features:	strong built-in carrying handle for adults
	hand screw cap – 55 mmØ
impact resistant:	resist a drop from minimum of 2.5m containing maximum volume.

UNDP / IAPSO (2000), p. 65

The UNDP / IAPSO specifications for semi-collapsible plastic jerry cans are as follows:

description:	plastic jerry can
material:	tough, flexible, food grade, low density polyethylene, UV stabilized
shipping weight:	0.5kg
shipping volume:	0.01m3
size:	10 litres
dimensions:	210 x 210 x 270mm (filled)
	210 x 210 x 80mm (empty)
features:	moulded carrying handle for adults. Built-in handle wide enough for male adult hand, without sharp edges. Hand screw cap. Linked to jerry can by a nylon string must stand by itself even when filled with less than 1/4 of its max. volume
operating temperature:	–20ºC to +50ºC
packed:	in wooden crates of 150
	970 x 680 x 645mm
weight:	approx 78kg

UNDP / IAPSO (2000), p. 66

7.6.8 fuel types

This section presents an overview of fuel types, to be used as part of an energy strategy. Section 7.6.9 presents options for stoves and heaters. The distribution of fuel and stoves should be considered when there is no sustainable source of fuel, and when fuel collection exposes people to security risks.

Household energy strategies in transitional settlement are usually complex, involving a number of projects which aim to make traditional local energy use as efficient and sustainable as possible. Specialist advice should be sought when selecting appropriate fuels and stoves. Local material resources need to be assessed, as do the fuel-use patterns of the displaced population. The use of familiar fuels should be promoted whenever possible.

7 distribution

Inappropriate stoves and fuels, combined with inadequate ventilation, are significant risks to health and safety: acute respiratory infections caused by cooking smoke account for up to 1.6 million deaths every year around the world (Warwick and Doig 2004). Consequently, the provision of adequate cooking facilities for displaced populations should be viewed as a major public-health issue. Poverty is the main factor that prevents people (both local and displaced populations) from upgrading their stoves and fuel sources. In the short term, improving ventilation may be the best way to improve respiratory health.

The amount of energy in each fuel is presented in table 7(b).

table 7 (b): energy value of fuels (based on UNHCR 1998c)

fuel type	heating value (mj/kg)
wet firewood	8
cow dung	10
tree residues (leaves, twigs, etc.)	13
agricultural residues (straw, stalks, etc.)	13
air-dried firewood	15
charcoal briquettes	16
oven-dried firewood	20
peat	21
lignite	24
bituminous coal	28
charcoal	28
densified carbonaceous briquettes	30
kerosene	44
liquid propane gas	46

It should be acknowledged that fuel-distribution projects require a significant logistics effort, as well as extensive harvesting. For example, it takes up to five person-days to cut, carry, stack, and load one ton of firewood, which then needs to be delivered and distributed under supervision. Such programmes may be a major recurrent cost in operating budgets. They should be initiated only if absolutely necessary.

wood Firewood is the most familiar fuel in most rural areas. Consumption depends in part on the type of stove used, whether the wood has been dried, and also the availability of the wood: if supplies are readily available at minimal cost and risk, consumption for cooking alone may exceed 4kg per person per day, compared with average use of 1–2kg per person per day.

charcoal Charcoal is lump wood converted to carbon by slow burning at high temperatures, with a very low level of oxygen. Traditional charcoal-production systems employ earth mounds or covered pits, into which wood is piled and burned. Traditional kilns are inefficient, because they retain about 40 per cent of the energy in the wood used. Charcoal making is illegal in a number of countries. However, charcoal has several advantages over firewood.

- The energy content is much higher, per unit of mass.
- It is easily handled, measured, and delivered in bulk.
- It can be burned more efficiently, because more heat is transferred to the pot by radiation from the fuel bed than by convection.
- Harmful emissions are typically much lower than those of other biomass fuels.
- Over long distances, it may prove more efficient to transport charcoal than fire wood, because of its higher energy content. However, it breaks up easily, and 10–20 per cent may be lost in transit, unless powders can be retained.

peat Peat is organic matter produced by incomplete decomposition of wetland vegetation, under conditions of excess moisture and oxygen deficiency. It occurs throughout the world in places where natural drainage is reduced or impeded, but is less common in warm climates where evapotranspiration rates are high. Peat produced from papyrus and other swamp vegetation is suitable as fuel. Air-dried peat has a higher energy content than wood.

Peat can be cut manually in sods from swampy areas and then, in ideal conditions, dried for at least three–five days before use. Wet peat emits more smoke than dry peat. Depending on the water level, there is a limit to the peat stock that can be removed sustainably. Cutting from undrained ground has a minor environmental impact, but natural regeneration will probably compensate for the loss. Wet peat sods can be compressed, using a manual press, to reduce their volume and optimise transportation.

kerosene Kerosene has a high calorific value, relative to other fuels, and can be burned in a good stove with good thermal efficiency. However, special stoves and fuel containers are required. Training may be needed if the displaced community is not familiar with the technology, because fire risks are significant.

The main disadvantage of kerosene is its cost. Negative impacts often result from the market created by its resale by beneficiaries, because this may destabilise local markets or more sustainable local energy-use patterns.

diesel and petrol

Diesel and petrol are normally used only by aid organisations themselves, in generators and for vehicles. Petrol is explosive and should not be distributed.

gas Bottled propane or butane gas under pressure is an efficient source of low-emission energy. Its thermal efficiency for cooking is very high; however, it is very costly and not a serious option for cooking in transitional settlement.

coal Bituminous coal has an energy content comparable to that of charcoal. It may be a realistic option if the transitional settlement is close to a source of coal. Pollutant emissions are high, and training may be required for its safe use and for the building of stoves.

dung Dried animal dung is used for heating and cooking in many areas where livestock is still present. Dung is sometimes combined with straw and other combustible agricultural residues. The calorific content is low, and smoke emissions tend to be high.

The Sphere Project standards for stoves, fuel, and lighting include the following:

> Each disaster-affected household has access to communal cooking facilities or a stove and an accessible supply of fuel for cooking needs and to provide thermal comfort. [...]
>
> **key indicators**
>
> Where food is cooked on an individual household basis, each household has a stove and fuel to meet essential cooking and heating needs.
>
> Environmentally and economically sustainable sources of fuel are identified and prioritised over fuel provided from external sources.
>
> Fuel is obtained in a safe and secure manner, and there are no reports of incidents of harm to people in the routine collection of fuel.
>
> Safe fuel storage space is available. [...]

Sustainable sources of fuel: sources of fuel should be managed, and measures taken to replenish and regenerate resources to ensure sustainability of supply.

Collecting fuel: women should be consulted about the location and means of collecting fuel for cooking and heating to address issues of personal safety. The demands of collecting fuel on particularly vulnerable groups, such as female-headed households and households caring for PLWH/A [people living with HIV/AIDS], should be addressed. Special provisions should be made where possible e.g. the choice of less labour-intensive fuels, the use of fuel-efficient stoves and accessible fuel sources.

Sphere Project (2004), chapter 4, pp. 234–6

7.6.9 stoves and heaters

This section offers an overview of stoves and heaters, to be used as part of an energy strategy. Section 7.6.8 presents options for fuels, and guidance on household energy strategies, with information on health and safety risks. The distribution of stoves and fuel should be considered when there is no sustainable source of fuel, and when there are security risks linked to fuel collection.

The choice of stoves and heaters should depend on the following factors:

- their impact on health
- safety considerations
- fuel cost and availability
- efficiency
- reparability.

The introduction of energy-saving practices is often more effective in reducing energy consumption than the use of improved stoves. Measures to improve efficiency of stoves include:

- cutting and drying fire wood
- careful control of the fire and its air supply
- pre-soaking of hard foods, such as pulses
- use of lids on pots.

7 distribution

Communal cooking is considerably more fuel-efficient than a system in which individual families cook their own food. However, it is rarely acceptable in cultural terms. The cluster-planning of camps (8.4.2) and the distribution of big pots increase opportunities for communal cooking, especially for extended families.

A stove that is improperly used may be no more efficient than a well-managed open fire. So stoves of a type that is familiar to the beneficiaries should be considered first. Alternatively, it may be appropriate to provide training in building, maintaining, and using the selected type of stove.

The Sphere Project standards for stoves, fuel, and lighting include the following:

> **Stoves:** existing local practices should be taken into account in the specification of stove and fuel solutions. Energy-efficient cooking practices should be promoted, including firewood preparation, fire management, food preparation, shared cooking, etc. This could include possible changes to the type of food to be prepared, such as any rations provided by food assistance programmes e.g. pulses require considerable cooking and hence fuel. Where displaced populations are accommodated in mass shelters, communal or centralised cooking and heating facilities are preferable to the provision of individual household stoves, to minimise fire risks and indoor smoke pollution.
>
> **Ventilation:** if used inside an enclosed area, stoves should be fitted with flues to vent exhaust gases or smoke to the exterior in a safe manner. Alternatively, the positioning of the stoves and weather-protected openings within the shelter enclosure should be utilised to ensure adequate ventilation and to minimise the risk of indoor pollution and respiratory problems. Stoves should be designed to minimise the risk of fire and of indoor and outdoor pollution.
>
> Sphere Project (2004), chapter 4, pp. 234–6

kerosene stoves

Multi-wick stoves are the most common, but they do not have flues and they need to be used in a well-ventilated space. If a wick is missing, the gases present in the combustion tank can enter the fuel tank and cause an explosion. Pressurised stoves should be avoided, because they are hard to light and prone to explosion if the seals fail.

Special fuel containers are required. Training may be needed if the displaced community is not familiar with the technology, because fire risks are significant.

The UNDP / IAPSO specifications for kerosene stoves are as follows:

type:	fuel efficient and low consumption stove non-pressurised wick type with incorporated fuel tank
fuel:	kerosene
burner:	minimum 8 wicks
dimensions:	approx length: 15cm
	approx. width: 15cm
	approx. height: 20cm
capacity of tank:	minimum 1 hour burning time
material:	sheet iron, rust- and heat-resistant
features:	wind safe, noiseless, odourless and smoke-less
shipping weight:	approx. 1kg
shipping volume	approx. 0.005m³

UNDP/IAPSO (2000), p. 63

The UNDP / IAPSO specifications for kerosene and diesel heaters are as follows:

type:	heaters for tents and buildings, with built-in hotplate
area of use:	as heater and as a stove
heating capacity:	min. 10kW consuming 10 litres kerosene/day
shipping weight:	approx. 10kg
shipping volume:	approx. 1m³
size:	approx. 50cm depth, 50cm width, 100cm height
features:	easy to install and operate low fuel consumption non-smoke producing non-corrosive materials wind safe supporting frame of steel fuel level gauge breather
accessories:	damper for air flow control, complete with ducting and piping, spare parts and cleaning instruments, small tool kit for repairs and maintenance, instructions for use and maintenance

UNDP / IAPSO (2000), p. 71

7 distribution

wood and charcoal stoves

When solid fuels such as wood and charcoal are available from sustainable sources (section 7.6.8), fuel-efficient stoves can greatly reduce consumption. Wood and charcoal stoves, including mud stoves and fired-clay stoves, are often the most flexible types to use. Local designs and fabrication should be adopted wherever possible, because they will be most appropriate for local cooking practices and repair.

The UNDP / IAPSO specifications for wood and charcoal stoves are as follows:

type:	fuel efficient cooking stoves
area of use:	for use in refugee camps where electricity or kerosene not available
fuel:	wood or charcoal
dimensions:	approx. diameter: 45cm
	approx. height: 50cm
material:	steel or stainless steel
features:	30-litre pot with furnace and wind protection cover
	furnace equipped with door fire grate and ash pan
	easily detachable parts for transport
	maximum fuel efficiency by means of controlled air inlet and flue gas outlet
shipping weight:	approx. 8 kg
shipping volume:	approx. 0.1m³

UNDP / IAPSO (2000), p. 63

mud stoves Mud stoves are easy to build, after simple training, and are ready to use after a few days. They are not made with mud alone, but normally with a combination of clay, sand, and straw or grass. Termite hills are a good supply of clay-rich soil. Sand is often mixed in, to improve the insulating properties and provide resistance to heat. Adding straw or grasses allows the stove to expand without cracking during thermal changes.

figure 7(d): mud and clay stoves

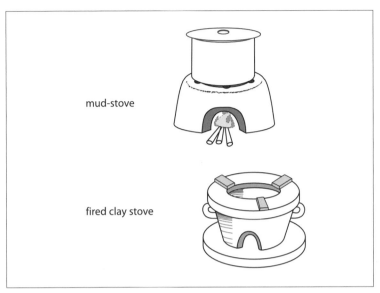

mud-stove

fired clay stove

fired clay or ceramic stoves

Mud stoves can be manufactured in portable forms, which are valued by displaced populations because they can be carried when moving from one TS option to another, or when moving towards a durable solution. Production processes need to be optimised locally to produce the best clay mixture for firing.

Fired clay or ceramic stoves are sometimes placed inside steel containers, similar to buckets, which are useful in protecting the ceramic, and in making the stove more portable.

7 distribution

solar cookers

Curved-reflector solar cookers use large reflective surfaces to collect, direct, and concentrate the rays of the sun.

Solar cookers are not usually easily compatible with cultural cooking practices: for example, they are not suitable for cooking food early in the day. Solar cookers have never replaced other stoves or fuels, but they can offer a supplementary heating method. Users must be properly trained, because solar cookers create hazardous glare at the focal point.

figure 7(e): solar cooker

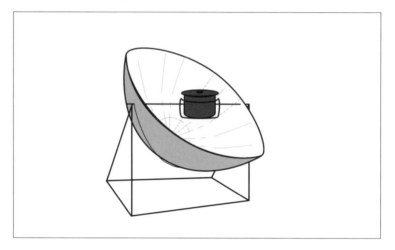

chapter 8 transit and camps

8 camps

8 transit and camps

This chapter offers guidance on establishing and supporting transit facilities and camps as part of transitional settlement (TS) programme options.

Support for planned or self-settled camps should be considered very carefully. In the majority of cases, camps are supported when other, more appropriate TS options are possible, but when these options are not supported by the aid community. UNHCR guidelines emphasise that camps should be supported only as a last resort. The reasons for this include security risks and potentially negative impacts on relations with the host population and the environment. In rare instances, however, camps may be the most appropriate transitional option, even when alternatives exist – if, for example, the displaced population significantly outnumbers the local population, and there is a history of antagonism between them.

Deng's 'Guiding Principles on Internally Displaced Persons' (1998) offer the protection framework within which all transitional settlement should be planned and implemented. Aid organisations should refer to them when planning any response in support of IDPs.

This chapter deals with several key issues which must be addressed if a camp is to provide a successful TS option. They are discussed in the following sections:

8.1 site selection presents a decision-making tool to help aid organisations to identify appropriate sites for transit facilities and camps.

8.2 transit offers guidance on managing the transit of a displaced population, with standards and typical layouts of facilities used in the transit process.

8.3 camp programme planning considers strategic planning issues specific to sites, building on the strategic planning information presented in sections 3.6 and 3.7.

8.4 camp site planning presents standards and guidance on developing a master plan for a site, with a detailed consideration of family plots, community and infrastructure layouts, and typical communal facilities.

8.5 community development discusses ways in which the displaced population can be supported within camps.

8.1 site selection

The process of selecting a site must determine the number, size, and location of transit facilities (8.2.2) and camps. It should also define the density of camps which in combination are intended to meet the objectives of a TS programme.

Poor site selection threatens the security of the displaced population and their hosts. It will probably also damage relations between the two populations, the sustainability of essential environmental resources, and the success of aid operations. In contrast, good site selection may have the opposite effects: for example, by increasing security, as part of the range of benefits of TS planning.

Site selection must be undertaken for self-settled camps as well as planned camps: if the process determines that the site of a self-settled camp is unsuitable, responsible agencies should initiate mitigating activities, or negotiate relocation of the population.

Careful site selection is important in different phases of operation for different types of camp, as listed below:

transit facilities (8.2)

- In the contingency phase, in order to form an understanding of the mechanisms of flight that may occur at a later date.
- In the emergency phase, siting facilities as part of influx management, to direct displaced groups towards safe transitional settlement.

self-settled camps (3.6 and 8.4.6)

- In the contingency phase, to determine whether or not particular areas or sites may be suitable for self-settlement, and the approximate capacity and combination of proposed camps.
- In the emergency phase, to determine whether a self-settled camp is appropriate for support or requires relocation.
- In later phases, to determine how to develop or expand a self-settled camp.

8 camps

- In the contingency phase, to identify potential sites and their capacities, and plan them in greater detail than for self-settled camps.

- In later phases, to determine how to develop or expand a camp.

In this section, and in this chapter, attention is not drawn to differences between self-settled camps, planned camps, and transit facilities unless specific distinctions need to be made.

site-selection process

The three steps in the site-selection process presented below follow the same structure as the profiling processes presented in chapter 2. Sections 8.1.1–8.1.3 explain how each of these steps should be adapted for site selection.

8.1.1 step 1: assessments

Site-selection assessment follows the same five steps as described in section 2.2, 'developing profiles', using criteria and tools presented in chapters 3 and 4.

- involvement: site-selection teams

- reference: strategic planning

- livelihoods: profiling local and displaced populations

- capacities: potential sites

- resources: the carrying capacities of the local environment.

involvement: site-selection teams

A site-selection team should ideally comprise representatives of the displaced and host populations, the host government, the lead agency, implementing aid organisations, and sector specialists, such as water engineers. The team needs a leader who is experienced in site selection and camp planning. There are two main reasons why all stakeholders should be involved from the beginning: the process introduces the various stakeholders to one another and, through the site-selection process, to the likely operational activities of establishing or supporting camps; and collective decision-making makes it more likely that decisions will be accepted and implemented.

The stakeholders represented in the site-selection team often form the basis of subsequent camp-management committees. However, rapid changeover of staff and responsibilities makes it essential to maintain a complete and accurate common record of commitments.

reference: strategic planning

Site selection and supporting camps should be considered only in the context of a wider TS strategy. The process of site selection must inform this strategy, quantifying capacities for self-settled and planned camps, identifying routes and locations for transit facilities, and analysing the context of such options, including the attitudes of the local and displaced populations.

Strategic planning should have already identified other major references, such as government development plans. Local references should also be sought – from local authorities, for example.

livelihoods: profiling local and displaced populations

It is essential to form an understanding of the type of camp that the displaced population would like to live in, regardless of the sites that are available: for example, are they mainly farmers bringing livestock with them, or traders who have lost everything?

It is equally important to form an understanding of the type of camp that the local population would like to have in their region: for example, would they like camps to be concentrated on one site, or dispersed across many sites?

Chapter 4 offers guidance on designing an assessment, identifying a list of appropriate criteria or questions (4.4), identifying appropriate tools with which to gather the information (4.5), and ways in which to analyse and present the final profiles (4.1).

When developing a list of criteria for assessing the displaced population, consider the criteria presented in sections 3.6 and 3.7, which include the following:

- their protection and security
- their origin, whether they are urban or rural, their livelihoods, the communal services and facilities in their settlements and how they were maintained, and the structure of their communities

8 camps

- the demographics of the group, the presence of subgroups and vulnerable families and individuals, different cultures and religions.

The resulting profile of the displaced population will describe how the displaced population should be living, socially and economically. This profile will help aid organisations to prioritise the needs of the displaced population within the sites of future camps, or discover more about what transit facilities they may need.

When developing a list of criteria for assessing the local population, consider the factors presented in sections 3.6 and 3.7, which include:

- their protection and security
- the size of the host population, and the size and dispersal of settlements
- the location of the host settlements in relation to the likely points of influx of the displaced population
- local livelihoods
- local community structures
- the natural-resource management strategies of the local population.

If the profiles of the local or displaced populations indicate that camps would be dangerous or unacceptable to either group, the results should be communicated immediately to those responsible for strategic planning.

capacities: potential sites

Identify as many potential sites as possible, provided that they seem appropriate and have sufficient capacity. These proposals will inform the scenarios planning to be undertaken in step 2 (8.1.2).

It is essential to involve local authorities and community leaders in the assessment of potential sites, partly because of their local knowledge, and partly because permissions and acceptance by the local community are required before any site can be used.

Even if self-settlement has already occurred, the same process of assessing potential sites should be used. Self-settled sites need to be assessed, to determine whether the site is appropriate, and to identify alternatives and opportunities for expansion.

When developing a list of technical criteria for assessing potential sites, consider the factors presented in sections 3.6 and 3.7, which include the following:

- security, which includes distances from borders and areas of conflict
- the accessibility of the site for displaced people in transit, for people living in local settlements, and for deliveries via all-weather roads, sea ports, rail heads, and air ports or air strips
- the availability of water, including the variety of sources
- the availability of other natural resources, such as fuel wood
- topographic characteristics, such as rocky ground, which complicates the construction of shelters and latrines, and the creation of kitchen gardens and very steep ground, which should be avoided for similar reasons.

The Sphere Project gives the following guidance in 'Shelter and settlement standard 2: physical planning':

Topography and ground conditions: for temporary planned camps the site gradient should not exceed 6%, unless extensive drainage and erosion control measures are taken, or be less than 1% to provide for adequate drainage. Drainage channels may still be required to min-imise flooding or ponding. The lowest point of the site should be not less than 3 metres above the estimated level of the water table in the rainy season. Ground conditions should also inform the locations of toilets and other facilities and hence the planning of settlements e.g. fissured rock may disperse toilet waste widely; fine clays provide poor percolation and the early failure of toilet pits; volcanic rock makes the excavation of toilet pits difficult.

Sphere Project (2004), chapter 4, p. 218

If no potential sites meet the technical criteria identified, the results should be communicated immediately to the strategic planning process.

resources: local environmental carrying capacities

The carrying capacities of the local environment are determined by the amount and volume of various resources that can be harvested sustainably. Assessment of these capacities is essential in order to determine the viability of TS options.

8 camps

The majority of resources necessary to construct and maintain camps must come from the local region, if supporting camps is to be a viable TS option. Importing all water, fuel, and construction materials would be a significant challenge, in practical and economic terms. If no alternative sites can be found, the importing of some resources may have to be considered. Importing drinking water by truck, for example, has been undertaken for extended periods, but at very high cost and with considerable damage to the road infrastructure.

The assessment of resources can be considered in two parts:

- the environmental resources available on the potential sites themselves; the likely impact of their use on the site and settlement; and the natural-resource management (NRM) strategy of the local population before the influx;

- the environmental resources available in the region; the likely impact of their use on the ecology and economy of the region; and the NRM strategy of the regional population before the influx.

Section 2.5.4 offers guidance on environmental management for all TS operations, including self-settled and planned camps. This section offers guidance that is specific to camps only.

When considering sites, profiling of local and displaced populations (see above, under 'livelihoods: profiling local and displaced populations') can simplify the tasks of estimating the environmental resources required and identifying opportunities for harvesting and management. Profiling will help planners to form a clear picture of the resources required by both populations (8.3), and the likely shortages. For example, a high demand for structural timber in the emergency phase may be anticipated by seeking supplies in the surrounding region. It will be necessary to establish projects which support the integration of the NRM strategy of the displaced population with that of their local host population.

Environmental assessment must be started at the site-selection stage, so that environmental management can be proactive and not reactive. Specialist guidelines are available (for example, UNHCR 1996, 1998a–e, 2002a, 2002c, 2002d); however, additional specialist advice should be obtained, if possible.

Site selection should take NRM into account, with the following aims:

- minimising negative impacts on the local host population
- avoiding damaging impacts on the local environment, by locating camps away from fragile ecosystems, ideally no less than one day's walk away
- controlling access to natural resources through the dispersal of camps, thereby determining, in consultation with all stakeholders, whether a given affected population will be settled in one large camp or in a series of smaller camps which will spread demands upon natural resources more widely
- locating a camp in an area where sufficient natural resources are available
- minimising distances travelled by displaced people to obtain basic natural resources, such as water and cooking fuel.

Once an appropriate site has been selected, site development may contribute to NRM in the following ways:

- minimising the clearance of on-site vegetation, in order to reduce soil erosion and to maximise shade and wind protection
- minimising soil erosion by building access roads along contour lines, or at a suitable gradient, with appropriate culverts, surface-water drainage, run-offs, and soak-aways
- minimising the amount of construction material that needs to be harvested locally: for example, by importing materials such as construction timber and plastic sheeting from the surrounding region, or from another country.

8.1.2 step 2: scenarios

The site-selection process seeks to identify a range of sites which will meet the requirements of the various likely scenarios (2.2.2) predicted by planners. It is very unlikely that the circumstances of a specific displacement of people will remain static, so scenarios must anticipate changes in circumstances, such as new influxes, or movements of displaced groups from one TS option to another.

The goal of scenario planning, both strategically and within the site-selection process, is to maximise the opportunities and options available to the displaced and local populations, while minimising the negative impacts on both.

8 camps

In general, scenario planning consists of considering possible changes in certain circumstances and assessing their likely effects on displaced and local populations. In the case of site selection, these changed circumstances are likely to include the following elements:

- regional and local security
- the numbers of displaced persons
- the demographic composition of the displaced population: for example, a predominance of young males fleeing conscription
- entry points across a border or from a conflict zone
- seasonal variations.

The circumstances that vary are different for each situation, so the assumptions that inform scenario planning must be described carefully. The results of scenario planning within site selection should be communicated immediately to the strategic planning process.

8.1.3 step 3: indicators

Within the site-selection scenarios, indicators should be identified and agreed, to enable planners to recognise when one scenario is becoming more likely than another: for example, if displaced people's rate of influx rises above, or drops below, an agreed figure.

As noted in section 2.2.3, identifying indicators has two main purposes: enabling the planners and implementers of aid operations to decide which scenario they should adopt as the basis for their decision-making; and determining whether additional key information should alter the scenario, add more detail to the scenario, or require more specific field assessment.

The site-selection scenario indicator should be communicated immediately to the strategic planning process, along with the details and assumptions of the scenarios.

8.2 transit

This section presents information for supporting the transit of displaced populations from a border area or front line to a safer place. Typical transit facilities (8.2.2), namely way-stations, transit centres, and reception centres, are described in detail, with accompanying plans.

8.2.1 influx management

Influx management is the process of supporting and guiding the transit of displaced populations away from danger, and towards appropriate TS options. Influx management is not possible without regular updating of sufficient, accurate, and timely information on the size, position, and composition of the influx of displaced people.

When influx management is adequate, it is possible to keep ahead of the arrivals, preparing for the reception of the displaced populations and ensuring that sufficient capacity exists in the TS options. However, when large-scale emergencies take place in a short and unpredictable timeframe, organisations may find it difficult to cope with the resulting influx. Under such circumstances, various options are open to organisations:

- requesting an increase in resources
- requesting support from other organisations
- improving field co-ordination, preventing duplication and inefficiency
- supporting low-cost self-settlement options, such as accommodation with host families
- supporting emergency provisions, such as defecation fields instead of latrines, with the aim of upgrading the latter in the care and maintenance phase.

influx checklist

To gain sufficient understanding for adequate influx management, the following questions should be considered:

- What is the rate of influx?
- What is the size of the displaced population?
- What is the likely size of the population in transit?

8 camps

- What are the circumstances of those who decided to remain in their homes?
- Are those circumstances likely to change?
- Is the displaced population in communication with those who decided to remain at home?
- What is the likelihood that the influx rate, and hence the number of displaced people, will increase, and what are the implications for strategic planning?

In addition it may be necessary to develop indicators (2.2.3) for the specific circumstances of any particular TS scenario.

8.2.2 transit facilities

The network of support and pre-registration facilities usually consists of way-stations, transit centres, and reception centres. Each facility must be sited and planned appropriately: for example, to ensure good access, sufficient waiting areas, and adequate services.

Figure 8(a) presents a fictitious situation which illustrates the relationship between various transit facilities.

locating transit facilities

Transit facilities should be established off the main track or road, leaving adequate space for vehicles to turn. Waiting areas should be separated from the main transport infrastructure, in order to prevent accidents: displaced people using transit facilities are often vulnerable, arriving in a confused state of exhaustion and shock.

When selecting a site for transit facilities, consider the following factors:

- protection and security: the transit facilities should offer safety, by being located near a police post, for example;
- ways of making the facilities serve as many displaced persons as possible: for example, by locating them at the intersection of several routes;
- the availability of water locally, and the treatment that it will require, or ways of delivering sufficient supplies of clean water to the site by truck.

figure 8(a): positioning transit centres and way-stations

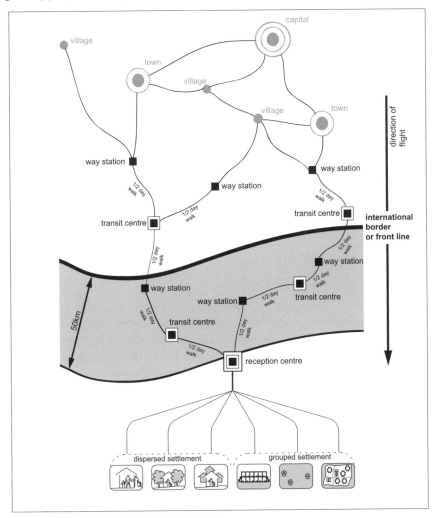

The movements of vehicles and people should be organised into an efficient system of arrival, disembarkation, registration, medical screening, distribution of rations, sanitation, and onward movement. Ideally, planning should ensure that the paths between these service points do not cross, for reasons of efficiency and pedestrian safety.

Way-stations, transit centres, and reception centres can often be hosted within facilities offered by the local authorities. When investigating this option, consider the following factors:

- Will the use of such facilities compromise the ability of the displaced population to make independent decisions about the form of transitional settlement most appropriate for them?

- What was the original function of the facilities? How will it be affected by the new use? (For example, schools should not be used unless absolutely necessary, because local education will be disrupted.)

- What actions will be required to return the facility to the local community or owner in its previous condition?

summary of standards

Table 8(a) summarises the UNHCR standards for transit facilities (UNHCR 2000, p. 146).

Transit facilities are an emergency provision. As such they are designed to accommodate the displaced population for only a few days, so they require lower standards of service provision than camps. However, capacity in transit facilities is often taken up by vulnerable groups or individuals who are awaiting other family members, or who wish to make use of the facilities. Depending on the situation, such use of capacity may slow or block the transit network for others. It is important to understand the reasons behind any blockage and to ensure that appropriate alternatives are in place for those who wish to remain in the transit facility.

The standards should take account of specific circumstances. For example, if food is provided by the transit centre, the displaced population has no need to cook. In this case, the amount of covered space provided for each person might be reduced from the area specified in the standards.

It is also important to ensure that longer-term options exist for meeting normal standards. The development of facilities should be phased, building upon emergency provision.

table 8(a): specifications for reception and transit camps

site	
primary criteria	good access (road, port, airport), availability of water, good drainage (minimum 2% slope), adequate conditions for sanitation
expected duration of stay	2–5 days, high turnover rate
security	fencing should be installed, depending on circumstances
space required	
accommodation	minimum of 3m² per person in barracks or long houses, subdivided for groups or families; for example, an 85m² tent can accommodate 14–25 persons approximately
food preparation	100m² per 500 persons
storage	150–200m³ per 1,000 persons
layout	arrival and departure zones separated from accommodation zones
water supply	
water supply per person	7 litres each per day minimum for survival, 15–20 if possible, plus water required for kitchens, cleaning, and sanitation
sanitation	
maximum no. per latrine	20 persons
maximum no. per shower	50 persons
other facilities	
equipment	lighting, public address system
health	a health post should be present
administration	office and staff accommodation

typical layout of transit facilities

Each of the transit facilities presented in the following pages is followed by a typical plan diagram. The diagrams are not prescriptive: they are intended only to illustrate a possible relationship between the various component elements. It is essential that appropriate transit facilities are designed in response to the specific features of each situation. The plans are not to scale, and they show no relation to context or topography.

8 camps

When transit facilities are planned, large waiting areas should be prepared outside the fenced areas of each facility. Displaced persons on the move need an opportunity to re-group, finding members of their family or community who have become separated. The waiting areas and the fenced areas should both be provided with services such as water and sanitation, and shading or some form of shelter from extreme climates.

The transit process should maximise the quantity of possessions and livestock that the displaced can take with them, to support them in maintaining their livelihoods. If people travel with belongings and livestock, they should be provided with space to keep both, making sure that the animals are kept separate from people, for reasons of hygiene. Livestock may require significant separate water supplies.

way-stations Way-stations are interim stopping points, set up between borders, transit centres, and reception centres at distances equivalent to about half a day's walk. They provide food and drink to displaced people *en route* to a transitional settlement, but they are not intended to offer accommodation, which should be provided at transit centres. The way-stations should offer the following forms of support:

- dry rations, such as high-protein biscuits
- clean water and sanitation
- preliminary registration or counting of the number of people passing, which is essential to forming an understanding of influx rates
- preliminary health screening, to assess who is able to travel onward
- transport for people unable to travel onward unaided.

figure 8(b):   example of a way-station

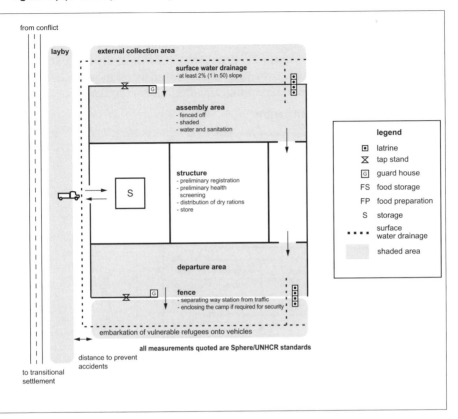

from conflict

layby   external collection area

surface water drainage
- at least 2% (1 in 50) slope

assembly area
- fenced off
- shaded
- water and sanitation

structure
- preliminary registration
- preliminary health
  screening
- distribution of dry rations
- store

S

departure area

fence
- separating way station from traffic
- enclosing the camp if required for security

embarkation of vulnerable refugees onto vehicles

all measurements quoted are Sphere/UNHCR standards

distance to prevent
accidents

to transitional
settlement

legend

▣   latrine
✖   tap stand
Ⓖ   guard house
FS   food storage
FP   food preparation
S   storage
‒ ‒ ‒ ‒   surface
    water drainage
    shaded area

8 camps

Transit centres should be set up on the route from a border or area of conflict to a transitional settlement. There is usually a complete day's travel between one transit centre and another, or between a transit centre and a reception centre. They provide short-term accommodation, usually overnight only, as well as clean water, cooked food, basic medical screening, and preliminary registration.

figure 8(c): example of a transit centre

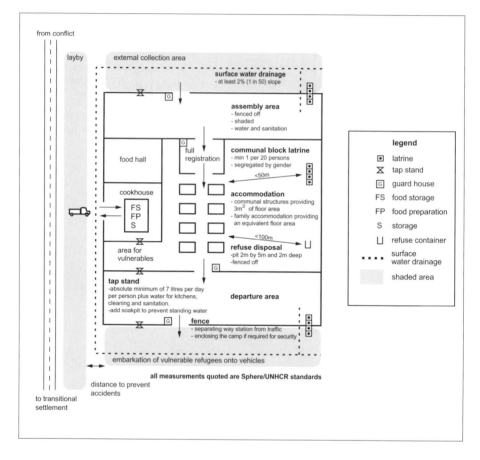

Reception centres are located in secure areas, at least 50km from an international border or the front line of conflict (8.3.2). They usually provide clean water, cooked food, non-food items, full medical screening, full registration, and wider assistance and social services. They should be planned to receive all displaced persons, and not just those entering planned camps. They should therefore be located near all of the TS options that are supported.

Reception centres are required in order to register displaced persons, for the following purposes:

- to evaluate their need for protection and security, especially asylum seekers, who should be interviewed by UNHCR
- to determine their status: for example, if they belong to a vulnerable group and require special support
- to issue them with ration cards, entitling them to distributed commodities and access to facilities and services
- to undertake medical screening, and possibly vaccination
- to distribute an initial package of food and non-food items
- to allocate a plot of land or a room if transitional settlement is offered in a camp or collective centre.

Information campaigns may be appropriate, to ensure that the displaced population is aware of what is on offer to them.

Once the significant influx is over, reception centres may still be used as distribution centres, or for other functions such as community centres. But take care to ensure that standards used during the emergency phase are not used in the long term.

The Sphere Project 'Shelter and settlement standard 3: covered living space' gives the following guidance:

> **Duration**: in the immediate aftermath of a disaster, particularly in extreme climatic conditions where shelter materials are not readily available, a covered area of less than 3.5m² per person may be appropriate to save life and to provide adequate short-term shelter to the greatest number of people in need. In such instances, the shelter response should be designed to reach 3.5m² per person as soon as possible, as longer durations may begin to affect the health and well-being of the people accommodated. If 3.5m² per person cannot be achieved, or is in excess of the typical space used by the affected or

8 camps

neighbouring population, consideration should be given to the impact on dignity, health and privacy of a reduced covered area. A decision to provide less than 3.5m2 per person should be highlighted, along with measures to mitigate against any adverse affects on the affected population.
Sphere Project (2004), chapter 4, p. 220

figure 8(d): example of a reception centre

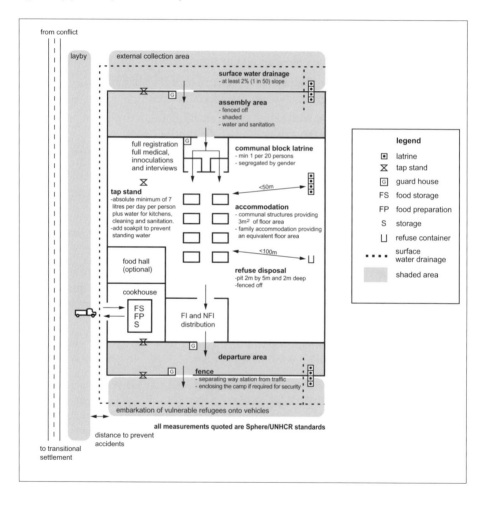

8.3 camp programme planning

This section presents the major practical factors to be considered when developing a transitional settlement programme for self-settled camps, planned camps, or facilities supporting the transit process (8.2). It builds on the strategic considerations presented in sections 3.6 and 3.7.

The planning process for a programme for camps involves the same steps as planning for other TS programmes (2.3): objectives (8.3.1), activities (8.3.2), and scheduling (8.3.3).

Camps and transit facilities are similar in nature to villages, cities, and their infrastructure. Specialist assistance should be sought from the local authorities, town planners, architects, engineers, physical or site planners, and shelter specialists.

8.3.1 step 1: objectives

It is essential to identify objectives for the camp programme plan that are consistent both with wider strategic objectives and with the objectives of other programmes and projects. Agreeing objectives for supporting camps, such as community development (8.5), offers a point of reference throughout the phases of operation (2.4), against which to develop appropriate activities (8.3.2) and schedule their implementation (8.3.3).

Section 2.3.1 presents a five-step process for defining objectives. This process should be used as a template for defining the objectives for a camp programme plan, while referring to site-selection profiles and scenarios (8.1). The five key steps of the process are as follows:

- involvement
- reference
- generic objectives
- situation-specific objectives
- quantifying objectives with planning indicators.

8.3.2 step 2: activities

Project activities to establish and support camps and transit facilities include the following:

- planning and building transit facilities (8.2)
- developing a master plan for a camp (8.4.2)
- building infrastructure and services in planned camps (8.4.5)
- upgrading infrastructure and facilities in self-settled camps (8.4.6)

Once the process of site selection has been completed, and appropriate resources have been identified (8.1), the remaining factors that should be considered when planning project activities include the following:

- security
- hazards and climatic design
- duration of camps
- contingency plans
- combinations of camps.

Project activities need to be based on a programme plan, which should agree the types of camp required: for example, small or large, high-density or low-density. These are discussed in detail later in this section.

security The location of transitional settlements, especially camps where displaced people are concentrated, is linked directly to issues of protection and security, both external and internal. Strategic security and protection considerations are presented in greater detail in section 2.5.1, while security, conflict, and ordnance are dealt with in more detail in section 6.3.3.

Security threats, both internal and external to displaced populations, are often linked to ethnic and religious differences. To minimise them, it is helpful to assess and monitor patterns of incidents: for example, identifying an informal 'front line' between different ethnic groups within a camp may suggest ways of reducing the internal security risk, such as installing street lighting or a security post.

UNHCR recommends that camps for refugees should be set back at least 50km from any international border, referring to the Organisation of African Unity (OAU) Convention:

> 31. In principle, the granting of asylum is not an unfriendly act by the host country towards the country of origin. However, to ensure the security and protection of the refugees, it is recommended that they be settled at a reasonable distance from international borders as well as other potentially sensitive areas such as military installations.
>
> The OAU Convention states: 'For reasons of security, countries of asylum shall, as far as possible, settle refugees at a reasonable distance from the frontier of their country of origin' (1.1 Article II, paragraph 6 OAU Convention).
>
> Exceptions should only be made to this rule where the interests of the refugees would be better served, for example if there are good prospects for early voluntary repatriation, and security and protection considerations allow.
>
> UNHCR (2000), chapter 2, p. 138

---

hazards and climatic design

When planning a camp or establishing whether to provide assistance to a self-settled camp, it is important to assess whether, in doing so, the displaced population would be at risk from natural hazards (6.3), such as flooding (6.3.11). Climate (6.4) influences site selection and the design of camps: for example, in cold climates (6.4.1) a different type of family-shelter support is required.

duration of camps

In most situations, it is impossible to predict how long a camp will be needed, so all camps should be planned to allow phased upgrading, development, and extension (8.4.7). Initial emergency provision must leave space for later upgrades, such as improved water-supply infrastructure.

Camps occasionally become permanent settlements. If this is foreseen before the camp is established, resettlement guidelines (UNHCR 1996) should be used instead of these guidelines. Considerable input is required if there is any likelihood that an existing camp may have to be developed into a permanent settlement. Transitional camps are not designed to guarantee sustainability or livelihoods. A permanent settlement would fail if,

8 camps

for example, there was insufficient work available for its inhabitants, or if there was insufficient water both for them and the local population.

contingency plans

Contingency plans, based on the scenarios compiled during site selection (8.1), may be required to facilitate responses to future events such as further influxes of displaced people, an outbreak of disease such as cholera, an earthquake, a violent attack, or spontaneous return. Likely eventualities should be identified, and detailed responses to them should be planned, with a series of indicators which would signal the need for the appropriate contingency plan to be implemented.

In certain situations the risks may be significant enough to require the development of contingency capacities, such as the preparation of cholera hospitals, or at least the preparation of sites for the rapid development of such facilities (MSF 1998).

combinations of camps

Different types of camp are often used in combination in order to spread the impacts of a displaced population on the local population and environment. This section presents some of the possible combinations and their implications.

Self-settled and planned camps can be arranged, developed, and expanded in a number of combinations, including the following:

- large camps
- a series of dispersed small camps, rather than one large camp
- camps with a high density of occupation, similar to a city
- camps with a low density of occupation, similar to a village or rural region.

For example, options might be combined to provide a single high-density camp, surrounded by smaller low-density camps. This might be appropriate in cases where the displaced population is from both rural and urban origins, or in response to a need for expansion.

There is no optimum size for camps. Although a maximum population of around 20,000 is discussed below, circumstances specific to each displacement will determine actual sizes. With both self-settled and planned camps, the site-selection process (8.1) makes these decisions about the combinations of camps necessary.

Security, social, environmental, physical, and local considerations should all be balanced as part of the selection process, to determine the number of camps required, their form, and their sizes.

Of paramount importance is the impact of the combination of camps on the local population. If the local population is settled in small villages, for example, a combination of camps should be considered in order to avoid overwhelming the villages or the natural resources on which the local population depends, such as fuel wood.

large camps

Large camps of more than 20,000 inhabitants should not be created, for the following reasons.

- They pose risks to security, because factions within a displaced population can more easily politicise and control the population when people are all together in one place.
- It is difficult to plan for expansion, because significant areas need to be left for future influxes and to allow communities to re-group next to each other.
- They expose the inhabitants to health risks, because communicable diseases spread more rapidly in a single population group, and because it is more difficult to maintain hygiene in large population groups.
- Risks of fire are greater, so well-equipped fire-control teams are essential; fire breaks can only slow the spread of a fire, but not prevent it.
- The local population may feel threatened by the population of a camp that is five or ten times bigger than an average town or village.
- They are difficult to supply safely with multiple natural resources, such as fuel wood and water: for example, there may be only one place to collect water and it may become polluted or it may run dry.
- They are hard to supply with natural resources on a sustainable basis: for example, the fuel wood within a half-day's walk from the camp will quickly be exhausted.

Large camps, accommodating up to about 20,000 inhabitants, also have some advantages:

- easier protection from insurgency and attack, in some situations, because the available security services can be concentrated in fewer places;

- more efficient infrastructure and facilities in some situations: for example, the logistics for distribution to feeding centres can be optimised.

small camps Small camps, similar in size to local villages, create the opposite conditions from those that are typical of large camps, as listed above: for example, epidemics and large fires are less likely in small camps; it is easier to use multiple sources for water; and relations with local communities may be more successful.

Dispersing small camps around a region generally increases the positive influences of small camps. For example, dispersal takes the pressure off natural resources by increasing the area of land accessible to the displaced population within a half-day walk: the radius of collection for harvesting fuel wood and construction materials is the same for a small camp as for a large camp, but smaller camps have fewer inhabitants, and hence lower demand.

Some small, dispersed camps have a unique influence on livelihoods. Restricted access to legal employment and capital often limits the already reduced opportunities available to displaced populations for agricultural activities. Small camps often result in more agricultural land being available per family, thus supporting livelihoods, increasing self-reliance, and contributing to the food basket available to displaced households. When it is legal and acceptable to the local population for displaced persons to work, displaced labour based in small camps has better access to local labour markets, for example during seasonal crop harvests.

high-density camps

High-density camps should be avoided, or attempted only when the security situation or host government does not offer any alternative. The implications of building high-density camps should be understood by all stakeholders.

High-density camps should not be considered unless very high levels of infrastructure, service, and utilities provision can be offered and maintained. In such circumstances, higher densities may reduce infrastructure costs.

The risks inherent in supporting high-density camps are the same as those for large camps, listed above, except that each risk is more likely. For example, in a high-density camp a fire is likely to spread more rapidly from shelter to shelter.

Many self-settled camps (3.6) begin with a high density of occupation; however, TS support should begin by considering the reduction of densities through phased infrastructure development and relocation projects (8.4.6).

low-density camps

Low-density camps create the opposite conditions from those that are typical of high-density camps, as listed above. They also offer unique opportunities, including the following advantages.

- The clearance of vegetation can be minimised, thus increasing shading and wind breaks, while reducing soil erosion.

- Site planning may be easier to achieve: for example, roads and buildings or family plots can be situated around natural topographic features, such as gullies, which is especially useful if works must be completed using manual labour only.

- A greater diversity of livelihoods activities is possible if family plots are larger.

- Good sanitation can be easier to achieve, because there are more options for locating a latrine on a family plot if the plots are bigger.

The UNHCR standards for 'Size of camp sites' are as follows:

24. (...) Ideally, the recommended minimum surface area is 45m^2 per person when planning a refugee camp (including garden space). However, the actual surface area per person (excluding garden space) should not be less than 30m^2 per person.(...)

25. Large camps of over 20,000 people should generally be avoided.

The size of a site for 20,000 people should be calculated as follows, assuming space for vegetable gardens is included: 20,000 people x 45m^2 = 900,000m^2 = 90ha (for example a site measuring 948m x 948m).

UNHCR (2000), chapter 12, p. 137

The Sphere Project gives the following guidance in 'Shelter and settlement standard 2: physical planning':

Surface area: the planning guideline of 45m² per person includes household plots and the area necessary for roads, footpaths, educational facilities, sanitation, firebreaks, administration, water storage, distribution areas, markets and storage, plus limited kitchen gardens for individual households. Area planning should also consider evolution and growth of the population. If the minimum surface area cannot be provided, consideration should be given to mitigating the consequences of higher-density occupation e.g. separation and privacy between individual households, space for the required facilities, etc.

Sphere Project (2004), chapter 4, p. 217

8.3.3 step 3: scheduling

A 'schedule of operations' (2.3.3) needs to be agreed and co-ordinated to determine the project activities (8.3.2) that are required to establish or support a camp.

The schedule of operations will ensure that the project activities can be undertaken within the time periods required, and with the resources available. It will help the project manager, contractors, labour leaders, and suppliers to know exactly who should complete each job and by when, and to understand the relevant risks and scenarios (8.1.2). Deadlines should be agreed, and a monitoring mechanism should be implemented.

To assist co-ordination, each project activity within the schedule of operations should follow consistent steps, such as those outlined in the checklist below:

• undertake an assessment
• define a brief
• survey and map the site
• present and develop options
• develop a plan, as part of the master plan (8.4.2)
• implement and manage the project on site
• hand over the facilities to the relevant organisation or authority.

undertake an assessment

Build upon site-selection assessment (8.1) to form a detailed understanding of the need for the project, its likely impacts, and local capacities for providing the required labour materials and tools. The assessment should inform the aid operation and provide the basis for the monitoring and evaluation of the project (4.1).

define a brief A project brief is a clear description of the phased functional, social, physical, and developmental requirements for the project, to be agreed by managers and users.

survey and map the site

Survey and map the site (6.1.2) to understand its size, topography, significant features, and relation to the camp, agreeing the legal and unofficial borders of the site with the local authorities and local population.

present and develop options

Present options to the camp planning committee (8.1.1), and develop these options until they are agreed by all stakeholders. Documents describing each option should include copies of the assessment, the brief, and the survey, along with designs, schedules of work, and lists of materials.

develop a plan

Drawings representing the project should be included in the master plan (8.4.2) of the camp. To support co-ordination, a central archive should be maintained, containing copies of the drawings and the associated project documents recording the option agreed, the assessment, the brief, and the survey.

implement and manage the project

After agreeing labour (chapter 5) and construction (chapter 6), and possibly putting the works out to tender to local companies (5.4), implement and manage the project on site. This will involve setting up an appropriate mechanism for monitoring and evaluation.

handover Hand over the project and its management to the relevant organisation, department, or authorities. It is important that documentation, such as the site master plan, is up to date and shows the process of development, to support a successful handover.

8.4 camp site planning

Once a site has been selected (8.1) and a transitional settlement programme for camps has been planned (8.3), the sites themselves need to be planned.

Camps are often comparable, both in size and in the facilities that they should offer, to towns or even cities, which usually have taken centuries to develop their layouts and infrastructure. Camps have to be planned rapidly, but they also need to respond to many of the same challenges that towns and cities face, such as the need to leave space within the original infrastructure for later expansion.

Site planning is a complex activity which should be undertaken only by experienced specialists. This section offers an overview of the process, in order to inform other staff and stakeholders participating in the process.

Site planning significantly influences the financial, social, and environmental impacts of a camp. Layouts that allow efficient delivery of services to the population will be easier to manage and cheaper to run, especially in the long term. Layouts that support social hierarchies already in place within the displaced population will encourage community development. For example, cluster planning (8.4.2) creates communal spaces used by only a few families, encouraging ownership and maintenance of facilities, and reducing opportunities for crime.

8.4.1 summary of terms and standards

This section presents internationally agreed standards for planning camps, collated from *The Sphere Project Humanitarian Charter and Minimum Standards in Disaster Response* (Sphere Project 2004), and from *Handbook for Emergencies* (UNHCR 2000). In addition to standards, the section introduces and illustrates the terms used. This section includes the following elements:

- a table of standards for the minimum provision of communal facilities
- a table of standards for camp-site layouts

- a diagram illustrating a camp sub-divided into sectors, blocks, and communities
- a diagram illustrating the standards for service provision for a community.

standards for camp-site layouts

table 8(b): minimum provision of communal facilities

facilities required	per number of sites	estimated population
1 hospital	10	200,000
1 health centre	1.5	30,000 (1 bed per 2,000–5,000 refugees)
1 health post or clinic	(per sector)	approximately 5,000 (1 community health worker per 1,000 and 1 traditional birth attendant per 3,000 refugees)
4 commodity distribution sites	1	20,000
1 market	1	20,000
1 school	(per sector)	5,000

(UNHCR 2000)

table 8(c): site layouts

	Sphere Project (2004)	UNHCR (2000)
space required		
minimum surface area of camp per person	45m², inc. infrastructure but excluding land for agriculture	45m² (30m² including infrastructure + 15m² for agriculture)
minimum covered floor area per person	3.5–4.5m²	3.5m² in warm climate 4.5–5.5m² in cold climate or urban area
fire breaks		
minimum distance between buildings	2m	2 times structure height 3–4 times structure height if highly flammable
minimum distance between clusters of dwellings	6m	
minimum distance between blocks of clusters of dwellings	15m	30m per built-up 300m
water supply		
minimum quantity of water available (litres per person per day)	15	7 minimum for survival 15–20 as soon as possible
people per tap-stand [1]	maximum 250	1 community, 80–100 persons [2] 200 per hand-pump/well
distance from dwellings to taps	maximum 500m	maximum 100m or a few minutes' walk
sanitation		
maximum people per latrine (UNHCR specifies in order of preference, 1–3	20 people (if sex-segregated public toilets)	(1) family (6–10 persons) (2) 20 persons (3) 100 persons (or a defecation field)

table 8(c): site layouts contd.

	Sphere Project (2004)	UNHCR (2000)
distance from dwelling to toilet (sited to pose minimum threats to users, esp. at nights)	maximum 50m or one-minute walk	6–50m
minimum distance between latrines and soak-aways and ground-water source [3]	30m	30m
distance from bottom of pit to water table[3]	minimum 1.5m	minimum 1.5m
refuse		
distance from dwellings to refuse disposal	<15m to container or household pit; or <100m to communal pit	
people per 100-litre refuse container	maximum 10 families	10 families or 50 persons
people per 2m x 5m x 2m communal refuse pit		500

Notes to table 8(c)

1   *Sphere elaborates:*
    people per 16.6 litres per minute (lpm) hand-pump = 500 max.
    people per 12.5 lpm well = 400 max.
    people sharing one washbasin = 100 max.

2   *UNHCR definition of groupings within camps:*
    family = 4–6 people
    community = 16 families = 80 people
    block = 16 communities = 1,250 people
    sector = 4 blocks = 5,000 people
    camp module = 4 sectors = 20,000 people

3   *Distances may be increased for fissured rock/limestone, or reduced for fine soil.*

8 camps

figure 8(e): camp sub-divided into sectors, blocks, and communities

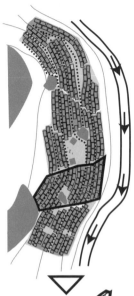

camp: approximately 20,000 inhabitants

4 sectors

- fire breaks: 30m per built-up 300m
- roads follow contours and lead out from centre
- run-off water also follows contours
- features used to break repeating pattern
- administrative centre located at the centre of the camp.

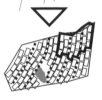

sector: approximately 5,000 inhabitants

4 blocks

- fire breaks: 15m between blocks
- should contain central recreational/commercial spaces

block: approximately 1,250 inhabitants

16 communities

- fire breaks: 6m (pathways)

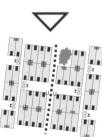

community: approximately 80 inhabitants

16 plots with 16 shelters

- fire breaks: 2m between dwellings
- drainage should be well planned and maintained
- drain water must not pollute existing surface water or groundwater, or cause erosion.

figure 8(f): standards for service provision for a community

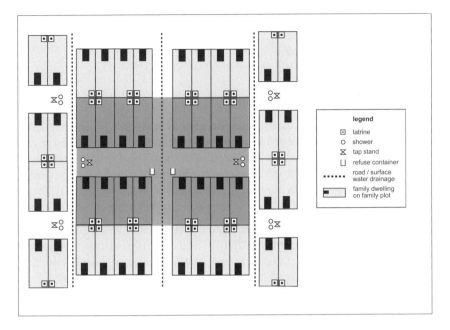

Figure 8(f) is a fictitious example to illustrate service provision.

tap-stands
- ideally one tap per community (UNHCR)
- absolute minimum 7 litres of water per day per person (Sphere)
- 15–20 litres per day per person as soon as possible (UNHCR)

living space
- minimum floor area per person should be 3.5m² (Sphere, UNHCR)
- 4.5m² in cold or built-up areas, where cooking takes place under cover (Sphere, UNHCR)

latrines
- latrines should be sited between 6 and 50 metres from dwellings (UNHCR)
- one latrine per family (UNHCR)
- no more than 20 people per latrine (Sphere)

8 camps

refuse • maximum 10 families per 100-litre refuse container (Sphere)

• every dwelling should be within 15 metres from a refuse container (Sphere)

• if there are no household waste containers, then every dwelling should be within 100m of a refuse pit (Sphere)

8.4.2 developing a site plan

The plan of a camp, like the plan of a town, should be a unique reflection of the people who live there and the area in which the camp is sited, informed by the profiles of the displaced population and of the site (8.1.1). Such assessments inform every aspect of the plan: for example, ensuring that the sizes of sectors and blocks reflect the sizes of communities that they will accommodate.

A master plan, a drawing which maps out the site boundaries and all sub-divisions, infrastructure, and facilities within it, should be created. Further guidance on camp set-up can be found in the Camp Management Toolkit (NRC 2004).

siting key facilities

Most traditional cities, towns, and villages have markets, town halls, and other communal facilities sited near their centres. This arrangement minimises the distance that each resident must travel to reach the facilities. For the same reason, it is a useful approach to siting key facilities in camps.

In some camps, distribution centres have been sited outside the accommodation area, because large convoys of vehicles supplying the warehouses pose a risk to children and create dust storms. It is important, however, to plan the camp around the needs of the displaced communities and not solely in order to facilitate logistics. Planning road layouts appropriately, for example by maximising visibility or defining clear pedestrian and vehicle routes, can help to overcome such problems.

figure 8(g): location of logistics area in camp

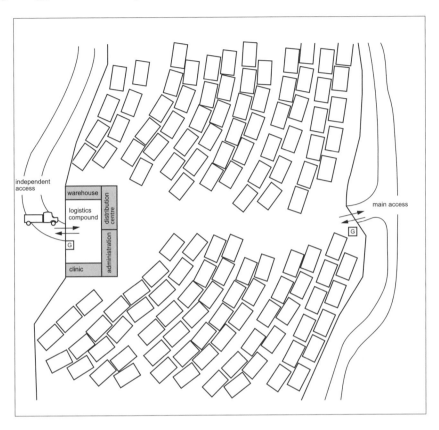

One reason for not siting facilities in a central area may be security, if internal conflict is likely and aid workers require reliable evacuation routes. Security considerations should be discussed with the appropriate experts.

grid and cluster planning

An approach to site planning that has often been used in the past is **grid planning**, which sets out the road infrastructure in a grid of roads, with communities, administrative facilities, and communal facilities placed in the gaps between the roads.

A different type of site planning is **cluster planning**. This involves setting out the major road infrastructure like branches of a tree, with

8 camps

roads radiating from central areas used for communal facilities. Road sizes may be varied, depending on the amount of use in each case, to create a hierarchy of road infrastructure, rather than an undifferentiated grid. On a smaller scale, cluster planning supports the use of varied types of community layout, creating semi-private roads on a cul-de-sac model for each community (see 8.4.4 – staggered square plan).

Grid planning is simple to design and can be easily marked out. It provides access to all family plots within a community. But a grid plan does not fit easily on sites with disrupted topography, such as hills or gullies. In contrast, cluster planning allows roads and community layouts to 'wrap' around topographic features, ideally following site contours. This approach allows roads to complement rather than disrupt natural drainage routes, reducing the drainage infrastructure required and the subsequent cost involved.

Cluster planning is preferable to grid planning for other reasons too, because it can have the following effects:

- reinforcing viable social communities, by creating 'private' areas
- encouraging communally shared activities and practices, from water collection to cooking
- supporting social hierarchy, which can improve the acceptance of extension programmes and the representation of the needs of the displaced population through committees.

figure 8(h): grid vs cluster planning

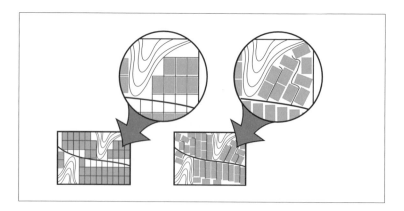

Whether a grid or cluster plan is used, accommodation areas should be sub-divided into sectors, blocks, and communities (8.4.1).

Communities should be arranged to form blocks, which in turn should be arranged to generate sectors. Again, these arrangements should be flexible. Sectors and blocks should be planned to follow the topographic contours of the land, in order to reinforce surface-water drainage measures. If soil erosion is likely, 'erosion belts' of undisturbed vegetation, following the contours of the site, may also be considered. Steep roads and paths should be avoided (8.4.5), and additional surface-water drainage and culverts should be considered on all gradients.

Section 8.4.4 presents three sample layouts which might be modified to meet local circumstances.

marking out the site

Once the overall site plan has been developed, the first step in implementation is to mark out the site boundaries and the sector and block divisions. This process requires conventional survey equipment or Global Positioning System (GPS) equipment, and carefully trained and managed teams – ideally professional surveyors.

In the emergency phase, there may not be time to mark out every block within the site before the first blocks are occupied. The site can be marked out incrementally, in pace with the influx, but it is easy to make mistakes when using basic surveying equipment in unfamiliar terrain, so it is important to mark out the boundaries of the site before the first blocks are occupied.

Marking out often begins with identifying a series of landmarks, such as large trees or rocks, as reference points. Marking-out teams can then move from these landmarks, marking boundaries with poles or stones. It is useful to colour-code markers to signify boundaries of sites, sectors, and blocks. It may also be useful to set poles in concrete and to mark immovable objects such as boulders, because local or displaced persons are likely to move marker poles: this may happen accidentally, for example in the process of clearing the site of undergrowth, or intentionally, either to disrupt the process, or to gain more land for their family plot.

The master plan should be maintained as the most up-to-date record of the physical development of the site, incorporating any new projects or other changes. The rapid changeover of staff and responsibilities in the TS sector makes it essential to maintain a complete and accurate master plan. To enable version control, the drawing should also contain an amendments table, describing each revision, the date that it was made, and the details of the person who made it.

8.4.3 family plots

Family-plot sizes are a major factor in determining the density of the camp. The minimum plot size, in accordance with standards on the overall area allowed per person (8.4.1), is approximately 200m². The size and orientation of family plots must be considered carefully. The space needs to accommodate a family shelter, a latrine, a shower or washing area, and space for child care, cooking, water storage, and a kitchen garden.

It is extremely important in regions of high rainfall that surface-water drainage is prepared before the rainy season. The drainage on the plot must be linked into the site-drainage infrastructure, such as soak-aways and run-offs. The clearance of vegetation, and especially trees, should be kept to a minimum.

kitchen gardens

Unoccupied space on a family plot is often used for kitchen gardens to supplement food distributions. Certain crops can also provide shade and erosion control. Specialist advice should be sought if livestock is present on site, because some animals may constitute a serious health risk in dense camps. It might be possible to provide additional agricultural and grazing land at a distance from the camp.

family shelter

Family shelter is more likely to take the form of a single room, made from local materials, than a tent. Material shelter non-food item (NFI) support (7.5) should be considered as a priority, especially in the emergency phase, when demand for construction materials is likely to exceed sustainable supplies, leading to conflicts with local populations or other displaced families.

An assessment should be made of the design of family shelter normally constructed by the displaced population, and the quantity of materials required. The assessment of local resources that was undertaken as part of site selection (8.1) will identify shortfalls in materials, and alternative solutions can then be initiated. For example, there may be a shortage of thatch, so plastic sheeting might be distributed as a supplement.

When tents are distributed, an extension project should be considered, to demonstrate how to prepare the sites for them, and how to erect them. The life of tents can be extended considerably if they are put up correctly: for example, if the canvas is not in contact with wet earth.

The Sphere Project gives the following guidance in 'Shelter and settlement standard 3: covered living space':

> **Household activities:** space should be provided for sleeping, washing and dressing; care of infants, children and the ill or infirm; the storage of food, water, household possessions and other key assets; cooking and eating indoors when required; and the common gathering of the household.
> Sphere Project (2004), chapter 4, p. 220

UNHCR standards give detailed specifications for shelter:

> 71. Shelter must, at a minimum, provide protection from the elements, space to live and store belongings, privacy and emotional security. Shelter is likely to be one of the most important determinants of general living conditions and is often one of the largest items of non-recurring expenditure. While the basic need for shelter is similar in most emergencies, such considerations as the kind of housing needed, what materials and design are used, who constructs the housing and how long it must last, will differ significantly in each situation.
> UNHCR (2000), chapter 12, p. 144

plots for vulnerable families

Consider ways of improving access to facilities for vulnerable families: for example, by allocating to them plots that are close to certain facilities. It is important that these families are integrated into community groups rather than concentrated in one place, which

8 camps

is likely to increase their dependence on outside assistance. Vulnerable families may have difficulty constructing their shelters. They should be identified and offered support through contract or incentive labour (5.4, 5.1.2), ideally supplied by the community itself.

8.4.4 layout options for communities

Communities should be developed by building a pattern of (approximately) 16 family plots with basic service infrastructure such as latrines. This pattern should be sufficiently flexible to allow it to 'wrap' around topographic features: for example, by omitting individual plots to protect a large tree which provides good shade and protection from the wind.

Generic layout options, such as those suggested in this section, offer useful reference, but they should not be copied without alterations to meet specific circumstances. The layout plans presented here are not drawn to scale. They represent the relationship between the different elements within each option only.

The UNHCR standards for the size of camp sites include the following:

24. While there are recommended minimum area requirements for refugee sites, these should be applied cautiously and with flexibility. They are a rule of thumb for an initial calculation rather than precise standards. The figure of 30m² surface area per person includes the area necessary for roads, foot paths, educational facilities, sanitation, security, firebreaks, administration, water storage, distribution, markets, relief item storage and distribution and, of course, plots for shelter. The figure of 30m² does not include, however, any land for significant agricultural activities or livestock. Although agricultural activities are not usually a priority during emergencies, small vegetable gardens attached to the family plot should be included in the site plan from the outset. This requires a minimum increase of 15m² per person, hence, a minimum of 45m² overall land allocation per person would be needed.
UNHCR (2000), chapter 12, p. 137

hollow square plan

The hollow square plan has certain advantages:

- There is a public side to each plot, facing the street, and a more private side, internal to the square. This private space can reinforce the community by increasing interaction within families.

- Tap-stands and latrines are situated away from the road, so they are less likely to be used by passers-by and are therefore more likely to be maintained by the community.

This plan has the disadvantage that the fronts of each family shelter face roads in a grid plan, limiting privacy. Often the nearest neighbour for each shelter is in an opposite block, a feature which disrupts the sense of community that this layout tried to create in the first place.

figure 8(i): hollow square plan

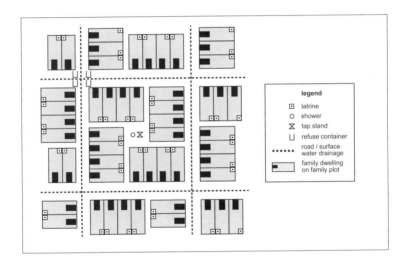

staggered square plan

The advantages of the staggered square plan are as follows:

- The front of each family plot faces a cul-de-sac road, which is used by the community residents only. This feature helps to improve social controls by enabling the residents to be aware of their neighbours, and by reinforcing the community through increased social interaction.

- The rear sides of the family plots face each other, improving privacy and security.

- Family latrines can be introduced gradually, starting with one latrine shared between four families. Building four latrines together is simpler than building separate latrines.

- 'Staggering' the communities prevents long straight roads. Long straight roads reduce privacy and flexibility, and increase the funnelling of wind, which increases dust and the spread of fires.

- Tap-stands and latrines are situated away from the road, so they are less likely to be used by passers-by and therefore more likely to be maintained by the community.

The disadvantage of the staggered square plan is that marking it out is more complicated than using a grid – although a grid can be marked and then the plots can be staggered within it.

figure 8(j): staggered plan

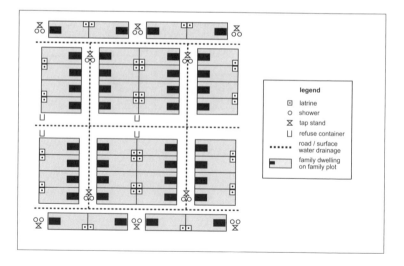

legend
- ⊡ latrine
- ○ shower
- ✕ tap stand
- ⊔ refuse container
- ••••• road / surface water drainage
- ▬ family dwelling on family plot

community road plan

The community road plan has several advantages:

- The front of each family plot faces a road which widens and narrows along its length, creating small communal open squares, linked by roads. Although the roads are used by everyone, the communal squares reinforce the sense of community by increasing social interaction.

- The rear sides of the family plots face each other, creating a sense of privacy and security.

- Family latrines can be introduced gradually, starting with one shared between four families. Family latrines can then be built in pairs.

The disadvantages are that tap-stands are situated in the road, and are likely to be used by people other than the community whom they serve, and so they are less likely to be maintained. Marking out the plan is more complicated than using a grid, because some family plots are sized differently from others.

figure 8(k): community road plan

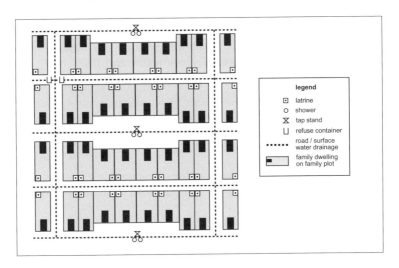

legend
⊡ latrine
○ shower
✕ tap stand
⊔ refuse container
...... road / surface water drainage
� family dwelling on family plot

8 camps

8.4.5 infrastructure and facilities in planned camps

This section offers an overview of infrastructure and facilities in planned camps, but it should also be useful when upgrading infrastructure and facilities in self-settled camps (8.4.6). Activities such as building roads, developing water-supply systems, and implementing sanitation programmes require specialist input.

phasing infrastructure development

Infrastructure should be designed so that it can be upgraded and extended. The functions of the transitional settlement will differ between the emergency phase and the care and maintenance phase. For example, defecation fields provided in the emergency phase should be upgraded into family latrines. Similarly, populations are unlikely to remain static, and the infrastructure may need to be extended into expansion areas.

surface-water drainage infrastructure

The pattern of surface-water drainage infrastructure can be a useful starting point in determining the orientation of roads and accommodation areas. Specialist engineers should advise on the size and positioning of run-offs required, and the use of options such as 'French drains' filled with stones, and soak-away pits.

Terracing slopes and planning drainage to follow the contour lines can help to prevent soil erosion and landslides, as can 'erosion belts' of undisturbed vegetation.

Surface-water drains require regular monitoring and maintenance, because they often become blocked with rubbish, or with earth dislodged by pedestrians creating paths across them.

roads and paths infrastructure

Infrastructure construction is usually well received by the local authorities, but such activities can easily become politicised and divisive.

Constructing or maintaining all-weather roads to be used by supply convoys is often the highest single cost in supporting camps; this fact reinforces the need for specialist advice. Keep pedestrians separate from vehicular traffic whenever possible, to prevent accidents. Ensure that the areas to the sides of vehicular roads are kept clear, to maintain good visibility for drivers and pedestrians. Steeply inclined roads should be avoided, especially if they carry vehicular traffic, because they can contribute to soil erosion by channelling surface water; to avoid this effect, consider incorporating 'switchbacks', building culverts, or following contours.

water sources, storage, and supply infrastructure

Involve sector specialists whenever available and refer to the existing literature (Adams 1999, House and Reed 1997). Specific considerations when planning water-supply infrastructure include the following:

- Infrastructure should ideally be useable by the local populations once the camp is closed, especially high-cost elements such as wells, boreholes, distribution systems, and collection pans.
- Pipes should be buried under 40–60cm of earth, to avoid damage by traffic.
- In cold climates, if frost is likely, pipes should be buried 60–90cm underground.
- The maximum distance between shelters and water-distribution points should not exceed 100m, or a few minutes' walk (UNHCR).
- Used water from tap stands should be used for gardens, or drained into soak-aways, because standing water encourages mosquitoes to breed.

sanitation infrastructure

Involve sector specialists whenever available, and refer to the existing literature (Adams 1999, House and Reed 1997). Specific considerations when planning sanitation infrastructure include the following:

- Support should be provided for the construction of showers or washing areas, including soak-aways to prevent standing water.
- Camp planning should allow space for one latrine per family.
- Sufficient space should be left for new latrine pits to be added.
- Composting or bucket latrines should be considered where the water table is high, to prevent contamination of the ground water.

refuse collection and disposal infrastructure

Maintaining a clean environment is important for the health of the camp population. Waste that accumulates in particular areas may

8 camps

pollute water sources and encourage vermin. Specific considerations when planning refuse collection and disposal infrastructure include the following:

- Badly sited and poorly managed refuse dumps and ineffective collection programmes can encourage vector infestation (6.3.5).

- Collected refuse should be sorted, to segregate materials for re-cycling, composting for fertiliser, burning, or safe disposal.

- Dumps should be sited away from dwellings and sealed with earth for vector control.

- Landfills are usually preferable to burning: many types of plastic release hazardous fumes (although polyethylene can be safely burned).

- Medical wastes, such as sharps and soiled bandages, should be incinerated and then buried deeply, in accordance with specialist guidance (MSF 1998).

market places and commercial facilities

Creating sufficient and appropriate areas for use as markets, both centrally and dispersed throughout the camp blocks and sectors, is essential to livelihoods and community development (8.5). Businesses, such as shops, restaurants, and milk-boiling services, will proliferate in the medium term. The structures that house these activities should receive as much attention as is given to dwellings. Latrines and water supplies are important. Fire risks should be evaluated.

cemeteries, crematoria, and mourning areas

Specific considerations when planning cemeteries, crematoria, and mourning areas include the following:

- Make sure that provision offered by aid organisations is in accordance with the customs of the displaced population, maintaining traditions and dignity, in a manner that is also acceptable to the local host population.

- Graveyards should be located at least 30m from groundwater sources used for drinking water, and at least 1.5m above the water table (Sphere Project 2004).

- Materials required for celebration rites, such as shrouds, should be provided whenever the displaced population has difficulty in procuring them or cannot afford them.

Medical infrastructure should be planned by specialists in close collaboration with the local authorities (MSF 1998). At least one health centre, capable of providing primary care, should be provided for every 20,000 displaced persons (8.4.1). If a camp is far from a referral hospital equipped with operating theatres, a larger clinic or camp hospital will be needed on site, to meet immediate health needs.

When local facilities are available, the local authorities may allow the displaced population to use them. If the local infrastructure is inadequate, support should be provided, in the form of medical staff and clinical materials and drugs.

If there are suitable hospitals within easy reach, only minor infrastructure will be required at the camp, such as:

• screening facilities within reception centres

• outreach clinics within blocks or sectors of the camp, with or without small surgery facilities

• dispensaries.

Medical facilities within a camp should be accessible by motorised vehicles and positioned in a central area. Minimum requirements for such facilities include the provision of the following:

• a waiting area

• a reception area

• examination rooms

• an in-patient room

• latrines and hand-washing facilities

• a reliable and adequate water supply

• a pharmacy.

feeding centres

In a feeding centre, vulnerable members of the refugee population will receive food in order to bring body weight to within a safe limit. Médecins sans Frontières divides feeding centres into two types (MSF 1998):

• supplementary feeding centres, which provide food to supplement the daily diet, and wet feeding: cooked meals that are consumed in the feeding centre before the patient returns home;

8 camps

- therapeutic feeding centres, which provide 24-hour care to the seriously malnourished; these operate on an in-patient system, where the patient will usually be accompanied by a carer.

Figure 8(l), which is not to scale, illustrates a typical layout of a supplementary feeding centre.

figure 8(l): example of a supplementary feeding centre

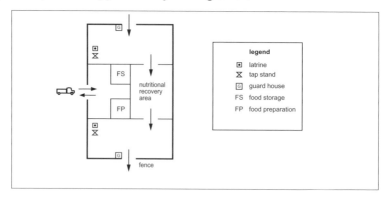

warehouses Warehousing may be located centrally, or in satellite facilities dispersed around the camp. Storage is discussed in section 7.3.4. Measures should be taken to ensure the security of staff and contents, together with measures to protect stored commodities from rodents, damp conditions, and fire.

Many materials have specific storage requirements, such as cement and foodstuffs: careful stock control and storage should be maintained. Periodic inventories should be carried out, and materials should be checked for signs of degradation: canvas tents, for example, may show signs of mildew and may need to be dried out.

Warehouses will generally be part of a logistics compound, comprising the following elements:

- indoor storage area: ideally a large unobstructed space, protected from rodents, well ventilated, lockable, and with easy access through large doors
- outdoor storage area
- delivery area, ideally with ramps or a high plinth to make loading and unloading easier; the area accessible to trucks should be well compacted or hard-surfaced and drained, to make it usable in all weathers

---

396

- guard shelters: allowing line-of-sight control around the entire perimeter.

Figure 8(m), which is not to scale, illustrates a typical warehouse layout.

figure 8(m): example of a warehouse compound

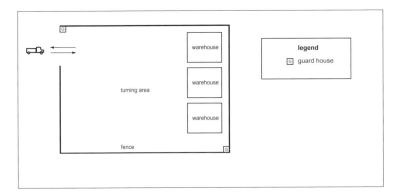

distribution centres

Site-planning considerations for distribution centres are similar to those for warehousing. Distribution centres require good access from all areas of the camp, especially for vulnerable families (8.4.3).

Distribution centres should be guarded. Water is required for cleaning purposes. A small amount of food may be kept in distribution centres, and protection from rodents and damp conditions should be considered, as in warehouses.

Depending on the size of the camp, there may be both centrally based and neighbourhood-based distribution facilities. A distribution centre will generally have the following features:

- **delivery area:** ideally well compacted or hard-surfaced and drained, to make it usable by trucks in all weathers

- **sorting area:** a lockable, well-ventilated space with a washable hard surface, preferably raised to facilitate unloading lorries, and to guarantee good drainage; space for scales and sorting tables

- **short-term storage:** a lockable space, rodent-proof and well ventilated, with pallets or shelves for the storage of foods

- an administration room.

figure 8(n): example of a distribution centre

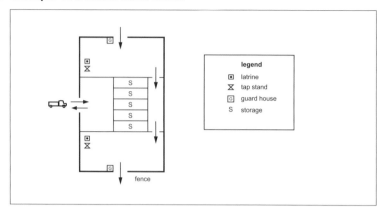

schools Local authorities may permit displaced children to use existing school infrastructure, in which case support should be provided to the local schools through the supply of teaching staff and teaching materials, such as desks, chairs, and blackboards.

If schools are to be built in the camp, provide one school for every 5,000 displaced children (8.4.1). Access by the local population may help to integrate the two communities, especially in areas where the local school infrastructure is poor.

If constructing a school building, choose a structure that could be used for a variety of purposes, and collaborate with the local authorities to make it possible to convert it to a different use when the camp closes.

Specific considerations when planning school buildings include the following:

- Provide indoor and outdoor spaces protected from the elements.
- Make sure the space is sufficiently ventilated, or heated in cold climates.
- Provide a sufficient number of latrines.
- Provide a source of water for washing and drinking.
- Consult education specialists to determine if classes could be taught in shifts, thus reducing the infrastructure required.

communal washing facilities

Communal or family facilities for bathing and laundry may require support. Appropriate drainage should be provided. Assess the general practices among the displaced community, in order to maximise hygiene and social benefits.

recreation facilities

Allow sufficient recreation space, both for children and adults, to be created as soon as the circumstances allow. These may be open spaces for sports, or meeting places located around communal facilities, such as market places. It is important to integrate these spaces within the initial site plan: they should not be simply added to the outside of the camp.

religious/ritual facilities

Aid agencies will have internal guidelines on supporting and planning for religious activities.

provision for livestock

Appropriate provision for livestock is fundamental to the continuity of the livelihoods of the displaced population.

- Provide or plan areas where livestock can be kept, at a distance from living areas, and possibly fenced.

- Do not provide individual fencing for the livestock of each family, because it can consume a significant proportion of available construction materials.

- Provide alternative water sources for livestock, situated away from human habitation and from sources of water for humans.

- Ensure that slaughter facilities are hygienic, easy to clean, and provided with traps and soak-aways for sedimentation, and facilities for disposal of wastes.

8.4.6 upgrading infrastructure and facilities in self-settled camps

Self-settled camps are established in an emergency phase without reference to international standards. The first action of the aid community in seeking to support transitional settlement must be to determine the appropriateness of each self-settled camp location. Site-selection assessment (8.1.1) should be undertaken, identifying issues such as risk from conflict or natural hazards. If a self-settled site is not appropriate, a new site should be selected, in consultation with the displaced and local populations.

Even if siting is appropriate, upgrading of infrastructure and facilities will probably be required, to improve safety and access to essential services, and to meet international standards. Upgrading can make external support easier: for example, by improving road infrastructure and hence improving access for emergency services.

Assuming that the site-selection process determines that siting is appropriate, the following considerations may be useful when upgrading self-settled camps.

upgrading self-settled camp layouts and family shelter

Determine the upgrading required to meet international standards, possibly including phased internal relocation, described in steps A– F in figure 8(o).

- Take into account local circumstances when considering the strict implementation of international standards; but respect the fact that the standards have been developed from extensive experience of risk management.

- Do a thorough assessment of localised risks, such as flooding and fire, and plan and implement appropriate provisions: for example, relocating some shelters to create fire breaks.

- Consider projects to upgrade family shelter, either by distributing construction materials or by contracting workers (5.4), with particular support given to vulnerable families.

upgrade health, water and sanitation, education, and livelihoods activities

- Consult health, water, and sanitation specialists to determine how best to support the upgrading of such services.

- Consult education specialists to determine how best to support access to the local school system and provide extra support.

- Consider with social-services specialists the best ways to support livelihoods.

plan environmental rehabilitation measures

- Ensure the removal of all the waste that cannot be reused and which might be polluting the environment.

- Begin regeneration programmes at points where the camp construction had a damaging impact on natural resources, such as reforestation.

figure 8(o): phased relocation of a self-settled camp

Figure 8(o) is a fictitious example, showing the phased relocation of a self-settled camp.

step A: Survey and map the camp, using either GPS or conventional measures, to determine boundaries and areas, and to explore potential sites for expansion.

step B: Identify the approximate borders between original communities, as they exist in the camp, and identify the largest community (marked as (a) in step D).

step C: Identify a site, larger than the original site for community (a), into which the camp can extend. (This may involve creating a new site.) Involve community (a) in planning and preparing the new site.

step D: Assist community (a) to move into the new site, which has planned infrastructure, fire breaks, and a reduced density of occupation, meeting international standards

step E: Identify the next community (b) for relocation. Involve community (b) in planning and preparing their new site, which is on the site previously occupied by community (a).

step F: Assist community (b) to move to the upgraded site that was once occupied by community (a), which now has planned infrastructure, fire breaks, and a reduced density of occupation, meeting international standards.

Steps E and F should be repeated until the entire camp is internally re-located with planned infrastructure, fire breaks, and a reduced density of occupation, meeting international standards. The final site, previously occupied by the smallest community, can be used for communal facilities, such as markets or recreation areas.

8 camps

8.4.7 developing and extending self-settled and planned camps

The circumstances that led to the planning and upgrading of self-settled and planned camps are likely to change during the life-span of the camps, requiring them to be developed or extended. Such circumstances include the following developments:

- natural population growth – in excess of 5 per cent each year in some cases
- spontaneous internal relocations, as communities rebuild
- new influxes of displaced persons, either from renewed conflicts, or from other TS options.

In planned camps, areas should have been left during the emergency phase for development and phased upgrading: for example, defecation fields, which will be covered over as family latrines are implemented.

If internal relocations resulting from reconstruction (8.5.1) affect a considerable proportion of a site, and if upgraded facilities are planned, phased relocation might be considered, as for that illustrated for self-settled camps (8.4.6).

If population pressures require the camps to be extended, or a new camp to be established, the site-selection process (8.1) should be repeated, making reference to the original assessments, profiles, and scenario options. Site-selection assessments should be undertaken, even if the extension under consideration is adjacent to the original site. Increasing camp populations should prompt a strategic planning review to support other TS options. The review should determine if the new influxes originate from different settlement options, and establish whether extending camps is the best response to the needs of the displaced population.

8.4.8 closing camps

The process of closing camps has very different implications for each of the stakeholders involved, but many of these implications are linked by common interests.

for the displaced population

Displaced families may leave camps gradually, in planned phases, or suddenly, depending on external events. Displaced families will choose one of the same durable solution options identified by

UNHCR for refugees (2.4.6): return to their homes; resettlement in the country or area where they are displaced; or resettlement in another country. These guidelines do not consider the return process; but the closure of camps must take into account the possible reluctance of displaced families to leave. The return process may be insecure, or not adequately supported. For example, to return even to subsistence agriculture may require two–three years of work to prepare the soil and develop sufficient food security. Returning families often take with them shelter NFIs such as tools and plastic sheeting, in addition to any return packages offered.

In rare circumstances, camps may be turned into permanent settlements. If this was not envisaged from the outset, and plans were not developed accordingly, serious consideration must be given to the livelihoods and sustainability of the camp population, and appropriate upgrading must be undertaken.

for the local population

Cleaning up the site to make it safe and usable by the local population is the responsibility of the lead aid organisation that established and supported the camp. It is likely that materials such as construction timber and latrine slabs can be recovered and handed over to the local population for re-use (2.4.7 exit strategies phase).

All infrastructure and facilities in camps should, whenever possible, be planned from the outset to be handed over to the local community or local authorities as resources for development. It may be, however, that the location of the camp, or its size in relation to the local population, means that infrastructure and facilities are inappropriate to local needs, in which case they should be dismantled and made safe, as part of the site clean-up. Any communal infrastructure that is likely to be useful, such as roads and wells, should be properly sited and built from materials appropriate to local maintenance capabilities. The final use of all communal facilities constructed should therefore be taken into account from the planning phase. For example, if camp schools will be used by local communities, consideration should be given to the question of who will pay for the teachers and for building maintenance.

8 camps

The lead agency is responsible for ensuring that the camp site is returned to the local authorities in the manner and condition initially agreed. It is common for camp sites, once they have been closed, to contain a considerable quantity of refuse, some of which may be hazardous, such as medical sharps. Abandoned pit latrines and surface-water drains may pose additional hazards to future users of the site.

Environmental degradation is likely to be considerable, and soil erosion may be expected. Reforestation or other mitigation programmes should have been considered from the establishment of the camp, to enable a smooth handover to the local authorities (UNHCR 1996, 1998a–e, 2002a, 2002c, 2002d).

Camp clean-up should include the following measures:

• sorting and stockpiling any reusable leftover material, such as pit-latrine slabs, which should be disinfected prior to handover for re-use;

• the closure and sealing of pit latrines, by backfilling with 75cm soil and compacting; active latrines should be disinfected, usually with lime;

• the incineration and burial of medical wastes, such as sharps and soiled bandages, in accordance with specialist guidance (MSF 1998).

As noted above, all communal infrastructure and facilities should be handed over to the local community, ideally in accordance with pre-defined agreements. Depending on the type of camp, the handover may include a range of buildings such as warehouses, camp clinics, and schools, in addition to water-supply infrastructure.

8.5 community development in camps

Camps and collective centres (3.5) accommodate entire communities of displaced populations in one place. This increases the control exerted over them (3.1.3) by community leaders, local authorities, and especially the aid community, which usually manages most community services, from water supply to food distribution.

When aid organisations are managing activities normally managed by the community itself, community structures and coping strategies may be undermined. Community-development activities may mitigate and even reverse such negative impacts, empowering and reinforcing community structures as a preparation for reaching durable solutions.

Community-development activities should begin with supporting the rebuilding of the community itself (8.5.1) and go on to support community livelihoods activities (8.5.2) and relations between the displaced and local communities (8.5.3).

Social-services departments of aid organisations and local authorities, where they exist, should be involved from the outset. Community-development activities require a detailed understanding of the communities involved. Badly defined activities can easily become counterproductive, with communities resisting the imposition of external perceptions of how they should develop.

The Camp Management Toolkit (NRC 2004) offers extensive guidance on community participation.

8.5.1 rebuilding community

Displacement often fragments communities and families. Rebuilding communities should be supported through activities such as site planning and transfers between TS options.

community development through site planning

The combination, planning, and development of camps influence the way in which the displaced population rebuilds and develops its communities, both as the population arrives and later on. It is important to support displaced families to rebuild and develop their communities, reinforcing traditional coping strategies in order that they can help each other.

Families and communities may not arrive all at the same time. Camp combinations, planning, and plot allocation need to be co-ordinated so that related families and families from the same community can settle in close proximity, which will support community development. One way to assist this process is to interview displaced persons to determine how many villages are likely to be displaced, and the size of their population: combinations of camps, or areas within a large camp, can then be planned with the appropriate capacities.

As displaced families arrive in self-settled camps, they tend to settle near relations and their own community, even if there is little space for them to do so. To ensure that sufficient service infrastructure can be provided, and fire breaks maintained, self-settled camps are often upgraded through phased relocation (8.4.6). Phased relocation projects are also opportunities for communities to rebuild at a more sustainable and equitable density.

transfers between settlement options

Movement by displaced individuals and families from one settlement option to another is often seen by aid organisations as opportunistic and inconvenient, complicating their attempts at giving support. While opportunism often plays a part in the decision of displaced persons to change their settlement option, the action is probably inconvenient for them too, and their reasons often deserve more attention.

It is likely that a significant proportion of the displaced population do not consider a self-settled or planned camp as their TS preferred option; however, their choices may be constrained. After the emergency phase, more choices may become available, or the circumstances of the displaced person may change. For example, members of the family may meet again after being separated during transit. Similarly, displaced persons living in settlement options other than camps may decide that camps offer the best alternative for them: for example, if they have been renting a room and they run out of funds. Lastly, events such as a monsoon season, changes in security in the region, or a harvest are likely to result in population movements between settlement options.

As a result, it is common for camps to experience a considerable turn-over of population, even in some cases where the overall population appears to be relatively constant. The demographic composition is also likely to change: for example, if young men move to the camps to avoid conscription into armed factions, or if there are employment opportunities in the region and most adults have left to seek work, leaving older people and children behind in the camps.

It is important to maintain an accurate profile of all groups within the displaced populations, both inside and outside the camps, to be able to predict or at least expect population movements into and out of the camps. Such population movements may involve a considerable proportion of the camp population and may have significant impacts on levels of infrastructure and support required.

It is also important to consider the community-development opportunities when displaced persons transfer from one settlement option to another. If such transfers have positive impacts on communities, consider making transfers easier, for example by developing assistance mechanisms such as ration cards that can be used in more than one TS programme option.

8.5.2 community livelihoods

Camps are not intended to be sustainable settlements, but every effort should be made to create and support livelihood opportunities for displaced populations, to empower them by increasing their self-sufficiency, and to reduce demands upon the aid community.

The assessment profile (2.2) of the displaced population will identify the range of livelihoods activities traditionally undertaken. The site-selection process (8.1) includes evaluating ways in which self-settled and planned camps can offer various opportunities for livelihoods, based on the assessment profile: for example, if the displaced population comprises predominantly farmers, the site-selection process should concentrate on identifying appropriate low-density, dispersed, small sites, in areas where there is land available for agriculture.

Camps are invariably established on marginal land, with little productive potential for agriculture or livestock; if the land was not marginal, the local population would probably be using it. When supporting self-settled or planned camps, it is therefore important to identify ways in which to make marginal land viable for the livelihoods of the displaced population. Ideally, as part of this process, the land should be made useful for the local population, so that it becomes a developmental resource for them, once the displaced population has achieved durable solutions. Examples include draining land that floods, or improving sustainable water sources on sites with little water.

8.5.3 community relations

Although displaced communities and local communities may not require external intervention in support of their relations, external support for TS does influence these relations. The way in which camps are planned and built, for example, affects relations between all stakeholders, but especially between the local and displaced populations, influencing activities such as natural-resource management (NMR).

Community-development activities to support positive relations between displaced and local populations may include the formation of joint committees to be responsible for managing disputes. Common concerns of displaced and local populations which may influence community relations, and may benefit from activities supporting community relations, include the following:

- the security of both communities
- the accessibility of the camp, and whether access is via local settlements
- the life-span of the camp
- support offered by the aid community and local authorities to displaced and local communities, and displaced and local households
- infrastructure, utilities, and services shared by the local and displaced communities: clinics, for example
- potential conflicts over the use of natural resources such as fuel wood.

chapter 9 resources

9.1 glossary

This glossary lists and describes a selection of agreed terms and definitions for use in the transitional settlement sector.

9.1.1 new terms

Table 9(a) lists the new terms that were developed and agreed during the shelterproject peer reviews held between June 2002 and October 2003.

table 9(a): transitional settlement – new terms

term	description
transitional settlement	settlement and shelter resulting from conflict and natural disasters, ranging from emergency response to durable solutions
transitional settlement sector	the field of work related to the provision of settlement and shelter needs resulting from conflict and natural disasters, ranging from emergency response to durable solutions; aim: to provide transitional settlement support to communities, families, and individuals affected by conflict and natural disasters, as well as any hosting populations, to ensure their security, good health, privacy, and dignity
transitional shelter	shelter which provides a habitable covered living space, and a secure, healthy, living environment with privacy and dignity to those within it, over the period between a conflict or natural disaster and achieving a durable shelter solution

9.1.2 commonly used terms

Table 9(b) lists selected terms frequently used in the transitional settlement sector.

table 9(b): transitional settlement – frequently used terms

term	description
family plot	a small piece of land allocated to an individual family for their own management
livelihoods	the ways in which people manage their lives in order to access the resources that they need, individually and communally, such as food, water, clothing, and shelter
local infrastructure	the facilities of a local or host population to meet their communal needs, such as schools, hospitals, water-distribution systems, electricity grids, market services, roads, and bridges
prefabricated shelters	shelters made in separate parts which need to be assembled on site upon delivery
settlement	a community of covered living spaces providing a secure, healthy living environment with privacy and dignity to the groups, families, and individuals residing within them
shelter	a habitable covered living space, providing a secure, healthy living environment with privacy and dignity to the groups, families, and individuals residing within it
shelter non-food item (shelter NFI)	an article that meets a need related to transitional settlement or shelter but is not structural, such as blankets, mattresses, mosquito nets, stoves, and fuels
shelter sector	an abbreviation of the term 'site selection, planning and shelter sector', describing the part of the 'transitional settlement sector' that responds to the transitional settlement and shelter needs of refugees, within the mandate of UNHCR
shelter system	the combination of structural shelter items and 'shelter NFIs' that create shelter, possibly including local materials, such as a tent with locally procured blankets, mattresses, and a stove appropriate to a cold climate
tent	a self-contained shelter, normally consisting of poles, pegs, ropes, and tailored material

9.1.3 formal terms

Table 9(c) lists a selection of terms with their formal definitions according to a particular source. Neither judgement nor endorsement is implied by the appearance of any definitions in this table.

table 9(c): transitional settlement – formal terms

term	description (verbatim quotation from source)
asylum UNHCR (2002b)	The grant, by a State, of protection on its territory to persons from another State who are fleeing persecution or serious danger. A person who is granted asylum is a refugee. Asylum encompasses a variety of elements, including non-refoulement, permission to remain on the territory of the asylum country, and humane standards of treatment.
camps UNHCR (2000)	Refugees find accommodation in purpose-built sites where a full range of services, for example water, sanitation, are provided, usually exclusively for the population of the site. High-density camps with very large populations are the worst possible option for refugee accommodation. However, this may be the only option because of decisions by the host country or simply because of a lack of alternatives. They are common in areas with little or no pre-existing infrastructure or where the size of the refugee population is such that it would put an intolerable strain on the local resources if [dispersed settlement or mass shelter] were used.

term	description (verbatim quotation from source)
cluster planning UNHCR (2002a)	Aims to create decentralised clusters of communities, where shelters are grouped together, to clearly define social units.
dispersed settlement UNHCR (2000)	Refugees find accommodation within the households of families who already live in the area of refuge. The refugees either share existing accommodation or set up temporary accommodation nearby and share water, sanitation, cooking and other services of the pre-existing households.
displaced persons UNDHA (1992)	Persons who, for different reasons or circumstances, have been compelled to leave their homes. They may or may not reside in their country of origin, but are not legally regarded as refugees.
grid planning UNHCR (2002a)	Creates repetitive patterns of long rows of plots and/or shelters.
internally displaced persons (IDPs) DFID (2003)	Persons displaced from their habitual place of residence by disaster, fear of persecution or fear of physical harm, but remaining within the territorial limits of their country of origin. Unlike refugees, IDPs have no internationally defined legal status.
mass shelter UNHCR (2000)	Refugees find accommodation in pre-existing facilities, for example, in schools, barracks, hotels, gymnasiums. These are normally in urban areas and are often intended as temporary or transit accommodation.

continued ...

9 resources

term	description (verbatim quotation from source)
physical planner UNHCR (2002b)	The UNHCR term for an aid worker specialising in temporary settlement and shelter, and specifically the layout of camps [supported temporary settlements]; also termed 'site planner' and 'camp planner'.
refugee UNHCR (1951/1967) [Due to the length of the full Definition of the Term 'Refugee', only the key passage is reproduced here.]	For the purposes of the present Convention, the term 'refugee' shall apply to any person who [...] owing to well-founded fear of being persecuted for reasons of race, religion, nationality, membership of a particular social group or political opinion, is outside the country of his nationality and is unable or, owing to such fear, is unwilling to avail himself of the protection of that country; or who, not having a nationality and being outside the country of his former habitual residence as a result of such events, is unable or, owing to such fear, is unwilling to return to it.
resettlement UNDHA (1992)	Actions necessary for the permanent settlement of persons dislocated or otherwise affected by a disaster to an area different from their last place of habitation.

continued ...

term	description (verbatim quotation from source)
shelter Sphere Project (2000)	Shelter is a critical determinant of survival in the initial stage of an emergency. Beyond survival, shelter is necessary to enhance resistance to disease and provide protection from the environment. It is also important for human dignity and to sustain family and community life as far as possible in difficult circumstances. The purpose of shelter, site selection and physical planning interventions is to meet the physical and primary social needs of individuals, families and communities for safe, secure and comfortable living space, incorporating as much self-sufficiency and self-management into the process as possible.

9.2 acronyms

AC	alternating current
BOQ	bill of quantities
CBO	community-based organisation
CESCR	Committee on Economic, Social and Cultural Rights
CGI	corrugated galvanised iron
CHF	Community Housing Foundation
CI	corrugated iron
COHRE	Centre On Housing Rights and Evictions
CRS	Catholic Relief Services
DFID	Department for International Development
DFID CHAD-OT	DFID Conflict and Humanitarian Affairs Department Operations Team
DGPS	Differential GPS
DMC	Disaster Management Centre (Wisconsin)
DP	displaced person
ECHO	European Commission Humanitarian aid Office
FHH	female-headed household
FI	food item
GBV	gender-based violence
GI	galvanised iron
GIS	Geographical Information Systems
GPS	Global Positioning System
GRP	glass-reinforced fibre plastic
HIC	Humanitarian Information Centre
HIV/AIDS	Human Immunodeficiency Virus/Acquired Immune Deficiency Syndrome
IED	improvised explosive devices
IOM	International Organization for Migration
ICRC	International Committee of the Red Cross
IDP	internally displaced person
IFRC	International Federation of Red Cross and Red Crescent Societies
IGO	inter-government organisation
IO	international organisation
INGO	international non-government organisation
IRC	International Rescue Committee
JICA	Japan International Cooperation Agency
LFA	Logical Framework Analysis
LNGO	local non-government organisation

LWF	Lutheran World Federation
MSF	Médecins Sans Frontières
MSF-B/NL	Médecins Sans Frontières – Belgium/Netherlands
NFI	non-food item
NGO	non-government organisation
NRC	Norwegian Refugee Council
NRM	natural resource management
OAU	Organization of African Unity (now the African Union)
OD	outside diameter
OHCHR	Office of the United Nations High Commissioner for Human Rights
PFA	Project Framework Approach
PLA	Participatory Learning and Action
POP	People-Oriented Planning
PRA	Participatory Rapid Appraisal or Participatory Rural Appraisal
RAP	Rapid Appraisal Procedures
RCD	residual current devices
RedR	Registered Engineers for Disaster Relief
RRA	Rapid Rural Appraisal
SAME	Shelter Assessment Monitoring and Evaluation
SCF	Save the Children Fund
SDC	Swiss Agency for Development and Cooperation
SNI/SFL	Shelter Now International / Shelter For Life
SWOC	strengths, weaknesses, opportunities, and constraints
SWOT	strengths, weaknesses, opportunities, and threats
UAM	unaccompanied minor
UN	United Nations
UNDP	United Nation Development Programme
UNDHA	United Nations Department of Humanitarian Affairs
UNDRO	United Nations Disaster Relief Organisation
UNEP	United Nations Environment Programme
UNHCR	United Nations High Commissioner for Refugees
UNICEF	United Nations Children's Fund
UN/ OCHA	United Nation Office for the Coordination of Humanitarian Affairs
UXO	unexeploded ordnance
UNOPS	United Nation Office for Project Services
VO	variation order

9 resources

9.3 training

This book is accompanied by a CD containing training modules which complement every aspect of these guidelines, including exercises, notes for trainers, and tips for giving a presentation. The Shelter Training modules can also be downloaded free of charge from www.sheltertraining.org.

9.4 annotated resource list

This section contains a compilation and short description of a few key texts relevant to decision making about transitional settlement in the field; only texts that are still in print or easily accessible over the Internet are included. General manuals and a number of relevant texts, such as the work of Fred Cuny, which are not easily accessible, have not been included.

Chalinder, A. (1998) 'Temporary human settlement planning for displaced populations in emergencies', *Good Practice Review* no. 6, ODI, London
This review aims to broaden contemporary thinking on temporary human-settlement planning in emergencies. The author distinguishes between the more technical aspects of site allocation and preparation when planning settlements, and decisions that take into account political, environmental, and economic-sustainability issues. The review contends that the long-term implications for emergency assistance programmes, resulting from the choice of area or region in which a displaced population is encouraged to settle, are frequently overlooked in the scramble to find a site. In addition, Chalinder asserts that more attention needs to be paid at a managerial level within both the development and humanitarian sectors to finding sustainable solutions.

RedR (2002) J. Davis and R. Lambert (eds.) *Engineering in Emergencies: A Practical Guide for Relief Workers*, 2nd ed., RedR/ITDG, London
A practical handbook for relief and development workers involved in providing humanitarian assistance. The information is focused on implementing an effective response in the aftermath of an emergency. Technical topics – such as water, sanitation, shelter

construction, and site planning – are combined with non-technical advice in areas such as managerial skills and personal effectiveness. Practical information on security, telecommunications, contracts, and logistics is also provided. For information on the print and CD-ROM versions, see www.redr.org/resources/Eng_Emergency/EngInEmergency.htm.

Sphere Project (2004) *Humanitarian Charter and Minimum Standards in Disaster Response*, Sphere Project, Geneva
This handbook specifies what disaster-affected people have a right to expect from humanitarian assistance. The Humanitarian Charter describes the core principles that govern humanitarian action. It asserts the right of populations to protection and assistance, based on international humanitarian law, human rights law, and refugee law, along with the principles of the Red Cross and NGO Code of Conduct. The Minimum Standards in Disaster Response describe five core sectors: water supply and sanitation, nutrition, food aid, shelter and site planning, and health services. Most of the standards, and the accompanying indicators, are not new, but consolidate and adapt existing knowledge and practice. They represent a consensus across a broad spectrum of agencies and mark a determination to ensure that humanitarian principles are realised in practice. The text is available in different languages and with training materials at www.sphereproject.org.

UNDRO (1982) *Shelter After Disaster, Guidelines for Assistance*, principal consultant I. Davis, UNDRO, New York
Although out of print, this book is available for free download from the website of UN/OCHA Online. Analysing shelter issues from the perspective of the survivor, rather than through the traditional perspective of donors and other assisting groups, Shelter After Disaster provides policy and programme guidelines on emergency shelter and post-disaster housing. It aims to cover the entire disaster spectrum, including disaster preparedness, disaster relief, post-disaster reconstruction, and prevention. The guidelines are intended for disaster-management personnel within the governments of disaster-prone countries, non-government, voluntary, and relief organisations, donor governments, the UN system, and other international organisations.

UNHCR (1951/1967) Convention and Protocol Relating to the Status of Refugees, UNHCR, Geneva

The 1951 Convention consolidates previous international instruments relating to refugees and provides a comprehensive codification of their rights. It lays down basic minimum standards for the treatment of refugees, without prejudice to the granting by States of more favourable treatment. With the passage of time and the emergence of new refugee situations, the need was increasingly felt to make the provisions of the Convention more widely applicable. As a result, the 1967 Protocol was prepared. By accession to the Protocol, States undertake to apply the substantive provisions of the 1951 Convention to all refugees covered by the Convention's definition. Although related to the Convention in this way, the Protocol is an independent instrument, accession to which is not limited to States parties to the Convention.

UNHCR (1996) *Environmental Guidelines*, UNHCR, Geneva

These guidelines offer comprehensive advice on environmental issues, including some advice on transitional settlement issues, mainly on refugee camps.

UNHCR (1998) *Key Principles for Decision-Making (Refugee Operations and Environmental Management)*, EESS / UNHCR, Geneva

This short booklet offers ten key principles for decision making on environmental issues, as well as a succinct overview of the practical relevance of the environment to humanitarian operations.

UNHCR (2000) *Handbook for Emergencies*, UNHCR, Geneva

This handbook is divided into four sections. Section One summarises UNHCR's mandate of international protection and the aims and principles of emergency response. Section Two describes emergency management. Section Three covers the problem areas related to refugee emergencies, including health, food, sanitation, and water. Key field activities underpinning the operations, such as logistics, community services, and registration, are also covered. Section Four gives guidance on the support to field operations, primarily administration and staffing. The appendices include UNHCR's 'Catalogue of Emergency Response Resources' and a 'Toolbox' listing the standards, indicators, and useful references used throughout the handbook.

Zetter, R. (1995) *Shelter Provision and Settlement Policies for Refugees: A State of the Art Review*, Studies on Emergency and Disaster Relief no. 2, Noriska Afrikainstitutet, Sweden

This review presents an overview and analysis of shelter and settlement policies for refugees.

9.5 bibliography and sources

Adams, J. (1999) *Managing Water Supply and Sanitation in Emergencies*, Oxfam GB, Oxford

Anderson, M.B. (1994) *People-Oriented Planning At Work Using POP to Improve UNHCR Programming*, Collaborative for Development Action, Inc./UNHCR, Cambridge, Massachusetts

Ashmore, J. (2004) *Tents, a Guide to the Use and Logistics of Tents in Humanitarian Relief*, UN/OCHA and shelterproject, Geneva

Aysan, Y. and P. Oliver (consultant I. Davis) (1987) *Housing and Culture after Earthquakes – A Guide for Future Policy Making in Seismic Areas*, Oxford Polytechnic Press, Oxford

Aysan, Y. and I. Davis (eds.) (1992) *Disasters and the Small Dwelling: Perspectives for the UN IDNDR*, James and James Science Press, London

Aysan, Y. and I. Davis (1994) *Rehabilitation and Reconstruction Disaster Management Training Programme* (DMTP), UNDP / UNDHA, Geneva and New York

Aysan, Y., A. Clayton, A. Cory, I. Davis, and D. Sanderson (1995) *Developing Building Improvements for Safety Programmes: Guidelines for organizing safe building improvement programmes in disaster-prone areas*, Intermediate Technology Publications, London

Bakhet, O. (1987) 'UNHCR Experiences in Implementing Rural Settlements for Refugees', paper delivered at International Conference on the Management of Planned and Spontaneous Refugee Settlements, 1–3 April 1987, Dar es Salaam

Barakat, S. (2003) *Housing Reconstruction after Conflict and Disaster*, HPN Network Paper, ODI, London

Bouchardy, J. Y. (1995) 'Use of GIS, Remote Sensing and GPS in Site Planning and Monitoring of Environmental Impacts of Refugees', unpublished report, UNHCR, Geneva

Catholic Relief Services (2001) *Post-earthquake Housing Reconstruction*, CRS, New York

Centers for Disease Control (2004) *Health Information for International Travel. The Yellow Book*, Centers for Disease Control, Atlanta (downloadable from www.cdc.go/travel/yb/index.htm)

Chalinder, A. (1998) *Temporary Human Settlement Planning for Displaced Populations in Emergencies*, Good Practice Review number 6, ODI, London

Chambers, R. (1979) 'Rural Refugees in Africa, What the Eye Does Not See', expanded version of a paper presented at the African Studies Association Symposium on Refugees, 13–14 September 1979, in *Disasters* 3:4, pp. 381–92, International Disaster Institute, London

Chambers, R. (1992) *Rural Appraisal: Rapid, Relaxed and Participatory*, IDS Discussion Papers 311, Institute of Development Studies (IDS), University of Sussex, Brighton

COHRE (2000) *Legal Resources for Housing Rights: International and National Standards*, COHRE, Geneva

Corsellis, T. (1996) 'UNHCR Guidelines Development: Shelter and Physical Planning Sector', unpublished consultancy report submitted to UNHCR, Geneva

Cosgrave, J. (1998) 'Refugee density and dependence: practical implications of camp size', *Disasters* 20/3: 260-70

Crisp, J. and K. Jacobsen (1998) 'Refugee camps reconsidered', *Forced Migration Review*, 3: 27–30

Cuny, F.C. (1977) 'Refugee camps and camp planning: the state of the art', *Disasters* 1/2:125–43

Cuny, F.C. and R. Hill (1999) *Famine, Conflict and Response: A Basic Guide*, Kumarian Press, West Hartford, Connecticut

Davis, I. (1978) *Shelter After Disaster*, Oxford Polytechnic Press, Oxford

Davis, I. (ed.) (1981) *Disasters and the Small Dwelling*, Pergamon Press, Oxford

Davis, J. and R. Lambert (2002) *Engineering in Emergencies: A Practical Guide for Relief Workers*, ITDG, London

Deng, F. (1998) 'Guiding Principles on Internal Displacement', Report of the Representative of the Secretary-General, Mr Francis M. Deng, submitted pursuant to Commission resolution 1997/39, www.unhchr.ch/Huridocda/Huridoca.nsf/0/d2e008c61b70263ec125661e 0036f36e?Opendocument

DFID (2003) 'Glossary of Development Terms and Abbreviations', DFID, London www.dfid.gov.uk/aboutdfid/files/glossary_r.htm

Dudley, E. (1991) 'The Critical Villager: Technical Aid for Rural Housing and the Characteristics of Indigenous Technology Change', PhD thesis submitted to the University of Cambridge

Edwards, M. and L. Gosling (2003) *Toolkits: A Practical Guide to Monitoring, Evaluation and Impact Assessment (Development Manual)*, Save the Children, London

Ellis, S. (1996) 'An Evaluation of Shelter Projects and Policies for Refugees and Displaced Persons Within the Republic of Croatia', PhD thesis, Faculty of Design and Technology, University of Luton

Goethert, R. and N. Hamdi (1988a) 'Refugee Camps, A Primer for Rapid Site Planning', unpublished draft manual prepared for UNHCR, Geneva

Goethert, R. and N. Hamdi (1988b) 'Refugee Settlements, A Primer for Development', unpublished preliminary outline prepared for UNHCR, Geneva

Goovaerts, P. (1993) 'Specifications and Standards, Emergency and Longer Term', unpublished paper presented at the First International Workshop on Improved Shelter Response and Environment for Refugees, UNHCR, Geneva

Gosling, L. (2003) *Toolkits: A Practical Guide to Monitoring, Evaluation and Impact Assessment*, Save the Children Fund, London

Hamdi, N. (1995) *Housing Without Houses: Participation, Flexibility, Enablement*, Intermediate Technology Publications, London

Hardin, D.K. (1987) 'Physical Planning', unpublished paper presented at the UNHCR/DMC Emergency Managers Workshop

Harris S.L. and D.L. Hulse (1977) 'Minimum Camp Standards', draft edition, J.F. Kennedy School of Government, Harvard University, Cambridge, Massachusetts

Hartkopf, V.H. and C.H. Goodspeed (1979) 'Space enclosures for disasters in developing countries', *Disasters* 3(4): 443–55

Harvey, P., S. Baghri, and B. Reed (2002) *Emergency Sanitation, Assessment and Programme Design*, Water Engineering and Development Centre, Loughborough University

House, S. and R. Reed (1997) *Emergency Water Sources, Guidelines for Selection and Treatment*, Water, Engineering and Development Centre, Loughborough University

Howard, J. and R. Spice (1989) *Plastic Sheeting: Its Use for Emergency Shelter and Other Purposes*, Oxfam Technical Guide, Oxfam GB, Oxford

IFRC (1997) *Camp Management Guide for Red Cross and Red Crescent National Societies in Eastern Africa*, Regional Disaster Preparedness Programme, IFRC, Geneva

IFRC (1999) *Battling the Storm. Study on Cyclone Resistant Housing*, German Red Cross and Bangladesh Red Crescent Society, Dhaka

IFRC (2000) 'Disaster Emergency Needs Assessment', Disaster Preparedness Training Programme, International Federation of the Red Cross and Red Crescent Societies, Geneva

Jacobsen, K. (1994) *The Impact of Refugees on the Environment: A Review of the Evidence*, Refugee Policy Group, Washington

Kelly, C. (2001) *Rapid Environmental Impact Assessment: A Framework for Best Practice in Emergency Response*, Benfield Hazard Research Centre, London

Khanna, P.N. (2001) *Indian Practical Civil Engineers' Handbook*, Engineers' Publishers, Delhi

Lambert, R. and J. Davis (2002) *Engineering in Emergencies: A Practical Guide for Relief Workers*, ITDG, London

Mellander, N. (1988) 'Can a refugee camp become a functioning community?', *Refugee Participation Network*, no. 2: 31–6, Refugee Studies Programme, Oxford

MSF (1994) G. Delmas and M. Courvallet (eds.) *Technicien sanitaire en situation précaire*, Médecins sans Frontières, Paris

MSF (1997) *Refugee Health*, Macmillan, London

MSF (1998) *Temporary and Semi Permanent Buildings for Health Infrastructures in Refugee Camps*, Médecins sans Frontières Building Department, Brussels

Narbeth, S. and C. McLean (2003) *Livelihoods and Protection. Displacement and Vulnerable Communities in Kismaayo, Southern Somalia*, HPN Network Paper, ODI, London

Nordberg, R. (1998) *Resettlement Planning Manual*, UNCHS, Nairobi

Norwegian Refugee Council (2004) *Camp Management Toolkit*, Norwegian Refugee Council/Camp Management Project, Oslo

OAU (1981) 'African Charter on Human and Peoples' Rights', Banjul http://textus.diplomacy.edu/Thina/thBridgeFset.asp?IDconv=2738OAU

OCHA (1999) *Manual on Field Practice in Internal Displacement*, Inter-Agency Standing Committee Policy Paper Series No. 1, UN/OCHA, Geneva

OFDA (1981) *Transition Housing for Victims of Disasters*, Padco Inc., Washington DC

Oger, P. (1995) 'Shelter International Research Project', draft report, MSF France, Mérignac

Payne, L. (1996) *Rebuilding Communities in a Refugee Settlement, A Casebook from Uganda*, Oxfam GB, Oxford

Setchell, C. (2001) *Reducing Vulnerability through Livelihoods Promotion in Shelter Sector Activities: An Initial Examination for Potential Mitigation and Post Disaster Application*, Working Paper No. 5, Feinstein International Famine Centre, School of Nutrition Science and Policy, Tufts University, Massachusetts

shelterproject (2003) 'Report on the Transitional Settlement Sector', unpublished report downloadable from www.shelterproject.org

Spence, R.J.S. and D.S. Cook (1983) *Building Materials in Developing Countries*, John Wiley and Sons, London

Sphere Project (2004) *Humanitarian Charter and Minimum Standards in Disaster Response*, Sphere Project, Geneva

Stulz, R. and K. Mukerji (1981) *Appropriate Building Materials – A Catalogue of Potential Solutions*, SKAT, IT Publications, London

Thomson, M.C. (1995) *Disease Prevention through Vector Control: Guidelines for Relief Organisations*, Liverpool School of Tropical Medicine, Oxfam GB, Oxford

UN (1992) 'Agenda 21, the Rio Declaration on Environment and Development', adopted at the United Nations Conference on Environment and Development (UNCED) held in Rio de Janeiro, Brazil, 3–14 June 1992, www.un.org/esa/sustdev/agenda21text.htm

UNDP / IAPSO (2000) *Emergency Relief Items – Compendium of Generic Specifications*, Volumes 1 and 2, UNDP, New York

UNDRO (1982) *Shelter After Disaster, Guidelines for Assistance*, principal consultant Ian Davis, UNDRO, New York (out of print, but downloadable free from the website of UN/OCHA Online)

UN–HABITAT (1995) *Shelter Provision and Employment Generation*, International Labour Office, Geneva

9 resources

UN–HABITAT/OHCHR (2002) *Housing Rights Legislation – Review of International and National Legal Instruments*, United Nations Housing Rights Programme: Report No. 1, Nairobi

UNHCHR (2005) webpage at www.unhchr.ch/housing on 'The Right to Adequate Housing', UNHCHR, Geneva

UNHCR (1951 / 1967) 'Convention and Protocol Relating to the Status of Refugees', www.unhcr.ch,UNHCR, Geneva

UNHCR (1987) 'Refugee Camp Planning', text prepared for Emergency Managers Training Workshop 15 June–3 July 1987, UNHCR/DMC, Geneva/Wisconsin

UNHCR (1993) 'Summary of Proceedings', First International Workshop on Improved Shelter Response and Environment for Refugees, 29 June–1 July 1993, UNHCR, Geneva

UNHCR (1994) 'Proposal for a Project Management Tool', UNHCR Programme and Technical Support Section, Geneva

UNHCR (1996) *Environmental Guidelines*, UNHCR, Geneva

UNHCR (1998a) *Refugee Operations and Environmental Management: Selected Lessons Learnt*, UNHCR Environment Unit, Geneva

UNHCR (1998b) *Environmental Guidelines: Forestry in Refugee Situations*, UNHCR, Geneva

UNHCR (1998c) *Environmental Guidelines: Domestic Energy in Refugee Situations*, UNHCR, Geneva

UNHCR (1998d) *Environmental Guidelines: Livestock in Refugee Situations*, UNHCR, Geneva

UNHCR (1998e) *Key Principles for Decision-Making (Refugee Operations and Environmental Management)*, EESS/UNHCR, Geneva

UNHCR (2000) *Handbook for Emergencies*, UNHCR, Geneva

UNHCR (2001) 'Practising and Promoting Sound Environmental Management in Refugee/Returnee Operations', paper presented at an International Workshop, 22–25 October 2001, UNHCR, Geneva

UNHCR (2002a) 'Environmental Considerations in the Life Cycle of a Refugee Camp', draft 2.2, UNHCR, Geneva

UNHCR (2002b) *Refugee Protection: A Guide to International Refugee Law*, UNHCR, Geneva

UNHCR (2002c) *Environmental Indicator Framework A Monitoring System for Environment-Related Activities in Refugee Operations*, EESS/UNHCR, Geneva

UNHCR (2002d) *Cooking Options in Refugee Situations*, UNHCR, Geneva

UNHCR (2002e) *Livelihoods Options in Refugee Situations*, UNHCR, Geneva

Warwick, H. and A. Doig (2004) *Smoke – the Killer in the Kitchen: Indoor Air Pollution in Developing Countries*, ITDG, London

Zetter, R. (1995) *Shelter Provision and Settlement Policies for Refugees: A State of the Art Review*, Studies on Emergency and Disaster Relief no. 2, Noriska Afrikainstitutet, Sweden

index

engineering 188, 194, 195, 199, 201, 367
  see also drainage; roads; sanitation;
    structural engineering
entry points 81, 356
environmental assessment 56, 354–5
environmental impact 21, 54–9
  collective centres 107
  dispersed settlements 70
  distribution projects 299
  exit strategies 58, 123, 132
  grouped settlements 56–7, 73
  information analysis 182
  materials sourcing 308, 309
  peat cutting 339
  planned camps 56–7, 132, 404
  self-settled camps 56–7, 123, 400, 404
  site selection 354
  up-grading urban facilities 103
  see also contamination; erosion; pollution;
    toxic environments; waste management
equal opportunities 188–9, 190
erosion
  drainage 392, 393
  exit strategies 58, 123, 132
  foundations 280
  grouped settlements 70
  low-density settlements 373
  roads 355, 393
  sand and gravel procurement 267
  site planning 355, 385
  see also environmental impact
erosion belts 385, 392
escape routes 217, 225, 231, 317, 382
ethical concerns 308
ethnic compatibility
  collective centres 107
  direct labour 196
  dispersed settlements 72
  feasibility assessment 80, 91, 99, 107,
    117, 126
  host families option 80, 82
  planned camps 126, 368
  rural self-settlement option 91
  security precautions 49
  self-settled camps 117, 368
  self-settlement problems 76
  urban self-settlement option 98, 99
ethnic groups
  distribution system design 303

  see also vulnerable people
evacuation 50, 225
  see also escape routes
evaluation
  camp projects 375
  direct labour 197
  distribution projects 300, 302
  host families option 82, 87, 88
  planning of 137–8
  rural self-settlement option 91
  stakeholders' interest in 13
  see also assessment; shelter assessment,
    monitoring, and evaluation
excavations 244, 281
execution plans, construction work 214
exit routes 217, 225, 231, 317
exit strategies 46–7
  collective centres 114
  financial management 62
  host families option 87–8
  planned camps 124, 132–3, 402–4
  rural self-settlement option 95
  self-settled camps 123–4, 402–4
  urban self-settlement option 104
expansion
  construction problem 280, 283, 285
  host families option 83, 84
  see also camp extensions
explosive materials
  storm protection 234
  see also landmines; unexploded ordnance
extended families 301, 334, 342
extension activities 296–7, 387
extensions *see* camp extensions; time
  extensions

families
  distribution channel 301, 302
  see also host families option
family agreements 83–4, 88
family plots *see* plots
family shelter 386–7, 401
family-shelter NFI packages 297–8, 386
farming *see* agriculture; food production;
  livestock; plots
'fast onset' emergencies 44
feasibility assessment
  collective centres 107
  host families option 80–1

early-warning mechanisms 41
environmental impact 59
heating and lighting provision 329
in profiles 29, 32
influx management 358
Logical Framework Analysis 172–3, 174
monitoring 38
objectives and 33, 34, 172–3
Participatory Learning and Action 175, 176
shelter assessment, monitoring, and
evaluation 137, 143
site selection 356
stoves and fuels 340
indirect water supply 251
industrial areas 221
see also reclaimed land; toxic environments
influx management 44, 402
access 91, 99, 110, 118, 126
capacity assessment 98
collective centres 110
community rebuilding 128
host families option 81, 357
planned camps 126, 128, 385
rural self-settlement option 91, 92
self-settled camps 118, 119, 385
site marking 385
transit facilities 357–8, 385
transit phase 42, 43
urban self-settlement option 98, 99
way-stations 362
informal settlements 96, 97, 99, 101
information analysis 180–6
information gathering 138, 141, 168–79
information plans 110
infrastructure
assessment 42
asset disposal 47, 123, 132, 403
availability 17
collective centres 108, 112, 114
community relations 408
damage 306, 355
definition 411
dispersed settlements 78, 88
high-density settlements 372, 373
host families option 81, 85–6, 87
host populations 112, 129, 132
land acquisition and 22
large camps 372
minefields and 218

planned camps 127, 129–30, 131, 392–9
planning 62, 382, 386, 388, 392–401
preparedness phase 41
rural self-settlement option 93, 95
security of 217
self-settled camps 115–16, 120, 121, 123, 406
self-settlement 76, 78
shelter requirement 17
stakeholders' interest in 12
transitional settlements' impact 8–9
urban self-settlement option 99, 101,
103, 104
see also services; transport
infrastructure
infrastructure up-grading
collective centres 112, 114
compensation, host populations 84
host families option 85–6, 87
informal settlements 101
planned camps 127, 129–30, 392
rural self-settlement option 93
self-settled camps 120, 121, 123, 399–401
urban self-settlement option 99, 101,
103, 104
insect control 278, 329–32
bamboo work 258, 259
clothing 327, 330
mud block walls 263
nets 63, 222, 329, 330, 331, 332
imber 257–8, 284
see also disease hazards
instantaneous water heaters 252
insulation see electrical insulation; frost;
thermal insulation
insurance 205, 244
integration
family-shelter NFI packages 298
host families option 87
host populations 42, 46
plans 26, 28, 29, 33
profiles 30
rural self-settlement option 95
schedules of operations 37
urban self-settlement option 104
see also resettlement
Inter-Agency Procurement Services Office
see UN Development Programme
Internally Displaced Persons 6, 348
definition 413

prefabricated shelters 322–3, 411
preferred settlement option 35
pregnant women 327, 328, 329, 330
preliminary handover 207
preparedness phase 40–1, 60
pressurised stoves 342
primary education 52
primary loads 280
prisons 86, 93, 101, 121, 130
privacy
  clothing and bedding standards 325
  cluster planning 384
  collective centres 105, 108, 109
  community road plans 391
  hollow square plans 389
  security, safety and 49
  shelter requirement 14, 17, 387
  staggered square plans 390
  stakeholders' interest in 12
  see also area per person; seclusion of women
procurement
  aggregates 267
  bamboo 258
  bricks and blocks 260
  cement 265
  concrete 271
  construction work documentation 213
  corrugated metal sheets 275–6
  distribution projects 295, 296, 297, 299,
    307–12
  economic stability and 296, 299, 308, 309
  lime 265
  mud blocks 262–3
  non-food items 307–12
  paint 278
  roof tiles 273–4
  steel reinforcement 272
  thatching materials 275
  timber 256–8
  see also sourcing
profiles and profiling 28–32, 33, 126, 131,
  177, 351–2, 354
programme aims and objectives 140–1
programme options 65–133
programme plans and planning
  collective centres 108, 110–11
  construction and 211
  definition 28
  development 32–3

health care 100, 111, 119, 127
host families option 82–3, 86
livelihoods and 24
local governments 82, 127, 367
NFI packages 299
planned camps 126–8, 365–75
rural self-settlement option 91–2
self-settled camps 118–19, 367–75
transit facilities 367–75
urban self-settlement option 96, 99–100
programme profiles 30
project briefs 36, 201, 211, 212, 316, 375
Project Framework Approach *see* Logical
  Framework Analysis
project framework matrix 171–3
project management 194, 195, 199
project objectives 172, 174
project plans and planning
  asset handover 47
  construction and 211
  definition 28
  development 33
  distribution projects 295–7, 299
  health and safety policies 244, 245
project profiles 30
project structure 171
protection *see* security
protective clothing 244, 249, 266, 271–2
  see also gloves; safety footwear; safety
    helmets; safety spectacles
protective treatments 263, 278–9, 284
Protocol Relating to the Status of Refugees 20
protocols of understanding 108
public address systems 361
public information campaigns 41, 42, 55, 81,
  365
public meetings
  collective centres 110, 112
  host families option 86
  planned camps 130
  rural self-settlement option 94
  self-settled camps 121
  urban self-settlement option 102
purchasing 61, 311–12
  see also procurement
purlins 276

quality control 213, 312
  see also inspection; monitoring

Please email any comments on this 2005 edition of the guidelines and CD-Rom to **guidelines@sheltercentre.org**.

Proposed revisions to the guidelines are reviewed by a panel of peer organisations at the Shelter Meetings, **www.sheltermeeting.org**.